Royal Society of New South Wales

Transactions of the philosophical Society of New South Wales

1862-1865

Royal Society of New South Wales

Transactions of the philosophical Society of New South Wales
1862-1865

ISBN/EAN: 9783337069919

Printed in Europe, USA, Canada, Australia, Japan

Cover: Foto ©ninafisch / pixelio.de

More available books at **www.hansebooks.com**

TRANSACTIONS
OF THE
PHILOSOPHICAL SOCIETY
OF NEW SOUTH WALES.

On the Vertebrated Animals of the Lower Murray and Darling, their habits, economy, and geographical distribution, by GERARD KREFFT.

[Read 10th September, 1862.]

SOME of the observations embodied in this paper date back as far as the year 1852, but the greater number are the results of a nine months' sojourn on the Lower Murray and Darling, where, encamped in the neighbourhood of Gol Gol, I was enabled, with the assistance of Messrs. Williams and their devoted natives, to thoroughly investigate the fauna of that part of Australia.

I cannot speak too highly of the valuable co-operation of these gentlemen, the same whom Mr. Landsborough met on his return journey at the Warrego pushing on towards the Gulf, and whom he designates "the best of Australian Bushmen."

The Placental Mammals of this district are of course few. They belong to the Bats, *(Nyctophilus, Scotophilus, Rhinolophus,)* the Rodents, *(Hydromys, Hapalotis, Mus,)* and the Carnivora, which are represented here, as in the rest of Australia, by the Dingo alone.

CHEIROPTERA.

The Bats of the Murray and Darling all belong to the family Vespertilionidæ, as the large so-called "Vampire Bat" or "Flying Fox" *(Pteropus)* is not found in those regions.

Owing to the superstitions of the natives, who look upon every Bat as a departed friend and relative, who, according to their ideas with regard to the transmigration of souls, has seen better days among themselves, has thrown spear and boomerang, and feasted upon Kangaroo, Wallaby, and Emeu, the number of Bats collected during my journey was very limited indeed.

When at Gunbower Creek I caught the first of these creatures, and I was seriously informed by the natives, that it was "brother belonging to black-fellow, who kill lubra if you kill him."

Farther down the river this superstition vanished more and more; still they never assisted in procuring specimens of this family.

The following are the species collected:—

1. NYCTOPHILUS GEOFFROYI.

Geoffroy's Nyctophilus—
observed at various places between Gunbower Creek and the Junction of the Darling.

2. SCOTOPHILUS PUMILUS.

The Little Bat—
of which a single specimen was caught near Milldura, 20 miles from the Darling.

3. SCOTOPHILUS MORIO.

Chocolate Bat—
specimens of which have been captured on the Lower Darling. I have been informed that a "tailed Bat" was also an inhabitant of that part of Australia, but I did not succeed in securing a specimen. I suppose that it is a new species of the genus Molossus, of which only a single representative is as yet described from this country, discovered some years ago by the late Dr. L. Becker, in the neighbourhood of Melbourne.

4. RHINOLOPHUS MEGAPHYLLUS.

The Large-leaved Horse-Shoe Bat—
frequently observed near Gunbower Creek.

CARNIVORA.

CANIS DINGO.

The Dingo, Warrigal of the natives, is the only Australian representative of the large Group of carnivorous animals inhabiting every other part of the globe; and as our "Native Dog" has already established a reputation for himself, I shall be as brief as possible. In spite of the many enemies of the Dingo he is as plentiful as ever on the Lower Murray and Darling; neither the strychnine of the settlers, nor the guns or spears of the Aboriginals could exterminate the breed : which no doubt is also maintained by stray shepherds' dogs—not all the so-called Dingos being of the pure "Warrigal" blood.

There is a black and tan coloured variety. Various litters taken by myself had generally four pups, sometimes a pair of each colour. The natives, who hate the Dingo most cordially for his living on the fat of the land, kill him on every opportunity and eat his flesh, which is by no means of ill flavour, though I have partaken of it under stress of hunger, and I will not vouch that I should sit down to roast Dingo with the same gusto now as ten years ago in the Murray scrub.

A question has been raised as to the origin of the Dingo in Australia, and several high authorities are of opinion that the dog was introduced there by man; if so, this must have been at a very remote age, as the first molar tooth of a dog has been found with other fossil remains in the breccia of the Wellington caves.

In those days of *Diprotodons*, not only did the Dingo exist, but also some of the animals now restricted to the island of Tasmania, as *Thylacinus* and *Sarcophilus*, teeth of which I have discovered in the same breccia, and which are now on view at the Australian Museum.

RODENTIA.

The third group of the Australian Mammalia consists of the Rodents, which are largely represented, and, to some extent, partake of the structure of the Kangaroo; many having their hind limbs much elongated, and moving by a succession of jumps, in which they use the hind legs only. A few (4 species) are aquatic *(Hydromys)*, expert swimmers and divers, and a great many are arboreal, and apparently the representatives of the squirrels in Australia.

All the species observed by me on the Lower Murray, are strictly nocturnal, and all bring forth 4 young ones (born blind) at a time.

1. HYDROMYS CHRYSOGASTER.

Golden-bellied Beaver Rat.

All the specimens of this rat procured by me are from Gunbower Creek and Lake Boga, where this animal is very plentiful.

It is strictly nocturnal, and was often observed after sundown, gambolling upon the shores of that beautiful lake. The Black Snake is a sore enemy to the young progeny of this *Hydromys*; for I captured a specimen, which, upon being opened, proved to have swallowed a full dozen young Beaver Rats, about the size of new-born kittens.

This Rat is not found on the Lower Darling, at least, I was assured by the natives that they had never seen it.

2. HAPALOTIS CONDITOR.

Building Hapalotis.
Koel or Kohl of the natives.

Captain Sturt described this animal first, though Sir Thomas Mitchell mentioned it before him.

It is one of the many species which will soon be extinct, as I found that it had already retreated before the herds of sheep and cattle across the Murray. Only a few empty nests were occasionally met with south of that river. The few specimens collected were captured by the natives about 10 miles north of the Darling Junction; though many empty nests, or rather huts, were met with, occupied by *Hapalotis apicalis*, which, it appears, often takes a fancy to the roomy structures of the building *Hapalotis*, and ejects the original inhabitant. I kept both species together in a box, but they never agreed, and, though the building *Hapalotis* is much larger in size, it could never hold its own against *Hapalotis apicalis*. They feed on various seeds, bulbous roots, insects, and the smaller species of *Hapalotis*, or birds' eggs, &c., and bring forth 4 young at a time.

3. HAPALOTIS APICALIS.

White-tipped Hapalotis.
Tillikin of the natives.

Mr. Gould figures this species, of which he mentions merely that he received it from South Australia. I observed the first specimens in the neighbourhood of Euston, and found it in great numbers upon Sir Thomas Mitchell's old track on both sides of the Murray. It also occurs on the Darling, and I have no doubt that the late lamented Explorers called Rat Point (in the neighbourhood of fort Bourke) after this *Hapalotis*.

They are gregarious in their habits. I have dislodged as many as 15 specimens from a single tree, and kept large numbers in captivity. They became quite tame; and many which had escaped would return to join my frugal supper at night, and help themselves, to damper especially. This is a very graceful animal, strictly nocturnal in its habits, and its flesh white, tender, and well-tasted.

4. HAPALOTIS MITCHELLII.

Mitchell's Hapalotis.

Kahlpere of the natives—

is another animal which the late Sir Thomas Mitchell first discovered. I have no doubt that it is widely distributed over the Australian continent, but I was not able to procure specimens at Gunbower Creek, or at the Junction of the Loddon. The first pair obtained were brought to me by natives in the neighbourhood of the Murrumbidgee. This animal is very plentiful on the Darling: and as many as 50 specimens were often procured by the native women in an afternoon. It burrows into the ground, and is dug out by them. *Hapalotis Mitchellii* is strictly nocturnal in its habits, and the female produces 4 young at a time. Though they are easily kept in captivity, they often kill each other, if not well supplied with food; they also have a disagreeable habit (to the naturalist, at least) of gnawing each others tails off.

5. MUS SUBRUFUS?

Dusky mouse.

Pethack of the natives.

Apparently an undescribed species (for which I would propose the name of *Mus subrufus*) is found in large numbers between Gol Gol Creek and the Darling; it is nocturnal and gregarious, and, like *Hapalotis Mitchellii*, burrows into the ground; 4 young are produced at a time by the female.

All the Rodents are eaten by the natives, but only in case of no other food being at hand, as a large number of these little creatures are wanted to satisfy the hunger of a black-fellow.

This closes the list of the Placental Mammalia, which I had

an opportunity of observing. But there are, no doubt, still many species of Rodents new to science; in fact, several skins of *Hapalotis* were received through native tribes living some 100 miles further north, but all were in such bad preservation, that it was found impossible to give a correct description of them.

MARSUPIALIA.

By far the larger number of animals inhabiting the extensive plains on the Murray and Darling are marsupial; and with a few exceptions truly *nocturnal* in their habits.

This accounts for the apparent scarcity of animal life; and often do travellers mention, that except an occasional Kangaroo, they have never met with any mammalian animal in the interior of the country.

Two-thirds of the smaller mammalia collected and examined by me on the Murray were new to many old residents, and even the natives, who, in many parts, have acquired habits different from their former mode of life, had almost forgotten the existence of some of these species. With the aid of the Messrs. Williams and the natives, I succeeded in procuring every species known to exist in that part of Australia; and in finding also a number of animals of this order which hitherto had been only known to frequent Western and South Australia.

The following are the different genera :—

Dasyuridæ	*Dasyurus.* *Phascogale.* *Antechinus.* *Podabrus.* *Myrmecobius.*
Peramelidæ	*Chœropus.* *Peragalea.* *Perameles.*
Phalangistidæ	*Phalangista.* *Belidæus.*
Macropodidæ	*Macropus.* *Onychogalea.* *Lagorchestes.* *Bettongia.*

I may also mention the Genus *Phascolomys* (the Wombat), as I know upon reliable authority that *P. latifrons* has been killed in the neighbourhood of the "North-west Bend" on the Murray.

The two genera *Petaurus* and *Phascolarctos*, the so called "*Flying Squirrels*" and "*Native Bear*," are not represented; both frequent the rocky and mountainous districts only.

1. DASYURUS GEOFFROYI.
Native Cat or Tiger Cat of the Settlers.
"Kettrie" of the Natives.

This is the most blood-thirsty of the Marsupial animals inhabiting the Murray scrubs, solitary in its habits, strictly nocturnal, and the terror of the feathered tribe, particularly of the yellow crested Cockatoo. Afraid of nothing, it will, when hungry, attack any other animal; a mother will eat even her own progeny, if she has nothing else to fall back upon.

I have often detected the lair of this *Dasyurus* by the heap of feathers and bones generally collected at the foot of the tree upon which it dwells; it is eaten by the natives. The female is not furnished with the usual pouch, and in June or July brings forth often as many as 6 young at a time, so that every teat is occupied, 6 being the number of mammæ generally observed in this species. The Native Cat of our neighbourhood (*Dasyurus viverrinus*) is somewhat smaller in size, with a more bushy tail, and the female furnished with 6 teats; this may not be constantly the case, though I am informed by my friend, Mr. E. P. Ramsay, that various specimens examined by him had not more than 6 teats, only 4 of which were in milk. Owing to the absence of a pouch, many of the weak young drop off, and only a few, generally 3 or 4, reach maturity.

All my attempts to domesticate the young have proved fruitless; they never learnt to recognise the hand that fed them, and though I kept a pair nearly six months, at the end of that time they were found only more ferocious than ever; having made their escape at last, they kept near the huts and tents of the camp, completely clearing the place of mice and other vermin. Wherever a spot is infested with mice or rats in the bush (and some of the stations are overrun with them) there is no better remedy than to procure a few young *Dasyuri*, which having been kept on the ground for a few months, and turned out into the store-house, will soon " effect a clearance."

The range of this species extends, according to Gould, as far as the West Coast.

The Natives inhabiting the country near the junction of the Darling, have some superstitions regarding this animal, and "Jacob," an old chief on the River, often assured me, that "Kettrie make rain and rainbow." As his kinsmen are not fond of rain, I suppose they kill as many Kettries as possible.

2. PHASCOGALE CALURA.

Handsome tailed Phascogale.

Kultarr, (native name.)

This is without doubt the most handsome species of the genus. It is ashy grey above, white underneath, with long bushy black tail, the upper half of the basal part of which is of a rich chesnut colour.

The few specimens which have found their way to Europe were procured at the Williams River, Western Australia; but when the intervening country between the Murray River and the West coast is better known to Naturalists, it will probably be found that the range of this beautiful creature extends over the larger half of the continent. The few specimens brought to me by the natives were generally found in hollow limbs of trees. I kept several alive for a considerable time, feeding them with live mice or small birds. Their movements were cat-like, but very graceful; like all the members of this genus they are strictly nocturnal in their habits. A female specimen, caught in the beginning of June, had 8 very small young ones attached to the teats, which were 10 in number: no regular pouch was observable, the long hair only covering the young progeny.

My specimens were captured near Williams' Station, Gol Gol Creek, about 10 miles from the Darling Junction.

3. PHASCOGALE PENICILLATA.

Brush-tailed Phascogale.

This species, nearly allied to *P. calura* is, no doubt, still more widely distributed. It is occasionally found in the neighbourhood of Sydney, and extends its range right across the continent to the west coast. On the Murray River, it is exceedingly rare; the only specimen I found was secured in the neighbourhood of Mount Hope. I have subsequently received specimens through the natives, when at Port Lincoln; and examined some which had been captured at Albany on King George's Sound, and have found them to be identical with the original Tapoa-Tafa of White.

The only female specimen I saw had no pouch, but 10 teats covered with long hair. I suspect that, as in the other species, a large number of young is brought forth; but how many reach maturity must yet be left to be determined.

4. PHASCOGALE LANIGERA.
Woolly Phascogale.
Kultarr (native name.)

Two single specimens of this little *Phascogale* were obtained through the natives at Gol Gol Creek: one a female with 10 teats and 7 young. The hind legs in this species are long and slender, and the natives informed me, that it lived upon the ground, unlike the other species of this genus; most of which are arboreal.

The little creature, which I kept alive for several weeks, was fond of flesh, and, when put into a box with a number of Rodents, attacked the frightened mice immediately.

The natives informed me, that the animal was very rare; in fact, they had a dispute about its name, and called it "Kultarr," just as they did with *Phascogale calura*, while some asserted they had never seen the animal before.

Though I offered high rewards for another specimen, I did not succeed in procuring any more than these.

This species is also strictly nocturnal in its habits.

5. ANTECHINUS FLAVIPES.
Rusty footed Antechinus,
Warum (native name.)

This lively little animal is the most abundant of the *Antechini*, and, though nocturnal, is often seen during the day time. Its range extends from the east to the west coast. It used to be so common near the camp on the Murray, that I have often captured several specimens whenever a load of wood was brought in. I kept many alive and always found that, like the species of the *Phascogale*, it would attack and kill any number of mice, if put into the same box. The shallow pouch of the female is provided with 10 teats, and as many young are sometimes attached to them. I find several entries in my diary corroborating these facts:—

Aug. 17. 1 female Antechinus flavipes with 10 young.
„ 19. 1 ditto „ 9 „
„ 20. 1 ditto „ 9 „

Several females procured in September had only 6 young, of much larger size, attached to the teats.

This animal is common on the North Shore, Sydney.

6. ANTECHINUS ALBIPES.

White-footed Antechinus,
Tram-Trammit (native name.)

One of the smallest of this genus, and widely distributed over the whole of the southern part of the continent from Swan River to Port Jackson. The specimens I obtained on the Plains of the Murray are identical with specimens from this Colony, and with those inhabiting South and Western Australia.

The female is furnished with a rather shallow pouch containing 10 teats; and in specimens captured in July and August, from 6 to 9 young, of the size of a pea. The Natives caught this species frequently on the Sand-hills near our camp, in King George's Sound. *A. albipes* frequents rocky places, and is often found under stones. I have also found specimens under stones near Manly Beach.

It bears captivity very well. I have lately found several specimens, and succeeded in keeping them about six weeks alive; they thrive very well, and I killed them only on account of their rather strong odour, if fed on flesh. Though small, they are very ferocious, and they will attack mice of double their size, without fear.

7. PODABRUS CRASSICAUDATUS.

Thick-tailed Podabrus.

Mondellundellun (native name.)

All the specimens of this species ever sent to Europe came from the West coast of this continent; but as I have obtained specimens from various parts of the Murray River, I doubt not that it inhabits the intervening country between the Swan River colony and New South Wales. I have never seen this handsome little Podabrus from the eastern part of Australia, though a species with a much longer tail *(Podabrus macurus)* occurs in the neighbourhood of Brisbane, and further north. I have kept several specimens alive for months, but always found it necessary to separate them on account of their ferocity. I have more than once lost a number of valuable Rodents through inadvertently adding a *Podabrus*, or any species of *Antechinus* to them; they fall upon the poor mice immediately, and kill many more than they can possibly eat. If not supplied with food, they attack and devour each other.

Females, which the natives brought in July and August, had from 6 to 9 young ones in the rather shallow pouch. The number of teats is 10; and, as I found several with the whole number in milk, I believe that as many as 10 young are brought forth at a birth.

All the species of the genus *Antechinus* are rather sensitive to cold; and, when the thermometer fell as low as 30° a great many perished.

Beyond a hoarse screech, I never noticed any voice. A singular peculiarity in all the Dasyuridæ is, that they carry their ears folded down, never erect, when alive: and, though I do not want to find fault with Gould's beautiful work, I must say, that, in this respect, the representations he gives of this tribe of the animals of Australia are not over true to nature.

8. MYRMECOBIUS FASCIATUS.

Banded Myrmecobius.

This singular animal which also inhabits the Plains bordering on the Murray and Darling, is not found close to the first named river: and, as far as my inquiries among the natives went, has never occupied that part of the country. It does not now inhabit any part of Victoria, and I think the Murray may be taken as its southern boundary. A quarrel existed between the Darling natives and the tribe which accompanied me, so that I was not able to procure any live specimens of this singular animal, but its existence is proved sufficiently. I have been informed by Mr. Scott, the owner of a Station at Tapio, about 80 miles from the Darling Junction, that the Banded *Myrmecobius* is by no means rare; and that the natives could procure specimens for me; but a few bad skins were all I obtained.

How many young ones the female produces, and with how many teats she is furnished, I am unable to say; the only fact proved is, that the range of *Myrmecobius fasciatus* is not limited to the West Coast, and, that according to the natives, it is not nocturnal in its habits.

9. CHŒROPUS OCCIDENTALIS.
The Eastern Chœropus.
Landwang (native name.)

This singular animal which Sir Thomas Mitchell first discovered in his expedition to the Darling, June 16, 1836, is still found on the plains of the Murray; though it is exceedingly rare, and is disappearing as fast as the native population. The large flocks of sheep and herds of cattle occupying the country will soon disperse those individuals which are still to be found in the so-called settled districts, and it will become more and more difficult to procure specimens for our national collection.

During a period of six months, I encamped not far from the spot where Sir Thomas Mitchell secured his tail-less animal. I had the greatest difficulty in obtaining a few specimens, but succeeded at last, and as I believe that nobody has ever been able to observe the habits of this singular creature in a state of nature, I will quote from my diary, October 4th, 1857:—

" After returning from a short excursion into the scrub, I fell in with a party of natives who had succeeded, at last, in securing a pair of the *Chœropus*, (male and female.) They wanted all manner of things for them, from a pair of blankets to a cutty pipe; and as I was very anxious to sketch them from life I emptied my pockets there and then; and promised a grand entertainment for the night with plenty of damper and sugar and tea."

On arrival at the camp, the two animals were secured in a bird cage; and I was busy for several hours sketching my charges in different positions.

Gould's figures of *Chæropus occidentalis* are spiritless, being taken from dry skins. I was in the habit of showing a copy of Sir Thomas Mitchell's tail-less specimen to the natives, urging them to procure animals of that description; of course, they did not recognize it as a "Landwang," and I was furnished in consequence with a large number of the common Bandicoot (*Perameles obesula*) minus the tail, which, to please me, had been screwed clean out.

About sun-down, when I was about to secure my animals for the night, one of the nimblest made its escape, jumping clean through the wires of the cage.

At a quick pace it ran up one of the sandstone cliffs, followed by myself, all the black-fellows, men, women, and children, and their dogs.

Here was a splendid opportunity for observing the motions of the animal; and I availed myself of it. The *Chæropus* progressed like a broken down hack in a canter, apparently dragging the hind quarters after it; we kept in sight of the fugitive; and, after a splendid run up and down the sand hills, our pointer, who had been let loose, brought it to bay in a salt bush.

A large tin case was fitted up for the habitation of these animals, and provided with coarse barley grass, upon which, as the natives informed me, they feed. Insects, particularly Grasshoppers, were also put into the box, and, though they were rather restless at first, and made vain attempts to jump out, they appeared snug enough in the morning, having constructed a completely covered nest with the grass and some dried leaves.

During the day time, they always kept in their hiding places, and, when disturbed, quickly returned to them; but, as soon as the sun was down, they became lively, jumping about and scratching the bottom of the case, in their attempts to regain liberty. I kept these animals upon lettuces, barley grass, bread, and some bulbous roots, for six weeks, until the camp was broken up, when they were killed for the sake of their skins.

I think that about 8 specimens of this species were secured during our stay; several of which, proved to be females with good sized young ones in the pouch, which is very deep and runs upwards, not like that of a Kangaroo. All were provided with 8 teats, and bore 2 young ones, only one pair of teats being drawn.

I may mention here that the *Chœropus* drinks a good deal of water, but will neither touch meat nor attack or eat mice, as the other members of this family do.

Their dung, which I often examined when out hunting, was entirely composed of grass, very dry, about the size of sheep's trundles, but much longer, so that I believe, that in a state of nature, they feed principally upon vegetables. They are very good eating, and I am sorry to confess that my appetite more than once over-ruled my love for science; but 24 hours upon "*pig face*" (*mesembryanthemum*) will damp the ardour of any naturalist.

The young which I took from the pouch of several females, never exceeded 2 in number, and were so far advanced, that I conclude that the breeding season is in May or June. It is a curious fact, that the third toe in the fore feet of the *Chœropus* is much more developed in the young than in the adult animal: in fact, the former looked more like a young *Perameles*, than a *Chœropus*; the limbs being short and strongly made—the basal half of the tail, which in the adult is covered with long black hair, is of a dark purple colour in the nude young animal: The eye of this species, which is very large and brilliant, is represented much too small in Gould's figures.

10. PERAGALEA LAGOTIS.
Rabbit Rat.
Wuirrapur, (Murray natives.)
Jecko, (Darling tribes.)

This beautiful animal, like many other species, has long ago retreated to the north of the Murray. It is social, not gregarious, in its habits, only found in pairs scattered over the wide plains formerly the sole domain of the Kangaroo and Emeu. It digs into the ground, forming a burrow like a rabbit, but with only one entrance, and differs herein from *Bettongia Graii*, the burrows of which are provided with several outlets, and may easily be distinguished from those of the *Peragalea*.

As this "Rabbit Rat" often prefers entering the ground on a hill side, and as hills, even of very slight elevation, are often scarce on these extensive plains, it will sometimes happen, that the *Peragalea* takes advantage of the mound raised upon a departed black-fellows grave, providing for itself a habitation beneath the natives weary bones. Upon this ground an investigator asserted, some years ago, that this animal dug out the dead bodies of the natives and fed upon them. I think that every naturalist that has the slightest knowledge of the habits of this animal, will agree with me, that it is no resurrectionist, and if it takes advantage of the "mound," it is only for convenience sake, and not for criminal purposes.

It is nocturnal in its habits, feeds upon grass, roots, insects, &c., and always retires before dawn. Its flesh is very good eating, though the fur has a peculiar sweetish smell which is retained for years after the skin has been cured.

The natives seldom unearth the animal; the holes being very deep, and often found to be uninhabited. I procured a few specimens only, among which, was an adult female, with a very deep pouch, 8 teats, and two large young.

All the spots which, in the adult, are covered with black hair, were of a purple colour in the nude young specimens, which appeared to be about four months old; so that, according to my diary, their breeding season will be about the beginning of May. The pouch runs upwards.

11. PERAMELES FASCIATA.

Banded Perameles.

Thill, (native name.)

Moncat (do.   do.)

One of the many animals whose range extends from the east to the west coast of the Continent, it is common on all parts of the Murray River, and is also found in Victoria, in South Australia, parts of Western Australia, and in the immediate neighbourhood of Sydney.

Though provided with strong claws it seldom burrows, except in search of its food, which consists of insects, bulbous roots, various herbs, &c. Nocturnal and social in its habits, the striped (so called) "Bandicoot" seeks shelter, during the day time, in hollow logs, or under stones, although sometimes it constructs a sort of nest like the *Chœropus*.

This animal bears captivity well, and becomes very expert in catching mice. I had several about the camp; and they proved as useful as cats.

I was in the habit of feeding the specimens kept in a large tin case with various kinds of Rodents, which they killed with astonishing quickness.

The *Perameles* would tumble the mice about with its fore paws, break their hind legs, and eat generally the head only. I have seen a single individual kill as many as twenty mice in a very short time, breaking their bones successively, after which it would begin to satisfy its hunger.

During the months of May, June, July, and August, female specimens provided with 8 teats, and containing from 2 to 4 young were captured by the natives. Those obtained in August, had grown to the size of a young rat; fur, cream coloured, without the markings upon the haunches, which appear at a more nature age.

The flesh is palatable. The pouch runs upwards.

12. PERAMELES OBESULA.

Short-nosed Perameles.
Bandicoot of the settlers.
Pirrikin, Murray natives.

This animal is the most common of the *Peramelidæ*, inhabiting the whole of the Southern part of the Continent and Tasmania. How far its range extends to the north, I have been unable to ascertain, though I know that it is frequently met with on the Clarence River.

The flesh is delicious, especially when *done* in the native style, that is, the hair removed, and the game roasted upon the coals. From May to September, females with from 2 to 3 young ones in the pouch were frequently captured. In October or November, the young progeny begin to shift for themselves.

The pouch is very deep, the entrance upwards, and contains 8 teats.

13. PHALANGISTA VULPINA.

Vulpine or Brush-tailed " Opossum "—

So well known to everybody, that I shall not enlarge upon it; but merely remark that this species is the staff of life to the natives.

I often admired my native friends, when after a hard day's unsuccessful hunting they dropped in at the camp empty handed; how carefully they would examine the large flooded Gum-trees *(Eucalyptus rostratus)*, fringing the river banks, how nimbly they would get a footing upon some hollow limb, and with what perseverance " Possum" was dislodged, and perhaps, accidentally dropped into the river, whence it had to be rescued by the blackfellow's better half: for it was the question of " to eat or not to eat."

How often the *Phalangista vulpina* produces young, I am not able to tell with certainty. I think, judging by the large numbers in every forest, several times a year. The female is provided with only 2 teats, and seldom carries more than one young one at the time.

14. PHALANGISTA VIVERRINA.

Ring-tailed Opossum.
Pirrath of the Murray natives.

A rare animal on the Murray and Darling. I secured no more than two specimens during my stay there. It is much lighter in colour than the species inhabiting the Swan River colony. The pouch in the female is provided with 2 teats.

It is one of the characteristics of the flat country traversed by the Murray and Darling, that no other species of the *Phalangistidæ* are found there.

The first *Belidæus* I captured on my return, at Mount Ida,

B

McIvor Range, 80 miles distant from the Murray, is, according to Gould, a new species, and is figured by him in part XI. of his Mammalia, 15, as "*Belidæus notatus.*"

As I made many enquiries of the Natives about the genus *Petaurus*, and found that these animals are not known to them, I do not hesitate to consider their range to be restricted to the mountainous coast districts.

All the members of this family are nocturnal, and the female is provided with one pair of mammæ only. In the "Flying Squirrels" the number of young is sometimes 2; but the Koala or "Native Bear" never produces more than a single young one at a time.

I now proceed to the Kangaroo, whose form and habits seem to have struck the discoverers of Australia with special wonder. Large Plains are admirably adapted to the habits of these animals, and the low lands of the Murray have once swarmed with their numbers as they do now with cattle and sheep. At the present time, large flocks of Kangaroos are a rare sight; and though I have seen as many as sixty or eighty together, I think that this is the exception, not the rule.

The most formidable, and no doubt the handsomest species of the whole tribe is,

15. Osphranter rufus.

The Great Red Kangaroo.
Bullucur of the Murray natives.

Which has become very scarce upon the left bank of the Murray, but is still found in considerable numbers in New South Wales and South Australia. The range of this species to the eastward does not extend much beyond Mount Hope.

This large beautiful animal, about which a great deal has been written, ought to be well known to every colonist, and yet it is only a few months ago that the very existence of such a creature was doubted by an enlightened "critic," who was pleased to designate this species as ante-diluvian; indeed it must sound like a fable to people who know little or nothing about such matters, if they are informed that the male of this species is of a foxy red, and the female of a bluish grey colour.

The Red Kangaroos, like the great Kangaroo, *(Macropus major)* feed in flocks, and, when disturbed, the old males cover the retreat of the fleet females who are off first, so that specimens of the latter sex are rare, the dogs generally stopping the progress of the rear-guard of the red "old men."

In wet weather, when the chalky top soil of the "Malley scrub" is softened, these Kangaroos are easily captured: they sink deep into the ground, and any black-fellow's cur, trained for such work, will stick to the tail of the Kangaroo until his master is able to come up and crack its skull, or run a spear through it.

The female produces one young at a time, which she carries in her pouch until it is of considerable size. As in all the other members of this family, the number of mammæ is four.

The flesh is very palatable—I prefer it to that of *Macropus major*.

16. MACROPUS MAJOR.

The Great Kangaroo.
Bullucur of the Murray natives.

A much more common species than the preceding, and similar in its habits, the female producing only one young one at a time. The pouch has 4 teats.

Dr. James C. Cox has lately presented two young of this species to the Museum, which were *both* taken from the same pouch. I mention this as being of very rare occurrence; they are about $\frac{1}{2}$ inch long.

17. ONYCHOGALEA FRÆNATA.

Bridled Nail-tailed Kangaroo.
Merrin of the Murray natives.

The most common of all the smaller species of the Kangaroo tribe; often seen out during the day-time, though, when observed in captivity, much livelier at night; gregarious, the female producing one young at a time, generally in the beginning of May; pouch containing 4 teats. Its flesh is white and well tasted.

18. LAGORCHESTES LEPOROIDES.
Hare Kangaroo.
Turatt of the Murray natives.

Common upon the level country between the Murray and Darling; strictly nocturnal and solitary in its habits; it is seen during the day-time only, and is generally found asleep under some salt bush, or in any other sheltered locality. The Hare Kangaroo is the fleetest of the whole tribe, and will, when hotly pressed, take leaps more than 8 feet high.

A single young one is produced at a time; pouch furnished with 4 teats. This species is easily tamed, and I have kept several at the camp, which lived well on biscuit, bread, or boiled rice.

Its flesh is delicious, in fact some of the best meat I ever tasted.

19. BETTONGIA RUFESCENS.
Rufous Bettongia.
Kangaroo Rat.

This animal, so common in the neighbourhood of Sydney, has not been observed by me to the westward of the Murrumbidgee, where *Bettongia penicillata* appears to take its place. Not a single specimen was procured by the natives during my stay at the Darling Junction; so that I have no doubt about the extent of its range. This animal is easily tamed, and I have kept a young one about the size of a large rat for several weeks. The little animal often followed me upon my excursions, seeking shelter upon the approach of danger by creeping between my boots and trousers.

Only one young is brought forth in June, though the pouch contains 4 teats. The flesh of this animal is also very palatable.

20. BETTONGIA PENICILLATA.
Pencil-tailed Bettongia.
Pattuck of the Murray natives.

The smallest of the whole family, nocturnal in its habits. Those occasionally seen during the day time have been disturbed.

It is not very quick, and is easily caught, even by common dogs. I have from time to time kept*numbers of these animals in captivity in an enclosure of pine logs about seven feet high, which they used to climb with a nimbleness truly astonishing, and thus often escaped. During the day time I always noticed these creatures crouching into some corner; the tail brought forward between the hind legs, the head between their paws; fast asleep. I noticed that they are very partial to the thick clusters of *Polygonum* scrub so frequent on the Murray.

Female specimens, with never more than 1 young attached to one of the 4 teats, were frequently brought to me by the natives. Single specimens, with a white brush at the end of the tail, occur occasionally.

This *Bettongia* and *B. Ogilbeyi* appear to be so closely allied to each other that I should consider them the same species.

21. BETTONGIA GRAII.

Gray's Jerboa Kangaroo,
Booming of the Murray natives.

This burrowing *Bettongia* has long retreated before the herds of cattle with which the plains bordering on the Murray are now stocked; and it is no longer to be found south of that river, so, at least, the natives assured me, and whenever we went out hunting for it, we always had to cross to the New South Wales side.

Not a single specimen of my collection was procured in Victoria. Although this species is constantly furnished with a brush of white hairs at the end of the tail, I consider it identical with Gould's *B. Graii*, in which the white mark is wanting.

It is a truly nocturnal animal, which always leaves its burrow long after the sun is down, in fact, never before it is quite dark. I often watched near their holes, gun in hand, listening to their peculiar call; but I always had great difficulty in procuring specimens, as they are very shy, and hardly to be distinguished from the surrounding objects.

The best plan is always to dig them out; an operation in which the black-fellows are very expert, though it is rather tedious work; the holes running into each other, and being sometimes ten feet deep; and several shafts may have to be sunk, before a couple of "Boomings" can be secured.

I have often seen several acres of ground covered with their holes.

I have no doubt that this, and, perhaps, many of the other species, breeds several times during the year, but brings forth one young only. The pouch of the female is furnished with 4 teats.

It is difficult to keep them in captivity, as they are very wild indeed; and either escape by a burrow, or kill themselves in running their heads against the enclosure.

These are all the Marsupial animals proper which I have observed; it will however be necessary to say a few words about the sub-class of the Marsupial Group, the Monotremata, which is represented by the following species.

22. Ornithorhynchus anatinus.

The Duck-billed Platypus.

This singular animal does still exist in most of the tributaries of the Murray, as the Loddon, Avoca, Campaspe, &c. It is extremely shy, and little is yet known about its habits and economy. It burrows into the river bank from below the water level, and according to Bennett, brings forth 3 young ones at a time; some found by that naturalist were one inch and seven-eighths in length. Its food consists of fresh water worms, mollusca, worms, insects, &c.

This is about all we know of the *Platypus*, and cannot I do better for the benefit of science than draw attention to Professor Owen's remarks in his elaborate paper on the monotremata; The great anatomist says:—

"The principal points in the generative economy of this paradoxical species still remain to be determined by actual observation.

1. Manner of copulation.
2. Season of copulation.
3. Period of gestation.
4. The nature and succession of the temporary structures developed for the support of the foetus during gestation.
5. The exact size, condition, and powers of the young at the time of birth.

6. The act of suckling.
7. The period during which the young requires the lacteal nourishment, and the age at which the animal attains its full size."

Knowing that many gentlemen in the country take great interest in Natural History, and have frequent opportunities of observing the *Ornithorhynchus*, I beg to draw their attention to the questions yet to be solved.

24. ECHIDNA HYSTRIX.
The Spiny Echidna.

This singular animal, of which I have seen two preserved skins at Mount Hope, is almost less known than the Platypus. Its geographical range does not extend far into the flat country, and it is generally found in mountain ranges among rocks and stones; a shepherd at Mount Hope assured me that the animals which he had preserved were captured at the mount; the natives further down the river did not appear to be aware of the existence of such an animal as the Echidna; their food is said to consist principally of ants and their eggs, though I have kept many in captivity and offered them the food mentioned, but without success. Upon hen-eggs they subsist for some time; they also like bread and milk, but seldom live longer than two or three months in captivity. I have reason to believe that, strange as it may appear, the Echidna lives upon grass also, as I have examined several which had the intestines full of digested grass or herbs.

Of the generation of this species nothing is as yet known, nor have I ever seen a very young Echidna, none at least less than six or eight inches long.

REPTILIA.

To investigate the Reptilian fauna of a country, a longer stay than six months is necessary, and the species which I am going to enumerate must be considered as but a small portion of the reptiles inhabiting those districts. The country consists of large plains without a stone upon them, studded with salt-bush, pine forests, or mallee scrub, affording the agile reptiles unusual facilities for escape during the summer. In the cold season these creatures, owing to the nature of the country, retreat into the ground, so that they can only be obtained with great difficulty; and this is the cause that the collection made during my sojourn on the Murray was but a scanty one.

Those which were observed belonged to the following genera:—

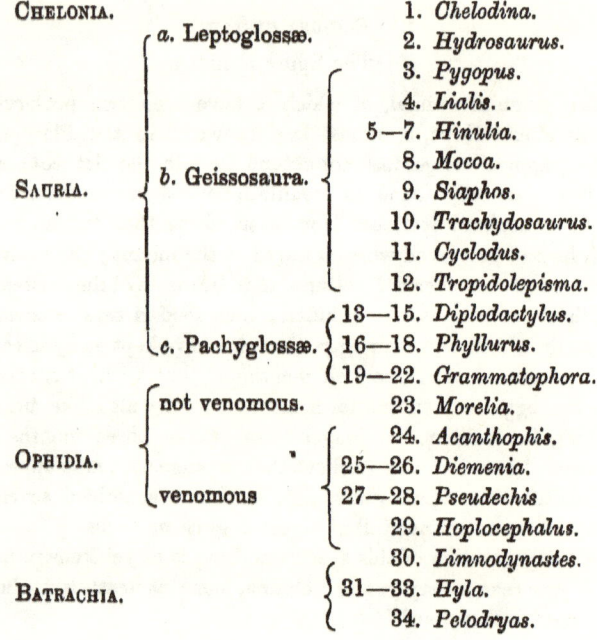

CHELONIA.
   1. *Chelodina.*

SAURIA.
 a. Leptoglossæ.
   2. *Hydrosaurus.*
 b. Geissosaura.
   3. *Pygopus.*
   4. *Lialis.*
   5—7. *Hinulia.*
   8. *Mocoa.*
   9. *Siaphos.*
   10. *Trachydosaurus.*
   11. *Cyclodus.*
   12. *Tropidolepisma.*
 c. Pachyglossæ.
   13—15. *Diplodactylus.*
   16—18. *Phyllurus.*
   19—22. *Grammatophora.*

OPHIDIA.
 not venomous.
   23. *Morelia.*
 venomous.
   24. *Acanthophis.*
   25—26. *Diemenia.*
   27—28. *Pseudechis.*
   29. *Hoplocephalus.*

BATRACHIA.
   30. *Limnodynastes.*
   31—33. *Hyla.*
   34. *Pelodryas.*

CHELONIA.

I. CHELODINA LONGICOLLIS.

The long-necked Tortoise.

This aquatic reptile is found in considerable numbers in the Murray and its tributaries. It affords food to the natives, especially during the summer, when the lagoons are dry, as it can then be procured in large numbers without difficulty. Their eggs, which are deposited in the beginning of January, amount to 15 or 20, perhaps even more, as the natives, who consume them in quantities, informed me.

Like all tortoises, the present species is very tenacious of life. On one occasion, a specimen was brought to the camp pierced by a spear: for the sake of experiment, it was put into a case, and kept for a few months, at the end of which, the wound was found completely closed, and the animal as lively as if nothing had happened to it.

SAURIA.

2. HYDROSAURUS VARIUS.
The Lace Lizard.

I believe the present striped species, and the large spotted or Gigantic Lace Lizard *(H. giganteus)* to be identical; this is one of the most common forms on the plains of the Murray; so common, in fact, that I have often captured half a dozen of them on my return to the camp; they were generally found basking in the sun, close to their holes, down which they disappeared with extraordinary swiftness when disturbed. They grow to a large size, as much as 7 or 8 feet long, and feed upon carrion, as well as upon living animals; on various occasions several pounds of bones, and once a large "opossum" was taken from the stomach of one of these reptiles.

Their eggs, of which they deposit some 10 or 15, are large, covered with a tough leathery membrane; the young lizards being more than 10 inches long, at the time of birth.

The present species is well distributed over almost every part of Australia.

3. PYGOPUS LEPIDOPODUS.
The Pygopus.

This, at first appearance, snake-like form, is occasionally met with, but not so frequently as other Lizards: its flat tongue, the two rudimentary limbs near the anus, and its ear-holes, easily distinguish it from a true snake.

The number of eggs deposited by the present species, seldom exceeds 3 or 4, they are of very elongate form, 3 or 4 times as long as they are broad, and are generally hatched by the powerful rays of the sun in 3 or 4 weeks. This lizard also has a very wide distribution.

There has been a second species of Pygopus observed on the Murray, marked with much more brilliant colours than any hitherto known; but owing to the mutilated state of the specimen which was captured by the natives, it was found impossible to preserve it or give a correct description thereof.

4. LIALIS BURTONI.
Burton's Lialis.

This is another snake-like form, with pointed muzzle, a single specimen of which came under my notice; its range is very extensive, as I have at various times received specimens from the Clarence River, and from farther north. Sir George Grey mentions its occurrence in Western Australia. In its habits, it is similar to the Pygopus.

5. HINULIA ELEGANS.
Elegant Hinulia.

6. HINULIA AUSTRALIS.
Australian Hinulia; and

7. HINULIA TENUIS.
Slender Hinulia.

Are three species of Scincoid Lizards, occasionally observed. The first is generally found beneath the rough bark of trees. I believe that there are many more representatives of the genus *Hinulia*, but owing to their nimbleness, it was impossible to capture many of them. The number of eggs deposited by these Lizards has not been ascertained correctly; perhaps they are viviparous, and if so, may bring forth 10 to 12 young.

8. MOCOA TRILINEATA.
New Holland Moco.

This widely distributed small Lizard has been frequently

captured, it is very common under bark, or among dead leaves or branches. Its eggs are deposited among decomposed leaves in moist places, and are from 10 to 16, and perhaps more in number. I have often taken as many as 50 out of one of these breeding places, but I believe that they were the produce of several lizards.

In the neighbourhood of Sydney, where *M. trilineata* is very common, the eggs are generally laid between the fronds of the so called " Staghorn fern."

9. SIAPHOS EQUALIS.

The Siaphos.

This is another small Lizard, with very short three-toed limbs ; it frequents shady or dark places, and lays but a limited number of eggs.

10. TRACHYDOSAURUS RUGOSUS.

Rugose Stump-tail.

A large, lazy, and very common kind of Lizard, generally known as the " Sleeping Lizard," which frequents open sandy plains, and may be captured in large numbers during a hot summer's day.

The number of young produced, seldom exceeds 4, those dissected by me had 2 embryos only. I believe these Lizards do not inhabit the east coast, at all events they are not found near Sydney, or at the Hastings or Clarence Rivers.

In Western Australia, particularly in the neighbourhood of King George's Sound they are very common.

11. CYCLODUS GIGAS.

Giant Cyclodus.

Whether this species is identical with the large *Cyclodus* of the east coast I cannot at present determine. Peters has described a *Cyclodus* from South Australia, and Dr. Schomburgk who discovered this new species informs me that our common Giant *Cyclodus* does not exist near Adelaide ; if this is correct, the *Cyclodus* found on the Murray, would be referable to Peters' *C. occipitalis*.

One or two specimens of this Lizard were captured by the natives.

I had been always under the impression that these reptiles produced 2 or perhaps 3 young only, but not long ago I dissected a large female specimen and took therefrom fifteen well formed young, each about from 5 to 6 inches long.

This species is prized by the natives as an article of food.

12. Tropidolepisma Kingii.
King's Tropidolepisma.

This species, (the smallest of the genus) is alone found on the Murray, its range extends almost from the east to the west coast, though in the immediate neighbourhood of Sydney it does not occur.

The number of eggs or young produced by this Lizard has not been ascertained.

13. Diplodactylus vittatus.
Yellow Crowned Diplodactyle.

This little Gecko is rather rare, as not more than 5 specimens were procured through the natives during my stay on the Murray; its distribution is very extensive, and, in fact, includes almost every part of Australia. The Australian Museum is in possession of specimens from the North East Coast, from the Murrumbidgee, and from South and West Australia. Near Sydney this species is tolerably common. It is oviparous, producing about 6 eggs.

14. Diplodactylus ornatus.
Beautiful Diplodactyle.

I do not think that there is another species of Lizard, so common and so widely distributed as this; every tree along the river banks harbours large numbers of them, and wherever a piece of dry bank is removed, this little Gecko is sure to be found beneath, in company with various species of Coleoptera, Blattæ, and spiders. In stony localities it frequents the shady side of rocks, &c. In its habits this Lizard is truly nocturnal.

15. DIPLODACTYLUS OCELLATUS.
The Eyed Diplodactyle.

Of this rare Lizard a few solitary specimens were captured, and these were in bad preservation and scarcely to be recognized. The Museum has, however, lately received well preserved specimens from the Murrumbidgee, through the kindness of Mr. William MacLeay, M.L.A., so that I am able to enumerate this Gecko, as inhabiting the Murray Plains.

16. PHYLLURUS PLATURUS.
Broad-tailed Gecko.
17. PHYLLURUS INERMIS.
Spineless Gecko.
18. PHYLLURUS MILIUSII.
Thick-tailed Gecko.

Have been obtained in the McIvor ranges and near Mount Hope; on the Murray Plains, no specimens were observed, though they may exist there. These three Geckos are common near Sydney and at the Clarence and Richmond Rivers; the last mentioned species also occurs in Western Australia.

19. GRAMMATOPHORA CRISTATA.
Crested Grammatophora.

The distribution of the present species does not extend, as far as my experience goes, beyond the mountainous districts; upon the dividing range specimens were frequently observed, but in the plain country they disappeared. The natives informed me that this lizard existed near Mount Hope, but they never captured it.

Near Sydney, where this species is common, it is generally found in the neighbourhood of water, diving into it when disturbed and remaining at the bottom for a considerable time. Specimens which I have in captivity, would lie at the bottom of a water vessel for hours without coming to the surface to breathe. I have watched one under water for more than forty minutes, I was then called away, but on my return half an hour afterwards I could not see the least indication that the lizard had stirred;

again I watched it for some twenty minutes longer, and gave it up at last, the reptiles being apparently under no necessity to breathe.

20. GRAMMATOPHORA MURICATA.
The Common Grammatophora.

This is a well-known and very common species found in nearly every part of Australia. It is fond of basking in the sun, and may be frequently observed sitting motionless on old stumps upon road side fences, &c. From 5 to 8 eggs are generally produced, and deposited in the sand.

21. GRAMMATOPHORA ORNATA.
Yellow spotted Grammatophora.

This species is found in large number upon all the open plains, every tuft of grass and every salt bush sheltering several of these gaily coloured creatures; they vary considerably in their markings, more so even than the previous species *G. muricata*. The number of eggs produced amounts to about 8.

22. GRAMMATOPHORA BARBATA.
Bearded Grammatophora.

This formidable looking reptile is better known under the name of "Jew Lizard." It cannot be considered a common form on the Murray, but its distribution extends from the East to the West Coast; how far it ranges North I have not been able to ascertain, I know however that it occurs at Wide Bay, and is probably found all over the continent.

The number of eggs produced by this reptile is most likely from 6 to 8, perhaps more.

OPHIDIA.

23. MORELIA VARIEGATA.
The Carpet Snake.

I am inclined to think that the Carpet Snake and the Diamond Snake are identical, varying in colour in different localities; Carpet Snakes occur in every part of Australia, the

South East Coast excepted ; they differ from the Diamond Snake in nothing but their markings, which consist of a series of brown blotches with darker margins, whilst the Diamond Snake is of a glossy bluish black, with a bright yellow spot in the centre of nearly every scale.

The Carpet Snake does not appear to be so common on the plains or in the mountain districts, and a single specimen only was secured ; this snake feeds upon birds, small mammals, &c., and produces a large number of eggs ; from 20 to 30 as the natives informed me.

24. ACANTHOPHIS ANTARCTICA.

The Death Adder.

Of this highly venomous snake, I obtained but a single specimen at Lake Boga ; it brings forth about 10 or 12 young ones.

25. DIEMENIA PSAMMOPHIS.

Grey Diemenia.

The present species so common near Sydney is not often met with on the Murray, only one specimen being secured during 6 months ; its bite is not considered dangerous, causing only a slight irritation, not as bad as the sting of a bee ; the total length seldom exceeds 3 feet.

26. DIEMENIA SUPERCILIOSA.

Brown Snake.

A species, which like many others, ranges from the East to the West Coast, and perhaps extends over the whole continent, as I have received specimens from Cape York. Near Sydney, and along the East Coast, the young are distinctly black, banded with a black patch upon the head ; but the young found on the Lachlan and in other localities to the westward are not banded. I have received specimens from Adelaide which are plain coloured with black patches upon head and neck, but without bands. In a few years these bands and black spots disappear more or less, and the adult snake is generally of an uniform brown color; there are some individuals on the coast, however, in which the bands may be traced when full grown. In the specimens taken on the Murray no bands or black marks could be detected.

This snake is highly venomous, and produces some 20 eggs, which are deposited in the sand under some bramble or decayed leaves; it is frequently confounded with the following species.

27. Pseudechis Australis.
Yellow-bellied Brown Snake.

Hitherto considered to be a variety of the Black Snake, from which it differs in nothing but the colour, being brown above and yellow or orange beneath. This Snake does not occur near Sydney; but it appears to be common as far north as Port Denison, from whence specimens have been obtained.

It is highly venomous.

28. Pseudechis porphyriacus.
Black Snake.

One of the most common and most venomous Snakes, distributed over almost every part of Australia, common on the Murray, and producing some twenty young annually.

29. Hoplocephalus curtus.
Brown-banded Snake.

This, the most vicious of all our reptiles, closely allied to the Indian Cobra, is very common on the plains, in particular in the reed-beds near Swan Hill, and in other swampy places; the natives appear to be in great dread of this reptile, and assured me that its bite was certain death.

This species is also found in almost every part of Australia.

These are all the Snakes actually observed by me, but no doubt they do not represent all the species which exist in these extensive plains.

BATRACHIA.
FROGS.

Of this order not many species were collected.

30. Limnodynastes dorsalis.
Striped Swamp Frog.

In a reed-bed near Lake Boga a single specimen was

obtained. It is a common species near Sydney, on the Clarence River, near Rylston, and in many other localities.

31. HYLA AUREA.
Common Golden Tree Frog.

This species, widely distributed over Australia, is the most common of all our Batrachians : the natives when pinched for food capture large numbers of it by the light of a torch at night; a supply of this frog can always be secured wherever there is fresh water near.

32. HYLA PERONII.
Yellow-Legged Tree Frog.

This species, which ranges also over a great part of the continent, is generally found during the day-time under the bark of the "Flooded Gum" (*Eucalyptus rostrata*).

33. HYLA ADELAIDENSIS.
Adelaide Tree Frog.

This species is not common on the Murray ; its range extends as far as Western Australia.

34. PELODRYAS CÆRULEUS.
Great Green Tree Frog,

The largest of our Batrachians, found in every part of Australia, and in New Guinea. I have seen specimens as large as a man's fist. This species feeds upon almost every living object that can be swallowed : lizards, frogs, all kinds of insects, and young birds—for I have once taken the nestling of a small honey-eater out of the stomach of one of these insatiable reptiles.

This concludes my notice of the reptilian fauna of the Lower Murray, which, as before mentioned, will prove much richer both in genera and species than it appears at present to be. I could enumerate some 5 or 6 more species, but these were in such bad preservation that it was found impossible to determine their character with certainty.

ON SNAKES

Observed in the neighbourhood of Sydney, by
GERARD KREFFT.

HAVING paid much attention to the reptiles found near this city, I am now able to give an account of the snakes to be met with in the vicinity, and to point out which of them may be considered dangerous to man or larger animals.

There are four highly venomous snakes observed to inhabit nearly every part of Australia, while a fifth large venomous species exists besides these on the North-west coast; and these are the only dangerous ones known to us as yet.

All the remaining species, as far as my knowledge goes, are too small to inflict a dangerous wound.

In the beginning of spring, when reptiles re-appear, there is generally a great supply of snake stories brought before the public by the daily press, but it is of very rare occurrence that we hear of death being caused by the bite of any of these animals.

If we compare our reptile-fauna with other countries under the same latitude, I think that we have sufficient reason to be thankful for the absence of the deadly Vipers, the Rattlesnakes and Puff-adders of India, America, and Africa—all of which have fangs an inch or more in length; we actually have not yet discovered a single species in which the teeth exceed one-fourth of an inch, and I doubt whether any of our snakes can inflict a wound through ordinary cloth or a common leather boot.

All our venomous snakes belong to the second sub-order of the class Ophidia, viz:—to the Colubrine snakes with permanently erect immoveable fangs in front. Of innocuous, or not venomous Colubrine snakes, we have three species near Sydney, all of which are Tree-snakes. If we except the Diamond snake, which belongs to the Boa family, we find that all not venomous

Colubrine snakes may be easily distinguished from the venomous species by the deep curve which the gape of the mouth forms; whilst, in the venomous snakes, the gape is always a more or less straight line. In the members of the Boa family the line is straight, as in venomous snakes, but these are easily distinguished by the rudimentary limbs, in shape like a small spur situated near the anus.

I have added Dr. Günther's description of the two species of Sea-Snakes which occur on our coast; both of which may be considered harmless, having only very small fangs—and I take this opportunity to thank that eminent naturalist for the kind assistance he has so frequently rendered me. I also beg to assure those contributors to the Museum who have furnished me with the means of adding to the knowledge of our Reptiles, that I shall always consider myself under deep obligations to every one of them.

FIRST SUBORDER.

OPHIDII COLUBRIFORMES INNOCUI.

INNOCUOUS COLUBRINE SNAKES.

Snakes without grooved fang in front, comprising the following families :—

1. *Typhlopidæ*, or Blind Snakes.
2. *Dendrophidæ*, or Tree-Snakes.
3. *Dipsadidæ*, or Nocturnal Tree-Snakes; and
4. *Pythonidæ*, or Rock-Snakes.

1.—TYPHLOPIDÆ; OR BLIND SNAKES.

Typhlops. *Schneid.*

Typhlops rüpelli. *Jan.*

The Blind Snake.

Scales in 22 rows. Rostral large and broad above, narrowing below; Preoculars much larger at the base than at the tip, third upper labial in contact with the ocular and preocular. Anterior scales smaller than the posterior ones. Tail short, cylindrical, very obtuse, three times the length of its diameter, and ending in a small spine.

The color of this harmless little reptile is brownish grey above, and yellowish below; each scale of the back being bordered with yellowish white, the markings becoming obsolete towards the tail; the form is cylindrical, enlarging towards the tail.

Of all our harmless snakes, the present species is the least offensive; it lives under ground, and is frequently found in Ants' nests, upon the larvæ of which it principally exists; its total length does not exceed 18 inches. I believe that the present species has a very wide range, and that it will be found to inhabit the greater part of the Australian Continent; specimens from the Murray River, from South Australia, and from Queensland are in the collection of the Australian Museum.

2.—DENDROPHIDÆ; OR TREE-SNAKES.

Dendrophis. *Boie.*

Dendrophis punctulata. *Gray.*

The Green Tree-Snake.

Scales in 12 or 13 rows.
Anal bifid.
Ventrals 207.
Subcaudals 106/106.

Of slender form, above green or pale olive brown, beneath bright yellow, sides and under parts of head the same colour; eyes large, pupil rounded. Outer edge of scales white, as may be seen on stretching the skin.

1 anterior 2 posterior oculars, scales smooth, those of the vertebral row much larger, polygonal; scales of outer rows elongated, narrow, quadrilateral, and very imbricated.

Maxillary teeth smooth and of equal length.

This snake, one of the few not venomous Australian species, is a gentle harmless creature, which at any time may be handled with impunity; it never attempts to bite, and of many hundred individuals which I had an opportunity to observe alive, not a single one could be induced to inflict a wound.

If we except Tasmania and the southern part of Victoria, we find the Green Tree Snake from north to south, and from east to west; it frequents trees, feeds upon insects, frogs, lizards, small birds and birds' eggs, and grows to a considerable length, but seldom if ever exceeding 6 feet.

I have reason to believe that the female is oviparous, laying about 20 or more eggs in November or December; young individuals differ considerably from the adult in colouring, being not of so bright a green; and having a grey instead of a light yellow belly. The winter is generally passed under hollow logs or beneath flat stones in sunny but often damp localities.

3. DIPSADIDÆ, OR NOCTURNAL TREE-SNAKES.

DIPSAS. *Auct.*

DIPSAS FUSCA *Gray;*

The Brown Tree-Snake.

Scales in 19 rows.
Anal entire.
Ventrals 236.
Subcaudals 87/87.

Form slender, body and tail compressed, elongate head much depressed, triangular, broad behind, very distinct from neck; scales on the vertebral line much larger, regularly six-sided, vertical shield broad, occipitals obtuse behind, one loreal; eight upper labials, the third and fourth and sometimes the fifth touching the orbit; one anterior two posterior oculars; eye large, pupil elliptical; nostril moderate, between two shields; posterior maxillary teeth longest and grooved.

Above, light brown or reddish brown, with numerous black rather oblique, sometimes obsolete cross bands; belly uniform salmon coloured.

The present species has not been so much noticed in the neighbourhood of Sydney as the Green Tree-snake, but this may be owing to its nocturnal habits; it is found along the East Coast, and ranges as far as Port Essington; individuals observed in captivity appeared very gentle in disposition, and could be freely handled without showing any inclination to bite, they passed the day coiled up amongst the branches of trees, but became very active at night, noiselessly gliding through the foliage in search of their prey, which, as in the Green Tree snake, consists of birds, birds' eggs, insects, frogs, lizards, and the smaller mammalia.

I am unable to state whether the female is oviparous or not; the number of young produced annually does probably not exceed 20. Total length of adult about 6 feet.

4. PYTHONIDÆ, OR ROCK-SNAKES.

MORELIA. *Grey.*

MORELIA SPILOTES. THE DIAMOND SNAKE.

> Scales in 47 rows.
> Ventrals 270.
> Anal bifid.
> Subcaudals 80/80.

Head shields small, scale-like; three pairs of distinct frontal plates, vertical plate indistinct, rostral shield with a pit on each side, first and second upper labials pitted; of the lower labials the first seven are smooth, then follow seven deeply pitted scales, and 3 or 4 smooth ones, nostrils lateral, in a single plate with a groove beneath; eyes lateral; pupil elliptical, erect; scales smooth; subcaudal plates in two rows, two spur-like appendages near the vent.

Coloration:—

Bluish black above, almost every scale with a yellowish (white in spirits) elongate spot in the centre; there is a series of dark-edged irregular blotches upon the back, each bearing in the middle a few very bright yellow-colored scales; these spots or blotches vary considerably in different individuals, specimens from Port Macquarie having almost the markings of the Carpet Snake, but still retaining the yellow spot in each scale, which in

M. variegata is wanting. Some specimens occur with a pale yellow streak from the side of the head to the vent: in fact we very rarely find two of these snakes which do not differ considerably in their markings.

The range of the Diamond Snake (*M. spilotes*) is restricted to a very limited area of country, being found in no other part of Australia than from Port Macquarie to Jervis Bay, or perhaps Cape Howe; and from the coast to the western slopes of the Blue Mountains and the Liverpool Range. In the plains watered by the Lachlan, the Murray and the Murrumbidgee, the present species is not found, the Carpet Snake *(Morelia variegata)* taking its place there.

The Diamond Snake is a common species in the county of Cumberland, in the Blue Mountains and the Illawarra district; it is a harmless creature, which may be picked up by any body without ever offering to bite; though it is a strictly nocturnal snake, individuals are nevertheless met with during the day-time, either basking in the sun and digesting their food, or, having been disturbed, in search of a place of shelter. Like the other species of the family Pythonidæ, they prey upon birds, and the smaller species of Mammals; young individuals feeding upon insects, frogs, or birds' eggs; the female deposits 30 or more eggs in December or January, which in a month or two the sun brings to maturity. I am not aware that the mother cares any longer about her progeny, after laying the eggs; and I have never seen or heard of a single instance where she coiled herself upon the eggs so deposited.

Diamond Snakes are found in almost every kind of country as long as it offers sufficient shelter; they prefer open stony ridges studded with low trees and well supplied with water, the edges of swamps and lagoons are frequented by them, as they find there a considerable supply of Water-rats (*Hydromys*), young Ducks, and other water-fowl; they also often visit the hen roosts of the farmer, or surprise " Opossums " (*Phalangista*) or " Flying Squirrels " (*Petaurus*), upon the branches of high *Eucalypti.*

The largest specimen, to my knowledge, that has been captured near Sydney, and properly measured, without being stretched, was 10 feet 3 inches long; that individuals of 11 feet or more in length occur, I doubt not, though they are very rare indeed, and have never come under my notice.

The way in which Diamond Snakes capture their prey is as follows :—

The snake suspends itself from the branch of some low bush or tree and watches for the victim, which often plays about near its unseen enemy. The reptile, with its neck and head bent into the form of an S, deliberately measures its distance, uncoiling more of its body if necessary, and often almost touching the animal it is in wait for ; as soon as the snake is sure to reach its victim, it darts forward, generally catching the prey by one of the hind legs, and instantly takes a turn around its body, soon extinguishing life through its powerful pressure. As soon as the animal is quite dead, the process of swallowing begins, the snake always commencing with the head ; this done, the reptile will often for days together bask in the sun, until the food is so far digested as to impede its movements no longer.

If a snake is disturbed during this state, it will almost always throw up the half digested carcass.

In a state of nature they never touch any food except living animals. I once, however, observed a Diamond Snake, which was kept in a cage, swallow a rat which had been killed by a Brown-banded snake (*Hoplocephalus curtus.*)

The present species is greatly infested by various kinds of Intestinal worms, including a Tape worm, clusters of which I have frequently taken from the stomach of this reptile.

Before concluding, a few remarks will be necessary with regard to the Carpet Snake (*Morelia variegata*).

There is very little, if any difference in the distribution and number of scales between the Diamond and Carpet Snakes, the only character in which both snakes vary, is the coloration; the first having a yellow spot in the centre of each scale, whilst the latter has the back ornamented with numerous irregular black edged brown blotches; the belly, as in the Diamond Snake, being yellowish. I have mentioned before the remarkable fact, that the Carpet Snake is found in every part of Australia, except the Coast District, say from Cape Howe to the Hastings, and about 100 miles inland ; at Port Macquarie both species occur, but at the Clarence River, according to Mr. James F. Wilcox, the Carpet Snake alone is found. Dr. J. E. Gray has indeed tried to distinguish the one from the other by the vertical plate, which he considers distinct in *Morelia variegata*, and indistinct in *M. spilotes*. But after examination of large numbers of both species, I do not think that the above is a character much to be relied upon, and I am led to believe that both Snakes are but varieties of the same species.

There is, according to Duméril and Bibron, the famous French Herpetologists, a second species of Snake of the Boa family to be found near Sydney, namely,

The Bolyeria, *D. & B.*

BOLYERIA MULTICARINATA. *D. & B.*

This, however, is not the case. I have hunted the country near Sydney for years, and have never come across a single snake of this description ; high rewards have been offered for it, with no better success, and no specimen ever existed in the Australian Museum. I have, however, lately purchased a snake which answers to the description given, and which was obtained at some of the islands near New Guinea.

SECOND SUBORDER.

OPHIDII COLUBRIFORMES VENENOSI.

VENOMOUS COLUBRINE SNAKES.

Snakes with an erect immoveable grooved or perforated fang in front of the maxillary.

Gape of mouth forming a straight line.

This suborder, if we include the genus *Acanthophis* with the first family, comprises the

1. *Elapidæ* or Elapides ; and the

2. *Hydrophidæ*, or Sea-Snakes.

1. ELAPIDÆ; OR ELAPIDES.

Diemenia. *Gray.*

Diemenia psammophis. *Schleg.*

The Grey Snake.

Scales in 15 rows.
Anal bifid.
Ventrals 177.
Subcaudals 85/85.

The present species has been described by Dr. Günther as *D. reticulata*, under which name I have frequently alluded to it. It appears, however, that the snake to which Günther refers in his *Cat. of Colubrine Snakes*, when quoting Schlegel's figure (*Abbildungen* Tab. 46, No. 14), is that author's *D. psammophis*, which name has the priority, and ought to be adopted instead of, *D. reticulata*. The coloration is a uniform grey above, and greenish below, the central part of the ventrals being conspicuously marked with green; tips of scales and skin between them, black; and of tail, salmon colour; a yellowish dark edged streak crossing the rostral shield. The eye is encircled first by a black and then by a yellowish line, both ending in a point below the orbit.

The present species is found in nearly every part of Australia, the extreme North and South excepted. I have taken it eight years ago on the Murray and Darling, and since then specimens have come to hand from Brisbane, Port Curtis, and Rockhampton. All these snakes differ no more from those of Sydney than these do amongst themselves. Much dependence can never be placed upon coloration as a distinguishing character in snakes, as in this no two reptiles vary so much as a snake about to shed its skin differs from itself after this operation has been successfully performed. I believe the present species to be the most common in our neighbourhood.

It frequents sandy localities, feeds on insects, small frogs, lizards, &c., and its bite does not cause any more irritation than the sting of a bee; from 15 to 20 eggs are deposited by the female under stones exposed to the sun, generally in the beginning of December, and perhaps earlier, as I have on more than one occasion taken the young snakes at the end of that month and in the beginning of January. This reptile is generally found from two to three feet in length, very rarely exceeding four feet. During the cold season the grey snake retires under flat stones exposed to the sun ; it very seldom, if ever, goes into the ground ; it is very sensitive to cold, and the least frost suffices to destroy it. I have found sometimes five and more of these reptiles under the same stone.

Diemenia Superciliosa. *Fischer.*

Ringed Diemenia.

Scales in 17 rows near neck.
Scales in 15 rows near tail.
Subcaudals 73/73.
Anal bifid.
Ventrals 228.

Superciliaries larger than vertical; occipitals widely forked, rounded, broad ; rostral high, reaching to the surface of crown ; one nasal, one anterior, two posterior oculars ; superciliaries prominent above the eye; anterior ocular grooved near the top; posterior frontals much larger than the anterior ones, bent down on the sides and with nasal, anterior ocular, and second and third upper labial replacing the loreal ; belly flat. Dark brown above, a lighter band just crossing behind the occipitals ; side of face and chin much lighter than the other parts of the body ; belly yellowish, sides of ventrals and lower edge clouded with purple grey, forming a series of irregular blotches, each ventral with a distinct darkish streak on its lower edge. Half-grown and sometimes adult individuals show traces of from seventy to seventy-five black rings, which in the young snakes are very distinct. The following description is applicable to young specimens up to three years old :—

Muzzle light brown ; a black triangular spot covering the region between the eyes and the occiput as far as the hinder margin of the occipitals—this streak is bent down on the sides of the face, and behind this dark spot is a white narrow streak and another broad dark band reaching down to the edge of the labial shields; then follows again a white streak and a second black band, but much smaller than the previous one, and so alternately a broader brownish and a narrow black band to within an inch of the apical half of the tail; the black bands are occasionally interrupted, leaving a blank on the other side of the body; including these interrupted streaks, from seventy to eighty may be counted upon body and tail, seventy-five is the usual number. The belly in young and half-grown individuals is covered with yellowish spots, which at a more mature age form into the black blotches mentioned in the description of the adult.

The great difference in the coloration of young half-grown and adult individuals has given rise to a variety of names: for some time I tried in vain to reduce them, but at last succeeded by bringing together a complete series of this snake in various stages of growth, from the egg upwards. Dr. Albert Günther to whom drawings as well as specimens in good preservation were submitted, states in a paper read before the Zoological Society of London,

"The young specimens, then, found by Mr. Krefft, do not belong to *Furina textilis*, Duméril and Bibron, which has three posterior oculars, but to *Diemansia annulata*, described by myself in ' *Colubr. Snakes*,' p. 213. And the old individual sent by Mr. Krefft is identical with *Pseudœlaps superciliosus*, Fisch. Mr. Jan, of Milan, (who says that he has examined the Snakes of the Hamburg Museum) describes the adult Snake under two names, *Pseudœlaps sordellii* and *Ps. kubinyi*, the latter being founded upon an accidental variety, in which some of the head shields are confluent. The synonomy of this species therefore would be:—

Diemansia superciliosa.

    an Adult.

  1856. *Pseudœlaps superciliosus*. Fisher in Abhandl. Geb. Naturwiss. III., part 107., taf. 2 fig. 3. (head not quite correct).

1859. *Pseudælaps sordellii.* Jan in Rev. and Magaz. Zool. pl. C. (head).

1859. *Pseudælaps kubinyi,* Jan, l. c. (founded on an accidental variety) C. (young).

1858. *Diemansia annulata,* Günth. Colubr. Snak., p. 2 B.

1862. *Furina textilis,* Krefft, Proc. Zool. Soc. p. 149."

The geographical range of this species extends over almost every part of Australia, as I have seen specimens from Cape York, Adelaide, the Murray, and other localities. When full grown, this Snake may be dangerous to man; in its habits it is diurnal, and found generally in rocky localities; young Snakes are frequently found under stones during the cold season, while those of a more mature age retire into the ground.

BRACHYSOMA. *Günther.*

Brachysoma diadema. *Günther.*

The Red-Capped Snake.

Scales in 15 rows.
Anal bifid.
Ventrals 175.
Subcaudals?

Body elongate and rounded; head flat, distinct from neck; muzzle broad and obtuse; rostral high, slightly grooved, reaching to surface of crown; one nasal pierced by the large nostril; anterior oculars triangular, posterior one much larger, five-sided and bent down on the sides; occipitals moderate, rounded, scarcely forked behind; 6 upper labials, the third and fourth forming the orbit; eye small, pupil sub-elliptical, erect. Two temporal shields, the upper in contact with both post oculars, the lower much larger, wedged in between the last two labials.

Above, purplish brown, each scale with yellow centre very distinct in the first 4 or 5 rows on each side; head and neck black above, except a lunated spot just behind the occiput, which is brick-red, and turns white in spirits.

Beneath yellowish, front of lower jaw with a black spot.

"Upper jaw with grooved fang in front, separated from the other teeth by an interval; an elongate series of six or seven teeth behind; palatine teeth equal in length; anterior teeth of lower jaw longest." (*Günther*.)

This very handsome little Snake is not uncommon near Sydney, though few people have ever seen it; during the cold season I have met with specimens under thin flat stones at Manly, Lane Cove, and other rocky localities; before I had an opportunity of proving its existence near Sydney, it had been known from Western Australia and the North East coast only. This Snake is venomous, but never offers to bite, and may be handled with impunity; it is oviparous, laying from 8 to 10 eggs. Its food consists, like that of other small species, in minute Blattæ, young frogs of the genus *Pseudophryne*, ants, ants' eggs, &c.

PSEUDECHIS. *Wagl.*

Pseudechis porphyriacus. *Shaw.*

The Black Snake.

Scales in 17 rows.
Anal bifid.
Ventrals 180 to 200.

Subcaudals 14, 41/41. Sometimes all subcaudals entire.

This snake is so well known that but a short description of it will be necessary. Body elongate and rounded; tail moderate, not distinct from trunk: head rather small, quadrangular with rounded muzzle; shields of crown regular; 2 nasals, no loreal; one anterior and 2 posterior oculars; scales smooth, imbricate, in 17 rows; anal bifid; first subcaudals entire, hinder ones two-rowed; in some individuals all the subcaudals are entire. Black above, each scale of the outer series, red at the base and black at the tip; ventral shields with black posterior margins; muzzle light brown; ventral plates from 180 to 200.

The Black Snake is, I believe, the most common of all our venomous snakes; it frequents low marshy places, is fond of water, dives and swims well, and subsists principally upon frogs, lizards, insects, and the smaller mammalia, in particular the young of *Hydromys leucogaster*. On one occasion 16 young of this rat were taken out of a single Black Snake, so that the reptile must have plundered four rats' nests.

When irritated the Black Snake raises about two feet of its body off the ground, flattens out the neck like a Cobra, and then darts at its prey or enemy. The bite of this snake is highly venomous, killing good sized dogs or goats within an hour.

The number of young brought forth in March generally amounts to 15 or 20. During the winter the Black Snake retires into the ground.

I believe that the Black Snake is found in almost every part of Australia. On the Murray and farther north a Snake occurs which has generally been considered a variety of the Black Snake; it is identical with it in almost every particular except colour, being brown instead of black, and orange beneath. Whether this is really a distinct species or merely a variety is not quite certain. Dr. Günther has distinguished the brown variety, however, as *P. australis*, and I mention this as it is a belief with some people that the Brown Snake and the Black Snake are identical, and the coloration sexual. It is to be remembered that the Brown Snake of Sydney, (*Diemenia superciliosa*) is generically distinct from the Black Snake.

HOPLOCEPHALUS. *Cuv.*

Hoplocephalus nigrescens. Gthr.

Black-backed Hoplocephalus.

Scales in 15 rows.
Ventrals 173 to 176.
Anal entire.
Subcaudals 37.

Scales in 15 rows, 6 upper labials, the second of which is pointed above, the third truncated. Uniform bluish grey or purple black above; ventral shields whitish, blackish on the sides. Description :—Body rather elongate, rounded; tail somewhat short, not distinct from trunk; head oblong, depressed, not distinct from neck; eye small, pupil sub-elliptical. Rostral shield, very broad and low, and very obtuse superiorly; anterior frontals moderate, broader than long, rounded in front; posterior frontals rather large, five-sided, each with two hinder edges forming together a right angle; vertical, six-sided, about as broad as long, with parallel outer edges, an obtuse angle in front, and a pointed one behind; occipitals oblong, obtusely rounded behind; superciliary moderate; two posterior oculars, one anterior just reaching to the upper surface of the head; the post frontal, nasal, anteorbital and second upper labial meet at a point and replace the loreals; six upper labials: the first is very low, situated below the nasal, the third and fourth enter the orbit; front series of temporals formed by two shields, one of which is in contact with the post orbitals. Chin-shields of nearly equal size, several scales between the hinder chin-shields and the first ventral; the median line of the upper part of the tail is occupied by a series of hexagonal scales; a series of small teeth behind the grooved front tooth.

The present species is subject to considerable variation of colours during the course of the year; sometimes before changing its skin the back and head are of a leaden hue, and the ventral scales uniform whitish; after the old skin has been cast off, the upper coat assumes a shining deep purple or bluish black; the ventral scales are at this time rose-coloured, which hue is invariably lost in spirits. The ventral scales of many subjects examined I found clouded on the sides; sometimes the greater part of the scales, in particular those near the vent, were blackish, and the subcaudals entirely so. I believe that this is the only snake of the genus *Hoplocephalus* in which the tongue is white.

The rocky neighbourhood of Middle Harbour (Port Jackson) is the locality where I first found this new species, but since then specimens have been obtained from Port Macquarie and the Clarence River, which do not differ in colour from those inhabiting the neighbourhood of Sydney; it is highly probable that the geographical distribution of this species extends still farther to the northward; but, owing to its nocturnal habits, collectors will experience great difficulty in capturing it.

During the cold season, from May to September, I have frequently found this Snake hybernating (if I may so express their dormant state) under loose flat stones, singly or in pairs, but never in company with other Ophidians; and more than once a dozen specimens were the result of a day's hunting.

It is very singular that no Snakes of this kind were ever met with between Sydney and Long-Bay, or towards the South-head, and I believe that they never frequented that district, otherwise the species would have been known long before this, as even White, in his Voyage to New South Wales, figures such rare Snakes as *Vermicella annulata*, and *Hoplocephalus variegatus*.

With regard to its habits, I may mention that it is strictly nocturnal, feeding on the smaller Batrachians, as *Pseudophryne australis*, and *Uperoleia marmorata*, specimens of which I have found in its stomach. It is rather sluggish in its disposition, and, though venomous, not dangerous to man or the larger animals.

The female produces about 20 young annually.

HOPLOCEPHALUS SIGNATUS. *Jan.*

Black-bellied Hoplocephalus.

Scales in 17 rows.
Ventrals 157.
Anal bifid.
Subcaudals 51.

Body short and rounded; tail short, distinct from trunk; head triangular, distinct from neck : above brownish olive, head much lighter coloured, with a white-edged dark streak from behind the eye to the back of the neck.

Description—head shields regular; vertical, six sided, with obtuse angle in front, and a sharp one behind; superciliaries rather large, nearly as long as the vertical occipitals; much forked behind, sometimes angular, but more generally rounded; nasal large, pierced by the nostril; one anterior, two posterior oculars; rostral high, with a groove along its lower edge; six upper labials, third and fourth coming into the orbit; a white or yellowish-edged dark streak from behind the eye to the back of the head, no collar; eye moderate, pupil rather sub-elliptical; in young individuals the pupil appears always quite rounded; scales six-sided, much larger on the sides than upon the back; skin between the scales black.

Young specimens have the whitish streak behind the eye very distinct and often extended on the other side as far as the nostril; the apical half of the tail is either whitish or salmon-coloured below; in other respects they do not differ from the adult in colour, except that the whitish hue on the sides of the neck is less distinct. In the adult subject the head is often much paler than the other part of the body, which is either olive brown or brownish black above, and bluish black or bluish grey below; the fourth part of each ventral scale is clouded with grey on the sides, leaving a much darker band in the middle, which, approaching the neck, diminishes in size; the sides of the neck below and the chin shields being of a yellowish hue. Individuals occur occasionally, which are almost black above; others, particularly those about to shed their skin, appear pale brown above, and bluish grey below; in removing any of the ventral plates, the skin below is always jet black.

Habitat.—

The present species abounds in sandy or swampy localities near Sydney; the country between the City and Botany is much frequented by these snakes; they appear to be nocturnal, and are seldom observed during the day-time; they often prey upon each other, but generally upon the smaller Batrachians *(Cystignathus* and *Pseudophryne)* which I have frequently taken from their stomachs; various kinds of insects, small lizards, &c., are also devoured by them. The venom of this snake does not effect the larger vertebrated animals. I have at various times experimented upon cats and goats with it, but without a single fatal result; in fact the animals bitten did not appear to be affected at all.

Mrs. Edw. Forde of Ash Island, to whom I am greatly indebted for much valuable information respecting the reptilian fauna of the Hunter River, informs me that *Hoplocephalus signatus* is the most common of the Snakes on Ash Island, and that it is frequently captured and carried about by domestic cats, generally at night, proving at once its nocturnal habits and the slight effect its venom has upon these animals.

At Port Macquarie, this Snake occurs in large numbers, also at the Richmond and Clarence Rivers, but from beyond Brisbane I have never seen any specimens. I believe that it is also found in the neighbourhood of Melbourne. It is probably identical with *Hoplocephalus flagellum* (M'Coy).

The female produces from 15 to 25 young ones annually, total length 20 inches, tail 4 inches, cleft of mouth ⅜ of inch.

HOPLOCEPHALUS VARIEGATUS. *D. and B.*

Broad-Headed Snake.

Scales in 21 rows.
Anal entire.
Ventrals 210.
Subcaudals 45 to 50.

Body and tail moderate ; head flat, broad behind, very distinct from neck, obtuse in front ; eye moderate, pupil sub-elliptical ; vertical shield rather small, six sided, frontals of nearly equal size, large posterior ones rounded behind ; occipitals regular, rather broad, forked ; large lower temporal shield wedged between fifth and sixth lower labial ; 6 lower labials, the last of which is the largest ; one large pre-ocular in conjunction with nasal ; anterior, frontal and second upper labial replacing the loreal.

Above black, irregularly spotted with yellow (white in spirits), forming a series of broad black blotches upon the back.

Beneath shining greyish black, each ventral plate with a large yellow spot on each side ; first and second row of scales yellow, with here and there a black one intermixed ; all the light scales more or less shaded towards the point.

We know little or nothing as regards the geographical distribution of this reptile ; the few specimens in European collections were obtained by Mons. Verreaux, near Sydney, and so rare has this snake always been that up to 1858 no specimen of it was to be found in the British Museum. Since then I have been able to collect several hundreds of these snakes, which are strictly nocturnal in their habits, and seldom if ever observed during the day time. They may be procured from under stones in sunny localities during the cold season, and all the stony ridges around Sydney have harboured them in large numbers. At the present time they begin to become scarce, many of their favourite haunts being invaded by the gardener or the builder.

The bite of this snake is not sufficiently strong to endanger the life of man. I have been wounded by it several times, and experienced no bad symptoms beyond a slight headache; the spot where the fang entered turning blue to about the size of a shilling, for a few days.

Cats, dogs, and goats have been frequently experimented upon without any fatal result.

In January or February the female produces from 15 to 20 young ones, which, though only a few inches long, will show fight if one attempts to lift them; the adults always look formidable if attacked.

The snake which Schlegel describes as *Naja bungaroides* Abbildungen, Tab. 48, fig. 17 and 18, is nothing but a variety of the present species. The Australian Museum is in possession of a specimen from the Hastings, which is banded instead of having the irregular blotches of *H. variegatus*.

HOPLOCEPHALUS CURTUS. *Schleg.*

The Brown-banded Snake.

Scales in 18 rows anteriorly, and in 19 posteriorly.

Ventrals 169.
Subcaudals 44.

Body rounded, rather depressed, tail moderate, not distinct from trunk; head large, broad, very distinct from neck, crown flat, muzzle rounded; superciliaries slightly prominent, and sometimes two grooves before the eye. All the shields of the head very broad, the vertical almost square, with an obtuse angle behind; occipitals deeply forked, sides sometimes jagged, with a broad scale fitting the notch. Scales never in less than 18 rows; above olive brown with from 60 to 70 darker cross-bands, in some specimens the scales between the dark bands are anteriorly edged with yellow, the two outer rows of scales yellowish, more or less clouded, but without any distinct spot in the centre of each scale as in *H. superbus*. Belly yellow, ventral plates frequently clouded or spotted with dark grey anteriorly, growing darker towards the tail; the subcaudals, which are entire, being almost uniform blackish.

The coloration of this snake varies considerably; on the East Coast light-brown specimens are much more frequent than dark ones, whilst Western Australian snakes of this species are very dark-brown, and the cross-bands remarkably distinct. This reptile has been frequently alluded to by some authors as *H. superbus*, but I have always maintained that no continental species has ever been found with 15 rows of scales, and the vertical shield more than twice as long as broad; the main characters by which the two snakes can easily be distinguished. I am certain that more than 300 specimens have passed through my hands, and in not one instance did they answer to Dr. Günther's description of *H. superbus*.

I will give here the main points in which both Snakes differ:

H. superbus.	*H. curtus.*
Scales in 15 rows.	*Scales* in 18 to 19 rows.
Tail short, distinct from trunk.	*Tail* not distinct from trunk.
Head remarkably small, scarcely distinct from trunk.	*Head* very broad, as large again as *H. Superbus*, and distinct from neck.
Neck rather rounded.	*Neck* very flat.
Scales of Head more or less elongate; vertical, more than twice as long as broad.	*Scales of Head* very broad, in particular the vertical, which without the anterior angle would form a square.
Coloration uniform brown, 2 outer rows of scales with reddish or yellow centre spot.	*Coloration* brown banded, 2 outer rows of scales paler, or clouded with yellow and greyish.
Habitat Tasmania.	*Habitat* Australian continent.
Synonym Diamond Snake of the Tasmanians.	*Synonyms* Brown Banded Snake, N. S. Wales; Tiger Snake, Victoria.

I have had some correspondence with Dr. Albert Günther regarding the habitat of the two Snakes, and I am glad to see the learned Doctor's statement in the *Annals of Natural History* for November, 1863, that "*Hoplocephalus superbus* proves to be a Tasmanian species."

It would be interesting to know whether the Tasmanian Snake is able to inflate the skin of the neck when irritated, but judging from its small size this is not likely to be the case, and we must leave to Tasmanian Naturalists the solution of this question. In the continental Snake the power to raise itself off the ground for half the length of the body, and to flatten out the neck like a Cobra, is well known, the Black Snake being the only other reptile which has been provided with the same power. A few words more and I have done with this, the most dangerous of all our Snakes.

Its habitat is, I believe, the temperate part of Australia from East to West. I have taken it on the Murray, in South Australia and Victoria, and received specimens from almost every part of New South Wales and from King George's Sound. The present species is not far removed from the Indian Cobra *(Naja tripudians)*, and its bite is as deadly. A good sized dog bitten became paralyzed within three minutes, and was dead in fifty minutes afterwards; a goat died in thirty-five minutes; another goat which escaped whilst experimented upon, was found dead in the street after a few hours; a Dingo met the same fate in forty-eight minutes; an Echidna *(Echidna hystrix)* lived six hours, and a Common Tortoise, an animal which will live a day with its head cut off, was dead in five hours after being bitten.

Antidote vendors seeing the effect of the poison, never dared to peril their reputation in the attempt to save the animals so bitten; I must mention, however, that in making these experiments, chance bites, where the snake makes a dart, bites, and retires, were out of the question, and I grant that under such conditions man or animal may recover; but if the snake's head is applied to the lip or ear of some animal and the fangs well pressed into the wound, there is little hope of recovery. Let me also give a few words of advice to such men as go about exhibiting these reptiles, and showing their prowess by allowing themselves to be bitten, professing that they possess an antidote against the poison; generally speaking, these persons are more or less impostors; they break off the fangs of the snake, but do not know how soon they are reproduced, and thus frequently fall victims to their ignorance. The Indian jugglers have more sense, and entirely remove the teeth, as most of the specimens of *Naja tripudians* prove which are received from India.

The young of this snake, from 15 to 20 in number, are generally observed about the end of February; they are then from 7 to 8 inches long, and subsist on small frogs, lizards, or insects. During the cold season this snake retires into the ground, as I have never met with half-grown or adult specimens under stones.

PETRODYMON. *Krefft.*

PETRODYMON CUCULLATUS.

Red-bellied Snake.

Scales in 15 rows.
Anal 1/1.
Ventrals 187.
Subcaudals 41/41.

Purplish brown above, with a series of darker longitudinal lines along the upper part of the body, leaving a light elongate mark in the middle of each scale. Beneath yellow, bright red in adult specimens, each ventral plate clouded on the upper edge with purplish brown, much interrupted on the posterior part of the body. Divisional line of subcaudal plates marked in a similar manner, leaving the outer edges of the plates yellowish. Upper part of head purplish brown as far as the middle of posterior frontals, covering the vertical part of superciliaries, and reaching beyond the occipitals; this elliptical spot is joined to the back by a narrow band of the same colour running along the median line of the neck. A light-greyish band encircles the dark-brown mark, divided by the narrow line by which this mark is joined to the back. Upper and lower labials dotted with brown spots. Body rounded, head rather flat, depressed; tail short, distinct from trunk, and ending in a conical spine or nail about a quarter of an inch long.

Scales in 15 rows (not in 13, as mentioned by Dr. Günther, whose description as *Diemenia cucullata* was taken from a very bad specimen); 6 upper labials, the third and fourth forming the lower edge of the orbit, the second labial *not* in contact with the posterior frontal; rostral broad, low, very obtuse superiorly; shields of the head regular, all more or less rounded posteriorly, and slightly imbricate, vertical twice as long as broad; one anterior and two posterior oculars, one temporal in contact with both oculars, four or five scale-like temporals behind; eye very small, pupil elliptical and erect.

About 3 years ago—in 1860—I captured a single individual of this species; since then, owing to the exertions of friends in the country, specimens from Ash Island, Hunter River, Port Macquarie, the Clarence River, and other localities have been received, so that its geographical range has been ascertained for many hundred miles along the east coast. This snake is strictly nocturnal in its habits, sluggish and of gentle disposition, never offering to bite when handled, and though venomous, it is so in a very slight degree only, as has been proved by experiments; its length seldom, if ever, exceeds 20 inches. Rocky and desolate places are frequented by it, and in such localities it is occasionally found under flat stones during the cold season.

VERMICELLA. *Gray.*

VERMICELLA ANNULATA

The Ringed Vermicella.

Scales in 15 rows.
Ventrals 225.
Anal bifid.
Subcaudals 18/18.

The following is Dr. Günther's description:—"Body elongate, rounded, slightly compressed behind; tail very short; head moderate, not distinct from neck, similar to *Elaps*; rostral shield very large, rounded, raised above the surface of snout; occipitals rather narrow; two posterior oculars; anterior large, replacing the loreal together with the nasal; nasal shield single, pierced in the centre by the small nostril; six upper labials, third and fourth coming into the orbit; one large temporal shield in contact with the upper posterior ocular, two smaller ones behind. Scales smooth, large, rather rounded behind, in fifteen rows. Anal and subcaudals bifid. Tail ending in an obtuse conical scale. Two small fangs in front of upper jaw, no other teeth behind; palatine and mandibulary teeth equal in length. Crown of head and muzzle black; a yellowish, in fresh specimens white, band across the posterior frontals, a second on the neck; body and tail encircled by alternate black and white (in spirits) rings. Length of cleft of mouth $\frac{1}{2}''$; length of tail $1\frac{1}{4}''$; total length 28''."

The ringed Vermicella, like all other nocturnal snakes, is very seldom met with, and apparently little known to the colonists. I often capture it during the cold season without taking any precaution whatever, as I know from experience that this gentle creature will never bite; but even if it should do so, the wound would be small and of no danger whatever. I have never succeeded to make it bite of its own accord, but had to open its mouth forcibly if I wished to try an experiment. White, in his Voyage to New South Wales, gives a figure of this interesting snake, but little was known until a few years ago with respect to its geographical range. We find it as far south as Eden, Twofold Bay; it occurs again in Western Australia, is tolerably common near Brisbane, and may probably be found much further north. Mr. William Taylor has lately presented a young specimen of this snake to the Museum, which was captured at the Culgoa River; it is not unlikely that this species is found all over the continent from east to west.

In its habits it is nocturnal, and closely allied to the genus *Elaps*, inhabiting South America; in fact it bears, like our Batrachians, according to Günther, a closer resemblance to the South American than to the Indian fauna.

ACANTHOPHIS. *Daud.*

ACANTHOPHIS ANTARTICA. *Wagl.*

. The Death Adder.

Scales in 21 rows.
Ventrals 127.
Anal entire.
Subcaudals 42.

Head large, depressed, broad behind, regularly shielded, no loreal, 2 nasals, nostrils between; 8 rows of dorsal scales, keeled to the root of the tail; grey, sometimes salmon coloured above, minutely punctulated; back and tail with about 4 or 5 white spots speckled with pink, lower lip flesh coloured (white or yellowish white in spirits), with a pale black dot in the centre of each scale; beneath salmon coloured (yellow in spirits); tail distinct from trunk, short, thin, and ending in a recurved soft spine.

The colour of the Death Adder is subject to a good deal of variation, northern specimens from Rockhampton and Port Denison have the dark cross-bands of the back considerably smaller than those from the neighbourhood of Sydney, and the markings in the centre of the upper and lower labials and chin shields are of a pale greyish hue in the former. Specimens of a copper-red colour, as occasionally occur near Richmond, Randwick, and Long Bay, have seldom come under my notice from other parts of the continent.

Its habits and economy are tolerably well known. It is fond of warmth and sunshine, frequents sandy localities, is sluggish in its movements, and does not jump backwards if going to bite. When irritated this snake flattens itself out generally in the form of an S, turning round to one side or the other with astonishing rapidity, but never *jumping* at its enemy. As regards the supposed venomous sting in the tail, I can assure everybody interested in this matter that the caudal appendage is a mere ornament, quite soft, which nobody could run into his finger if he tried, and I am astonished that the fables which ignorance has circulated in a former and darker age, have not been exposed long before this.

In April or May they go into winter quarters, having during the summer months accumulated a sufficient quantity of fat, to be under no further necessity of catching frogs, grasshoppers, or field-mice during the next season. The burrow of some small rodent, or the hole furnished by a decayed root, is selected and taken possession of until the warm sunshine of spring recalls the sluggish reptile to fresh activity.

I believe that the Death-adder is found in almost every part of Australia north of 36°. The Australian Museum is in possession of specimens from many parts of New South Wales and from various localities in Queensland. The British Museum received this snake from Port Essington and the north-west coast, and I have taken it myself on the Murray and Darling. Its length seldom exceeds 30 inches. A very large specimen measured 2 feet $2\frac{1}{2}$ inches to the vent, and $4\frac{1}{4}$ inches to the tail; total, 2 feet 7 inches; around the body, 6 inches.

2. HYDROPHIDÆ, OR SEA SNAKES.

PLATURUS. *Latr.*

PLATURUS SCUTATUS. *Laur.*

The Ringed Sea Snake.

Scales (front part) 21 to 23 series.
Ventrals from 213 to 241.

Body subcylindrical, of moderate length, shields of the head subnormal in number and arrangement, nostrils lateral, in a single nasal shield, both nasals being separated from each other by a pair of anterior frontals. Scales imbricate, smooth, ventral shields well developed, tail with 2 series of subcaudals (Gthr.)

Body covered with a series of black rings, 20 to 50; crown of the head black, the first and second black mark of the head and neck are joined below by a longitudinal band commencing from the chin; snout and side of the head yellow, with a black band running through the eye (Gthr).

This Snake is frequently thrown ashore after stormy weather near Manly Beach, Coogee Bay, Botany, and other localities. Its range is very extensive, and it is common in the Bay of Bengal, the China Seas, and on the Australian and New Zealand coast; it lives on fishes, and is not much dreaded by the natives of the South Sea Islands who, I am told, handle this snake with impunity.

PELAMIS. *Daud.*

Pelamis bicolor. *Daud.*

The Black and Yellow Sea Snake.

"Head long, with very long spatulate snout; neck, rather stout; body of moderate length; nasal shields contiguous, longer than broad, pierced by the nostrils posteriorly; only one pair of frontals; scales not imbricate, not polished, tubercular or concave; ventral shields none or very narrow; lower jaw without notch in front; 2 or 3 postorbitals; neck surrounded by from 45 to 51 longitudinate series of scales: from 378 to 440 scales in a lateral longitudinal series between the angle of the mouth and the vent." (Günther.) The coloration of this snake varies considerably; the most prevailing colour is, the upper part of the head and the back uniform black, the sides and belly uniform brownish olive or yellow, the latter colour predominating just after the snake has shed its skin. Both the black and yellow colours are sharply defined. Tail with a series of black spots. This snake, which occasionally occurs on our shores, has a wide range, and appears to be as common on the Indian Ocean as it is here. The coast of New Zealand may be taken as its most southern limit. Dr. Gray, speaking about the Hydridæ in the *Brit. Mus. Cat. of Snakes*, remarks "that they are true Sea-Snakes; that they coil themselves up on the shore, living on sea-weeds, and lay their eggs on the shore." This observation is not correct if applied to the present species, as I have more than once taken gravid females with from four to six well-developed young of such a size as are sometimes met with swimming about, and apparently a few days old only. That they live on sea-weed is doubtful also, for though I have dissected almost every specimen which has come into my hands, I have found nothing but fishes or the remnants of such in the stomach.

These are all the specimens of Snakes observed near Sydney; and as the country has been well searched for more than five years, it will be difficult to discover new species.

" Geometrical Researches" in four papers, comprising numerous
new theorems and porisms, and complete solutions to celebrated
problems, by MARTIN GARDINER, C.E.

DEFINITIONS.

1. If A, B, O, be any three points, then by "*angle* O·AB"
we mean the angle formed by the revolution of a rigid straight
line round O as centre from a position coincident with O A to a
position coincident with O B, the method of movement being such
as to sweep direct across the straight line A B from A to B.
And according as the revolution is right-handed or left-handed
we say the angle is of *right formation* or of *left formation*.

2. The "*rotative*" of a straight line A B in respect to a
point O, is *the method* of rotatory movement of a rigid straight
line round O as centre when the movement is such as to sweep
direct across the straight line from A to B. And according as the
revolution is right-handed or left-handed we say that A B is of
right rotative or *left rotative* in respect to O.

3. By the *rotative of a tangent* drawn from a point to a curve,
we mean its rotative in respect to the centre of the osculating
circle at the point of contact of the tangent and curve.

4. By the term *n'gon*, we mean a figure composed of *n* connected portions of straight lines which we can conceive to be
formed by *n* successive movements of one point.

5. The lines composing any n'gon are called *sides*; and the
first point of the 1st side, and the final point of the nth side are
called *extremities*.

6. A *closed* n'gon has its extremities coincident; and an *open*
n'gon has its extremities distinct.

7. When any n'gon is represented by means of the letters
which indicate its first extremity and its various other angular
points and last extremity written in successive order, we say it is
of *prescribed formation*.

E

8. If O be a point, and A B a straight line: then by "*rectare* $O \cdot A B$" we mean $\frac{1}{2} OA \cdot OB \cdot \sin(O \cdot AB)$ in which the lines O A, O B are regarded as of like signs, and in which account is taken of the formation of the angle $O \cdot A B$.

9. By the "*rectare*" of any closed n'gon $A_1 A_2 \ldots A_n A_1$ we mean the sum of the n products.

$$\frac{1}{2} OA_1 \cdot OA_2 \cdot \sin(O \cdot A_1 A_2)$$
$$\frac{1}{2} OA_2 \cdot OA_3 \cdot \sin(O \cdot A_2 A_3)$$
$$\cdots \cdots \cdots \cdots \cdots$$
$$\frac{1}{2} OA_n \cdot OA_1 \cdot \sin(O \cdot A_n A_1)$$

in which O is any fixed point in its plane, and in which all the straight lines issuing from O are regarded as of like signs

☞ The rectare of a closed n'gon of prescribed formation is constant in sign and magnitude.

10. If S represents any straight line or plane, and that p represents any point; then p, S represents the length of the perpendicular from p on S.

I think it proper to mention, that early in 1862 I forwarded enunciations of the theorems in papers 2 and 3, and some of those of paper 4 to the President of the Queen's College Galway, and to Professor Chasles. I sent also enunciations of the principal porisms and theorems in papers 1 and 2 to Sir James Cockle, the Chief Justice of Queensland, immediately after his arrival in the Colony.

PAPER No. 1.

Researches concerning figures peculiarly derived from other figures
by MARTIN GARDINER, C.E.

[Read 9th July, 1862.]

Given a closed n'gon $A_1 A_2 \ldots\ldots\ldots A_n A_1$, to find the locus of a point O, such, that if we join the successive points $B_1, B_2, \ldots\ldots B_n, B_1$, of the feet of perpendiculars from it on the respective sides $A_1 A_2, A_2 A_3, \ldots A_n A_1$, of the given n'gon, then will the rectare of the new n'gon $B_1 B_2 \ldots B_n B_1$, thus derived (which we will call the *derived figure*) be of a given magnitude, Σ.

PROCESS OF INVESTIGATION.

Let $a_1, a_2, \ldots, a_n$, be the centres of the circles circumscribing the quadrilaterals

$$O\,B_n A_1 B_1,\ O\,B_1 A_2 B_2, \ldots\ldots O\,B_{n-1} A_n B_n.$$

Now, paying attention to the formations of magnitudes, and looking on the quadrilateral $O\,B_n A_1 B_1$, we at once perceive that
$\tfrac{1}{2}$rectare$(O \cdot B_n A_1 + O \cdot A_1 B_1)$ = rectare $(O \cdot B_n B_1)$ − rectare $(a_1 \cdot B_n B_1)$.

And from the quadrilateral $O\,B_1 A_2 B_2$, we have
$\tfrac{1}{2}$rectare$(O \cdot B_1 A_2 + O \cdot A_2 B_2)$ = rectare $(O \cdot B_1 B_2)$ − rectare $(a_2 \cdot B_1 B_2)$.

And in the like manner we get the following equations from the other $n-2$ quadrilaterals:—

$$\ldots\ldots \quad \ldots\ldots \quad \ldots\ldots$$
$$\ldots\ldots \quad \ldots\ldots \quad \ldots\ldots$$

$\tfrac{1}{2}$ rectare $(O \cdot B_{n-1} A_n + O \cdot A_n B_n)$ = rectare $(O \cdot B_{n-1} B_n)$ −
rectare $(a_n \cdot B_{n-1} B_n)$.

Therefore as the sum of the first sides of these n equations is obviously equal half the known rectare of the given n'gon

$A_1 A_2 \ldots A_n A_1$, it follows that by putting Σ'' to represent the rectare of this n'gon, we will have $\frac{1}{2} \Sigma'' = \Sigma -$ rectare $(a_1 \cdot B_n B_1 + a_2 \cdot B_1 B_2 + \ldots + a_n \cdot B_{n-1} B_n)$; and therefore rectare $(a_1 \cdot B_n B_1 + a_2 \cdot B_1 B_2 + \ldots + a_n \cdot B_{n-1} B_n) = \Sigma - \frac{1}{2} \Sigma''$.

And since the squares of diameters of circles are four times the squares of the radii, it is evident this last equation may be written:
$(A_1 O)^2 \cdot \sin(a_1 \cdot B_n B_1) + (A_2 O)^2 \cdot \sin(a_2 \cdot B_1 B_2) + \ldots + (A_n O)^2 \cdot \sin(a_n \cdot B_{n-1} B_n) = 8 \Sigma - 4 \Sigma''$.

But if we assume any point p in the plane, and draw the perpendiculars $p C_1, p C_2, \ldots p C_n$, to the respective sides $A_1 A_2, A_2 A_3, \ldots A_n A_1$; and that we find the centres $c_1, c_2, c_3, \ldots c_n$, of the circles which circumscribe the quadrilaterals $p C_n A_1 C_1, p C_1 A_2 C_2, \ldots p C_{n-1} A_n C_n$: it is evident we have

$$\text{angle}(a_1 \cdot B_n B_1) = \text{angle}(c_1 \cdot C_n C_1).$$
$$\text{angle}(a_2 \cdot B_1 B_2) = \text{angle}(c_2 \cdot C_1 C_2).$$
$$\ldots\ldots\ldots\ldots\ldots\ldots\ldots\ldots\ldots\ldots$$
$$\text{angle}(a_n \cdot B_{n-1} B_n) = \text{angle}(c_n \cdot C_{n-1} C_n).$$

Hence it is obvious we may write the last general equation in in the form $(A_1 O)^2 \cdot \sin(c_1 \cdot C_n C_1) + (A_2 O)^2 \cdot \sin(c_2 \cdot C_1 C_2) + \ldots + (A_n O)^2 \cdot \sin(c_n \cdot C_{n-1} C_n) = 8\Sigma - 4\Sigma'$.

And from this we learn that the locus of the point O is a known circle. Moreover, it is evident (see Salmon's Conic Sections, pages 88 and 89) that if M indicates the centre of this circle, and that ρ^2 represents the square of its radius, then we can write the preceding equation under the form

$\rho^2 (\sin c_1 \cdot C_n C_1 + \sin c_2 \cdot C_1 C_2 + \ldots + \sin c_n \cdot C_{n-1} C_n)$
$+ (A_1 M)^2 \cdot \sin c_1 \cdot C_n C_1 + (A_2 M)^2 \cdot \sin c_2 \cdot C_1 C_2 + \ldots + (A_n M)^2 \cdot \sin c_n \cdot C_{n-1} C_n = 8\Sigma - 4\Sigma'$.

☞ It is also well to remember that the position of the centre M is independent of the value of Σ.

1. If all the given straight lines forming the closed n'gon pass through one point, it is obvious the locus of O has this common point of intersection for centre. In this case $\Sigma' =$ zero; and, when the point of intersection is at infinity, Σ has no real value but zero; and, for such value of Σ, the problem is porismatic,—for any straight line cutting the given ones perpendicularly may be regarded as belonging to an infinite circle whose centre is at the point of intersection.

And when the first half of the closed n'gon $A_1 A_2 \ldots A_n A_1$ is coincident with the second half (taken in order as indicated) then also Σ' and Σ must be each $=$ zero, and the locus of O is unrestricted.

2. If the closed n'gon be a triangle $A_1 A_2 A_3 A_1$, then it is evident that for each of the angular points of the triangle, considered as a position for O, we have Σ equal zero; $\therefore$ it is obvious that for all values of Σ the centre of the locus must be coincident with the centre of the circle circumscribing the triangle. And putting R for the radius of the circle circumscribing the triangle, we have the relation—

$$(\rho^2 + R^2) \cdot (\sin c_1 \cdot C_3 C_1 + \sin c_2 \cdot C_1 C_2 + \sin c_3 \cdot C_2 C_3) = 8\Sigma - 4\Sigma';$$

but $\quad R^2 (\sin c_1 \cdot C_3 C_1 + \sin c_2 \cdot C_1 C_2 + \sin c_3 \cdot C_2 C_3) = -2\Sigma'$

$\therefore \rho^2 (\sin c_1 \cdot C_3 C_1 + \sin c_2 \cdot C_1 C_2 + \sin c_3 \cdot C_2 C_3) = 8\Sigma - 2\Sigma'$

and $\therefore \dfrac{\rho^2 - R^2}{R^2} = \dfrac{4\Sigma}{-\Sigma'}$

But if m_1, m_2, m_3, represent the feet of perpendiculars from the centre of the circumscribing circle on the sides $A_1 A_2$, $A_2 A_3$, $A_3 A_1$, of the triangle and that we put Σ'' to represent the rectare of the triangle $m_1 m_2 m_3 m_1$, then $-\Sigma' = -4\Sigma''$, and therefore we have

$$\dfrac{\rho^2 - R^2}{-R^2} = \dfrac{\Sigma}{\Sigma''}.$$

3. If the figure $A_1 A_2 \ldots A_n A_1$ is a complete regular polygon of n sides; than the centre M of the locus of O is coincident with the centre of the circle which circumscribes the polygon. And if we represent the radius of the circumscribing circle by R, it is evident we can write the equation of the locus in the form
$n \cdot \sin \left(\frac{2}{n} \text{revolution}\right) \cdot \rho^2 + n \cdot \sin \left(\frac{2}{n} \text{revolution}\right) R^2 = 8\Sigma - 4\Sigma'$
in which the involved angle is of like formation with Σ'.

From this we at once see that when $n = 2$, we must have $8\Sigma = 4\Sigma'$; and $\therefore$ as Σ = zero, so also must Σ' = zero.

When $n = 4$, then we must have $8\Sigma = 4\Sigma'$, or $\Sigma' = 2\Sigma$; and the problem is porismatic.

4. Again, since $\sin \left(\frac{2}{n} \text{revolution}\right) = \frac{1}{2}$ chord $\left(\frac{4}{n} \text{revolution,}\right)$ and that $\frac{n}{4}$ chord $\left(\frac{4}{n} \text{revolution}\right)$ = perimeter of polygon of $\frac{n}{4}$ sides; therefore it is evident that $n \cdot \sin \left(\frac{2}{n} \text{revolution}\right)$ is equal to twice the perimeter of a polygon of $\frac{n}{4}$ sides. And $\therefore$ it is evident that when $A_1 A_2 \ldots A_n A_1$ is a regular polygon, and n = infinity, we have $n \cdot \sin \left(\frac{2}{n} \text{revolution}\right) = 4\pi = 4 \, (3\cdot 1416)$

and $4\pi \cdot \rho^2 + 4\pi R^2 = 8\Sigma - 4\Sigma'$

$$4\pi \cdot \rho^2 = 8\Sigma - 8\Sigma'$$

$$\pi \cdot \rho^2 = 2 \, (\Sigma - \Sigma')$$

And, putting Σ''' to represent the rectare of the circle which constitutes the locus of O, we can write the last equation in the form

$$\Sigma''' = 2\Sigma - 2\Sigma'$$

When we suppose $\rho = R$, then the derived figure of the circle $A_1 A_2 \ldots A_n A_1$ is a *cardoid* whose rectare is represented by Σ; and therefore, as in this case, the point O has the circle $A_1 A_2 \ldots A_n A_1$ as locus, we have

$$\Sigma = \tfrac{3}{2} \Sigma'$$

5. It is evident we can investigate in like manner (and that the locus of O will be a circle) when, instead of one closed n'gon, we are given any number of closed n'gons, and that the sum of the products of the rectares of their *derived figures* and given numbers of known signs, is to be of a given magnitude.

And it is also evident the locus of O is a circle when the sum of the products of the rectares of some of the derived figures and given numbers, has a given ratio to the sum of the products of given numbers and the rectares of the remaining derived figures.

6. Again (owing to the nature of the investigation, and to our knowledge of the relative properties of approximate figures) it is evident the principle of continuity justifies the extension of our results to the more comprehensive propositions in which given straight lines are replaced by curves of any kind whatever in a plane. And (remembering that the curvatures at points in curves are proportional to the angles between tangents at the extremities *of equally long elements*) we may announce the following important porisms :—

PORISM I.

Given any lot of closed figures of prescribed formations in a plane, then will the locus of a point o *be a determinable circle when the sum of the products of given numbers and the rectares of the derived figures of the lot in respect to this point is of a given or determinable magnitude* Σ. *And, for all values of* Σ, *the centre of the determinable circle (whose circumference is the locus of* o) *is a fixed point, with which the locus of* o *is coincident when* Σ *is a minimum, and which point is the mean centre of the curvatures when the given figures are closed curves and the given numbers all equal.*

PORISM II.

Given a lot of closed figures of prescribed formations, and given also a second lot of closed figures of prescribed formations; then will the locus of a point o *be a determinable circle when the sum of the products of given numbers and the rectares of the derived figures of the first lot in respect to the point, has a given or determinable invariable ratio to the sum of the products of other given numbers and the rectares of the derived figures of the second lot in respect to this same point.*

7. These porisms give immediate intimation of numerous interesting theorems, of which the two following are examples:—

THEOREM I.

The rectare of the derived figure of any conic in respect to any point in the circumference of a circle having the line joining the foci as diameter, is equal the rectare of the circle.

THEOREM II.

If any number of conics have a common focus; then will the locus of a point o be a determinable circle, passing through this focus, when the sum of the rectares of the derived figures of the conics in respect to the point o is equal to the sum of the like rectares of the circles having the transverse axes of the conics as diameters.

8. In respect to the general problem, it is evident that when the given data is wholly or partly curve, the exact locus of O cannot be (unless in some particular cases) obtained without the aid of the infinitesimal calculus.

It is also obvious that in cases in which some points of the given data are at infinity, the co-ordinate methods will afford the best means of actual solution, though of course the principle of continuity justifies us in predicting the *nature* of the locus, even when the manner of approximating to its position (as indicated in our general investigation) may not be intelligible to our limited understanding. However, to clear all doubt on this point, we can easily find the equation of the locus of O without paying attention to the rectare of the given figure $A_1 A_2 \ldots A_n A_1$.

This may be done in various ways, but the following is sufficient:—

Assuming rectangular axes of reference, let

$$G_1 x + H_1 y + K_1 = 0$$
$$G_2 x + H_2 y + K_2 = 0$$
$$\dots\dots\dots\dots$$
$$G_n x + H_n y + K_n = 0,$$

be the equations of the n successive straight lines $A_1 A_2$, $A_2 A_3$, ... $A_n A_1$, taken in order. Then putting x', y', to represent the co-ordinates of any one of the positions of O, it is evident we can express the equations of perpendiculars from this point to the lines represented by the above equations, and that we can find the co-ordinates of the feet B_1, B_2, ... B_n, of these perpendiculars in terms of x', y', and known quantities. Hence it is obvious that if we indicate the co-ordinates of B_1, B_2, ... B_n, by (x_1, y_1), (x_2, y_2), ... (x_n, y_n), in the equation

$$(x_1 y_2 - y_1 x_2) + (x_2 y_3 - y_2 x_3) + \dots + (x_n y_1 - y_n x_1) = 2\Sigma,$$

then by substituting the values of $x_1 y_1$, $x_2 y_2$, &c., implicating x', y', and known quantities, we will have the equation of the circle which is the locus of O.

And by expressing the equations of the sides of the given figure $A_1 A_2 \dots A_n A_1$ in terms of the co-ordinates of the points A_1, A_2, ... A_n, we can arrive at the theorems already found, but not so obviously as by the method already exposed.

9. Theorems pertaining to *all kinds* of plane figures are very limited in number, owing no doubt to the bias for investigations concerning peculiar forms which the minds of geometers suffer in learning the science of geometry.

When theorems of such a general nature are discovered they should not be passed unnoticed in elementary class-books; for they show to us that in geometry (as in nature) we may have forms of the most irregular character adapted to fulfil definite relations in as complete a manner as forms definable by words or equations.

In addition to the theorems given in the preceding investigation, I would direct attention to the following general theorem.

THEOREM.

If a rigid tangent of fixed length perform (as tangent) a movement round any given complete curvilinear plane figure so that the point of contact continues at the extremity of the tangent; then if m *denote the number of right loops, and* n *the number of left loops which constitute the given figure, the rectare of the track of the outward extremity of the tangent will differ from the rectare of the given figure by* (m—n) *times the area of a circle having a radius equal in length to the tangent.*

Note.—The porisms evolved in this paper cannot fail to be interesting to geometers who apply themselves to questions in Speculative Astronomy.

Paper No. 2.

Researches concerning n'gons inscribed in other n'gons by
Martin Gardiner, C.E.

[Read 9th July, 1862.]

Given n straight lines $L_1, L_2, \ldots\ldots L_n$, and the like number of points $o_1, o_2, \ldots o_n$ in a plane; to describe a closed n'gon $p_1 p_2 \ldots p_n p_1$, which will have its points $p_1, p_2, \ldots p_n$, on the straight lines $L_1, L_2, \ldots L_n$ taken in order, and its successive sides $p_1 p_2, p_2 p_3, \ldots p_n p_1$ passing in order through the n respective points $o_1, o_2, \ldots o_n$.

PROCESS OF INVESTIGATION.

1. If we assume any three points a_1, b_1, c_1, in the line L_1, and that we draw the straight lines $a_1 o_1$, $b_1 o_1$, $c_1 o_1$ to cut L_2 in the points a_2, b_2, c_2; then

$$\frac{a_1 p_1}{b_1 p_1} : \frac{a_2 p_2}{b_2 p_2} = \frac{a_1 c_1}{b_1 c_1} : \frac{a_2 c_2}{b_2 c_2},$$

Similarly, if we draw $a_2 o_2$, $b_2 o_2$, $c_2 o_2$, to cut L_3 in points a_3, b_3, c_3; and that we draw $a_3 o_3$, $b_3 o_3$, $c_3 o_3$, to cut L_4 in a_4, b_4, c_4; and that we proceed thus until $a_n o_n$, $b_n o_n$, $c_n o_n$, cut L_1 in a_{n+1}, b_{n+1}, c_{n+1}; then evidently we have the following relations (each one of which is similar to the above):—

$$\frac{a_2 p_2}{b_2 p_2} : \frac{a_3 p_3}{b_3 p_3} = \frac{a_2 c_2}{b_2 c_2} : \frac{a_3 c_3}{b_3 c_3}$$

$$\ldots \quad \ldots \quad \ldots \quad \ldots$$
$$\ldots \quad \ldots \quad \ldots \quad \ldots$$

$$\frac{a_n p_n}{b_n p_n} : \frac{a_{n+1} p_1}{b_{n+1} p_1} = \frac{a_n c_n}{b_n c_n} : \frac{a_{n+1} c_{n+1}}{b_{n+1} c_{n+1}}$$

And from these n equations we at once derive the equation:—

$$\frac{a_1 p_1}{b_1 p_1} : \frac{a_{n+1} p_1}{b_{n+1} p_1} = \frac{a_1 c_1}{b_1 c_1} : \frac{a_{n+1} c_{n+1}}{b_{n+1} c_{n+1}}, \ldots \ldots (1).$$

From this we learn that p_1 is known (by the problem of "determinate section" of Apollonius, or because it is a double point of known homographic divisions on L_1); and therefore also the n'gon $p_1 p_2 \ldots p_n p_1$.

Moreover, we learn that in the non-porismatic state of the data, there are two and but two positions for p_1, both real or both imaginary.

2. When the data is so related that the points a_{n+1}, b_{n+1}, c_{n+1}, fall on the respective points a_1, b_1, c_1; then evidently the problem is porismatic; for equation (1) assumes the form

$$\frac{a_1 p_1}{b_1 p_1} : \frac{a_1 p_1}{b_1 p_1} = 1,$$

which holds when p_1 has any position whatever in L_1.

Hence we may announce the following theorem:—

THEOREM I.

If there be n *straight lines and* n *points in a plane, and that any three closed* n'*gons can be described, such that each one of them has its* n *angular points in the* n *respective lines, and its* n *sides passing in order through the* n *points, then will any point in any of the fixed lines be an answerable position for the prescribed angular point (resting on that line) of a closed* n'*gon fulfilling the like conditions with the three others.*

3. Theorem 1 will enable us to arrive at some interesting porisms and theorems.

Firstly.—Suppose we were given all the data but the two points o_{n-1} and o_n, and that it is required to find such positions for these points as will render the problem porismatic.

Here our object is to form 3 closed n'gons $a_1 a_2 \ldots a_n a_1$, $b_1 b_2 \ldots b_n b_1$, $c_1 c_2 \ldots c_n c_1$, (subject to the imposed conditions as respects the given data) whose sides $a_{n-1} a_n$, $b_{n-1} b_n$, $c_{n-1} c_n$ will pass through one point, and whose sides $a_n a_1$, $b_n b_1$, $c_n c_1$, will pass through another point: for these two points would evidently be answerable positions for o_{n-1} and o_n. If we take b_1 in the intersection of L_1 and L_n, we can find the corresponding point b_{n-1} on L_{n-1}. If we take a_{n-1} in the intersection of L_{n-1} and L_n, we can find the corresponding point a_1 on L_1. And if we take c_1 anywhere in L_1, we can find the corresponding point c_{n-1} on the line L_{n-1}. Now if we take any point in $b_1 \, b_{n-1}$ as a position for o_{n-1}, and that we draw $o_{n-1} \, c_{n-1}$ to cut L_n in c_n; and then draw $c_n \, c_1$ to cut $a_1 \, a_{n-1}$ in o_n; it is evident o_{n-1} and o_n so determined are answerable positions: for we have the three closed n'gons, $a_1 \, a_2 \ldots a_n \, a_1$, $b_1 \, b_2 \ldots b_n \, b_1$, $c_1 \, c_2 \ldots c_n \, c_1$ fulfilling the conditions.

Hence in the general states of the data, we have the following porism:—

PORISM I.

If a closed n'*gon have its* n *angular points on* n *given straight lines, and have its first* n-2 *sides passing through* n-2 *given points; then its* n-1th *and* nth *sides will cut two determinable straight lines* XX, YY *in points* o_{n-1} *and* o_n, *such that if we look on these points as fixed, we can " deform" the* n'*gon so that its angular points will move along the* n *given straight lines, and its sides continue through the* n *fixed points.*

In respect to this porism it may be proper to observe that when the two lines L_{n-1} and L_n are parallels (and therefore a_{n-1} at infinity) and that a_1 is at infinity on L_1, then the line $a_1 \, a_{n-1}$ is at infinity; and the point o_n where $c_1 \, c_n$ cuts $a_1 \, a_{n-1}$ is at infinity; and therefore the last sides of the n'gons (the sides through o_n) must be all parallels to each other. And if L_n, L_{n-1}, and L_1 be parallels, and that a_1 is at infinity, then $b_1 \, b_{n-1}$ and $a_1 \, a_{n-1}$ are at infinity; and it is evident we can assume c_n anywhere on L_n, and that $c_{n-1} \, c_n$ and $c_n \, c_1$ will continue through o_{n-1} and o_n at infinity.

4. We arrived at porism 1 under the hypotheses that L_1, L_{n-1}, and L_n do not intersect each other in one point; and therefore it is necessary to inquire into the nature of the relations when these three lines pass through one point.

When such is the case, it is evident the line $b_1 \, b_{n-1}$ (or XX) becomes co-incident with L_{n-1}, and that the line $a_1 \, a_{n-1}$ (or YY) becomes co-incident with L_1).

It is also evident o_{n-1} can be taken anywhere in L_{n-1}; and that o_n can be taken anywhere in L_1. It is also evident the nth angular points of the n'gons are all co-incident in the common point of intersection of the lines L_1, L_{n-1}, and L_n. Moreover, we arrive at this under the hypotheses that *all* the given straight lines do not pass through one point.

Hence we infer the following theorem :—

THEOREM 2.

Given n *straight lines* L_1, L_2, ... L_n, *of which the first, the* n $-$ 1th, *and the* nth *pass through one point,—the rest not all passing through this point ; and given likewise* n $-$ 2 *point* o_1, o_2, ... o_{n-2}, *of a series of* n *points : if positions for the* n $-$ 1th *and* nth *points* o_{n-1} *and* o_n *of the series be such that any point whatever in the line* L_1 *is an answerable position for the first angular point of a closed* n'*gon* $p_1 \, p_2 \, ... \, p_n \, p_1$, *having its* n *angular points* p_1, p_2, ... p_n *on the* n *respective lines* L_1, L_2, ... L_n, *and its* n *sides* $p_1 \, p_2$, $p_2 \, p_3$, ... $p_n \, p_1$, *passing in order through the* n *respective points* o_1, o_2, ... o_n, *then will the points* o_{n-1} *and* o_n *be situated in the given straight lines* L_{n-1}, L_n, *each in each respectively.*

5. When all the given straight lines L_1, L_2, ... L_n, intersect in one point q, then it is obvious that the infinitely small n'gons $a_1 \, a_2 \, ... \, a_{n-1} \, a_n \, a_1$, $b_1 \, b_2 \, ... \, b_n \, b_1$ are not distinct, and that $b_1 \, b_{n-1}$ and $a_1 \, a_{n-1}$ (XX and YY) are not determined in position. In this case we may evidently assume o_{n-1} anywhere in the plane (because $a_1 \, a_{n-1}$ is not restricted in position) and find corresponding answerable positions for o_n in the intersection of the sides $c_1 \, c_n$, $d_1 \, d_n$, of any other two closed n'gons $c_1 \, c_2 \, ... \, c_{n-1}$

$c_n c_1, d_1 d_2 \ldots d_{n-1} d_n d_1$, fulfilling the conditions (because the three n'gons including these two and the n'gon $a_1 a_2 \ldots a_n a_1$ fulfil the conditions). Moreover it is evident that if we draw any straight line XX through q; then for all points o_{n-1} assumed in XX, the corresponding points o_n will be on a determinable straight line passing through q.

Hence we have the following porism :—

PORISM 2.

If all the angular points of a closed n'gon move on n given straight lines meeting in a point q, and that all its sides but the nth pass through determinable fixed points; then if the point through which the $n-1^{th}$ side passes be situated on a known straight line passing through q, so will the point through which the nth side passes be on a determinable straight line passing through q. (See Mulcahy's "Modern Geometry," page 77.)

6. If we have the $n-2$ given points $o_1, o_2, \ldots o_{n-2}$, in directum with the intersection of L_1 and L_n; then (no matter how general otherwise the given lines may be) it is evident the straight line X X will pass through these $n-2$ given points; and therefore o_{n-1} will be in directum with the $n-2$ given points.

Hence we may announce the following porism :—

PORISM 3.

If all the angular points of a closed n'gon move on given straight lines, and all its sides, except one, pass through given points which lie in a straight line passing through the intersection of the lines on which the extremities of the free side move, then this side also passes through a fixed determinable point. (See Mulcahy's "Modern Geometry," page 77.)

7. When the given points $o_1, o_2, \ldots o_{n-2}$, are in one straight line, and that the three lines L_1, L_{n-1}, L_n, pass through one point in this line; then XX and YY are evidently both coincident with the straight line $o_1, o_2, \ldots o_{n-2}$; and we infer the following theorem :—

THEOREM 3.

If a closed n'gon $c_1 c_2 \ldots c_n c_1$, have its angular points $c_1, c_2, \ldots c_n$ on n fixed straight lines $L_1, L_2 \ldots L_n$, of which any three L_{n-1}, L_n, L_1, taken in successive order meet in one point q: then $o_1, o_2, \ldots o_n$ being the n points in which any straight line through this point q cuts the respective sides $c_1 c_2, c_2 c_3, \ldots c_n c_1$ of the n'gon, we can (if we conceive these points to become fixed) deform the n'gon, so that its sides will continue through these fixed points, and its angular points move on the fixed straight lines.

8. If all the given straight lines but L_n pass through one point q; then, from the general investigation, it is evident the straight line $b_1 b_{n-1}$ (or XX), is indeterminate, and may have any position we wish with respect to q. And it is also evident that by giving $b_1 b_{n-1}$ any fixed position through q, then will $b_n b_1$ be coincident therewith; and o_n and o_{n-1} will be in directum with q. Hence we have the following porism:—

PORISM 4.

If all the sides of a closed n'gon $c_1 c_2 \ldots c_n c_1$ pass through given points, and all its angular points except one c_n move on given straight lines meeting in a point q which is in directum with the points through which the sides containing the free angle pass; then the locus of this angular point c_n is a determinable straight line.

9. *Secondly.*—When the data is all given but the straight lines L_{n-1} and L_n; to find positions for these two lines so as to render the problem porismatic.

Here, if we assume a_1 in the intersection of the lines $o_{n-1} o_n$ and L_1, it is evident the corresponding point a_{n-1} must be on the line $o_{n-1} o_n$, and also on the line $o_{n-2} a_{n-2}$: and therefore it must be (generally) their point of intersection. And it follows that any answerable straight line L_{n-1} must pass through the point of intersection of the lines $o_{n-1}\, o_n$ and $o_{n-2}\, a_{n-2}$.

And if we take the point in which the straight line $o_{n-1}\, o_{n-2}$ cuts L_{n-2} as an angular point b_{n-2} of an answerable n'gon, we can find the corresponding point b_1 in L_1. Moreover, it is evident that b_n must be co-incident with the known intersection of $o_{n-2}\, o_{n-1}$ and $b_1\, o_n$; and therefore any answerable straight line L_n must pass through the point of intersection of the lines $o_{n-2}\, o_{n-1}$ and $b_1\, o_n$. Now let $c_1\, c_2 \ldots c_n\, c_1$ be any other closed n'gon, having its n sides passing in the prescribed manner through the n given points, and its first $n-2$ angular points $c_1, c_2 \ldots c_{n-2}$ resting on the $n-2$ given lines $L_1, L_2, \ldots L_{n-2}$.

It is evident that if we draw the two straight lines $a_{n-1}\, c_{n-1}$ and $a_n\, c_n$, and look on them as fixed, they will be answerable positions for L_{n-1} and L_n, because the three closed n'gons $a_1\, a_2 \ldots a_n\, a_1, b_1\, b_2 \ldots b_n\, b_1, c_1\, c_2 \ldots c_n\, c_1$ fulfil the prescribed conditions.

Hence (in the general state of the data) we may announce the following

PORISM 5.

If a closed n'*gon have its* n *sides passing through* n *given points, and have its first* n—2 *angular points situated on* n—2 *given straight lines: two points can be found, such that if we draw a straight line from the first of these determined points through the* n—1th *angular point of the* n'*gon, and that we draw another straight line from the second determined point through the* nth *angular point of the* n'*gon, and look on these drawn lines as fixed; then we can deform the* n'*gon so that its* n *sides will continue through the* n *given points, and its* n *angular points move along the* n *straight lines composed of the* n—2 *given ones, and the two determined ones.*

F

10. If, in the investigation to the preceding porism, we consider the particular state of the data in which all the given points o_1, o_2 .... o_n are in one straight line, it is obvious that the intersection of the lines $o_{n-1} o_n$ and $o_{n-2} a_{n-2}$ becomes indeterminate, as also that of $o_{n-2} o_{n-1}$ and $b_1 o_n$. However, it is evident that if we fix on any point in the straight line $o_1 o_2 \ldots$, as the point through which L_{n-1} must pass, then there corresponds another point in the same line through which L_n must pass. And we have the following porism:—

PORISM 6.

If all the sides of a closed n'gon pass through given points which lie in one straight line, and that all its angular points except one move on given straight lines: then will the locus of the free angle be a determinable straight line (see Mulcahy's Geometry, page 75).

11. Porisms 5 and 6 can be easily derived from those which precede them by the usual method of reciprocation; and other particular theorems and porisms can be deduced from these, &c. However, I will not enter more into details in the present paper, as my chief object is to get at the more general relations.

12. *Thirdly.*— Given all the data but the point o_n and the line L_n to find positions for these which will render the problem porismatic.

Let $a_1 a_2 \ldots a_{n-1} a_1$, and $b_1 b_2 \ldots b_{n-1} b_1$, be the two known closed $(n-1)$'gons, having their sides passing in the prescribed manner through the $n-1$ given points, and their angular points on the $n-1$ given straight lines. If we put b_n for the point in which the straight line $b_{n-1} b_1 o_{n-1}$ cuts L_n; then evidently (o_n having any position not in $b_{n-1} b_1 o_{n-1}$) we must have b_n coincident with b_1, or, in other words, we must have L_n passing through b_1, the first angular point of one of the known closed $(n-1)$'gons. And, putting a_n the point in which the straight line $a_{n-1}\, a_1\, o_{n-1}$ cuts L_n, it is evident that for the n'gon $a_1\, a_2 \ldots a_{n-1}\, a_n\, a_1$, we must have any answerable point o_n situated on the straight line $a_{n-1}\, a_1\, o_{n-1}$ which is the last side of the other known closed $(n-1)$'gon.

And if $c_1\, c_2 \ldots c_n\, c_1$ be any closed n'gon, having its first $n-1$ sides passing through the $n-1$ given points, and having its first $n-1$ angular points on the $n-1$ given lines; it is evident that by drawing a straight line from b_1 through c_n, and by producing $c_n\, c_1$ to cut the line $o_{n-1}\, a_{n-1}\, a_1$; then will this point of intersection and the line $b_1\, c_n$ be answerable positions for o_n and L_n: (because we have the three closed n'gons $a_1\, a_2 \ldots a_n\, a_1,\ b_1\, b_2 \ldots b_n\, b_1$, $c_1\, c_2 \ldots c_n\, c_1$, fulfilling the conditions).

Hence the following porism:—

PORISM 7.

If a closed n*'gon have its first* n -1 *angular points on* n -1 *given straight lines, and its first* n -1 *sides passing through* n -1 *given points: then two straight lines and a point in each of them can be found, such that if from either one of these determined points (in a determined line) we draw a line* L_n *through the* nth *angular point of the* n*'gon, and that we produce the* nth *side of the* n*'gon to cut the other of the two determined lines in a point* o_n, *and that we regard the line* L_n *and point* o_n *as fixed: we can deform the* n*'gon so that its* n *sides will continue through the* n *points composed of the* n -1 *given ones and the determined one* o_n, *and its angular points move along the* n *straight lines composed of the* n -1 *given ones and the determined one* L_n.

13. Re-considering the problem, it is evident we can use the following system of equations:—

$$\frac{a_1\, p_1}{b_1\, p_1} : \frac{a_2\, p_2}{b_2\, p_2} = \frac{a_1\, o_1}{b_1\, o_1} : \frac{a_2\, o_1}{b_2\, o_1}$$

$$\frac{a_2 p_2}{b_2 p_2} : \frac{a_3 p_3}{b_3 p_3} = \frac{a_2 o_2}{b_2 o_2} : \frac{a_3 o_2}{b_3 o_2}$$

... ...
... ...

$$\frac{a_n p_n}{b_n p_n} : \frac{a_{n+1} p_1}{b_{n+1} p_1} = \frac{a_n o_n}{b_n o_n} : \frac{a_{n+1} o_n}{b_{n+1} o_n}$$

And from these we at once obtain the equation :—

$$\frac{a_1 p_1}{b_1 p_1} : \frac{a_{n+1} p_1}{b_{n+1} p_1} = \frac{a_1 o_1}{b_1 o_1} \cdot \frac{b_2 o_1}{a_2 o_1} \cdot \frac{a_2 o_2}{b_2 o_2} \cdot \frac{b_3 o_2}{a_3 o_2} \cdots$$

$$\cdots \frac{a_n o_n}{b_n o_n} \cdot \frac{b_{n+1} o_n}{a_{n+1} o_n}.$$

In the porismatic states of the data it is obvious the second side of this equation must $= 1$, since a_{n+1} & b_{n+1} must be coincidents with a_1 & b_1.

14. We may also remark that if $a_1 a_2 \ldots a_n a_1$ & $b_1 b_2 \ldots b_n b_1$ are two closed n'gons, and that $o_1, o_2, \ldots o_n$ the intersections of their pairs of sides (of their first sides; of their second sides, &c.) are in one straight line; then, drawing straight lines through a_1 and b_1, through a_2 and b_2, &c., to cut the line $o_1 o_2 \ldots o_n$; it is evident the line $o_1 o_2 \ldots o_n$ has coincident with it a third closed n'gon inscribed in the n lines $a_1 b_1, a_2 b_2$, &c. And therefore we must have :—

$$\frac{a_1 o_1}{b_1 o_1} \cdot \frac{b_2 o_1}{a_2 o_1} \cdot \frac{a_2 o_2}{b_2 o_2} \cdot \frac{b_3 o_2}{a_3 o_2} \cdots \frac{a_n o_n}{b_n o_n} \cdot \frac{b_1 o_n}{a_1 o_n} = 1$$

or

$$\left(\frac{a_1 o_1 \cdot a_2 o_2 \cdots a_n o_n}{a_2 o_1 \cdot a_3 o_2 \cdots a_1 o_n} \right) \cdot \left(\frac{b_2 o_1 \cdot b_3 o_2 \cdots b_1 o_n}{b_1 o_1 \cdot b_2 o_2 \cdots b_n o_n} \right) = 1$$

And as the third or *single-line* closed n'gon can be substituted instead of either of these, we must have each of the two factors of the first side $= 1$.

15. The problem can be investigated in the following manner :—

Looking on the four successive sides $p_1 p_2, p_2 p_3, p_3 p_4, p_4 p_5$ let us see whether we could replace them by a less number of sides passing through determinable points, and having their intersections on determinable straight lines, and their extremities in p_1 and p_5.

Let i_1 be the point of intersection of the straight lines $o_1 o_2$ and $o_4 o_3$. Then since o_1, o_2, i_1, are in one straight line, it follows that the intersection r_1 of the straight lines $o_1 p_2$ and $i_1 p_3$ is in a known straight line R_1. And since o_3, o_4, i_1, are in one straight line, it follows that the intersection s_1 of the straight lines $o_4 p_4$ and $i_1 p_3$ is in a known straight line S_1.

Hence it is evident the solution of the problem is reduced to that of describing a closed $(n-1)$'gon $p_1 r_1 s_1 p_5 p_6 \cdots p_n p_1$, whose sides $p_1 r_1, r_1 s_1, s_1 p_5, p_5 p_6, \cdots p_n p_1$ pass through the $n-1$ known points $o_1, i_1, o_4, o_5, \ldots o_n$, and whose angular points $p_1, r_1, s_1, p_5, \cdots p_n$ will rest on the $n-1$ known straight lines $L_1, R_1, S_1, L_5, \cdots L_n$. Similarly, by proceeding with the first four sides of this closed $(n-1)$'gon as with those of the n'gon, we can reduce the solution to that of describing a closed $(n-2)$'gon $p_1 r_2 s_2 p_6 \cdots p_n p_1$ whose sides pass in order through $n-2$ known points $o_1, i_2, o_5 \ldots o_n$, and whose angular points $p_1, r_2, s_2, p_6 \cdots p_n$ rest on the $n-2$ known straight lines $L_1, R_2, S_2, L_6, \ldots L_n$.

And thus, step by step, we can proceed until we make the solution of the problem depend on that of describing a triangle $p_1 r_{n-3} s_{n-3} p_1$ whose sides $p_1 r_{n-3}, r_{n-3} s_{n-3}, s_{n-3} p_1$, will pass through known points o_1, i_{n-3}, o_n, and whose angular points $p_1, r_{n-3} s_{n-3}$, will rest on known straight lines L_1, R_{n-3}, S_{n-3}.

16. To arrive at porismatic relations of the data let us consider the question when we arrive at that point in the investigation where we have reduced the solution to the forming of a quadrilateral $p_1\ r_{n-4}\ s_{n-4}\ p_n\ p_1$ whose sides pass in order through the known points $o_1,\ i_{n-4},\ o_{n-1},\ o_n$, and whose angular points rest in order on the known straight lines $L_1,\ R_{n-4},\ S_{n-4},\ L_n$. It is evident our method of investigation leaves the point o_n and the lines L_n, L_1, unimplicated; and therefore it follows that if we give such positions to these as will render the forming of the quadrilateral porismatic, then will the problem of the forming of the n'gon $p_1\ p_2 \ldots p_n\ p_1$ be porismatic. Now, if we assume any two positions for L_1 and L_n which pass through q the point of intersection of R_{n-4} and S_{n-4}, then (by a well-known porism) we can find a position for o_n which will render the problem of the forming of the quadrilateral porismatic.

Hence we may announce the following porism:—

PORISM 8.

If a closed n'gon have all its angular points but the 1st and n^{th} resting on given straight lines, and have all its sides but the nth passing through given points: a point q can be found, such that if we look on straight lines from it through the 1st and n^{th} angular points as fixed, and that we deform the n'gon so that its n angular points will move along the n straight lines composed of the n $-$ 2 given ones and the two described ones, and so that its first n $-$ 1 sides continue through the n $-$ 1 given points, then will the nth or last side of the n'gon continue through a fixed determinable point.

17. The problem can be investigated in the following manner:

Suppose we draw the straight line Q_1 containing the intersection of L_1 and L_2, and that of L_3 and L_4. And let q_1 be the point of intersection of $p_2\ p_3$ and Q_1.

Then since L_1, L_2, and Q_1 pass through one point, it follows (by a well-known porism) that $p_1\, q_1$ cuts the line $o_1\, o_2$ in a known point r_1. And since L_3, L_4, and Q_1 pass through one point, it follows that $p_4\, q_1$ cuts the line $o_2\, o_3$ in a known point s_1.

Hence evidently the solution of the problem is dependent on that of forming a closed $(n-1)$'gon $p_1\, q_1\, p_4\, \ldots\, p_n\, p_1$ whose successive sides pass through the $n-1$ known points r_1, s_1, o_4 $\ldots\, o_n$, and whose angular points taken in order rest on $n-1$ known straight lines L_1, Q_1, L_4, $\ldots\, L_n$.

And, proceeding with this closed $(n-1)$'gon as we have done with the closed n'gon, we can reduce the solution of the problem to the forming of a closed $(n-2)$'gon $p_1\, q_2\, p_5 \ldots p_n\, p_1$, whose sides pass in order through $n-2$ known points r_2 (in line $s_1\, r_1$), s_2 (in line $s_1\, o_4$), o_5, o_6, $\ldots\, o_n$, and whose angular points rest in order on $n-2$ known straight lines L_1, Q_2, L_5, $\ldots\, L_n$.

And thus, step by step, we can proceed until we make the solution depend on that of forming a triangle $p_1\, q_{n-3}\, p_n\, p_1$, whose sides pass in order through three known points r_{n-3}, s_{n-3}, o_n, and whose angular points rest in order on three known straight lines L_1, Q_{n-3}, L_n.

18. To arrive at porismatic relations, we will (as in last method) consider the question at that point in the investigation where we have reduced the solution of the problem to the forming of the quadrilateral $p_1\, q_{n-4}\, p_{n-1}\, p_n\, p_1$, having its angular points, taken in order, on known straight lines L_1, Q_{n-4}, L_{n-1}, L_n, and its successive sides passing through four known points r_{n-4}, s_{n-4}, o_{n-1}, o_n. For, as the method leaves the points o_n, o_{n-1}, and the line L_n unimplicated, it follows that if we give these such

positions as will render the quadrilateral porismatic, then will the problem of the forming of the complete n'gon be porismatic.

But it is evident (from a well known porism) that if we assume any two points in the straight line $r_{n-4}\, s_{n-4}$ as positions for o_{n-1} and o_n, then we can find a position for L_n so as to render the problem of the forming of the quadrilateral porismatic.

Hence we may announce the following porism:—

PORISM 9.

If a closed n'gon have its first $n-2$ sides passing through $n-2$ given points, and have its first $n-1$ angular points resting on $n-1$ given straight lines: a straight line can be found, such that if we look on the two points in which it is cut by the two last sides of the n'gon as fixed, and that we deform the n'gon so that its sides will continue through the n points composed of the $n-2$ given ones and the two determined ones, and that its first $n-1$ angular points move on the $n-1$ given straight lines, then will the locus of the nth angular point of the n'gon be a determinable straight line.

This porism is evidently derivable from Porism 8 by reciprocation:

19. It is evident from the properties of homographic pencils and divisions (see Chasles' "Géométrie Supérieure"), that we can solve the more extended problem, in which all or any number of the entities $o_1, o_2, \ldots o_n$ may be replaced by conics to be touched by sides of the closed n'gon, provided these conics touch the respective pairs of given straight lines on which the extremities of the touching sides are to rest. And all the data but the conic o_n being given, the method of finding this conic so as to render the problem porismatic is evident.

And if instead of requiring all the angular points of the closed n'gons to rest on straight lines, we were to have all or any number of them rest in given circles, or other given conics passing through the pairs of given points through which the sides of the n'gon forming such angular points pass, then also we can solve.

The numerous problems which may be formed by diversifying the data give rise to porisms which may be easily evolved. I will not enter on their investigation in this paper; but the following porism, comprising a multitude of particular cases, can be easily deduced:—

PORISM 10.

If there be a closed n'gon, having its 1st and $n-1^{th}$ angular points resting on given straight lines L_1, L_{n-1}, and that the nature of the conditions imposed on the $n-2$ first sides and angles be such that by forming the open $(n-2)$'gons according to these conditions, we shall have the given straight lines L_1 and L_{n-1}, divided homographically by their extremities: two straight lines XX, YY, can (generally) be found, such that if we look on the points o_{n-1} and o_n in which they are cut by the $n-1^{th}$ and n^{th} sides of the closed n'gon as fixed points, and that we "deform" this n'gon so that its sides and angles continue subject to the imposed conditions, and that its $n-1^{th}$ and n^{th} sides continue through the determined points o_{n-1} and o_n, then will the nth angular point of the n'gon describe a determinable circle passing through o_{n-1}, and o_n (see Porism X. in Transactions of the Royal Society of Victoria for 1859).

20. From the well-known properties of three pairs of points in one straight line, which are in involution (see "Géométrie Supérieure") we infer the following theorem:—

THEOREM 4.

If we can form one closed 2 n'gon whose first n sides and whose second n sides pass successively through n fixed points taken in prescribed order, and whose first n angular points rest in succession on n given straight lines taken in prescribed order: then any point whatever in any of the lines is an answerable position for an angular point of a like closed 2 n'gon; or which amounts to the same—we can deform the 2 n'gon subject to the imposed conditions, so that its angular points will move along the n straight lines.

21. The problem solved at the commencement of this paper may be regarded as strictly analogous to the following one:—

"Given a system of n straight lines $L_1, L_2, \ldots L_n$ in space, and given also a second system of n straight lines $K_1, K_2, \ldots K_n$ in space; through the lines of the second system taken in order to draw n planes forming a closed planes n'gon whose n angular joints will rest on the n lines of the first system taken in order."

To those who understand the homographic theory (and possess the ability to conjure up figures in the air) the method of solution is obvious; and the following theorems and porisms are evident consequences.

THEOREM 5.

If we can form three closed planes n'gons, such that the n planes of each contain n fixed straight lines in space (each plane containing a certain line), and the n joints rest on n other fixed straight lines in space; then will any point whatever in any straight line of the second system of n lines be an answerable position for an angular point of a closed planes n'gon fulfilling the like conditions.

THEOREM 6.

If we can form one closed planes 2 n'gon, whose first n planes and whose second n planes contain n fixed straight lines (in space) taken in prescribed order, and whose first n angular joints and second n angular joints rest on n other fixed straight lines taken in prescribed order; then we can deform this planes 2 n'gon so that its sides will contain the straight lines of the first system, and its angular joints move along the straight lines of the second system.

PORISM 11.

Given a system of n *straight lines in space, and given the first* n—2 *straight lines of a second system of* n *straight lines in space:*

Innumerable straight lines (contained in the surface of a determinable hyperboloid of one sheet) can be found, such that if we chose any two of them, and draw a plane through each, we can find two points R and S, one in each plane, and through these points draw innumerable pairs of corresponding straight lines (the line through each point being in the plane in which the point lies), such that if we chose any pair of the corresponding lines as the n—1th and nth straight lines of the second system, we shall render porismatic the problem of the construction of the closed planes n'gon, whose n planes contain the n lines of the second system, and whose n angular joints rest on the n lines of the first system.

PORISM 12.

Given the first n — 1 of a system of n straight lines in space, and given also the first n — 1 of a second system of n straight lines in space :—

If a closed planes n'gon have its first n — 1 angular joints on the respective n — 1 lines of the first system, and its n — 1 first planes containing the respective n — 1 lines of the second system; two straight lines and a point in each can be found, such that if from either of these two points we draw any staight line L_n through the nth angular joint of the n'gon, and that through the point where the other found line pierces the nth plane of the n'gon, we draw any line K_n in that plane; then by taking the lines L_n and K_n as fixed nth lines of the first and second systems, we can deform the n'gon so that its n planes will continue to contain the n straight lines of the second system, and its angular joints move on the n straight lines of the first system. Moreover, we can give any position to K_n, and find innumerable corresponding answerable positions for L_n (all in the surface of a determinable hyperboloid of one sheet.)

The following theorems are also obvious consequences from the theory of homographic figures :—

THEOREM 7.

If there be three distinct closed straight line n'gons having their first angular points in one straight line xx, each n'gon of which has its sides passing through n fixed points, and its angular points in n fixed planes; then will any point in the straight line xx be an answerable position for the first angular point of another such closed n'gon, and any other point in the plane containing xx

will be an answerable position for the first angular point of a straight line closed 2 n'gon, whose two successive series of n sides will pass in order through the n fixed points, and whose two successive series of angular points will be situated in the n fixed planes. And, reciprocally, if we can form one closed 2 n'gon having its first n sides distinct from its second n sides, &c.

THEOREM 8.

If there be 4 closed straight line n'gons, each one of which has its sides passing in order through n fixed points, and its n angular points resting on n fixed planes, and that the first angular points (all in one plane P) of these closed n'gons are not all in one straight line; then will any point in the plane P be an answerable position for the first angular point of another such closed n'gon.

NOTE.

The principal porisms (concerning plane straight line n'gons) envolved in this paper contain as particular cases all those of a kindred nature, said to have been comprised in the writings of the ancient Greek Geometers.

They contain also as particular cases all those concerning polygons which are given in the works of Professors Simson, Mulcahy and Chasles.

PAPER No. 3.

Researches concerning n'gons inscribed in curves of the second degree, by

MARTIN GARDINER, C.E.

---

1. Let S represent any fixed curve of the second degree; and let $o_1, o_2, \ldots o_n$ represent n fixed points of a series, which, taken in order, may be designated the 1st, 2nd, 3rd, ... and n^{th} points respectively.

Suppose $a_1\ a_2\ \ldots\ a_{n+1},\ b_1\ b_2\ \ldots\ b_{n+1},\ c_1\ c_2\ \ldots\ c_{n+1},\ d_1\ d_2\ \ldots\ d_{n+1}$, &c., to be inscribed n'gons, the successive sides of each of which pass in order through the n points of the series.

If we regard the point o_1 and its polar as vertex and axis to homologic figures whose homological ratio is -1, and that we look on the points a_1, b_1, c_1, d_1, &c., as belonging to one figure, then will a_2, b_2, c_2, d_2, &c., be the corresponding points in the other figure.

Similarly, if we regard the point o_2 and its polar as vertex and axis to homologic figures whose homological ratio is -1, and that we look on the points a_2, b_2, c_2, d_2, &c., as belonging to one figure, then will a_3, b_3, c_3, d_3, &c., be corresponding points in the other figure.

We may thus proceed from the extremities of sides of the n'gons of like subscript numbers to those of higher subscripts until we arrive at the final extremities of the n'gons. And as homologic figures are homographic, and that figures homographic with any figure are homographic with each other, therefore it is evident the first points a_1, b_1, c_1, d_1, &c., of the inscribed n'gons, and their final points $a_{n+1}, b_{n+1}, c_{n+1}$, &c., are corresponding points of homographic figures. Moreover, it is evident that the tangents to the curve S, at the corresponding points of these homographic figures, are corresponding lines of the figures.

2. By indicating tangents to the curve by capital letters of like names and subscripts to the small letters indicating the points of contact, we at once infer the following important theorem :—

THEOREM I.

If in a curve of the second degree there be three n'gons $a_1\ a_2\ \ldots\ a_{n+1},\ b_1\ b_2\ \ldots\ b_{n+1},\ c_1\ c_2\ \ldots\ c_{n+1}$, inscribed so that the n

successive sides of each pass in order through n *fixed points* o_1, o_2, ... o_n; *then,* d_1 d_2 .... d_{n+1} *representing an inscribed* n'*gon whose sides pass in like manner through the fixed points, and which we may conceive to be deformed so as to assume the position of all the* n'*gons which can be so inscribed, we will have*

$$\frac{d_1, A_1}{d_1, B_1} : \frac{d_{n+1}, A_{n+1}}{d_{n+1}, B_{n+1}} = \frac{c_1, A_1}{c_1, B_1} : \frac{c_{n+1}, A_{n+1}}{c_{n+1}, B_{n+1}}.$$

3. We know that the first extremities of the inscribed n'gons are corresponding points to their last extremities in a pair of homographic figures. We know also that according as these homographic figures are homologic or not homologic so accordingly will the closing chords of the n'gons all pass through one point or be tangents to a conic T having double contact with S, (in the points which are answerable positions for first extremities of inscribable closed n'gons whose sides pass in order through the given points) and of like or unlike rotatives, (reckoning from the final extremities of the n'gons) just according as the final extremities of the n'gons are on the same side or on opposite sides of the line of contact of the conics T and S. But, when we can interchange the distinct extremities of one of the inscribable n'gons, we know that the figures are homologic. Hence we have the following theorems :—

THEOREM 2.

If in a curve of the second degree there can be one inscribed closed 2 n'*gon whose two successive series of* n *sides pass in order through* n *fixed points, and are not co-incident; then will any point in the curve be an answerable position for the first extremity of another inscribable closed* 2 n'*gon whose sides will pass in like order through the* n *fixed points.*

And the closing chords of the inscribable n'*gons the sides of each of which pass in order through the* n *fixed points will all pass through one point, whose polar cuts the curve in the answerable positions for first extremities of inscribable closed* n'*gons whose sides pass in order through the points.*

THEOREM 3.

If in a conic S *there can be inscribed one open* 2 *n'gon whose first* n *sides and whose second* n *sides pass in order through* n *fixed points, then will the closing chords of all the inscribable* n'*gons whose sides pass in order through the* n *fixed points be tangents to a conic* T *having double contact with the given conic* S, *and they will be of like or unlike rotatives in respect to* T *(reckoning from the final extremities of the* n'*gons) just according as the final extremities of the* n'*gons are on the same side or on opposite sides of the line of contact.*

THEOREM 4.

If there be a curve of the second degree and a series of n *points and that the problem of the inscription of closed* n'*gons the sides of each of which pass in order through the* n *points is non-porismatic, there are two and but two answerable positions for the first extremities of such closed* n'*gons.*

THEOREM 5.

If three closed n'*gons be inscribable in a curve of the second degree so that the sides of each pass in order through* n *fixed points of a series of* n *points; then will any point in the curve be an answerable position for the first extremity of an inscribable closed* n'*gon whose sides pass in like manner through the* n *points.*

☞ This theorem is otherwise evident from the well-known relations of homographic divisions in a conic. It can also be easily deduced from the formula of theorem 1 by supposing a_{n+1}, b_{n+1}, and c_{n+1}, to be co-incident with a_1, b_1, and c_1 respectively. For as

$$\frac{d_1, A_1}{d_1, B_1} : \frac{d_{n+1}, A_1}{d_{n+1}, B_1} = 1, \text{ and that } \frac{d_1, A_1}{d_1, C_1} : \frac{d_{n+1}, A_1}{d_{n+1}, C_1} = 1,$$

it would follow that if d_1 and d_{n+1} be supposed distinct, the chord $d_1 \, d_{n+1}$ should pass through the points of intersection of A_1 with B_1 and C_1.

4. If o_{n+1} be any point in the straight line containing the first extremities a_1 and b_1 of the two inscribable closed n'gons, whose sides pass in order through the n fixed points $o_1, o_2, \ldots o_n$, of a series of n points, it is evident $a_1 \; a_2 \ldots a_n \; a_1 \; b_1 \; b_2 \ldots b_n \; b_1 \; a_1$ is a closed $2(n+1)$ 'gon whose two series of $n+1$ successive sides pass in order through the $n+1$ points $o_1, o_2, \ldots o_n, o_{n+1}$.

Moreover, it is evident (by making a_1 the first point of an inscribed $2(n+1)$ 'gon) that if the point o_{n+1} be such as to render any point in the curve answerable for the first point of an inscribable closed $2(n+1)$'gon whose sides pass in the prescribed manner through the $n+1$ points $o_1, o_2, \ldots o_n, o_{n+1}$, then will o_{n+1} be situated in the straight line containing a_1 and b_1. Hence we infer the following theorems:—

THEOREM 6.

If in a curve of the second degree we inscribe any three distinct n'gons $e_1 \; e_2 \ldots e_{n+1}, \; f_1 \; f_2 \ldots f_{n+1}, \; g_1 \; g_2 \ldots g_{n+1}$, the sides of each of which pass in order through n given points; then will the three pairs of straight lines $e_1 \; f_{n+1}, \; f_1 \; e_{n+1}$ and $e_1 \; g_{n+1}, \; g_1 \; e_{n+1}$ and $f_1 \; g_{n+1}, \; g_1 \; f_{n+1}$, cut each other in three points in the straight line which contains the first points of the two inscribable closed n'gons whose sides pass in order through the n points.

☞ This theorem is otherwise evident, since homographic pencils having a common vertex in a conic, are such that by taking any two pairs of the corresponding radiants and coupling them transversly they will form an involution with the double radiants of the pencils.

THEOREM 7.

Any point in the straight line containing the first points of the two closed $(n-1)$ 'gons inscriptible in a curve of the second degree so that the sides of each pass in order through $n-1$ fixed points, will be an answerable position for the nth point of the series so as to *render any point in the curve an answerable position for the first extremity of an inscribable closed* 2 n'*gon whose two successive series of* n *sides will pass in order through the* n *points. And no point outside the straight line containing the first extremities of the two closed* (n — 1) '*gons will possess this property.*

5. If we have a curve of the second degree and the first $n-2$ points of a series of n points, and that we assume the $n-1^{th}$ point o_{n-1} anywhere in the straight line containing the first extremities p_1 and q_1 of the inscribable closed $(n-2)$ 'gons whose sides pass in order through the $n-2$ given points and that we assume the nth point o_n co-incident with the pole of the straight line containing the first extremities of the inscribable closed $(n-1)$ 'gons whose sides pass in order through the $n-1$ points $o_1, o_2, \ldots o_{n-2}, o_{n-1}$, it is obvious from theorems 6 and 2 that any point in the curve is an answerable position for the first extremity of an inscribable closed n'gon whose sides pass in order through the n points of the series. Moreover, it is evident (by considering p_1 or q_1 as first points of inscribable n'gons) the nth point o_n lies in the line $p_1\, q_1\, o_{n-1}$. Hence

PORISM 1.

If any closed n'*gon inscribed in a a curve of the second degree have its first* n — 2 *sides passing in order through* n — 2 *given points; then a straight line* xx *can be found such that if we look on the points in which it is cut by the* n — 1th *and* n^{th} *sides of the* n'*gon as fixed, we can deform the* n'*gon so that its angular points will move along the curve and its* n *sides continue through the* n *fixed points composed of the* n — 2 *given ones and the two determined ones.*

☞ In respect to this porism it is well to remember that the straight line xx cuts the given curve in the answerable positions (real or imaginary) for the first extremities of the inscribable closed $(n-2)$ 'gons, the sides of each of which pass in order through the $n-2$ given points. And when the problem of the inscription of the closed $(n-2)$ 'gons is porismatic, then o_{n+1} and o_n must be coincident though otherwise unrestricted in the plane.

6 If we have a conic and any even number of points in one straight line, it is evident the points in which this line cuts the conic, are answerable positions for first angular points of inscribable closed n'gons, whose sides pass in order through the n points.

Hence from porism 1, we infer the following theorem:—

THEOREM 8.

If n be any even number, and that in a conic there be inscribed a closed n'gon having $n-1$ of its sides passing through $n-1$ fixed points in one straight line; then will the remaining side pass through a point in the same line, such that if we suppose it fixed, we can deform the closed n'gon so that its angular points will move along the curve, and its n sides continue through the n fixed points.

And from theorem 2 or 7, we at once infer the following

THEOREM 9.

If n be any odd number, and that in a conic there be inscribed any closed 2 n'gon such that $n-1$ pairs of its opposite sides cut each other in $n-1$ points situated in one straight line, then will the remaining pair of opposite sides cut each other in a point of this same straight line.

☞ The particular case in which $n = 3$ is identical with Pascal's famous theorem concerning an inscribed hexagon.

7. In applying theorem 6 to the finding of the first angular points of the inscribable closed 1'gons, the side of each of which must pass through a given point o_1, we immediately perceive that the polar of the point o_1 cuts the curve in the answerable positions for these angular points. And from this, and porism 1, we have

THEOREM 10.

If we have a conic and three points, each point of which is the pole of the straight line containing the other two; then will any point in the conic be an answerable position for the first angular point of an inscribable closed 3'gon whose sides pass through the three points taken in any order whatever.

8. The theorem inverse to that made use of in establishing theorem 3 may be enunciated in the following manner:—

THEOREM 11.

If two conics, S and T, have double contact (real or imaginary), and that from any four points in the conic S there be drawn tangents to the conic T of like or opposite rotatives just according as the points lie on the same side or on opposite sides of the straight line (always real) containing the points of contact of the conics : then will the anharmonic ratio of the four points whence the tangents are drawn be equal to the anharmonic ratio of the four points in which the tangents touch the conic T, and also to the anharmonic ratio of the other four points in which these tangents again cut the conic S.

This theorem is given in a very imperfect form in Chasles' " *Géométrie Supérieure*," and also in Salmon's " *Conics*," where its discovery is said to be due to Mr. Townsend, of Trinity College, Dublin. The CORRECT THEOREM is now given for the first time.

9. It is evident, from this theorem, and from the preceding portions of the paper, we can form theorems in respect to extended data, analogous to those arrived at. I will give the following one as an instance :—

THEOREM 12.

If the n angular points of a closed n'gon rest on a curve S of the second degree, and that its first $n-1$ sides pass through $n-1$ points, or that all or any number of them, not passing through fixed points, are tangents of certain prescribable rotatives to fixed conics having double contacts with S; then if we deform the n'gon subject to these imposed conditions, the envelope of the nth side will be a conic having double contact with S, or it will be a determinable point, just according to the possibility of inscribing in S an open $2(n-1)$ 'gon or a closed $2(n-1)$'gon whose two successive series of n sides are distinct and meet in orderly succession with the $n-1$ entities in the manner prescribed for the closed n'gons.

PROBLEM.

10. Given a conic and a series of n points $o_1, o_2, \ldots o_n$; to inscribe the closed n'gons, in the conic, the sides of each of which will pass in order through the points.

Now it is evident that if we can find the answerable positions for the first angular points of the closed n'gons our object will be attained.

First method of solution.

If n be an odd number, it is obvious from theorem 10 that we can replace the point o_n and the side of any of the closed n'gons which passes through it by two other points and two chords cutting each other in the curve and passing through the determined points and the extremities of the side which passed through o_n. Hence we may consider n to be an *even* number.

Analysis.—Let $a_1 a_2 \ldots a_n a_1$ be one of the inscribed closed n'gons whose sides pass in order through the n points $o_1, o_2 \ldots o_n$.

Looking on the first four sides of this n'gon, let us designate by i_1 the intersection of the lines $o_1 o_2$ and $o_3 o_4$; and let b_1 be the point in which $i_1 a_3$ again cuts the conic. Then, $a_1 a_2 a_3 b_1 a_1$ being an inscribed 4'gon, it is evident from theorem 8, that the point r_1 in which $a_1 b_1$ cuts the line $o_1 o_2 i_1$ is known. And, since $a_3 a_4 a_5 b_1 a_3$ is an inscribed 4'gon, and that o_3, o_4, i_1, are in one line, therefore the point s_1 in which the line $a_5 b_1$ cuts the line $o_3 o_4 i_1$ is known. Hence we perceive that the inscription of the closed n'gons is reduced to that of the inscription of the closed $(n-2)$'gons $a_1 b_1 a_5 \ldots a_n a_1$ whose sides pass in order through the $n-2$ known points $r_1, s_1, o_5, \ldots o_n$.

And thus, step by step, we can reduce the number of sides repeatedly by two until we arrive at a closed 4'gon $a_1 b_{\frac{1}{2}n-2} a_{n-1} a_n a_1$ whose sides pass in order through four known points $r_{\frac{1}{2}n-2}, s_{\frac{1}{2}n-2}, o_{n-1}, o_n$.

Now let $i'_{\frac{1}{2}n-1}$ be the intersection of the lines $r_{\frac{1}{2}n-2}\, s_{\frac{1}{2}n-2}$ and $o_{n-1}\, o_n$; and let $b'_{\frac{1}{2}n-1}$ be the point in which $i'_{\frac{1}{2}n-2}\, a_{n-1}$ again cuts the conic. Since $a_1\, b_{\frac{1}{2}n-1}\, a_{n-1}\, b_{\frac{1}{2}n-2}\, a_1$ is an inscribed 4'gon, it follows that the point (see theorem 8) $r_{\frac{1}{2}n-1}$ in which $a_1\, b_{\frac{1}{2}n-1}$ cuts $r_{\frac{1}{2}n-2}\, s_{\frac{1}{2}n-2}$ is known. And since $a_{n-1}\, b_{\frac{1}{2}n-1}\, a_1\, a_n\, a_{n-1}$ is an inscribed 4'gon, the point $s_{\frac{1}{2}n-1}$ in which $a_1\, b_{\frac{1}{2}n-1}$ cuts $o_{n-1}\, o_n$ is known. Hence, as the points $r_{\frac{1}{2}n-1}$ and $s_{\frac{1}{2}n-1}$ are known, the points a_1 in which the straight line $r_{\frac{1}{2}n-1}\, s_{\frac{1}{2}n-1}$ cuts the conic are known.

☞ I may also remark that porism 1 is prominently evident from this method of solution—for (from the well-known case of theorem 8 in which $n = 4$) the straight line $r_{\frac{1}{2}n-2}\, s_{\frac{1}{2}n-2}$ is such that if we assume one of the points o_{n-1}, o_n, anywhere therein, we can find a corresponding position for the other one in the same line which will render porismatic the inscription of the closed 4'gon, and ∴ also that of the closed n'gon.

Second method of solution.

Analysis.—Let $a_1\, a_2 \ldots a_n\, a_1$ be a closed n'gon inscribed in the desired manner (n being regarded as an even number). Suppose that through a_1 we draw the chord $a_1\, b_2$ parallel to $o_1\, a_2$. Then it is evident (from the well-known particular case of theorem 8 in which $n = 4$) that the point p_2 in which $b_2\, a_3$ cuts $o_1\, o_2$ is known.

And if we suppose the chord $b_2\, b_3$ parallel to $p_2\, o_3$, and that we draw $b_3\, a_4$ to cut $p_2\, o_3$ in p_3, then for like reasons the point p_3 is known. Similarly, if we draw the chord $b_3\, b_4$ parallel to $p_3\, o_4$, and that we draw $b_4\, a_5$ to cut $p_3\, o_4$ in p_4, then will the point p_4 be known.

And proceeding thus, it is evident we at length arrive at the known point p_n in which the chord $b_n\, a_1$ cuts the straight line $p_{n-1}\, o_n$.

The result of these operations is obviously an inscribed closed n'gon $a_1 \, b_2 \, b_3 \, \ldots \, b_n \, a_1$ whose first $n-1$ sides are parallels to known straight lines $o_1 \, o_2$, $p_2 \, o_3$, $p_3 \, o_4$, $\ldots p_{n-1} \, o_n$, and whose last side $b_n \, a_1$ passes through the known point p_n.

Now $n-1$ being an odd number, we know that the chord $b_n \, a_1$ will be parallel to a fixed determinable direction; and, therefore, as the side is also a transversal through the point p_n, we know the point a_1 of its intersection with the conic. Moreover, it is obvious that the point b_n will also be an answerable position for the first angular point of an inscribable closed n'gon fulfilling the conditions. It is also evident that when the point p_n is at infinity and indicated by the infinite production of the chords $b_n \, a_1$, the problem will be porismatic.

Third method of solution.

Theorem 6 intimates to us Poncelet's elegant method of arriving at the first angular points of the closed n'gons fulfilling the imposed conditions.—Inscribe any three distinct n'gons $a_1 \, a_2 \, \ldots \, a_{n+1}$, $b_1 \, b_2 \, \ldots \, b_{n+1}$, $c_1 \, c_2 \, \ldots \, c_{n+1}$, the n sides of each of which pass in order through the n given points $o_1, o_2, \ldots o_n$; find i, the point of intersection of the chords $a_1 \, b_{n+1}$ and $b_1 \, a_{n+1}$; find k, the point of intersection of the chords $a_1 \, c_{n+1}$ and $c_1 \, a_{n+1}$; find l, the point of intersection of the chords $b_1 \, c_{n+1}$ and $c_1 \, b_{n+1}$. Then will the three points i, k, l, be in one straight line which is such that its points of intersection with the conic (real or imaginary as may be) are answerable positions for the first angular points of the inscribable closed n'gons.

☞ This method holds whether n is odd or even, and from the present paper it is obvious it holds in the following more extended problem:—Given a conic S and n entities $o_1, o_2, \ldots o_n$, any number of which represent given points, and the rest given conics having double contacts with S; to inscribe in S the closed

n'gons, the n sides of each of which will meet with the entities taken in order, in such a manner as that the sides meeting with the entities which are conics will be tangents of prescribed rotatives thereunto. (Remembering that when we fix on the rotative of any particular numbered sides of the n'gons whose first points lie on one side of the line of contact of the entity which they touch, we must have them of opposite rotative when the first points fall on the other side of the line of contact.)

Fourth method of solution (for particular case).

When the given conic is a circle, the problem of the inscription of the closed n'gons whose sides pass in order through the n given points $o_1, o_2, \ldots o_n$ can be investigated in the following manner (which is worthy of particular attention as an illustration of the importance of conceiving the methods of *rotatives* of segments of lines in respect to particular points, and by such means eliminating uncertainty as to which of two straight lines is the answerable one to the object in view.) *Method of investigation*:—Suppose $p_1 p_2 \ldots p_n p_1$ an inscribed closed n'gon whose sides pass in order through the n points.

Let $a_1 a_2 \ldots a_{n+1}$ and $b_1 b_2 \ldots b_{n+1}$ be two inscribed n'gons, formed at random, the sides of each of which pass in order through the n points. From the properties of similar triangles we have

$$\frac{a_1 p_1}{b_1 p_1} : \frac{a_2 p_2}{b_2 p_2} = \frac{a_1 o_1}{b_1 o_1}$$

$$\frac{a_2 p_2}{b_2 p_2} : \frac{a_3 p_3}{b_3 p_3} = \frac{a_2 o_2}{b_2 o_2}$$

$$\ldots \quad \ldots \quad \ldots$$

$$\frac{a_n p_n}{b_n p_n} : \frac{a_{n+1} p_1}{b_{n+1} p_1} = \frac{a_n o_n}{b_n o_n},$$

holding in signs when the *rotatives* of the involved lines are taken in respect to any point in the circumference. And from these we have

$$\frac{a_1 p_1}{b_n p_n} : \frac{a_{n+1} p_1}{b_{n+1} p_1} = \frac{a_1 o_1}{b_1 o_1} \cdot \frac{a_2 o_2}{b_2 o_2} \cdots \frac{a_n o_n}{b_n o_n}.$$

the rotatives of the involved parts being taken in respect to any point in the circumference.

Now since the product of two sides of any plane triangle is equal in *magnitude* to the product of the diameter of the circumscribing circle and the perpendicular from their point of intersection on the third side; it is evident from the last equation that the perpendiculars from p_1 on the straight lines $a_1 b_{n+1}$ and $b_1 a_{n+1}$ have to each other a known numerical ratio; and, therefore, all the answerable positions for p_1 must be included amongst those given by the intersections of the given circle with two known straight lines passing through the intersection of the chords $a_1 b_{n+1}$ and $b_1 a_{n+1}$. Moreover, since *one only* of these two straight lines gives points p_1 fulfilling the equation of conditions when the *rotatives* of the involved portions are taken in respect to any point in the circumference, it is obvious that the point p_1 is an intersection of the given circle with one known straight line.

By forming another inscribed n'gon $c_1 c_2 \ldots c_{n+1}$ whose sides pass in order through the given points, it is evident the point p_1 must be in a determinable straight line through the intersection of the chords $a_1 c_{n+1}$ and $c_1 a_{n+1}$. And hence we infer Poncelet's method of finding the straight line $x\,x$ containing the answerable positions for p_1.

When a_{n+1} and b_{n+1} are co-incident with a_1 and b_1 then evidently the first side of the last equation is equal unity, and therefore so also the second side. And in this state of the data it is evident that any point in the circumference will be an answerable position for p_1. Hence we re-arrive at theorem 5, and also at the following :—

THEOREM 13.

If $a_1 \ a_2 \ \ldots \ a_n \ a_1$ *and* $b_1 \ b_2 \ \ldots \ b_n \ b_1$ *be two closed* n,*gons inscribed in a circle, the sides of each of which pass in order through* n *fixed points* $o_1, o_2, \ldots o_n,$ *and that*

$$\frac{a_1 \ o_1}{b_1 \ o_1} \cdot \frac{a_2 \ o_2}{b_2 \ o_2} \ldots \frac{a_n \ o_n}{b_n \ o_n} = +\ \vdots 1$$

when the rotatives of the involved lines are taken in respect to any point in the circumference; then will any point in the circumference be an answerable position for the first angular point of an inscribable closed n'*gon whose sides pass in order through the* n *fixed points.*

12. When the data is such as to render the problem porismatic when the number of points is even, and that they are all in one straight line; then, by supposing the points a_1 and b_1 co-incident with the points in which this line cuts the circle, it is obvious from the last theorem that

$$\frac{a_1 \ o_1 \cdot a_1 \ o_3 \ \ldots \ a_1 \ o_{n-1}}{a_1 \ o_2 \cdot a_1 \ o_4 \ \ldots \ a_1 \ o_n} = \frac{b_1 \ o_1 \cdot b_1 \ o_3 \ \ldots \ b_1 \ o_{n-1}}{b_1 \ o_2 \cdot b_1 \ o_4 \ \ldots \ b_1 \ o_n}$$

which is a formula already arrived at by Chasles, on page 465 of his treatise on "*Géométrie Supérieure.*"

13. Again (since the extremities of all the inscribable n'gons belong to homographic figures) the following theorem can be easily deduced :—

THEOREM 14.

If there be given a circle and n *points in a plane, two straight lines,* X *and* Y *can be found, such that if* a_1 *and* a_{n+1} *be the extremities of any inscribed* n'*gon whose sides pass in order through* the n *points, then will the product of the perpendiculars from* a_1 *and* a_{n+1} *on* X *and* Y, *respectively, be of constant magnitude.*

The lines are equidistant from the centre of the circle, and are those corresponding to infinity in the homographic figures to which the extremities of the inscribable n'gons belong.

14. By the well-known process of reciprocation we can at once form theorems which are the "*duals*" or "*correlatives*" of those investigated, or we can arrive at them by steps correlative to those already used. It is also obvious we can make the solutions of the problems subservient to the solutions of their "*duals*," or we can arrive at solutions to the dual problems by steps correlative to those used. As an example of the latter mode of proceeding, I will enunciate the dual problem, and give the method of solution correlative to the first.

PROBLEM.

To exscribe a closed n'gon to a given curve of the second degree, so that its n successive angular points will be situated in n given straight lines L_1, L_2, ... L_n taken in order.

Analysis.—Let n be considered an even number; and let $a_1 \, a_2 \, ... \, a_n \, a_1$ be an exscribed closed n'gon whose angular points $a_1, a_2, ... a_n$ rest on $L_1, L_2, ... L_n$ respectively.

Suppose we draw a straight line I_1 through the points of intersection of L_1 and L_2, and of L_3 and L_4; and let i be the point in which this line cuts $a_2 \, a_3$. Then if r_1 be the point in which the other tangent from i cuts $a_1 \, a_2$, it follows that the straight line R_1 through r_1 and the intersection of L_1 and L_2 is known. And if s_1 be the point in which the other tangent from i cuts $a_4 \, a_5$, it follows that the straight line S_1 through s_1 and the intersection of L_3 and L_4 is known.

Hence we see that the problem is reduced to the exscribing of a closed $(n-2)$'gon $r_1 s_1 a_5 \ldots a_n\, r_1$ having its successive angular points on the $n-2$ known straight lines R_1, S_1, L_5, ... L_n.

And thus, step by step, we can reduce the problem until we make the solution dependent on that of exscribing a closed 4'gon $r_{\frac{1}{2}n-2}\, s_{\frac{1}{2}n-2}\, a_{n-1}\, a_n\, r_{\frac{1}{2}n-2}$ having its angular points on the four known straight lines $R_{\frac{1}{2}n-2}$, $S_{\frac{1}{2}n-2}$, L_{n-1}, L_n.

Now our object is to find out how to form this closed 4'gon.

Suppose we draw the straight line which contains the intersection of the lines $R_{\frac{1}{2}n-2}$ and L_n, and the intersection of $S_{\frac{1}{2}n-2}$ and L_{n-1}; and suppose x to be the point in which this line cuts the line $r_{\frac{1}{2}n-2}\, s_{\frac{1}{2}n-2}$.

Then as the point in which the other tangent from x cuts the side $a_{n-1}\, a_n$ must be on each one of two known straight lines (one through the intersection of $R_{\frac{1}{2}n-2}$ and L_n, and the other through that of $S_{\frac{1}{2}n-2}$ and L_{n-1}) it is known. And therefore the tangent $a_{n-1}\, a_n$ through it is known, &c. Moreover it is evident the point x is such that if L_{n-1} and L_n pass through it, the problem of the construction of the closed 4'gon will be porismatic, and therefore also the construction of the exscribed closed n'gon. Hence we may announce the following porism, which is the *dual* of porism 1 already given :—

PORISM 2.

If a closed n'*gon be exscribed to a fixed conic, and have its first* n—2 *angular points on* n—2 *fixed straight lines; a point* x *can be found, such that if we draw straight lines from it through the* n—1th *and* nth *angular points of the* n'*gon, and regard these two lines as fixed, we can deform the* n'*gon so that its angular points will move along the* n *fixed straight lines, and its* n *sides continue tangents to the fixed conic.*

15. It is evident, from the projective properties of figures, that analogous theorems and porisms, to those established concerning plane conics, can be established in respect to "*spherical conics.*" It is also obvious that analogous problems concerning spherical conics can be solved by analogous processes.

HISTORICAL NOTES :—

The problem solved in this paper is famous from having been the chief instrument in unfolding the *theory of poles and polars* amongst the matchless geometers of France.

In 1776, Castillon gave a solution to the particular case in which the conic is a circle and $n = 3$, which appeared in the "*Memoires of the Academy of Berlin.*"

In 1776, Lagrange indicated a method of arriving at a solution to the particular case considered by Castillon, by means of rather complicated trigonometrical equations.

In 1776, the porism pertaining to this case appeared in the "*Opera Reliqua*" of Professor Simson, of the University of Glasgow. Simson solved the problem in 1731.

In 1784, Ottajano and Malfatti (two distinguished Italian Geometers) gave excellent solutions to the more general case in which the curve is a circle and $n =$ any whole number whatever. These solutions were published in the "*Memorie della Societa Italiana*" of Naples.

In 1796, Lhuilier gave a solution to this case, or rather he showed how its solution might be made dependent on the solution of trigonometrical equations.

In 1803, the illustrious Carnot (the republican statesman chosen by Napoleon I. to rally the shattered power of the empire against the combined feudalism of Europe) gave a similar solution to this particular case in his work entitled "*Géométrie de Position.*"

In 1810, Brianchon solved the general problem, in which the curve is any conic, and n any whole number. This solution appeared in the "*Journal de l' Ecole Polytechnique.*"

In 1817, Poncelet (the celebrated French Engineer) gave an

elegant and simple method of solution to the general problem in the "*Annales des Mathematiques.*"

In 1847, Mr. Townsend (of Trinity College, Dublin) pointed out an easy method of demonstrating the correctness of Poncelet's process by means of anharmonic properties of conics.

In 1847, Mr. Gaskin (of Jesus College, Cambridge) furnished a solution which was edited by Professor Davies (of the Royal Military Academy) and published in the "*Mechanics' Magazine.*" This method of solving the general question is evidently nothing more than an extension of the methods of Castillon and Ottajano.

Mr. Gaskin has also paid much attention to this problem in an appendix to his work entitled "*Solutions to Geometrical Problems;*" and he is unquestionably the first geometer who succeeded in arriving at a true conception of the contingent porismatic relations of the data.

The inquisitive reader may consult the third volume of "*The Mathematician*" for a more detailed history, including the labours of Euler, Lexell, Fuss, Gergonne, Servois, Econtre, Rochat, Noble, Wallace, Lowry, Swale, Hearn, &c.

PAPER No. 4.

Researches concerning n'gons inscribed in surfaces of the second degree

by MARTIN GARDINER, C.E.

[Read 17th June, 1863.]

---

1. Let S represent a surface of the second degree; and let $o_1, o_2, \ldots o_n$ be a series of n fixed points, designated as first, second, &c., according to the subscript numbers. Let $a_1 a_2, \ldots a_{n+1}, b_1 b_2 \ldots b_{n+1}, c_1 c_2 \ldots c_{n+1}, d_1 d_2 \ldots d_{n+1}$, &c., be inscribed n'gons, the sides of each of which pass in order through the n points.

If we regard the point o_1 and its polar plane as vertex and axis to homologic figures whose homological ratio is -1, and that we look on a_1, b_1, c_1, d_1, &c., as belonging to one of these figures, then will a_2, b_2, c_2, d_2, &c., be their corresponding points in the other figure. Similarly, by regarding o_2 and its polar plane as vertex and axis to homologic figures whose homological ratio is -1, and looking on a_2, b_2, c_2, d_2, &c., as belonging to one of these figures, then will a_3, b_3, c_3, d_3, &c., be their corresponding points in the other figure. And it is evident we may thus proceed until we arrive at the final extremities of the inscribed n'gons. But, as homologic figures are homographic, and that figures homographic with any figure are homographic with each other, it is evident the first extremities of the inscribed n'gons belong to a figure which is homographic with a figure to which the final extremities of these n'gons belong. Moreover, it is evident that the first and last extremities of each n'gon are corresponding points in the homographic figures, and that the tangent planes at the extremities of each n'gon are corresponding planes.

Hence we may announce the following theorem :—

THEOREM 1.

If in a surface of the second degree there be inscribed n'*gons such that the* n *successive sides of each pass in order through a series of* n *fixed points; then will the first extremities of these* n'*gons belong to a figure which is homographic with a figure to which their final extremities belong; moreover, the extremities of each* n'*gon will be corresponding points in the homographic figures, and the tangent planes at these extremities will be corresponding planes.*

2. The two following theorems are immediate consequences from theorem 1 :—

THEOREM 2.

If in a surface of the second degree n'gons be inscribed whose first extremities are all in one plane, and whose sides pass in order through n fixed points, then will their last extremities be all in one plane.

THEOREM 3.

If in a surface of the second degree there can be inscribed 3 closed n'gons whose sides pass in order through n fixed points, then will any point in the trace of the plane containing their first extremities be an answerable position for the first extremity of another such inscribable closed n'gon.

3. If in addition to having 3 inscribed closed n'gons, whose sides pass in order through the n fixed points, we were to have another such inscribed closed n'gon whose first extremity x_1 is not in the trace of the plane containing the first extremities of the other three, then obviously any point y_1 in the surface is an answerable position for the first extremity of a closed n'gon whose sides pass in order through the n points.—For through x_1 and y_1 we can conceive a plane whose trace cuts the trace of the plane containing the first extremities of the other three closed n'gons; and therefore, from theorem 3, it follows that y_1 is an answerable position for the first extremity of an inscribable closed n'gon. Hence we have—

THEOREM 4.

If in a surface of the second degree there can be inscribed 4 closed n'gons whose sides pass in order through n fixed points, and that the first extremities of these closed n'gons are not all in one plane, then will any point in the surface be an answerable position for the first extremity of another such inscribable closed n'gon.

4. Again (as a consequence from theorem 1) we have the following :—

THEOREM 5.

If in a surface of the second degree there be inscribed four n'gons $a_1\ a_2 \ldots a_{n+1}$, $b_1\ b_2 \ldots b_{n+1}$, $c_1\ c_2 \ldots c_{n+1}$, $d_1\ d_2 \ldots d_{n+1}$, *whose sides pass in order through* n *fixed points; then, representing tangent planes by capital letters of like names and subscripts with the small letters indicating the points of contact, we have*

$$\frac{c_1, A_1}{c_1, B_1} : \frac{c_{n+1}, A_{n+1}}{c_{n+1}, B_{n+1}} = \frac{d_1, A_1}{d_1, B_1} : \frac{d_{n+1}, A_{n+1}}{d_{n+1}, B_{n+1}}$$

$$\frac{c_1, A_1}{c_1, D_1} : \frac{c_{n+1}, A_{n+1}}{c_{n+1}, D_{n+1}} = \frac{b_1, A_1}{b_1, D_1} : \frac{b_{n+1}, A_{n+1}}{b_{n+1}, D_{n+1}}$$

5. If in the equations of the last theorem we suppose a_{n+1}, b_{n+1} and d_{n+1}, to be respectively coincident with a_1, b_1, d_1; and that c_1 and c_{n+1} are distinct. Then, evidently

$$\frac{c_1, A_1}{c_1, B_1} = \frac{c_{n+1}, A_1}{c_{n+1}, A_1}, \text{ and } \frac{c_1, A_1}{c_1, D_1} = \frac{c_{n+1}, A_1}{c_{n+1}, D_1}.$$

From these equations we at once perceive that the closing chord $c_1\ c_{n+1}$ passes through the common point of intersection of the planes A_1, B_1, D_1.

Hence, from this and theorem 4, we infer the following:—

THEOREM 6.

If in a surface of the second degree there can be inscribed 3 *closed* n'*gons, whose sides pass in order through* n *fixed points; then according as any other inscribed* n'*gon having its sides passing in order through the points and not having its first extremity in plane with those of the others, is an open* n'*gon or a closed* n'*gon, so accordingly will the entire locus of all the answerable positions for first extremities of inscribable closed* n'*gons (whose sides pass in* order through the n points) be the trace of the plane containing the first extremities of the 3 closed n'gons or the entire surface—in other words—so accordingly will the problem of the inscription of the closed n'gons be partially porismatic or fully porismatic.

THEOREM 7.

If the problem of the inscription of closed n'gons (whose sides pass in order through n fixed points) in a surface of the second degree be partially porismatic, then will the closing chords of all the inscribable open n'gons (whose sides pass in order through the n points) pass through the pole of the plane whose trace is the locus of the first extremities of the inscribable closed n'gons.

THEOREM 8.

If there be a surface of the second degree and n fixed points, such as to render partially porismatic the problem of the inscription of the closed n'gons whose sides pass in order through the points; then will any point whatever in the surface be an answerable position for the first extremity of an inscribable closed 2 n'gon whose first n sides and whose second n sides pass in order through the n fixed points.

6. Suppose we have a surface of the second degree and n fixed points, such that in addition to two inscribed closed n'gons whose sides pass in order through the points, we have an inscribed closed 2 n'gon whose two successive series of n sides pass in order through the n points. And let a_1 and b_1 be the first extremities of the closed n'gons, and c_1 the first extremity of the closed 2 n'gon.

Then d_1 and d_{n+1} being the extremities of any inscribed open n'gon whose sides pass in order through the n points, we have (from equations of theroem 5)

$$\frac{c_1, A_1}{c_1, B_1} : \frac{c_{n+1}, A_1}{c_{n+1}, B_1} = \frac{d_1, A_1}{d_1, B_1} : \frac{d_{n+1}, A_1}{d_{n+1}, B_1}$$

And as we can interchange the extremities $c_1, c_{n...1}$, it is evident that

$$\frac{c_1, A_1}{c_1, B_1} = \frac{c_{n+1}, A_1}{c_{n+1}, B_1} \text{, and that } \frac{d_1, A_1}{d_1, B_1} = \frac{d_{n+1}, A_1}{d_{n+1}, B_1}. \text{ And from}$$

this we learn that the closing chords of all the inscribable open n'gons must pass through the straight line zz of intersection of the planes A_1 and B_1.

Now, if we conceive a plane through zz and the line c_1 c_{n+1}, it follows that all the inscribable open n'gons (whose sides pass in order through the points) whose first extremities are in the trace of this plane, will have their final extremities in the same trace. And as the extremities of the n'gons form homographic divisions in the trace, and that two distinct corresponding points c_1 and c_{n+1} are interchangeable in these divisions, therefore it follows that all the closing chords of these inscribable open n'gons will pass through one point v (in the line zz). Moreover, it is evident that the points of contact of the tangents from v to the trace are answerable positions for first extremities of inscribable closed n'gons whose sides pass in order through the n fixed points. Hence, from this and theorem 6, we infer

THEOREM 9.

If there be a surface of the second degree and n *fixed points, such that one closed* 2 n'*gon can be inscribed whose two successive series of* n *sides pass in order through the points and are not coincident; then will any point in the surface be an answerable position for the first extremity of an inscribable closed* 2 n'*gon whose sides pass in like manner through the points; and the problem of the inscription of the closed* n'*gons whose sides pass in order through the* n *fixed points is partially porismatic.*

THEOREM 10.

If there be a surface of the second degree and a series of n *fixed points such that the problem of the inscription of the closed* n'*gons whose sides pass in order through the* n *points is fully porismatic; then any one of the points of the series being omitted will render partially porismatic the problem of the inscription of the closed* (n—1)'*gons whose sides pass in the same order through the* n—1 *remaining points. And according as the omitted point is inside or outside the surface so will the closed* (n—1)'*gons be imaginary or real.* ☞ The trace of the polar plane of the omitted point being the locus of an extremity of a side of the (n—1)'gons.

THEOREM 11.

If there be a surface of the second degree and n *fixed points, such as render partially porismatic the problem of the inscription of the closed* n*'gons whose sides pass in order through the* n *points; then by adopting the pole of the plane whose trace is the locus of the first extremities of the inscribable closed* n*'gons, as the* n $+ 1^{th}$ *point of the series, we render fully porismatic the problem of the inscription of the closed* (n $+$ 1)*'gons whose sides pass in order through the series of* n $+$ 1 *points.*

THEOREM 12.

If there be a surface of the second degree and a series of n *fixed points, such that the problem of the inscription of the closed* n*'gons whose sides pass in order through the* n *points is non-porismatic; then there can be two and not more than two answerable positions (real or imaginary as may be) for the first extremities of the closed* n*'gons.*

7. Let us have a surface of the second degree and n points o_1, o_2, ... o_n, such as to render non-porismatic the inscription of the closed n'gons whose sides pass in order through these points. And let $x\,x$ be the straight line containing the first extremities of these closed n'gons.

If o_{n+1} be any point in the line $x\,x$, then evidently the points in which xx pierces the surface are answerable positions for first extremities of inscribable closed 2 ($n + 1$)'gons each of which has its two successive series of n sides passing in order through the $n + 1$ points o_1, o_2, ... o_n, o_{n+1}. Therefore (theorem 9) the problem of the inscription of the closed ($n + 1$) 'gons whose sides pass in order through the $n + 1$ points is partially porismatic. Moreover, we know that the line xx is a closing chord of an inscribable ($n + 1$)'gon, and must, therefore, pass through the pole of the plane whose trace is the locus of first extremities of the inscribable closed ($n + 1$)'gons. Hence we have the following theorems :—

THEOREM 13.

If there be a surface of the second degree and n points such as to render non-porismatic the problem of the inscription of the closed n'gons whose sides pass in order through the points; then by assuming any point in the straight line containing the first extremities of the two inscribable closed n'gons as the $n+1^{th}$ point of the series, we will render partially porismatic the problem of the inscription of the closed $(n+1)$'gons whose sides pass in order through the $n+1$ points.

THEOREM 14 *(porism)*.

If there be a surface of the second degree and n fixed points, such as to render non-porismatic the problem of the inscription of the closed n'gons whose sides pass in order through the points; then, assuming any point in the straight line xx containing the first extremities of the two inscribable closed n'gons, as the $n+1^{th}$ point of the series, we can find a position for the $n+2^{th}$ point of the series in the same straight line which will render fully porismatic the problem of the inscription of the closed $(n+2)$'gons whose sides pass in order through the $n+2$ points of the series.

8. And from theorem 14 we at once infer the following theorems:—

THEOREM 15.

If an open n'gon be inscribed in a surface of the second degree so that its n sides pass in order through n fixed points, and that the problem of the inscription of the closed n'gons whose sides pass in like manner through the points is non-porismatic; then will the closing chord of the open n'gon be in plane with the straight line xx which contains the first extremities of the two inscribable closed n'gons whose sides pass in order through the n fixed points.

THEOREM 16.

If in a surface of the second degree there be inscribed an open 2 n'gon whose two successive series of n sides pass in order through n fixed points; then will the plane containing its extremities and the first point of its $n-1^{th}$ side pass through the two answerable positions for the first extremities of the inscribable closed n'gons whose sides pass in order through the n points of the series.

9. And from theorems 3 and 15 we infer—

THEOREM 17.

If there be a surface of the second degree and n *fixed points, and any odd number* k; *and if in the surface there can be inscribed one closed* k.n'gon *whose* k *series of successive* n *sides pass in order through the* n *fixed points so that no two of the series are co-incident; then will the first points of the* 1st, $n + 1^{th}$, $2n + 1^{th}$, ... $(k-1)n + 1^{th}$, *sides lie all in the trace of one plane; and any point in this trace will be an answerable position for the first extremity of an inscribable closed* k.n'gon *whose sides pass in order through the* n *fixed points.*

10. The following theorem (of which theorem 9 may be regarded as the particular case in which $k = 2$) is evident.

THEOREM 18.

If there be a surface of the second degree and n *fixed points, and any even number* k; *and if in the surface there can be inscribed a closed* k.n'gon *whose* k *series of successive sides pass in order through the* n *fixed points so that no two of the series of sides are co-incident; then will the first points of the* 1st, $n + 1^{th}$, $2n + 1^{th}$ .... $(k-1)n + 1^{th}$ *sides lie all in the trace of one plane; and any point in the surface will be an answerable position for the first extremity of another inscribable closed* k.n'gon *whose sides pass in like manner through the* n *fixed points; and the problem of the inscription of the closed* $\frac{1}{2}$.k.n'gons *whose* $\frac{1}{2}$.k *series of sides pass in order through the* n *fixed points is partially porismatic.*

11. Now let us have a surface S of the second degree and the first $n-2$ points $o_1, o_2, \ldots o_{n-2}$ of a series of n points, such as to render porismatic the problem of the inscription of the closed $(n-2)$'gons whose sides pass in order through the $n-2$ given points.

First, it may be observed that when the inscription of the closed $(n-2)$'gons is fully porismatic, *then* no distinct fixed positions can be found for the $n-1^{th}$ and n^{th} points which will render porismatic the inscription of the closed n'gons whose sides pass in order through the n points of the series. But it is evident that answerable *coincident* positions have unlimited space as locus.

When the problem of the inscription of the closed $(n-2)$'gons is partially porismatic, we know that the closing chords of inscribed $(n-2)$'gons will pass through the point x which is the pole of the plane X whose trace is the locus of the first extremities of the inscribable closed $(n-2)$'gons. And it is evident that x and X may be real even though the closed $(n-2)$'gons be imaginary.

Now if $a_1 \, a_2 \, \ldots \, a_{n-1}$ be one of the inscribed $(n-2)$'gons, it is evident that in order to render porismatic the inscription of the closed n'gons we must have o_{n-1} and o_n in such positions that by drawing $a_{n-1} \, o_{n-1}$ to cut the surface in a_n, then will $a_n \, o_n$ cut the surface in a_1. This can be effected by taking o_{n-1} anywhere in the plane X, and by then taking o_n anywhere in the polar line of the point o_{n-1} in respect to the trace of X.

Hence we have the following theorem :—

THEOREM 19 *(porism)*.

Given a surface of the second degree and the first n $-$ 2 *points of a series of* n *points such as to render partially porismatic the problem of the inscription of the closed* (n $-$ 2)*'gons whose sides pass in order through the* n $-$ 2 *given points: a plane* X *can be found such that by taking the* n $-$ 1th *point of the series anywhere therein we can find a corresponding straight line in the same plane, any point in which line being made a position for the* nth *point of the series will render partially porismatic the problem of the inscription of the closed* n*'gons whose sides pass in order through the* n *points of the series.*

12. In the investigation of the preceding theorem I have used a theorem arrived at in the researches concerning n'gons inscribed in curves of the second degree, viz. :—" If there be any line of the second degree and 3 points in its plane such that each one has its polar line passing through the other two, then will any point in the curve be an answerable position for the first extremity

of an inscribable closed 3'gon whose sides pass in *any* order through the three points o_1, o_2, o_3."

Now, if we assume the pole of the plane $o_1\ o_2\ o_3$ as a fourth point, then evidently (see theorem 7) we have

THEOREM 20.

If there be a surface of the second degree and four points, such that each one is the pole of the plane containing the other three, then will any point in the surface be an answerable position for the first extremity of an inscribable closed 4'gon whose sides pass in order through the four points taken in any order. ☞ The centre of the surface and the three points at infinity indicated by the productions of any system of conjugate diameters, are evidently four points such that each one is the pole of the plane containing the other three.

13. And from theorems 20 and 10 we have

THEOREM 21.

If there be a surface of the second degree and three points such that the polar plane of each one contains the other two points, then will the problem of the inscription of the closed 3'gons, the sides of which pass in any order through these points, be partially porismatic. ☞ These closed 3'gons will be imaginary when the trace of the plane through the three points is imaginary.

THEOREM 22.

If there be a surface of the second degree and three points such that the polar plane of each one contains the other two points, then any point in the surface is an answerable position for the first extremity of an inscribable closed 6'gon whose first three sides and whose second three sides pass through the three points taken in any order.

14. Now if we have a surface of the second degree and any odd number n of points in one straight line, it is evident that the points in which the straight line pierces the surface are answerable

positions for first extremities of inscribable closed 2 n'gons whose first n sides and whose second n sides pass in order through the n points.

Hence (see theorem 9) we infer the following:—

THEOREM 23.

If there be a surface of the second degree and a series n *of points (*n *being an odd number) in one straight line, then will the problem of the inscription of the closed* n'*gons whose sides pass in order through the* n *points be partially porismatic; and any point in the surface will be an answerable position for the first extremity of an inscribable closed* 2 n'*gon whose first* n *sides and whose second* n *sides pass in order through the* n *fixed points.* ☞ It is evident that when $n=1$, the locus of the extremities of the inscribable 1'gons will be the trace of the polar plane of the point through which the sides all pass.

15. The following theorem (of which Pascal's is but a particular case) is an evident consequence.

THEOREM 24.

If n *be an odd number and that in a surface of the second degree there be inscribed a closed* 2 n'*gon such that all its pairs of opposite sides, with the exception of one pair, cut each other in* n−1 *points lying in one straight line, then will this remaining pair of opposite sides cut each other in a point in the same straight line.*

16. If $n-2$ be an even number, and that the inscription of the closed $(n-2)$'gons whose sides pass in order through $n-2$ fixed points in one straight line xx is non-porismatic; then (see theorem 14) by assming any position in xx as a $n-1^{th}$ point, we can find a corresponding position for a nth point in the same line so as to render fully porismatic the problem of the inscription of the closed n'gons whose sides pass in order through the n points of the series.

This may be formally enunciated, thus :—

THEOREM 25.

If n be any even number, and that we have a surface of the second degree and n—1 points in one straight line; then a position for a nth point can be found in the same straight line which will render fully porismatic the problem of the inscription of the closed n'gons whose sides pass in order through the n points of the series

17. If there be n fixed points in the plane of a conic, we know that the problem of the inscription of closed n'gons in the conic is either non-porismatic or fully porismatic; and in the non-porismatic state of the data we can always find a real line containing the two answerable positions for the first extremities of the closed n'gons.

Hence we easily arrive at the following theorem.

THEOREM 26.

If a gauche closed n'gon inscribed in a surface of the second degree be cut by a plane, and that we conceive the points of its intersection with the plane to become fixed, then the problem of the inscription of the closed n'gons whose sides pass in order through these n fixed points is partially porismatic or fully porismatic, just according as the problem of the inscription of the closed n'gons in the trace of the plane containing the points is non-porismatic or porismatic.

18. Let the surface S and the n points $o_1, o_2, \ldots o_n$ be so related that the problem of the inscription of the closed n'gons whose sides pass in order through the n points is non-porismatic.

Let p_1 and q_1 be the first extremities of inscribable closed n'gons; and let xx be the straight line containing these points.

Through xx conceive any plane cutting the surface S. Now if in the trace of this plane we assume points as first extremities of inscribable open n'gons whose sides pass through the n fixed points, then will the final extremities of these n'gons be in the same trace. And, as the extremities of each of these n'gons are corresponding points in homographic divisions in a conic such that we cannot interchange them in the divisions, we know that the closing chords of these n'gons are tangents of like or unlike rotatives to a conic k having double contact with the trace in the points where xx pierces it (reckoning from the final extremities of the n'gons) just according as the final extremities of the n'gons are on the same side or on opposite sides of the straight line xx. Similar remarks evidently apply in respect to the traces of all other planes drawn through the line xx. And we know that the conics to which the closing chords are tangents belong to a surface having double contact with S in the points where xx pierces it.

Again by assuming o_{n+1} in any particular position in xx, it is evident that the tangent lines from this point to the various conic sections, made in the surface S by planes through xx, are all closing chords to n'gons inscribable in the surface so that the sides of each pass in order through the n fixed points $o_1, o_2, \ldots o_n$. And we perceive that we can have any number of closed $(n + 1)$ 'gons inscribed in S so that the sides of each pass in order through the $n + 1$ points $o_1, o_2, \ldots o_n, o_{n+1}$; we perceive also that the problem of the inscription of these closed $(n + 1)$'gons is partially porismatic. Hence we learn that the point o_{n+1} is the vertex of a cone of the second degree enveloping the surface which has double contact with S in the points where xx pierces it. This is also evidently true for all other points in xx. Therefore we infer that the envelope of the closing chords of all the inscribable n'gons, whose sides pass in order through the n points, is a surface T of the second degree having double contact with S in the points in which the line xx pierces it.

Moreover, it is evident that when we have the rotative of any one of the closing chords (reckoning from the final extremity of the n'gon) in respect to a section of T made by a plane through xx, we can determine on the rotatives of all others by conceiving the plane to revolve round xx as axis and the chord to be deformed so as to move tangentially to the various conic sections of T but not to have either of its extremities pass through the points in which xx pierces the surface. Hence we may announce—

THEOREM 27.

If there be a surface S *of the second degree and a series of* n *fixed points such as to render non-porismatic the problem of the inscription of the closed* n'*gons whose sides pass in order through the* n *points of the series; then will the closing chords of the inscribed open* n'*gons whose sides pass in order through the fixed points be tangents to a surface of the second degree having double contact with the surface* S *in the two points which are answerable positions for first extremities of the inscribable closed* n'*gons whose sides pass in order through the* n *fixed points.*

THEOREM 28.

If two surfaces of the second degree have double contact; and that from points in one of the surfaces we draw chords tangent to the other surface in plane with the line xx *of contact of the surfaces, and of such rotatives (in respect to the plane sections in this other surface made by the planes through* xx *containing these tangents) as are indicated by any one of the chords we conceive to revolve with the plane which contains it round the line* xx *as axis, in such a manner as to be always tangent to the surface but not to have either of its extremities pass through the points where* xx *pierces the surface; then will the final points of the chords belong to a figure which is homographic with a figure to which the first extremities of these chords belong.*

THEOREM 29.

If two surfaces of the second degree have double contact, and that any point in the line of contact is the vertex of a cone enveloping one of the surfaces, then will the traces of this cone on the other surface be plane curves. And the poles of the planes containing these traces are situated in the line of contact of the surfaces.

THEOREM 30.

If there be a surface S *of the second degree, and* n *entities, each entity of which is either a fixed point or a conicoid having double contact with* S ; *and if there be* n'*gons inscribed in the surface* S *so that each side of every* n'*gon will meet with the entity of the series which is of like rank in the series which such side is in the* n'*gon, and in such a manner as to pass through the entity if it be a point or, if the entity be a conicoid, to be tangent of certain prescribable rotative to the trace made on this conicoid by a plane containing the first point of such side and the line of contact of the conicoid with* S : *then will the extremities of each* n'*gon be corresponding points of homographic figures. And when we cannot interchange the extremities of any of the* n'*gons so as to have them still corresponding in the homographic figures, then will the closing chords of the* n'*gons be tangents of determinable rotatives to the traces made on a certain conicoid having double contact with* S *by planes containing the final extremities of the* n'*gons and the line of contact of such conicoid with* S. *But when we can interchange the distinct extremities of the* n'*gons so that they still remain corresponding points of the homographic figures, then will the closing chords of the* n'*gons all pass through one point.*

19. It is evident we can extend many of the preceding theorems by a substitution of such entities as those implicated in the theorem just enunciated for some of the entities which we considered as all composed of points.

It is also obvious that all these theorems have "duals," which are easy of formation by well known methods—or which can be arrived at by steps correlative to those we have employed in the preceding investigations.—As it would be superfluous to repeat the "duals" of all the theorems, I will content myself by giving that of theorem 20 in order to exhibit a sort of nomenclature which may be found convenient in enunciating the duals of the others.

THEOREM 31.

If there be a surface of the second degree and four fixed planes such that each plane is the polar of the point common to the other three planes; then any straight line in any of the planes is an answerable position for an angular joint of a closed planes n'*gon whose* n *planes are tangential to the surface, and whose four successive angular joints lie in the four fixed planes taken in any order whatever.*

20. I will now proceed to indicate methods by which we can graphically find the positions for the first extremities of the closed n'gons inscribable in a surface of the second degree so that the sides of each will pass in order through n given points. And (in doing so) I would have the reader remember that when I speak of a closed n'gon, or of any n'gon, I refer to a n'gon inscribed in the surface whose sides pass in order through the n point of the series; and when I speak of a 2 n'gon, I refer to one inscribed in the surface whose first n sides and whose second n sides pass in order through the n points of the series, and are not coincident in pairs.

PROBLEM.

Given a surface S of the second degree, and a series of n points o_1, o_2, ... o_n; to inscribe in the surface the closed n'gons the sides of each of which will pass in order through the n fixed points.

Analysis of a first method of Solution.

Suppose a_1 a_2 .... a_n a_1 to be a closed n'gon such as required, —the sides a_1 a_2, a_2 a_3, ... a_n a_1 passing through the respective points o_1, o_2, ... o_n.

Now let us see whether we could reduce the inscription of this closed n'gon to that of another having a less number of sides.

If o_1, o_2, o_3 are in one straight line we know that in this line we can determine a point g such that a_4 a_1 g will be a straight line. And therefore evidently we can reduce the solution of the problem to the inscription of the closed $(n-2)$'gon a_1 a_4 a_5 .... a_n a_1 whose sides pass in order through the $n-2$ known points g, o_4, o_5, ... o_n.

If o_1, o_2, o_3 be such that each one of them has its polar plane passing through the other two, we know that the point h which is the pole of the plane o_1 o_2 o_3 is such that a_1 a_4 h is one straight line. And therefore evidently we can reduce the solution of the problem to the inscription of a closed $(n-2)$'gon whose sides pass in order through the $n-2$ known points h, o_4, o_5, ... o_n.

If o_1, o_2, o_3, be neither in one straight line nor such that the polar plane of each one passes through the other two, then we can find the straight line xx such that by assuming q any point therein, we can find a corresponding point r, in the same line, such that $q\,a_1$ and $r\,a_4$ will cut each other in a point p in the surface S. And therefore evidently we can reduce the solution of the problem to the inscription of the closed $(n-1)$'gon $a_1\,p\,a_4\,a_5\,....\,a_n\,a_1$ whose sides pass in order through the $n-1$ known points q, r, o_4, o_5, ... o_n.

So now it is evident we can reduce the solution of the problem of the inscription of the closed n'gons to that of the inscription of closed $(n-2)$'gons or to that of the inscription of closed $(n-1)$'gons. And thus, step by step, we can reduce the problem until we make its solution depend on that of the inscription of closed 3'gons, or 2'gons whose sides are required to pass through known points.

When we reduce the problem to the inscription of closed 3'gons whose sides are required to pass through 3 known points, and that these points are in one straight line or that each one of them has its polar plane containing the other two; then will the problem of the inscription of the closed n'gons be partially porismatic; and the locus of the first extremities of the closed n'gons is the trace of the polar plane of the point through which the closing chords of the inscribable open n'gons all pass.

When we reduce the problem to the inscription of closed 2'gons whose sides are required to pass through 2 known points, and that these points are co-incident, then we know that the problem of the inscription of the closed n'gons is fully porismatic.

☞ I need scarcely state that the method of solution just indicated is complete, though it is obvious there are many peculiar states of the data from which we can at once pronounce on the nature of the solution without going through all the indicated operations or processes.

Analysis of a second method of solution.

From theorems 9 and 16 we learn that according as we can inscribe one open 2 n'gon or one closed 2 n'gon, so will the problem of the inscription of the closed n'gons be non-porismatic or partially porismatic.

When the data is in the non-porismatic state, it is evident that if we inscribe an open 2 n'gon, and draw the plane which contains its extremities and the first point of its $n + 1^{\text{th}}$ side; and that we then inscribe another open 2 n'gon whose first extremity is not in this plane; then will the plane through the extremities and first point of the $n + 1^{\text{th}}$ side of this last 2 n'gon cut the other plane in a straight line xx which pierces the surface in the points (real or imaginary as may be) which are the answerable positions for the first extremities of the inscribable closed n'gons.

When we can inscribe a closed 2 n'gon; it is evident that we can inscribe open n'gons, and that the closing chords of these will intersect in a point the trace of whose polar plane is the locus of the answerable positions for the first extremities of the closed n'gons.

When the problem is fully porismatic, the fact will be intimated to us by our being enabled to inscribe 4 closed n'gons whose first extremities are not all in one plane.

☞ This method of solution is also complete, and is applicable to the following more general problem :—" *Given a surface* S *of the second degree, and* n *entities in prescribed order, each entity being either a given point, or a conicoid having double contact with* S; *to inscribe in the surface* S *closed* n'*gons such that each side of each* n'*gon will meet with the entity of the series which is of like rank in the series with such side in the* n'*gon, and in such a manner as to pass through the entity if it be a point, or to be tangent of certain prescribable rotative to the trace made on the conicoid by a plane containing the first point of such side and the line of contact of the conicoid with* S *if it be a conicoid."*

Third Method of Solution.

The following method of finding the first extremities of the inscribable closed n'gons is applicable to the more general problem when the data is in the non-porismatic state :—

Inscribe three n'gons such that the first extremity of the second n'gon coincides with the final extremity of the first n'gon, and that the first extremity of the third n'gon coincides with the final extremity of the second n'gon ; draw the plane which contains the extremities of these n'gons, and find its trace on the given surface ; find i the point of intersection of the straight line through the first extremity of the first n'gon and the final extremity of the second n'gon with the tangent line to the trace at the junction of these n'gons; find k the point of intersection of the straight line through the first extremity of the second n'gon and final extremity of the third n'gon with the tangent line to the trace at the junction of these n'gons : then will the points in which the straight line ik pierces the surface be the answerable positions for the first extremities of the closed n'gons. The proof is obvious from theorem 8, and the properties of the homographic figures in which the extremities of the n'gons are corresponding points.

21. Various simple solutions can be given to the problem when all the entities are points and that the surface is either spherical, cylindrical or conical. However their exhibition requires much more room than can be accorded in this paper, so that I will finish by showing how theorem 5 can be arrived at when the surface is spherical.

22. When the surface is spherical and the entities $o_1, o_2, \ldots o_n$ all points, we can easily derive theorem 5 independently of homologic or homographic considerations.

Thus.—Let $d_1\ d_2 \ldots d_{n+1}$ be any variable inscribed n'gon ; and let $a_1\ a_2 \ldots a_{n+1},\ b_1\ b_2 \ldots b_{n+1},\ c_1\ c_2 \ldots c_{n+1}$, be three n'gons (inscribed at random).

From similar triangles we immediately deduce the following relations :—

$$\frac{(d_1 a_1)^2}{(d_1 b_1)^2} : \frac{(d_2 a_2)^2}{(d_2 b_2)^2} = \frac{(c_1 a_1)^2}{(c_1 b_1)^2} : \frac{(c_2 a_2)^2}{(c_2 b_2)^2}$$

$$\frac{(d_2 a_2)^2}{(d_2 b_2)^2} : \frac{(d_3 a_3)^2}{(d_3 b_3)^2} = \frac{(c_2 a_2)^2}{(c_2 b_2)^2} : \frac{(c_3 a_3)^2}{(c_3 b_3)^2}$$

... ...
... ...

$$\frac{(d_n a_n)^2}{(d_n b_n)^2} : \frac{(d_{n+1} a_{n+1})^2}{(d_{n+1} b_{n+1})^2} = \frac{(c_n a_n)^2}{(c_n b_n)^2} : \frac{(c_{n+1} a_{n+1})^2}{(c_{n+1} b_{n+1})^2}$$

From these we at once obtain the relation—

$$\frac{(d_1 a_1)^2}{(d_1 b_1)^2} : \frac{(d_{n+1} a_{n+1})^2}{(d_{n+1} b_{n+1})^2} = \frac{(c_1 a_1)^2}{(c_1 b_1)^2} : \frac{(c_{n+1} a_{n+1})^2}{(c_{n+1} b_{n+1})^2}$$

And now since the square of a chord of a sphere is equal to the product of the diameter and the perpendicular let fall from one extremity of the chord on the tangent plane at the other extremity, we perceive (from the last formula) that the following relation (adopting the notation employed in theorem 5) subsists,

viz. : $$\frac{d_1, A_1}{d_1, B_1} : \frac{d_{n+1}, A_{n+1}}{d_{n+1}, B_{n+1}} = \frac{c_1, A_1}{c_1, B_1} : \frac{c_{n+1}, A_{n+1}}{c_{n+1}, B_{n+1}}$$

NOTE.

Sir William Hamilton, the Astronomer Royal of Ireland, has given much attention to the problem of this paper. He published the results of his researches in the Philosophical Magazine for July 1849, and afterwards drew the attention of the Mathematical Section of the British Association to the subject. He succeeded in solving only the particular case in which the surface is an *ellipsoid* and the closed *n'*gon *even sided*.

It seems that his "*Quaternion*" and other symbolical methods led him to infer that independent of the two positions for the first angular points of the closed *n'*gons, which may be real or imaginary according to peculiar states of the data, there are also two necessarily imaginary positions. But it is clearly evident from this paper that such is not the case; and that his symbolical analysis labours under the defect of grasping some extraneous kindred problem. However, Sir William's method led him to discover theorem 27 as respects the particular state of the data considered: but he does not seem to have observed that the closing chords are all *in plane* with the line of contact of the surfaces.

The solutions which I give to the general problem are extremely simple; and the numerous new and beautiful theorems unfolded bear testimony to the power of the system of "Géométrie Supérieure" of the modern French School.

On the desirability of a systematic search for, and observation of variable stars in the Southern Hemisphere, by MR. JOHN TEBBUTT, JUNR.

[Read August 13th, 1862.]

THE department of Astronomy relating to variable stars was very little followed up before the middle of the present century. The most complete catalogue that I have yet seen of such objects is that contained in Mr. George F. Chambers' admirable handbook of Astronomy, published at the close of last year. It comprises 99 stars. Of 22 the dates of discovery are not given, 18 were discovered previous to 1800, and the remaining 59 were discovered during the present century. If we divide the elapsed portion of the present century into periods of ten years, we shall find the following table for the number of variable stars discovered in each period:—

Periods.	Number discovered.
1811—1800	2
1821—1811	0
1831—1821	4
1841—1831	4
1851—1841	18
1861—1851	31
Total	59

It will be observed from the above statement, that within the last twenty, and especially within the last ten years, the zeal of Astronomers in this department of research has been rapidly increasing. Observations of variable stars furnish employment for some of the most distinguished Astronomers of Europe, and as a consequence, we frequently find communications with reference to such objects in the pages of that valuable scientific journal, the *Astronomische Nachrichten*. Now, considering the additions to our knowledge in this department of Astronomy which have been made during the past twenty years, and are constantly being made by Northern observers; and, also, taking into account the fact that so few stars of high south declination are to be found in the catalogue, the question might well be asked, how is it that so little has been done for the cause in this hemisphere? Surely we are not to suppose that our Southern heavens do not furnish as fertile a field for such discoveries as the Northern Hemisphere does. This scarcity of results does not proceed from any peculiar barrenness of the Southern heavens, but rather from the great want of Southern observers. On an examination of the above mentioned catalogue, it will be seen that out of the 99 stars that it contains, 25 only are situated in the Southern Hemisphere, and of these only two are south of the 23rd parallel of declination, namely : Eta (η) Argus, and Kappa (κ) Coronæ Australis. I may, however, remark that the star B. A. C. 5656, not contained in that catalogue, is variable, on the authority of the British Association Catalogue. Of Eta (η) Argus I shall speak presently, suffice it just now to say that it is one of the most, if not the most remarkable, in the whole heavens. It cannot be expected that this department of the science can receive many accessions at the hands of professional Astronomers in this Hemisphere, they being too much occupied with the advancement of *standard astronomy* to devote much time to the search for variable stars. It is, however, a department in which a great deal might be done by amateurs. Intelligent persons, even if unprovided with instrumental means, might, by means of good eyes, work with considerable advantage, so far as the observation of stars from the first to the fifth magnitude is concerned. Observation of fainter stars will, of course, require telescopic aid, and it sometimes happens that a star, which at its maximum is a brilliant object to the naked eye, dwindles to a telescopic object as it advances towards its minimum. But telescopes of three or four inches aperture would be of great assistance, and these are within the means of many amateurs. I shall now treat of my subject under three different heads, namely :—

I. The observation of particular stars known to be variable.
II. The examination of stars suspected to be variable.
III. A general survey and comparison of all the stars of the Southern Hemisphere.

And first, the observation of Stars known to be variable. This course of observation should be pursued in order to determine with increased accuracy the law or progress of increase and decrease of their lustre, together with the exact epochs of their maxima and minima. Mr. Pogson, the present director of the Madras Observatory, who has hitherto taken much interest in this department of Astronomy, forwards periodically to the *Astronomische Nachrichten* ephemerides of the observed variable stars to assist observers in their researches. We must not infer from the fact of a star being observed to go through its variations in a certain period that it will continue to do so. Some of the stars that were originally thought to undergo fluctuations of brightness in regular periods have been found from continuous observation to go through those variations in irregular intervals of time. Thus I may instance the case of the distinguished star Algol in the constellation Perseus. From careful continuous observation of this star by Argelander, Heis, and Schmidt, its period is found to be shorter now than when it was first discovered.

The period is found to diminish, not progressively, but with accelerated rapidity. It is impossible to foresee what the final result of this gradual diminution will be. The star may eventually become of *constant* lustre, or its period, after having arrived at a certain state, may again lengthen with accelerated rapidity. The law and cycles of its variations have, of course, to be determined from a long course of future observation. There are also great apparent irregularities attending the variations of Omicron (*o*) Ceti, another remarkable star in the class we are considering. The maximum of this star for 1862, according to Pogson's Ephemeris, occurred on July 3rd, its magnitude then being the second; it is well known that at its minimum it becomes invisible to the naked eye. It is a star which commends itself to the close attention of Southern observers. Although it is within reach of European observers, still the conditions under which it is seen by most of them are not so favourable as those under which it is seen in this latitude. Few Northern observers have the advantage of clear skies like those of Australia. No observations, perhaps, are more difficult of accurate performance than those attending variable stars, both on account of the many sources of error to which they are liable, and because so much depends on the observer's judgment. The more numerous, then, the observers of a particular star, the greater reliance is to be placed on the general result. Every variable star should, if possible, be observed about the time of its superior meridian transit, as atmospheric causes interfere much with the accuracy of the results. I should be trespassing beyond the limits of a paper were I to enter into a description of all the known variable stars.; it will be sufficient to give a table of those which are advantageously situated for observation in this hemisphere. Such a table will be found appended to this paper. But after having spoken of Algol and Mira Ceti, I must not forget to say a few words with reference to our remarkable Southern star Eta (η) Argus, which more nearly concerns us in this latitude. This star has, for the last thirty-five years, been known to be variable.

The following extract, from Sir John Herschell's "Outlines of Astronomy," shows the changes that have been recorded of it previous to 1844:—

"In the time of Halley (1677) it appeared as a star of the fourth magnitude. Lacaille, in 1751, observed it of the second. In the interval from 1811 to 1815 it was again of the fourth; and again, from 1822 to 1826, of the second. On the 1st of February, 1827, it was noticed by Mr. Burchell to have increased to the first magnitude, and to equal Alpha (a) Crucis. Thence, again, it receded to the second; and so continued until the end of 1837. All at once, in the beginning of 1838, it suddenly increased in lustre so as to surpass all the stars of the first magnitude except Sirius, Canopus, and Alpha (a) Centauri, which last star it nearly equalled. Thence, it again diminished, but this time not below the first magnitude until April, 1843, when it had again increased so as to surpass Canopus, and nearly equal Sirius in splendour."

I have myself watched the variations of this star for some years past with considerable interest. In 1854 it was a very conspicuous object west of the Southern Cross, equilibrating as it were the two bright stars of the Centaur with that constellation. The most casual observer of the heavens might now miss the bright object which was then so conspicuous. The following comparisons, made by me in July of that year, may be interesting in conjunction with the present insignificant appearance of the star:—Of Alpha (a) Centauri, Beta (β) Centauri, Alpha (a) Crucis, and Eta (η) Argus, the first was by far the brightest. Beta (β) Centauri and Eta (η) Argus were about equal in brilliancy. It was difficult to judge of the comparative brightness of these two, but I considered the latter to be somewhat the brighter. Eta (η) Argus was somewhat brighter than Alpha (a) Crucis. The star in question now appears as one of about the $4\frac{1}{2}$ magnitude. A marked diminution of its lustre has taken place since May, 1860. About that time I pointed out to the Rev. W. Scott, the Government Astronomer, the remarkable changes that had taken place in its lustre; and at his recommendation I compared its magnitude with stars within range of the European observatories. I found some difficulty in making this comparison, owing to the stars being situated in different parts of the heavens, my observations being made without the assistance of an astrometer. From very careful comparisons, however, I considered its lustre to be equal to that of Beta (β) Canis Minoris. I, at the same time, compared it with Delta (δ) Crucis and Theta (θ) Argus, to which I found it equal. This latter estimate may be considered as accurate as can be formed by the unaided judgment, the stars of comparison being moreover in the same part of the heavens. At the close of January, of the present year, I compared Eta (η) Argus with Sigma (σ) Orionis, u Carinæ, Theta (θ) Argus, and Beta (β) Canis Minoris. It was not so bright as the last mentioned two; the difference between it and Sigma (σ) Orionis was scarcely perceptible, though the latter may have been somewhat the brighter. It appeared to be exactly equal to u Carinæ, which is a small star distant about a degree and a half from it in a north-easterly direction. From observations during last month, I find that its magnitude is perceptibly less than that of u Carinæ, which, being very close to it, can easily and accurately be compared with it. I have not contented myself with a comparison between it and one or two stars near it, but have extended my observations to several others, in order to avoid any errors which might arise from the standard of comparison itself being variable. I am devoting considerable attention to this star, with a view to the determination of its time of minimum, magnitude at minimum, and ratio of decrease and increase. It is very probable that the minimum is not far distant; the time however, cannot be predicted, as the changes of this star have hitherto been very irregular. From what has been said it appears that Eta (η) Argus is one of the most interesting of the class to which it belongs, and deserves continuous and close observation. So far as the contrast between its maximum and minimum magnitudes is concerned it may be regarded as the Algol of the Southern Hemisphere. It appears from the notices of the Royal Astronomical Society for February last that the variations of Eta (η) Argus have been made the subject of papers by Mr. Abbott and Mr. Powell read before the Society. It is a remarkable fact that the variable character of this star has so far escaped the knowledge of Mr. Hind, the celebrated Astronomer and superintendent of the Nautical Almanac, as to be still denoted in that valuable work as a star of the second magnitude. Several stars of a character far less marked are designated in that work as variable. The other variable stars of high south declination are Kappa (κ) Coronæ Australis, and B.A. C. 5656. The former was discovered to be variable by Halley, in 1676. The latter is variable on the authority of the British Association catalogue: it is one of the stars forming the tail of the Scorpion, and is, like Eta (η) Argus, situated within the Via Lactea. I have no knowledge of its period and limits of variation. It does not appear to have been observed by Lacaille.

II. The next subject to which I would direct your attention is the examination of stars suspected to be variable. In the *Astronomische Nachrichten*, No. 1311, May 29, 1861, is a communication from M. Secchi, an Astronomer at Rome, from which I give the following extract:—

"On m'écrit du Chili que l'étoile Canopus brille actuellement d'un éclat qui plusieurs fois est superieur a Sirius: cela prouverait une variabilité."

It appears, then, that our bright star Canopus has surpassed Sirius even in splendour. M. Secchi does not give his authority, nor is his statement accompanied by any definite observations. I have not hitherto paid much attention to the subject of variable stars, but it occurs to me that I have often been struck with the great brilliancy of Canopus, and I believe I have even given expression to my thoughts on the subject. I have not, however, instituted any comparisons between it and Sirius. It was only very recently that I became aware of M. Secchi's communication, so that I was unable to verify the statement, Sirius being then too near the vapours of the horizon to afford a trustworthy comparison. I trust to be able to make some comparisons in the course of a short time. Canopus may, therefore, at least be regarded as belonging to the class of stars suspected to be variable. There are some circumstances connected with the conspicuous star Beta (β) Argus, which should make it the subject of careful observation. The catalogue of the British Association imitating, I presume, that of Lacaille, represents this star as of the first magnitude; whereas, it is at the present time only an average star of the second magnitude, being about equal to Alpha (a) Trianguli Australis. It was observed by Taylor, Brisbane, Johnson, and Rumker; but I cannot speak as to their estimation of its magnitude, as I have not their catalogues at my command. According to the photometric observations made by Sir John Herschell at the Cape of Good Hope, its magnitude was somewhat greater than that of Alpha (a) Trianguli Australis. I cannot for a moment suppose that Lacaille committed an error in recording Beta (β) Argus in 1751 as of the first magnitude. Considering, then, the circumstances connected with this star, we may regard it also as belonging to the list of stars suspected to be variable. There are other Southern stars which might well claim attention if the magnitudes assigned to them in the catalogues of Lacaille and the British Association are to be relied on.

I shall here advert to an interesting discovery which I made on the evening of the 25th July, and which suggests the conclusion that Eta (η) Argus is not the only variable star in that part of the heavens which it occupies. On comparing the stars of the sixth magnitude in its neighbourhood with a chart constructed from data afforded by the British Association catalogue, I was struck with the fact that B.A.C. 3679, a star of the sixth magnitude, had vanished from its place in the heavens. At all events it was not visible in my telescope of $3\frac{1}{4}$ inches aperture, which is capable of showing stars down to the ninth and tenth magnitudes. Instead also of finding both B.A.C. 3680 and 3683, I could distinguish one only. The distance between these two stars, according to the catalogue just mentioned, is rather more than a minute of arc, a quantity appreciable in a small telescope, yet an instrument furnished with a power of 120, and capable of separating easily Alpha (a) Crucis and Alpha (a) Centuri exhibited the star under the single aspect. Possibly B.A.C. 3680 and 3683 may be members of a double star and now in the same visual line. This is a subject which I should like to have investigated by means of the large equatorial telescope of the Observatory. The only remaining star of the three in question is situated about half a degree north-west of Eta (η) Argus, and is surrounded with several stars of the ninth or tenth magnitude. That all three of the stars formerly existed there can be no doubt, for B.A.C. 3679 and 3683 were observed by Taylor and Brisbane, and B.A.C. 3680 by those two observers and also by Lacaille.

III. I will now direct your attention to the desirability of a complete naked eye examination of all the stars in the Southern Hemisphere to the fifth magnitude. As a general rule the best months for comparison observations in this latitude are May, June, and July; the atmosphere at that period of the year being peculiarly steady and transparent; observations should, however, be made at all available opportunities, as variable stars of short period might thus be earlier detected. The stars at the time of comparison should be at a considerable altitude. In my short experience I have found that a star, as it approached the horizon, sometimes became fainter and at other times brighter. The former effect is probably produced by thin clouds near the horizon, the latter by diffused particles of matter in the atmosphere causing the well-known phenomenon of scintillation, which is very apt to produce an exaggerated impression of its lustre on the judgment of the observer. Care should be exercised that the portions of the heavens occupied by the compared stars be equally clear, as inequality in that respect might seriously affect the results. Comparisons should also be repeated at different hours on the same night, in order to the elimination of any errors which might arise from the source just mentioned. Attention should also be paid to the position of the moon on the nights of observation. It is well known that an observer's estimate of the brilliancy of a star is considerably influenced by the degree of illumination of the sky on which it is projected; consequently he should not compare stars in the neighbourhood of the moon with those more remote from her. An inexperienced observer would hardly credit the amount of error incurred by a neglect of these precautions. The observer must, in fact, in this, as in every other department of Astronomy, pay the most scrupulous attention to all probable sources of error. In instituting a set of naked-eye comparisons, a number of standard stars must be selected for the epoch, in a descending scale of magnitude, from the star of the greatest brilliancy to one that can only be perceived with difficulty by the naked eye; the difference between any two consecutive magnitudes should be so small as not to admit with accuracy of any intermediate order of magnitude. All the other stars should then be arranged under the standard stars to which they are respectively considered to be equal. A mere isolated comparison of two stars, without reference to other stars of the same class, and to the higher and lower orders of magnitude, would hereafter leave the observer in doubt as to which of the two stars was the variable one, and as to their limits of magnitude. In making a series of comparisons recourse might be had to the very simple and inexpensive astrometer devised and employed by Sir John Herschell at the Cape of Good Hope. A description of this instrument may be found in his "Outlines of Astronomy," or in his "Results of Observations made at the Cape of Good Hope," &c. To those amateurs who would undertake a comparison of the stars in the Southern Hemisphere, a study of Sir John Herschell's "Method of Sequences" will be profitable, and the results of the labours of that great authority valuable for reference.

A new and interesting feature in the department of stellar astronomy has, I believe, been brought to light by the observations of Mr. Abbott, of Tasmania, as the following extract from the *Herald*, of June 23rd last will show :—

"At a meeting of the Royal Society of Tasmania, on the 3rd instant, Mr. Abbott read some notes on a drawing of the 'cluster of coloured stars surrounding Kappa (κ) Crucis,'—the object being to show that considerable alteration had taken place both in the position and colouring of its component stars since it was observed by Sir John Herschell at the Cape of Good Hope."

If the component stars of the cluster Kappa (κ) Crucis have really undergone changes in their position and colouring, surely it is a discovery of the highest interest in stellar astronomy. May we regard the cluster in question as a system of coloured suns, revolving round their common centre of gravity, thus adding one more example to the known variety and beauty of the Great Creator's works?

It would be foreign to the object of this paper for me to enter into any speculations regarding the causes of the phenomena of variable stars. Observations of such objects have been too few and disconnected to admit of our forming any satisfactory hypothesis. My object is to draw attention to this department of Astronomy, in order, if possible, to induce some to follow it up more systematically in this hemisphere. I trust my humble efforts may succeed. Searching for variable stars and observing them, may appear a useless labour to the minds of some persons; but we must remember that in the history of Astronomy many researches, which at the outset appeared to be fraught with no great result, eventually contributed much to the advancement of the science. Let us contemplate the grand fact, that within the past seventeen years 68 planets have been discovered between the orbits of Mars and Jupiter. Or again, let us consider what delicate instruments of inquiry comets have become. The celebrated periodical comet of Encke has not only informed us of the extreme probability of a resisting medium in the interplanetary spaces, but has also afforded us the means of determining with unprecedented accuracy, the mass of the planet Mercury. And great results may be predicted for the branch of science we have been treating of. The inquirer, in any department of the science, must not be discouraged in his efforts because he cannot see grand results looming in the future. The experience of Astronomers for ages past he must make his own, and it will teach him to press onward to the invisible goal. Faith, in fact, must be an ingredient in the intellectual constitution of the scientific man, as it is in the spiritual constitution of the religious man. It is sufficient that observers work zealously and intelligently in any field that may be open to them; or, rather, in those fields for which they are respectively peculiarly fitted, and the future will be certain to bring forth some not only interesting, but valuable result. A high authority has said " In all labour there is profit." Let this, then, be the motto of the observer, and if he adhere to it he need not despair of eventual success.

TABLE OF VARIABLE STARS ADVANTAGEOUSLY SITUATED FOR OBSERVATION IN NEW SOUTH WALES.

Stars.	1860. R. A.	1860. Declin.	Period.	Change of Magnitude.		Times of Maxima, according to Pogson's Ephemeris for 1862. Astr. Nach. No 1350.
	h. m. s.	° ′	days.	from	to	
T Piscium	0 24 46	+ 13 46	242 +	9.5	11	April 24. Sept. 14.
S Piscium	1 10 15	+ 8 11	..	9	13	
R Piscium	1 23 25	+ 2 9	343	7	0	
o Cœti	2 12 17	— 3 37	331.3	2	12	July 3.
λ Tauri	3 52 55	+ 12 5	3.95	4	4.5	
R Tauri	4 20 38	+ 9 51	327	8	13.5	May 7.
S Tauri	4 21 32	+ 9 38	375	10		March 11.
R Orionis	4 51 22	+ 7 55	327 ?	9	12.5	June 19.
R Leporis	4 53 14	— 15 2	..	7		
a Orionis	5 47 36	+ 7 23	196 +	1	1.5	Jan. 9. July 24.
R Canis Minoris	7 1 0	+ 10 14	1 yr. +	8	10	April, uncertain.
S Canis Minoris	7 25 7	+ 8 37	340	7.5		July 3.
R Cancri	8 8 57	+ 12 7	380	6	10	Jan. 17.
S Hydræ	8 46 16	+ 3 36	256	8.5	13.5	Jan. 22. Oct. 5.
T Hydræ	8 48 51	— 8 37	292	6.5	10.5	Feb. 22. Dec. 11.
a Hydræ	9 20 42	— 8 3	55	2.5	3	
R Leonis	9 40 2	+ 12 5	324	5	10	Oct. 13. min. 10·0 May 29.
η Argus	10 39 38	— 58 56	irreg.	1	4	
R Virginis	12 31 24	+ 7 46	146	6.5	11	Jan. 1. May 27. Oct. 19.
U Virginis	12 44 0	+ 6 19	..	7.5		July 28.
21 Virginis	12 26 33	— 8 40	..	5.5		
V Virginis	13 20 36	— 2 28	8m. +	7		March, Nov.
R (v) Hydræ	13 22 4	— 22 33	440	4	10	Not until Feb., 1863.
S Virginis	13 25 42	— 6 28	380.11	6	11	May 21, min. 11·0 Nov. 17.
* in Libra	14 44 39	— 11 45	..	8	9.5	
R Libræ	15 45 40	— 15 49	722	10		April, uncertain.
R Scorpii	16 9 19	— 22 35	..	9		April, very uncertain.
S Scorpii	16 9 20	— 22 33	1 yr. +	5	12	April, uncertain.
* in Ophiuchus	16 25 43	— 15 49	..	7	10	
S Ophiuchi	16 26 12	— 16 52	232	9.3	13.5	August 5.
Hind's Nova (1848)	16 51 39	— 12 40	..	4.5	13.5	
R Ophiuchi	16 59 44	— 15 54	301	7.6	13	June 25.
* in Serpens	18 21 59	+ 6 12	..	11	14	
κ Coronæ Australis	18 23 48	— 38 49	years.	3	6	

Table of Variable Stars—*(Continued.)*

Stars.	1860. R. A.	1860. Declin.	Period.	Change of Magnitude,	Times of Maxima, according to Pogson's Ephemeris for 1862. Astr. Nach. No. 1350.
			days		
R Scuti Sobieskii	18 40 1	— 5 50	71.75	5 9	Jan. 8. March 21. May 31. Aug. 11. Oct. 26.
R Aquilæ	18 59 38	+ 8 1	352	6.5	May, uncertain.
R Sagittarii	19 8 28	— 19 33	467	8 12.8	May 19, irregular.
S Sagittarii	19 11 14	— 19 16	..	.. ..	Dec.
η Aquilæ	19 45 9	+ 0 38	7.18	3.6 4.4	
R Capricorni	20 3 28	— 14 41	..	9.5 13.5	Sep. 25.
U Capricorni	20 40 22	— 15 18	420	10.5 13	April, irregular.
T Capricorni	21 14 13	— 15 45	274	9 14	July 26.
S Pegasi	22 15 9	+ 7 19	..	8.5 13.5	
* in Aquarius	22 21 0	— 10 42	..	8 0	
R Pegasi	22 59 37	— 19 46	378	8.5 13.5	April 28.
R Aquarii	23 37 15	— 16 3	354	7 10	June 28.

APPENDIX.

Since the preceding Paper was written I have obtained the following ring-micrometer observations of the star of the sixth magnitude, about half a degree north-west of Eta (η) Argus, which afford satisfactory proof that it is B. A. C. 3680.

Date.	Star of Comp.	B. A. C. 3680—Star of Comp.		Resulting Mean Places.	
		Diff. of R. A.	Diff. of Declin.	R. A. of B. A. C. 3680.	Declin. of B. A. C. 3680.
1862.		m. s.	m. s.	h. m. s.	deg. m. s.
Aug. 4.	B. A. C. 3655.	† 3 50·6	—1 41	10 37 21·7	—58 29 48
		† 3 50·6	—1 43	10 37 21·7	—58 29 50
		† 3 51·6	..	10 37 22·7	..
		† 3 50·6	..	10 37 21·7	..
		Mean result		10 37 21·9	—58 29 49
Aug. 7.	B. A. C. 3655.	† 3 50·6	—1 47	10 37 21·7	—58 29 54
		† 3 50·6	—1 53	10 37 21·7	—58 30 0
		† 3 51·1	—1 47	10 37 22·2	—58 29 54
		† 3 50·1	—1 44	10 37 21·2	—58 29 51
	B. A. C. 3721.	—6 37·1	..	10 37 20·9	..
		—6 37·1	..	10 37 20·9	..
		Mean result		10 37 21·4	—58 29 55

Note.—Where the difference of declination is not given, it is to be understood that one of the stars crossed the ring too near its centre to afford a trustworthy determination of difference.

MEAN PLACES OF THE STARS OF COMPARISON DEDUCED FROM THE B. A. CATALOGUE.

B. A. C. 3655 R. A. = 10 33 31·1   Declin. = 58 28 7
B. A. C. 3721 R. A. = 10 43 58·0   Declin. = 58 35 44

MEAN PLACES OF B. A. C. 3680 AND THE MISSING STARS DEDUCED FROM THE SAME CATALOGUE.

B. A. C. 3679 R. A. = 10 37 22·1   Declin. = 58 34 46
B. A. C. 3680 R. A. = 10 37 22·2   Declin. = 58 29 39
B. A. C. 3683 R. A. = 10 37 30·1   Declin. = 58 29 45

Since my arrival in Sydney to-day, the Rev. Mr. Scott has kindly drawn my attention to Mr. Maclear's report of a "Comparison of the Southern Stars of the B. A. Catalogue with the Heavens, made at the Cape of Good Hope," which report is published in the 20th volume of the "Memoirs of the Royal Astronomical Society." It contains the following note with reference to the stars B. A. C. 3679 and 3683 :—

"There are no stars in the catalogue positions. The modern authorities are Taylor and Brisbane, but Taylor gives no polar distance of 3679, and his position of 3683, is approximate. They will agree with B. A. C. 3680, by assuming an error of 5 minutes of arc, and of 10 seconds of time respectively in the places of Brisbane, 3174 and 3177."

From this it will be seen that the observations of Taylor and Brisbane most probably refer to B. A. C. 3680. I regret I had not the "Memoirs of the Royal Astronomical Society" at command when engaged in the composition of my paper. The only works I had for reference on the point were the catalogues of Lacaille and the British Association.

On the Comet of September 1862. No. 1.
By Mr. John Tebbutt, Jun.
[Read October 8th, 1862.]

THE object of the present paper is to furnish the members of the society with some popular information respecting the comet which has been visible during the past month. The paper is a short one, owing to the whole of my available time having been occupied in making and reducing observations and performing other necessary calculations. So far as I can learn from the newspapers, the comet appears to have been seen at Brisbane in the neighbouring colony of Queensland, at the close of the last week in August. A letter from Mr. Biden, dated from the ship "Stornoway," and also a telegram from Brisbane appeared in the *Herald* of the 1st ultimo, announcing its visibility. I may here remark, in passing, that when a comet makes its appearance, the fact should, if possible, be at once communicated to those stations where the instruments necessary for observation are located, in order to ensure complete and accurate observation of the stranger while it is within reach of the telescope. It was through a neglect of these precautions that a large comet seen at Brisbane in the beginning of November last, altogether escaped observation, so that we remain in utter ignorance of the elements of its orbit. But to return to our subject. On seeing the announcement in the *Herald*, I made preparations for observing the new visitor with the best instrumental means at command. This consisted of a telescope of $3\frac{1}{4}$ inches aperture and 4 feet focal length, provided with a ring-micrometer constructed by Mr. Tornaghi of Sydney. The comet was first detected with the naked eye at twenty-six minutes past six o'clock on the evening of the 1st, the twilight being pretty strong at the time. This circumstance proved our new visitor to be one of more than ordinary brilliancy. As the twilight declined the comet's head became, of course, more distinct, but no portion of the tail could be distinguished with the naked eye, owing to the presence of the moon, then in her first quarter, and shining brightly. The comet would have been in every way well situated to serve as a striking object, were it not for the unfortunate circumstance that the moon was approaching her opposition; altogether it does not appear to have attracted much attention. Mr. Biden mentions in his letter that the comet's tail was about five degrees in length, but then he saw it under more favourable circumstances, namely, when the moon was comparatively young. On the evening of the 1st the nucleus was about equal to a star of the fourth magnitude. It was of a dull lead colour, large, and of a very elliptical form, but not of a character calculated to afford very precise determinations of position. A conspicuous star of the sixth magnitude was fortunately found near the comet, which served as a standard of comparison. The observations of that evening gave the following result :—

September 1st, 7h. 33m. 13s., Windsor M.T. R.A. 15h. 46m. 53.8s. Declination, 20° 28′ 32″ N. This corresponds to a position a little south of or above the constellation Corona Borealis. Comparisons, repeated at short intervals, showed that the comet was moving slowly in right ascension, but very rapidly in declination. The rapid movement of the comet thus indicated gave ground for hope that observations extending over a few days would afford a tolerable approximation to the orbit. This, you will remember, was not the case with the great comet of last year; that body moved over a space of only a few minutes of a degree during the week succeeding its discovery, so that nearly a month elapsed before a determination of the orbit could be attempted. Such was also the case of Donati's comet of 1858. On the following evening (the 2nd), the comet was found to have moved between five and six degrees in declination, and in a direction nearly due south. On this occasion it presented a rather curious aspect in my telescope. The nucleus was more distinct than on the preceding evening, but it appeared as two bright points connected by a slender thread of light. I was at first disposed to regard this phenomenon as the result of some defect in the object-glass of the telescope, but was soon satisfied that such could not be the case. The Rev. C. F. Garnsey, of Windsor, assures me that he observed the same phenomenon some days later, but with a telescope of smaller dimensions.

The line connecting the two nuclei appeared to be nearly coincident with a parallel of declination, having, in fact, the same direction as the major axis of the large elliptical nucleus of the preceding evening. On the evening of the 3rd the nucleus was scarcely distinguishable, in consequence partly of the increase of the moon's light, partly of the increase of the comet's distance from both the earth and the sun, and partly of the haziness of the atmosphere. The evening of the 4th was very cloudy. The clouds broke once and revealed the comet, but it again clouded over before I could make any observation. Some good observations were made on the 5th, but the stars of comparison cannot be identified with any in the catalogues in my possession. The comet's nucleus on this occasion was much more sharply defined, and presented a very interesting appearance. It appeared single, but there extended from it a narrow beam of light in the direction of the sun. The beam gradually increased in breadth as it extended from the nucleus, and resembled that seen on July 4th, 1861, in the great comet of that year, by the Rev. T. W. Webb, of Hardwick, Herefordshire, England. I estimated it to be about two minutes of arc in length. The physical changes of the comet during the first week of September were remarkable, and an account of them will be awaited with interest from those possessed of more powerful instrumental means. The nebulosity surrounding the nucleus was pretty extensive, being upwards of six or eight minutes in diameter. The observations of the first three evenings being carefully reduced, a process rather troublesome, owing to the rapid movement of the comet in declination, the calculation of the orbit was immediately proceeded with. Mr. Hawkins of Goulburn, published an approximation on the 13th, which, though based on rough observations, was sufficiently accurate to show that the comet was not to be identified with any whose elements had hitherto been computed. On the 16th, my first approximation appeared as deduced from the observations of the first three evenings. [See the set of elements marked I., at the end of this paper.] These were found to represent the observations of the 7th within a few seconds of arc; those of the 11th, within about three minutes; and, finally, on the 17th, the discrepancy between the observed and computed places amounted to upwards of a degree. I accordingly proceeded to a closer approximation founded on the observations of the 1st, 11th, and 20th, and arrived at the second set of elements here given. I have not yet had an opportunity of comparing these elements with the intermediate observations, but hope to be able to do so in time for the next meeting of the Society. On the whole, I think set II. will be found to be as close an approximation as can be obtained from the first three weeks observations uncorrected for parallax. I hope to be able to enter more at length into the subject when the observations of the comet have been completed and fully reduced. I shall also then have an opportunity of comparing the results with those derived from the more accurate and extended observations of European and American astronomers. No notice of the discovery of the comet has appeared in the *Astronomische Nachrichten* up to the 14th June, the latest date received; but in the *Illustrated London News* of July 12th, I find the following item of news :—

" A new comet was discovered on the 3rd instant at Marseilles, by M. Tempel, in the constellation Cassiopea. It is rapidly journeying towards the polar star, and will soon, it is believed, be visible to the naked eye."

On calculating back for Greenwich mean midnight, July 3rd, from elements II, I obtain the following for the apparent place of the comet :—R.A., = $76\frac{1}{2}$ degrees; declination = 64 degrees north.

This position is on the confines of the constellation Cassiopea, so I think there can be little doubt that the comet discovered by M. Tempel is the same as that which is now the subject of observation here. The next mail from England will probably satisfy us on that point. From the date of discovery till about a week before it became generally visible here, the comet was traversing the northern hemisphere beneath our horizon.

I will now give a few interesting particulars, founded on the elements. The comet when first seen, on the evening of the 1st, was distant about thirty-three millions of miles from the earth, and was slowly receding from us. It passed its perihelion on the evening of the 23rd August, its distance from the sun then being ninety-one and a-half millions of miles. There is no comet in the tables to whose elements those of the present one bear a complete resemblance. There is a rough coincidence between its perihelion distance, position of orbit-plane, and direction of heliocentric motion, and the corresponding elements of the great comet of 1811; the greater axes of the two orbits are, however, at right angles to each other. The most remarkable feature of the orbit of the present comet is the fact that it nearly intersects that of the earth at the descending node, or point where the comet crosses from the north to the south side of the plane of the ecliptic. The value of the comet's radius vector, at the node, expressed in parts of the earth's mean distance from the sun, is 1·0191352. The radius vector of the earth, corresponding to the same point, is 1·0132944. If we multiply the difference 0·0058408 by ninety-five millions of miles, the assumed mean distance of the earth from the sun, we have very approximately the distance between the two orbits, as measured in the plane of the ecliptic—namely, 554,876 miles. Now, it will be remembered that when the great comet of last year crossed the plane of the earth's orbit on the 29th June, the earth and comet had nearly the same longitude as seen from the sun. The comet's head, however, was thirteen millions of miles within the line of the earth's orbit; consequently the earth merely performed a journey through the more diffused part of the comet's tail. Had the earth and comet in the present instance been in heliocentric conjunction at the time of the nodal passage, we should have witnessed a phenomenon surpassing, it may be, the magnificent apparitions of ancient times. The condition necessary to have brought the two bodies into such close neighbourhood would be that the perihelion passage should occur about thirty-two days earlier than it actually did. If we assume six minutes of arc as the apparent diameter of the comet's head on the evening of the 1st September, we have 58,000 miles as the real diameter of the nebulosity surrounding the nucleus, and this would subtend an angle of six degrees, supposing the earth and comet to be both in the line of nodes at the same time. An object like this would strike even the enlightened people of the nineteenth century with amazement. The earth, however, had passed the point on the 10th of August, or thirty-two days before the comet came down to it, and as a consequence the distance separating the two bodies at the time of the nodal passage was about fifty-two millions of miles. It is of course utterly impossible to predict what would be the result of a transit of the earth through the head of a comet. It is commonly supposed that results of a disastrous character cannot be produced by collision with a comet, because it is composed of matter very highly rarified and diffused. We are, however, acquainted with some natural agents which, though ethereal in their constitution, are capable of producing very disastrous effects. The earth passed through a very diffused part of the tail of the last great comet, and the result was a universal magnetic storm. What might be the degree of electric disturbance should the earth pass through the densest portion of a comet may well form a subject for speculation. The earth has, however, for ages past in its successive revolutions round the sun, escaped entanglement with these wanderers of the skies. Considerations such as these are not unprofitable. They teach us our utter dependence on the power and goodness of the great Being who "hath measured the waters in the hollow of his hand, meted out heaven with the span, comprehended the dust of the earth in a measure, weighed the mountains in scales, and the hills in a balance." They serve to impress us with a sense of the wisdom and good providence of Him who has adjusted the orbits of countless revolving worlds, and regulated their motions therein.

On the 20th ultimo the comet had increased its distance from the earth to seventy-six millions of miles, and by the 27th it had become quite invisible to the naked eye. It has been traversing the constellation Scorpio during the past three weeks, and is now on the borders of the Milky Way. It will probably continue visible in the telescope for some days to come.

ELEMENTS OF THE COMET.

	Set I. Aug. 23.	Set II. Aug. 23.
Perihelion passage, 1862, G. M. T.,	·0530	·13478
Perihelion distance	0·96264	0·962905

	deg.	min.	sec.	deg.	min.	sec.
Distance of perihelion from ascending node in the direction of motion	152	40	20	152	49	46
Longitude of ascending node ..	137	8	33	137	13	37
Inclination of orbit	65	41	39	66	9	35
Motion	Retrograde.			Retrograde.		

NOTE.—The longitude of the ascending node in Set I. is reckoned from the mean equinox of September 1st, 1862; that in Set II., from the mean equinox of January 1st, 1862.

On the Comet of September 1862. No. 2.
By MR. JOHN TEBBUTT, JUN.

[Read November 12th, 1862.]

IN the course of the last paper which I had the pleasure of reading before the Society, I mentioned that, in all probability, the comet which formed the subject of the paper was identical with one discovered by M. Tempel, at Marseilles, on the 3rd July. The intelligence we had received from Europe respecting the discovery of the latter was very vague, consisting merely of a brief announcement in the *Illustrated London News*, of 12th July, that a comet had been discovered as above in the constellation Cassiopea. You will remember, that on calculating back from the elements in the last paper, it was found that the comet seen here was, on the 3rd July, in R.A. $76\frac{1}{2}$ degrees; Declin. 64 degrees north. Finding this position was near Alpha and Beta Camelopardi, and therefore not far from the constellation Cassiopea, and making some allowance for the indefinite character of the announcement in the *Illustrated London News*, I naturally, but, as the sequel will shew, rather hastily concluded that Tempel's comet and our own were one and the same. With this conclusion I rested satisfied till the *Illustrated London News* came to hand of the 2nd August, which contained the following more precise notice respecting the discovery of Tempel's comet.

" The new comet discovered by M. Tempel at Marseilles, on the night of the 2nd and 3rd instant, near Beta, in the constellation Cassiopea, we learn, was previously observed on the 2nd, by M. Seeling, at Athens. It was seen by M. Tempel, with difficulty, with the naked eye. With a glass it presented the appearance of an irregular oval-formed nebulosity, without any trace of a tail. On July 5th, at eleven o'clock, p.m., it was near to Eta in the Great Bear."

On reading this notice, it immediately occurred to me that, either the elements contained in the last paper were not so accurate as I had supposed, or that the comet discovered by MM. Tempel and Seeling was totally distinct from that which had been the subject of observation here. My attention was at once drawn to the subject. On discussing the whole series of observations from the 1st September to the 15th October, I found no reason to doubt the accuracy of the elements. By means of the elements I found the following for the approximate places of the comet which has been visible here :—

July $3^d.$ 5. G.M.T. R.A.=$76° 27'$ Declination=$64° 6'$ N.
July $7^d.$ 5. G.M.T. R.A.=$77° 24'$ Declination=$64° 52'$ N.

The distances of the comet from the sun and earth at those times were respectively as follows :—

July $3^d.$ 5. Distance from Sun 123 millions of miles ; from Earth 171 millions of miles.

July $7^d.$ 5. Distance from Sun 119 millions of miles ; from Earth 162 millions of miles.

Now from the known brilliancy of the comet in that portion of its orbit which it traversed while above our horizon from the 1st September to the middle of October it is obvious that it must at the above dates have been far beyond the limits of unassisted vision. In this circumstance, then, it differs from the comet discovered by MM. Tempel and Seeling, which is stated to have been just visible to the naked eye. Again, it will be observed that the motion of our comet, although nearly in the direction of the pole-star, was only a few minutes of arc daily, whereas the other comet moved over the large arc of about seventy degrees in three days. Here, then, is conclusive evidence that the two comets were pursuing totally different orbits. On making known this circumstance to a friend my attention was drawn by him to the *Illustrated London News* of August 16th, a later date than I myself had received. It was therein stated that a comet had been discovered by Rosa at Rome, on the 25th July, which became distinctly visible to the naked eye on the 3rd August. The notice is accompanied with a rough chart showing the comet's apparent track among the stars from the night of discovery to the 20th August. The chart enables me at once to identify this comet as the one observed here, for on calculating back from the elements, I find our comet occupied precisely the positions indicated in the chart, and must have become visible to the naked eye in the beginning of August. On the night of discovery, the comet was distant one hundred and three millions of miles from the sun, and one hundred and eighteen millions from the earth. The comet discovered by MM. Tempel and Seeling might have been seen in the colony after the first week in July; but I am not aware that it has been seen by any one. It is usual for Astronomers to designate the comets of any particular year according to the order of their times of perihelion passage. Taking, therefore, into account the fact that the two comets under consideration appeared in Europe almost simultaneously, and our present ignorance respecting the time of the perihelion passage of the one, I am not yet justified in designating our comet as " I. of 1862." I hoped the October mail would bring us a considerable amount of intelligence respecting the late comet, but that hope has not been realised. In the *Herald* of the 20th ultimo, there is an extract of a letter from Mr. Hind to the *Times*, which confirms to some extent the results contained in my last paper. He states the comet will be nearest to the sun on the 23rd, (August is implied, though not expressed, in the extract), and distant thirty-two and a half millions of miles from the earth on the 30th. He says, further: "the comet will traverse the plane of the ecliptic on the 11th September, at a point distant rather more than two millions of miles from the earth's path." Now, it will be remembered that, in my last paper, I stated that the nearest approach of the comet to the earth's path had occurred on the 11th September, but that the distance between the two orbits was rather more than half a million of miles. This is about one-fourth of the distance which Mr. Hind gives. It is, however, very probable that Mr. Hind's are only approximate results, based on a few observations taken at the comet's first appearance: it is, of course, usual for astronomers to give rough results at the beginning, to be gradually corrected from future observations. I think, therefore, it will be found, when more mature results reach us from Europe, that the comet actually approached the earth's orbit much nearer than two millions of miles. I speak thus confidently because the elements which I have given satisfy pretty nearly observations extending over six weeks. Further on I will give a comparison of the parabola, with the results derived from observation. From the meagre accounts that have reached us, it appears that the phenomena mentioned in my last paper as attending the comet were also observed in Europe during the month of August. These phenomena are described as most extraordinary, so we may expect some interesting information respecting them by the next mail from Europe. There is a drawing of the comet in the *Illustrated London News* of August 16th, from which it will be seen that the comet in its general appearance resembled that of Halley, as figured by Struve on October 8th, 1835.

Since the last meeting of the Society I have slightly corrected the elements contained in my former paper. My latest approximation, uncorrected for aberration and parallax, is as follows:—

Perihelion passage, 1862, August 23rd, ·1340 Greenwich mean time.
Perihelion distance 0.96290
Distance of perihelion from ascending ⎱ Deg. min. sec.
   node, according to the order of the signs ⎰ 207 10 12
Longitude of perihelion on orbit........ 344 23 48 ⎱ Mean equinox of
Longitude of ascending node .... 137 13 36 ⎰ 1st January, 1862.
Inclination of orbit   66   9 36
Motion, retrograde.

Adopting the above elements, we have the following expressions for the comet's heliocentric co-ordinates referred to the plane of the Equator and the two corresponding planes:—

Log sin λ = [—9·9976609] + log sin (191°23′.96 + v.)
Log tan A = [+ 9·0149823] + log tan (191°23′.96 + v.)
  $x = r \cos (141° 21′ 22 + A) \cos \lambda$
  $y = r \sin (141° 21′ 22 + A) \cos \lambda = x \tan (141° 21′ 22 + A)$
  $z = r \sin \lambda$

where r is the comet's radius vector and v the true anomaly, reckoned according to the order of the signs, or contrary to the direction of the comet's motion.

I believe the elements above given, will be found to be a pretty close approximation to the true ones, considering the difficulty attending exact observations of the comet, and the liability to error of the positions of the stars of comparison. In all cases, I have adopted the best authorities at command for the positions of the stars of comparison. In three instances, I have been enabled to avail myself of corrections deduced from meridian observations made at the Sydney Observatory in 1859 and 1860. As an instance of the liability to error of the Southern catalogues, I may refer to my observations of the 13th October. In the comparisons of that evening, I employed B. A. C. 5558 a star of the sixth magnitude, and Lacaille 6907 one of the seventh. The latter corresponds with 5789 of the Brisbane Catalogue. My comparisons of the two stars showed that Lacaille 6907 was thirty-five seconds of time west of B. A. C. 5558. Lacaillle's catalogue gives the same result, but Brisbane makes it only sixteen seconds west of B. A. C. 5558. The position of Brisbane 5789 depends on one observation only, and this is the case with many other stars in that catalogue. It appears, therefore, we must be cautious in placing much dependence on the star positions of the Southern catalogues. A complete and accurate re-observation of the Southern stars, down to the eighth magnitude inclusive, more especially those between the parallels of 20 and 50 degrees declination, is a work of the highest importance, and without which we cannot expect any great advance in the astronomy of this hemisphere. The best observations of a planet or comet cannot be made available for any accurate purpose till the origins from which its position are measured are known with certainty. For the accomplishment of this great work, we must, in a great measure, look to our observatory: a valuable instalment of it has already been presented to the scientific world in the three volumes of observations for 1859, 1860, and 1861.

The following table contains the results of my observations, with the exception of those where the stars of comparison could not be found in the catalogues of the British Association, Brisbane, and Lacaille. The later observations will prove useful in the event of the comet not being more accurately observed elsewhere. The positions are uncorrected for parallax, and referred to the mean equinox and mean equator of January 1st, 1862. The last two columns of the table exhibit a comparison of some of the places derived from observation with the corresponding positions deduced from the parabola. In order to this comparison, the comet's places have been corrected for parallax. C and O denote respectively the calculated and observed places of the comet, and Δa, $\Delta \pi$, the differences of right ascension and north polar distance. The October comparisons indicate the necessity of a further slight correction of the elements, but it would be a waste of time to attempt extreme accuracy, considering the probable amount of the errors of the catalogues, and of the comparison observations themselves. The positions of the 15th October, are the latest that can be depended on for a comparison; the comet's distances from the sun and earth, were then respectively, one hundred and twenty-five and one hundred and forty-six millions of miles. I succeeded in making some observations on the evening of the 21st, but the results, owing to the excessive faintness of the comet, are liable to errors of upwards of a minute of arc; they are, therefore, not sufficiently accurate for a correction of the orbit.

Having now given you as much information as I can under the circumstances, I must take leave of the subject. The members of the Society will, doubtless, find much to interest them in the intelligence which will be received respecting the comet by the English mail, now due, and that of December next.

152   ON THE COMET OF SEPTEMBER 1862.—No. 2.

PLACES OF COMET (UNCORRECTED FOR PARALLAX) REFERRED TO THE MEAN EQUATOR AND EQUINOX OF JANUARY 1st, 1862.

Greenwich Mean Time, 1862.	No. of Comps.	Star of Comp.	Authority for Star's Place.	Comet's R.A.	Comet's N.P.D.	C—O $\Delta\alpha \sin \pi$	C—O $\Delta\pi$
d. h. m. s.				h. m. s.	° ′ ″	′	′
August...31 21 29 31	2	B. A. C. 5273	B. A., Catalogue	15 46 53·6	69 31 16		
September. 1 21 6 58	4	,, 5293	,,	15 50 8·4	75 6 46	—0·20	+0·26
,, ..2 22 28 56	2	,, 5270	,,	15 53 12·7	80 45 21		
,, ..6 21 21 66	3	,, 5387	,,	16 2 14·0	98 8 29		
,, ..8 21 32 20	1	,, 5420	,,	16 2 14·1	98 8 65		
,, ..10 22 39 65	3	,, 5337	,,	16 8 47·9	110 14 32	—0·27	+0·09
,, ..14 22 14 17	2	,, 5342	Sydney Obs., 1859	16 8 48·0	110 14 28	—0·29	+0·16
,, ..14 ,, ,,	2	,, 5429	Catalogue	16 13 43·9	118 12 28		
,, ..16 23 37 21	3	,, 5433	B. A. ,,	16 13 43·1	118 12 16	—0·14	—0·14
,, ..16 23 41 9	2	,, 5468	,,	16 16 54·9	121 18 69		
,, ,, ,, ,,	3	,, 5471	Sydney Obs., 1859	16 15 54·4	121 18 48	—0·01	—0·19
,, ..19 22 13 28	3	,, 5538	B. A., Catalogue	16 18 44·4	124 66 8		
,, ..25 23 47 16	2	,, 5593	Sydney Obs., 1860	16 23 54·4	130 23 7	+0·38	—0·18
,, ..26 22 13 33	2	,, 5683	B. A., Catalogue	16 24 40·6	131 0 22	+0·20	+0·05
,, ,, ,, ,,	2	,, 5684	Brisb. Catalogue	16 24 41·6	131 0 8		
October....3 22 6 10	1	Brisb. 5799	B. A. ,,	16 30 11·6	135 2 22	+1·06	—1·16
,, ..12 22 18 17	1	,, 5754	B. A. ,,	16 30 13·7	135 3 1		
,, ..12 21 52 10	1	*B. A. C. 5568	B. A. Catalogue	16 37 36·3	138 40 29	+1·08	—0·70
,, ..14 21 44 34	4	,, 5661	,,	16 39 16·8	139 20 50	+1·48	—1·38

* B. A. C. 5568, is a double star; the *following* or easternmost star was employed in the comparison of the 13th October. Position of place of observation:—
Longitude 10h. 3m. 43s. E.   Latitude 33° 30′ 30″ S.

On Australian Storms.
By Mr. John Tebbutt, Jun.

[Read 7th September, 1864.]

THE public for the past few months have been rejoicing in the acquisition of another lunar theory for the prediction of weather, which, like all its predecessors, will, I fear, be eventually thrown aside as useless. But, there is a weather system in full operation in England, which, though not so ambitious in its pretentions as the various lunar theories, is nevertheless logically deduced from observation, and therefore of great value. I refer to the method of forecasting weather, as daily practised in England by Admiral Fitzroy. His theory does not profess to determine months beforehand, when and where storms will occur, but a storm having once begun in the vicinity of the British Isles, it fixes, with a very tolerable approach to accuracy, its velocity and the course it will pursue. These desiderata being obtained, it is an easy matter to forewarn by the electric telegraph those places on the coasts which will probably feel the effects of the storm. The general principles on which forecasts of weather are drawn by Admiral Fitzroy, and the way in which these principles have been discovered, are soon explained. For some time before the system of weather warnings was established, the Board of Trade had maintained a system of simultaneous meteorological observations throughout the United Kingdom. The regular observations of the astronomical establishments and the lighthouses were supplemented by those of a large corps of earnest and devoted private observers. These observations were regularly forwarded to a central office for correction and discussion. Very little insight into the law of atmospheric changes could be obtained by the mere inspection of a mass of tabular records, but when the simultaneous observations were exhibited in a series of curves and charts a very interesting fact was elicited. On a careful comparison of the diagrams during periods of marked atmospheric disturbance, it was found, that storm phenomena, barometric and otherwise, did not remain stationary on the spot where they originated, but gradually shifted eastward. A storm, for instance, which originated in the Atlantic off the west coast of Ireland, would be found to cross over Ireland and England, towards the North Sea. It was in fact discovered, that the atmosphere of the north temperate zone had a slow circulation eastward, carrying with it its disturbances, just as the tidal current of a river carries with it, the eddies that are formed in it. The general direction, and velocity, of this grand circulation, and the modifications which they undergo from various circumstances, having been satisfactorily ascertained from numerous systematic observations, the electric telegraph furnished the means of carrying out the great principle into practice. The consequence now is, that forecasts of weather are daily telegraphed to all parts of the British coasts from one to three days in advance, such forecasts being drawn from previous states of weather, reported to the central office also by telegraph. Suggestions have been thrown out from time to time in our daily papers, as to the advisability of establishing in these colonies the system above described. But I think it would be premature, to attempt its introduction here, until the meteorological observations, already available have at least been systematically and carefully discussed as were those which furnished the principle on which the daily forecasts of Admiral Fitzroy are founded. I believe it has always been assumed, that the atmospheric disturbances affecting these colonies, have an eastward tendency, as in the north temperate zone, but at the same time, beyond the tracing of a few isolated gales, nothing has been done by comparison of observations, to show, that as a general rule, our gales and storms are so translated. The observations already available are sufficient to show roughly their general direction and average velocity. But in order to trace them out with all desirable accuracy, together with the modifications which they undergo from the influence of the physical geography of the colonies, we require observations more numerous and extended than those made at present. It is here we feel the great want, which is not experienced in the mother country, of a large corps of amateur observers, to supplement the efforts of the government. There is, too, another disadvantage attending any operations here, but it is one which might easily be remedied. A little more care in the preparation, or publication, of the telegraphic weather reports is necessary. Their frequent inaccuracy is an evil, which is the more serious, on account of the fewness of the stations. Where the places of observation are numerous, and therefore not so widely separated from one another, an accidental error in a report from any one station is easily detected by comparing it with the reports from the other stations in its immediate vicinity.

My present object is to lay before the Society a series of diagrams, which I humbly hope may throw some light on the manner in which barometric changes are propagated over the Colonies. The area of the Colony of New South Wales being so limited, and the observations at seven out of the nine meteorological stations being made only once a day, it is obviously impossible to trace any atmospheric disturbance with satisfaction. This difficulty is especially obvious if the movement of the disturbance be from west to east, because the stations differ so little in longitude. The observatory at Adelaide is then of great importance in the solution of this question. Its distance westward from our own Colony is sufficiently great to enable us to detect any deviation from actual synchronism of barometric changes. Mr. Todd has kindly supplied me with his observations made at the Adelaide Observatory, during the years 1861 and 1862. I have employed those for 1861, together with the observations made at Deniliquin, Sydney, and Brisbane, for the same year, in laying down the barometric curves appended to this paper. The curves for Adelaide and Sydney have been projected from the 9 a.m. observations at those places; the Brisbane and Deniliquin curves are copied from those contained in the Volume for 1861 of the Sydney Astronomical and Meteorological observations. No corrections have been applied to the observations for difference of longitude or height above sea level, as such corrections would not materially affect the conclusions to be arrived at. The diagrams require very little explanation. The vertical lines represent the days of the month, and the horizontal ones the heights of the barometers at the four stations. The vertical lines at their intersections with the curves indicate the simultaneous height of the barometers. Now a cursory glance at the four curves is enough to satisfy any person of their general similarity, but on a closer inspection it will be seen that the barometric maxima and minima, which are of course the prominent features of the curves, are not simultaneous over the large area embraced between the observatories at Adelaide and Brisbane, but have a gradual progression from west to east, or rather perhaps from south-west to north-east. On the average, they occur at Sydney and Brisbane respectively about one and two days later than at Adelaide. The principal corresponding maxima and minima at the four stations are pointed out in the diagrams by the red lines. If we may take the observations for 1861 as sufficient to demonstrate the rule as to the propagation of our barometric changes, and I think we may, it is incontestably shown by the diagrams that they are propagated gradually over the colonies from about south-west to north-east. The wind phenomena attending these alterations of tension are made up of the two great polar and tropical currents. In the winter months the gradual shifting of these streams of air over the colonies, is as distinctly marked by the observations as the propagation of their accompanying barometric phenomena. The alternation of the tropical and polar winds is distinctly marked at Sydney through the whole year, the former corresponding to a falling and the latter to a rising barometer. During the summer months at Adelaide the tropical currents appear in a great measure to fail, polar winds being remarkably prevalent. This fact may be simply accounted for, by the position of Adelaide with reference to the great Australian Continent. During the summer the atmosphere over the vast area of land to the north is greatly rarified by radiation, and consequently ascends. The tropical streams of air instead of passing over Adelaide are arrested in their progress by this partial vacuum and are met by the polar winds, which are also hastening to restore equilibrium at the same point. Thus it is that polar winds are so remarkably prevalent at Adelaide during the summer. In order to illustrate the way in which our storms are propagated, I may briefly trace out the progress across the colonies of one of the most conspicuous instances of bad weather in the year 1861. In glancing over the Adelaide observations, the first bad weather which would particularly attract our attention would perhaps be that of April 13th—18th. It appears from Mr. Todd's observations, that after a fine day and nearly cloudless night, the morning of the 13th at Adelaide was ushered in with thin *cirro-stratus* cloud and a falling barometer, both phenomena being marked characteristics of tropical currents of air. During the night of the 12th the polar currents had failed, and the opposite or tropical ones commenced. Northerly winds prevailed on the 13th, 14th, and 15th, the barometer still falling, with indications of heavy weather: the tropical winds were also marked by the thermometer, the temperature being high on those days. The lowest recorded reading of the barometer occurred at 6 p.m. on the 14th, being 29·523 (corrected for temperature). On the morning of the 16th the tropical current was met and overcome by its polar opponent, the wind changing to south-west, the barometer rising, and the thermometer falling. Strong gales and heavy weather from the polar quarter prevailed throughout the colony of South Australia on the 16th, 17th, and 18th, moderating towards evening of the 18th. A heavy storm of wind and rain swept over Melbourne and the adjacent country in the afternoon of the 16th, which coming from a southerly direction, appears from the newspaper accounts to have been only a temporary advance of the polar current. We learn from a telegram in the *Herald* of the 17th, that a N.N.E. gale with squalls, was blowing at Melbourne at 8 p.m. on the 16th. Hence it appears, that while the tropical current which had passed over and altogether ceased at Adelaide, was prevailing at Melbourne, the opposite or polar current was severely felt at the former place. On the night of the 17th, however, Melbourne in its turn experienced the conflict of the two great currents, in the shape of violent westerly gales, trees being uprooted and other damage done. It was in Bass' Straits during the fearful weather of the 16th—18th that the ill-fated ship "Rembrandt" foundered, taking down with her eleven out of the fifteen souls she had on board. The newspapers describe these gales as being remarkably violent. Now let us turn to the state of the weather in our own colony. From the observations at the Sydney

Observatory and South Head, it will be seen that tropical winds prevailed throughout the 14th, 15th, and 16th. The prevalence of these winds was made manifest by a falling barometer, and rising thermometer. The lowest recorded reading of the former instrument occurred at three p.m. on the 16th, being 29.587, differing only 0·064 from the minimum at Adelaide. These values are at once comparable, because the heights of the Sydney and Adelaide Observatories above the sea are nearly equal. During the night of the 16th the polar winds were first felt at Sydney, blowing strong from the west during the forenoon of the 17th, the barometer rising and the thermometer falling. On referring to the account of the gale at Adelaide, it will be seen that the least pressure of the atmosphere and the reversal of the wind occurred there many hours earlier. And probably if the wind observations at Brisbane were before us, we should find that the polar winds were not experienced there till the 18th, that is, if the storm had not expended itself before reaching so far north. However, we perceive from the diagrams that the least pressure occurred on the 17th, or one day later than at Sydney. On the whole, it would appear, that the barometric oscillations decrease as we advance towards the tropics. An inspection of the curves contained in Mr. Scott's Volume of observations for 1861, will make this circumstance at once apparent.

It is unnecessary for me to go into a consideration of the other period of great atmospheric disturbance, which characterized the year 1861. Those who wish to go further into the subject, may profitably examine the following storm periods:—May 21st—24th, June 15th—26th. During the latter period the barometer remained low for several days, owing to the remarkable persistency of the tropical winds. There is one thing that cannot have escaped the observation of those who have studied the winds, that their effects are different in different places owing to local influences, such as coasts and mountains. On comparing my own observations with those made at the Sydney Observatory, I find that all winds blowing from the eastern semi-circle between north and south, are felt with much more effect at Sydney than at Windsor. This circumstance, I have no doubt, is owing to the winds from the sea being deflected or thrown upwards by the high coast line, the scud during heavy gales on the coast being often seen at Windsor, to move with great rapidity, while light winds only prevail on the earth's surface. An easterly gale is, I believe, a thing of very rare occurrence at Windsor. The strength of the different winds in various localities is a subject that should be studied, as one means of enabling us to forecast the probable effects of weather at such places. In an interesting communication in the *Illustrated London News* of December last, on the subject of the gales which marked the last three months of 1863, a writer referred to the circumstance, that the greatest violence of gales might be expected to occur about the time of minimum barometric pressure. Heavy gusts are commonly experienced shortly after the time of least pressure. In connexion with this subject I may say, I have observed that it is not only about the time of the minimum barometric pressure in *great* storms that the greatest force of wind is experienced. It is well known that in ordinary fine weather the chief daily barometric minimum occurs regularly about 3 p.m., and it happens that this is precisely the hour at which the average strength of the winds is a maximum. In support of this statement I may give the following as the mean force of air currents at Windsor at 9 a.m. noon, 3, 6, and 9 p.m. for the first seven months of the present year. The scale employed in the observations was 0—6.

MONTH.	9 a.m.	NOON.	3 p.m.	6 p.m.	9 p.m.
January	1·3	1·7	2·3	2·3	1·3
February	1·6	1·9	2·0	1·9	1·4
March	1·3	1·8	2·1	1·5	1·1
April	1·3	1·6	1·9	1·2	1·3
May	0·8	1.2	1·6	1·0	0·9
June	1·0	1·7	1·7	1·2	1·3
July	1·2	2·0	2·1	1·7	1·1
Means	1·2	1·7	2·0	1·5	1·2

The wind observations of last year were only made at 9 a.m., 3 p.m., and 9 p.m., but a comparison of these as also of the observations made at the Sydney Observatory during the past eight years will show that the mean force is greater at 3 p.m. than at 9 a.m. or 9 p.m. The least pressure of the atmosphere and the greatest activity in air currents occurring at the same time as the highest temperature would seem to point to the conclusion that the sun is the primary and chief agent in the production of all our atmospheric commotions.

One of the most interesting examples I have met with of the propagation of storm phenomena over the colonies, was on the occasion of the remarkable gales of the 25th and 26th October last. In the *Sydney Morning Herald* of the 27th October, appeared the following telegram from Adelaide:—

"Heavy gale here yesterday, (25th) commencing at N.N.E., min. bar. 29.150 at 4.15 p.m.; wind soon after veered round to W., blowing very hard throughout the night. Bar. at 10 p.m., 29.310, but falling after midnight; 28.990 at 9 a.m. (26th) at Mount Gambier; 29.160 at Adelaide at 11 a.m., still falling slightly." The dates in parenthesis are inserted by me for the sake of explanation. Compare the above observations with the state of the weather as recorded by myself at Windsor. Light north-easterly winds prevailed on the 25th, with a falling barometer; at 9 a.m. on that day, it stood at 29.906, (corrected for temperature) and during the following twenty-four hours, fell to 29.342 or 0.564 of an inch. The wind freshened at 9 a.m. on the 26th, and blew a gale, varying from N.E. to N.W., the barometer in the meantime falling rapidly. The wind was remarkable for its numerous circuitous sweeps, blowing frequently from every point of the compass in succession. From half-hourly observations on the 26th, the lowest corrected reading of the barometer was found to be 29.021 at 3 p.m. Forty-five minutes after the minimum was attained, the wind veered to west, and blew in heavy gusts during the afternoon, the barometer oscillating, but on the whole, rising slowly. It, however, began to go down rapidly again after 9 p.m., falling 0.08 inch in an hour and a half, the wind, then light, having backed to N.W. It rose slowly after 2 a.m. on the 27th. Heavy W. and W.S.W. winds continued throughout the 27th, the barometer still rising. Now it fortunately happens, that at both Adelaide and Windsor, three prominent features of the storm were recorded, viz:—a first and second minimum of the barometer, and the change in the direction of the wind. The principal minimum occurred at Adelaide and Windsor as reduced to the meridian of Windsor, as follows:—

At Adelaide, October $25^d\ 5^h\ 4^m$ Windsor mean time.
„ Windsor „ $26^d\ 3^h\ 0^m$ „ „ „

The difference gives twenty-two hours as the interval of absolute time occupied by the phenomenon in its propagation over the space separating the two observatories. Again, we find that soon after the principal minimum of atmospheric pressure, the wind at both places veered to the west, and that in about eight hours at Adelaide, and six at Windsor, the barometer again began to fall. We have here a well defined instance of the gradual shifting eastward of the two great air currents in connection with their corresponding atmospheric pressures, and it is evidently in accordance with the rule derived from the consideration of the curves. And the observations recorded at Windsor on this occasion, afford a very striking illustration of the influence of tropical currents of air on the barometer, for no sooner did the tropical current gain a temporary ascendancy over its polar opponent, as shown by the backing of the wind to northwest on the evening of the 26th, than the instrument again began to fall. I have received observations of the same storm from Brisbane and Cape Otway. The observations at Cape Otway are made three times a day, and show that the storm at that place, slightly preceded in point of time the same phenomenon at Windsor. The lowest reading of the barometer occurred early in the afternoon of the 26th, the wind also shifted about the same time. The observations at Brisbane are also made three times a day, viz:—at 9 a.m., 3 p.m., and 9 p.m. N.N.E. and N.N.W. winds prevailed there on the 26th, the barometer falling from 29.924 at 9 a.m. on the 25th, to its lowest recorded point 29.440 at 3 p.m. on the 27th. Strong polar winds from W.S.W. prevailed on the 27th. Thus, it appears, that the principal features of the storm occupied about two days in shifting north-easterly from Adelaide to Brisbane.

From what has been said we should infer that if a system of weather warnings were established along our eastern sea-board, Adelaide would form an admirable out-post to warn us of approaching danger. But it does not follow that the Adelaide reports are sufficient for this purpose. It is said by some persons that the prevailing gales of these Colonies originate in the Southern Indian Ocean, and pass over Adelaide before reaching us. Although this may be true in the majority of cases, it will sometimes happen that our east coasts are subject to gales from which Adelaide either wholly or in part escapes. Admiral Fitzroy has shown that a polar current advancing from the north towards the British Isles, is sometimes carried so far eastward by the general movement of the atmosphere as to pass between Norway and the east coast of Scotland, spreading itself over the North Sea, and there encountering the tropical current from the southwest; both being deflected westward by Danish and Dutch shores, and combined producing those violent easterly gales which are so destructive to the shipping along the east coast of Great Britain. Such easterly gales are not first felt at the meteorological stations in Ireland and the west of England. The approach of the two great currents would be first announced from the north of Scotland and from the French coasts. Instances analagous to this occur in these Colonies. Let us suppose an area of diminished pressure with northerly winds to be passing over Adelaide eastward, and a powerful current to be advancing from the south-east towards this point. Before the extremity of this current can reach Adelaide it is carried eastward by the general circulation, and so passes over Tasmania along our eastern coast, meeting, probably, the warm moist current from the north, and so producing one of those terrific easterly gales which are so remarkable for their down-pour of rain. In such a case as this we must not trust to Adelaide alone for warning; the reports from that station must be supplemented by those from the Tasmanian coasts. We have before us a very striking exemplification of the case I have just mentioned. If we examine the curves at the close of April, we shall find what appears at first view an exception to the theory of eastward circulation, namely—the barometric minima at Sydney and Brisbane precede those at Adelaide and Deniliquin. At Adelaide northerly winds were remarkably prevalent with high temperature throughout the 27th, 28th, 29th, and 30th April and 1st

May; the barometer attaining its minimum at 6 p.m. on the 30th April. Mr. Todd on the 30th describes the barometer as falling, with every appearance of high winds. But let us see what was going on along our east coast at this time. The lowest recorded reading of the barometer at Sydney was 29,444 at 3 p.m. on the 29th; and throughout the 27th and 28th the polar and tropical currents were in violent conflict, producing gales between E.S.E. and N.E. of no ordinary character. A reference to the newspapers of that period will show that floods were very prevalent in the Colony. On the 29th the polar winds appear to have gained the mastery for a short time, and the barometer rose a little. On the 1st May the polar winds were first felt at Adelaide; the tropical ones at the same time prevailing at Sydney. This second advance from the southward, which had reached Adelaide, was afterwards slightly felt at Sydney.

Although we have apparently arrived at the rule for the propagation of our atmospheric disturbances, still it cannot be denied that there are some remarkable exceptions. Take for example the weather of the middle of February of last year, which was marked by successive heavy rains and floods from Queensland to Bass' Straits. A rather lengthy account of that storm, which bore strong marks of the cyclonic character, is contained in the *Sydney Morning Herald* and the *Empire* of the 11th and 10th June, 1863, respectively. The gradual progression southward of the barometic phenomena in connexion with the changes of the wind and weather are remarkably well shown by the scattered observations available. As then there are exceptions to the rule just mentioned for the propagation of our storms, it becomes us before attempting to apply the system of Admiral Fitzroy to our own coasts, to make at least some effort to establish special observations during periods of remarkable atmospheric disturbance. The discussion of such data might acquaint us with the conditions under which the exceptions to the rule are produced. The effects of local influence on the wind and weather would also have much light thrown upon them. It is much to be regretted that special observations were not instituted for the months of October and December last, which were marked by extraordinary disturbances in the atmospheric elements. It is of course impossible to announce long beforehand the day on which such observations should be made; this is not required. Sufficient warning is given by the barometer, and if the instrument is found at any time to be falling rapidly, a series of hourly or two-hourly observations should be at once commenced in order to secure the gradual variations of the atmospheric pressure, together with the corresponding changes of the wind. Especially should the time and amount of the least pressure be secured. At the chief observatories in England, self-recording instruments are established. The principal instruments are the barograph and the anemometer; the former registers the gradual march of the atmospheric pressure, and the latter the direction and velocity of the wind. These records being continuous and unbroken, the slightest and briefest changes are traced with accuracy. It is much to be regretted that the expensive character of these instruments prevent their general adoption. I am happy to say that a self-recording anemometer was erected at the Sydney Observatory about twelve months ago, which I believe, gives entire satisfaction.

In concluding this paper, I think I may reasonably urge upon you the claims which Australian meteorology has upon you as a scientific Society. We are in a position to lend a helping hand to a science, the promotion of which is of the highest importance to the interests of the colonies. It is much to be regretted that some of our colonists who have plenty of leisure and means, do not come forward in the cause as earnestly as the many in the noble country from which we are sprung, but it must be remembered they have no encouragement. A noble example would be shown by our Philosophical Society, if we should only establish one meteorological station, and invite the co-operation of observers in the colonies. The Government have done all that can be expected of them, for, in addition to the Sydney Observatory, they support meteorological stations at Armidale, Newcastle, Bathurst, Goulburn, Deniliquin, Albury, and Cooma.

Remarks on the preceding paper, made at the Meeting of 7th September, 1864, by

THE REV. W. B. CLARKE, M.A., F.G.S. &c., V.P.

IN the paper just read there are 31 distinct propositions or statements, with an appeal to the public, and especially to this Society, to aid in researches such as those in which the author of that paper is so usefully engaged.

It may not be, perhaps, impertinent to mention this appeal before I proceed to notice the other very interesting subjects discussed by Mr. Tebbutt. There have been several writers in this colony already on the science of Meteorology or on some of its most important branches. Count Strzelecki, in his "*Physical Description of New South Wales and Van Diemen's Land*, published in 1845, entered on the Climatology of these colonies, and discussed the nature of the atmospheric currents from his own personal observations. He gives a table of monthly currents contrary in direction to surface winds; attributing some of the observed phenomena to increase or decrease of the Sun's declination, showing that a cold current moves frequently between two warmer currents entirely by virtue of its volume.

He further shows from his own observations, that at Port Phillip the rule adduced by Mr. Tebbutt for Adelaide obtains, viz.: polar winds prevail in summer; but he appears to oppose Mr. Tebbutt's solution of a *rise* of the equatorial current, stating that there is no proof of this from observation. Further, he shows that the rule stated for Port Phillip and now for Adelaide, is not maintained either in Tasmania, Port Jackson, or Port Macquarie, of which in the former the equatorial prevails both in summer and in winter, and in the latter two localities the winter is distinguished and not the summer by polar winds. He infers that such variations must depend on something more than a local cause, and probably belong to the influence of monsoons and winds existing within a certain distance of Terra Australis. He gives also skeleton charts of the prevailing winds in New South Wales and Tasmania, during the winters of 1840-1-2, and during the summer of 1840, by which we are to assume that, depending on the monsoons, the *winter* winds veer round and within Australia from *right* to *left*, and the *summer* from *left* to *right*.

Since the date of that work, the subject of *Cyclones* or Circular storms has been amply discussed, and among other writings a treatise on "*Australasian Cyclonology, or the law of storms in the South Pacific Ocean*," was put forth in 1853 by Mr. Dobson, of Hobart Town, in which he endeavours to show that the great storms of the Southern Pacific rotate from *left* to *right*, beginning near the Equator, progressing first westerly, then to S.W., and recurving towards S.E. He shows also, that the general storm track of the South Pacific Ocean appears to follow the curvature of the East Coast of Australia, as the storm track of the South Indian Ocean does that of the West Coast of Australia. He further points out that Bass's Strait is subject to two kinds of Cyclones, one changing from N.W. to S. and S.W., and the other from N.E. to E. and S.E. The work of Mr. Dobson is filled with examples from log-books and other data which, certainly, in many instances, justify his conclusions.

In 1859, Mr. W. S. Jevons, then a member of this Society, published in *Waugh's Almanac* an elaborate collection of data concerning the climate of Australia and New Zealand. These were collected from contributions to newspapers and other sources and from his own recorded observations. So far as they bear on the question immediately before us, he adopts the conclusion, that his "facts fall into beautiful harmony on the single supposition of two antagonistic winds."

He speaks, firstly, "*of the Great westerly wind of the Southern Hemisphere*," secondly, of the "*monsoon-like summer wind on the S.E. Coast*." I quote one passage from this essay, because it fitly introduces what I have to say respecting my own opinions. Speaking of the ultimate causes of the changes of weather, he says :—

"The rain-bearing winds of New South Wales may be connected with the S.E. trades, which, according to common rule, commence a little north of Moreton Bay, but move up and down with the sun. Now, if these winds at any time extended themselves unusually far south, a wet season might be produced along the S.E. coast. This theory finds support, I believe, from the Rev. W. B. Clarke, who has watched and investigated the climate many years.

"Just the same effect would be produced, if any cause acted from the centre of Australia to hinder the advent of sea winds, and project the fiery breath of the sun-heated plains upon the unexpecting coast lands, or during hot winds." And then he adds, with needful caution, "these are mere speculations; to *reason* accurately upon such wide-acting causes, will not be within any person's power till meteorology is quite another thing. Australia is more sea-surrounded than any other large surface of land, and, as it is only over the wide ocean that the winds perform their normal course, meteorology is, perhaps, a simpler problem in this land than anywhere else."

There is a fact also mentioned by Mr. Jevons, which must be borne in mind, that in Australia similar phenomena are apt to prevail almost synchronously over very wide areas. On one occasion, at least, a severe hot wind was felt from Moreton Bay to Port Phillip, a distance of at least 800 miles; rains are equally general at times, and what I have already pointed out in comparing the weather near Sydney with that in Mr. Kennedy's experience in the interior, and what the late Admiral King found in comparing Paramatta with Sir T. L. Mitchell's experience in Tropical Australia, the laws affecting the barometer are nearly constant.

In any discussion on storms in Australia these facts should be borne in mind.

I must now apologise for referring to my own individual efforts in this region of science. Probably, from their distant date and the manner in which they were published, my earlier attempts to interest the Australian community in the laws of storms may have passed somewhat out of view. And it is probable, that at that time Mr. Tebbutt may have been too young to notice such a subject in the columns of a public journal. But, twenty-two years ago, in the month of January, 1842, I published the particulars of a great storm that had just traversed the whole of the eastern portion of New South Wales; and I think it was the first attempt of the kind bearing on the wide area often visited by such atmospherical derangements. As this account attracted some notice, I commenced a series of papers on all the general topics of Meteorology, which were published in the *Sydney Herald* in that year, 1842, in which, among other things, I proposed to show that our Eastern Australian storms revolve from *left* to *right*, and that the conflict of opposing winds is the principal agency employed. I will quote a few remarks to show how far Mr. Jevons's notion of monsoon-like winds and the easterly set of the atmosphere alluded to by Mr. Tebbutt, were anticipated by me 22 years ago, in connection with the South and East Coasts of what was then altogether New South Wales.

"In Bass's Strait a sort of monsoon prevails at certain periods of the year, the wind blowing from the east for a time, though generally from the westward at the other season; and so powerful is the westerly wind that the trees upon Kent's Group point to the east.

"Beyond this, the great westerly circuit winds which travel round the earth have their full influence, affected only by the great southerly currents of air which sometimes—as well as the northern ones—produce derangements in the ordinary phenomena of the winds.

"It may be assumed, therefore, that as easterly and southerly winds are the most prevalent on the east side of the dividing mountains; so on the south-west side of these ranges the prevalent winds inland ought to be from westerly points. Such is the case, for there is direct evidence to show that the south-westerly winds blow over the land from about the Gulf of Alexandria to the Blue Mountains; and north and north-westerly from the N. W. interior to the Blue Mountains,—the least violent of them becoming *west winds* when they reach the mountains, and descending into the seaward country to the east as west winds, yet slightly deflected according to the passes through which they descend.

"The course of both N.W. and S.W winds seems to be defined pretty accurately in the above statements as *circuit winds* meeting somewhere about 147° and 150° E., and about that point turning seawards as west winds, the curves, as it were, touching at the point where a common tangent would stretch away towards the West Coast, and where, according to observation, the trees lean from the west."

One of the points which I proposed to elucidate, was that "some of the southerly gales off the East Coast of Australia come from the north (as they should do), if there be any truth in the laws affirmed for the southern hemisphere."

In allusion to the prevalence of winds on the south coast, I have cited several instances in which, what is general for *South Australia*, the winds veered from *left* to *right*.

In subsequent papers during several years I published observations on the storms along the east coast, and especially on thunder-storms; and of these I had logged down carefully with barometers, thermometers, and time-keeper close at hand, every few minutes or seconds, every change that occurred. Many of these I now produce. Much, however, of the matter I had prepared I sent, at the request of Admiral Erskine and by his hands, to the late Colonel Reid.

My object in alluding to these descriptions is to show that during the time when meteorological observations had not been commenced here as a public duty and the facilities were far less than they are at present, private observers were at work and recorded their discoveries, just as Mr. Tebbutt is now doing with such praise-worthy industry. The appeal to private observers, at the close of his paper, has therefore already had encouragement beforehand.

Another object in referring to my own pursuits, in connection with the study of storms, is to justify the observations which I wish to offer on Mr. Tebbutt's paper,—as proving that I enter upon its discussion with some claim to offer an opinion, inasmuch as I speak as much from observation as from theoretical views. And I may say that I have recorded far more observations on this subject than I have ever had leisure to put in print. What I have been enabled to do in the latter way has, I am happy to know, met the approval of others; and not only has Dr. Leichhardt, but Mr. Piddington of Calcutta has also mentioned my old labours with approval.—*(Sailor's Horn Book*, 2nd *Ed.*, p. 631.)

Mr. Tebbutt commences his paper with a remark relating to what is called Saxby's system. I agree with him in thinking, that whatever merit there may be in proving that derangements of the atmosphere are often coincident with certain epochs of the moon, there is nothing yet sufficiently known to authorise any dicta on the subject and to justify predictions of weather in Australia as deduced from it. Nay, many allotted days have indicated nothing of fulfilment.

Two suggestions occur to me—that if there be any truth in the idea that the passage of the moon over the equator is the sole cause of storms and changes of weather, it must have also been so from the beginning of creation, and no such thing as irregular variations could ever have occurred in the state of season; and that if the moon's influence affect any portions of the earth beneath her attraction, all ought to be equally affected in the same way in succession.

Now, facts certainly not fully coinciding with the theory, we need not look about for arguments to justify it. Noah Webster has a far greater belief in the lunar influence than Mr. Saxby;—but it may be safe to reject it as the main agent with Sir J. Herschel and M. Arago, who both deny it on convictions derived from a consideration of all the phenomena presented to their enquiry. Nevertheless, I would speak with the highest respect of Mr. Saxby who is not, as some imagine, a mere pretender, but a man of science and well versed in all appliances to illustrate his subject: but he appears to me to have ridden his hobby a little too hard, as at present there is not evidence enough to sanction his conclusions.

Admiral Fitz Roy who, Mr. Tebbutt thinks, has established a system which we should also initiate in New South Wales appears to me to have deserved the great credit which is assigned to him as a most diligent and indefatigable observer, and a very practical and useful guide in directing others to observe and utilise their observations. But, it is not yet acknowledged that his system is perfect, or altogether to be depended on. I might quote on this head evidence that cannot be refuted. But I would guard these remarks on the conscientious labours of such men as Fitzroy and Saxby, by saying that I have read very carefully and with much advantage the extensive lessons of the former, and that I name the latter author only in connection with what has been observed in Australasia ; and that it is not in a spirit of presumption that I venture to make the following remarks.

I can, of course, have no objection to the establishment here of Observatories or Meteorological stations to test any of these views. Therefore, my remarks must not be interpreted into a denial of the value of such stations, could we only discover where they could be placed. Together with the late Admiral King, I waited on a late Governor, Sir Charles Fitz Roy, to urge the establishment of an Astronomical Observatory near Sydney, and if our recommendation, backed as it was by Capt. Owen Stanley, R.N., had been attended to, the present Astronomer would have been saved much inconvenience, and the Observatory would have been placed where it ought to have been, on the Silica Range, on the North Shore.

I do not, therefore, object to fresh stations, but, with my views relating to storms, I do not yet see where we could place these stations, so as to become fore-casters of change. And the adoption of these is the main object, as I take it, of Mr. Tebbutt's paper.

In order to show this, I have entered into so much preliminary matter, before I examine the grounds of his argument.

The first point noticed is the easterly tendency of the atmosphere in this hemisphere as well as in the northern, the latter of which is dwelt on by Admiral Fitz Roy, though it must be added that his synchronous curves are very irregular in this respect. .

That the atmosphere partakes of the earth's motion there can be little doubt : I have shown this in my *Herald* essays. The upper wind in all known temperate latitudes is generally from the west, and of examples of this I would mention the dust (with American infusoria) so constantly falling over the Cape de Verd Islands, of which I have been eye witness ; and the volcanic ashes from South American eruptions which, falling upon the trade wind, were carried by it to the westward back again towards Jamaica.

Mr. Tebbutt shows in his diagrams that there is, apparently, an easterly set in this way between the S.W. and N.E. points of a line joining Adelaide and Brisbane. But, whether this is due to the general atmospheric translation from west to east, or to the influence of a compound motion or resolution of forces of a southerly wind and a westerly wind during gales, does not appear.

That gales which come in at Adelaide from the S.W. and blow towards the N.E. in a right line, must by necessity have a seeming tendency to the east, is clear ; but, it may be open to conjecture whether gales which blow fiercely from the south would progress to the eastward, unless the general westerly current could overpower them.

All this is on the supposition that such gales are *right-lined*, It is doubtful, however, whether they are not actually circular. and if it be so (and there can be no comparison as to the changes of wind following the same order at Sydney as well as at Adelaide and Brisbane, unless they are) the easterly progression must be due to some other cause.

I will state what I believe the cause to be.

In dealing with storms in Australia we must well weigh all the local conditions. Surrounded by wide oceans its coasts are exposed to the prevailing ocean winds. Along the east coast, at a moderate distance from it, runs a barrier of high land from 3,000 to 7,200 feet in elevation, separating the eastern coast from the low interior, the southern part of which is exposed to the S.W.,—say about Adelaide.

The tendency of the drainage of the northern part of the mountain barrier is (as shown by the Darling) in the same N.E. and S.W. line of which, in reversed direction, storms are assumed to travel from Adelaide to Brisbane.

Now, it is reasonable to assume, that unless a storm has a vertical thickness greater than the height of the Cordillera it cannot cross it ; and, therefore, only such storms as are more than from 3,000 to 7,200 feet thick can cross the mountains, even if their area be wide enough : and thus many storms bringing heavy rains from S.W. never cross to the eastward at all, but travel along the western slopes of the Cordillera, leaving all the eastward dry and only slightly affected by other atmospherical conditions consequent on the passage of the eastward edge of the gale.

Similarly, if gales come in from the N.E., unless they are vertically thick enough, they also travel southwardly along the eastern slopes of the Cordillera, and never water the western interior.

I have collected examples of numerous gales which, although violent along the coast and up to the slope of the mountains, deluging the sea board with rain, have only been recognised at Bathurst or Wellington by a slight shower or Scotch mist, or a gently disturbed atmosphere. Such was the case during some of our late tempestuous weather; for, whilst the Coast was under floods, patches of the western country were suffering from drought, being cut off by the high lands from access of the easterly winds.

Mr. Tebbutt's mention of *scud* at Windsor when there is a storm at Sydney, and of only rare westerly gales at the former place, is thus to be explained. The *scud* being probably only evaporated moisture is borne on the very top of a thin gale; and he, no doubt, rightly admits such local influences from the coasts and mountains.

Mr. Tebbutt quotes the case of the storm of 25th and 26th October, 1863, showing that the same changes of wind and barometrical oscillations occurred between Adelaide and Windsor at an interval of 26 hours, and about a day later at Brisbane.

Now, these successive changes prove that that gale was a Cyclone,—having probably a diameter of about 250 miles, and a mean progress of about 24 miles per hour (which is in remarkable agreement with the rate of numerous great East Pacific storms and cyclones), the eastern edge of which grazed and came over the summit of the Cordillera where it was about 4000 feet above the sea; the thickness of the storm being about 5000 feet, which is the height, as obtained by measurement by myself, of very many of the gales in this colony. Mr. Redfield and Mr. Piddington assume a thickness of a mile (280 feet more) for several known cyclones.

On the east coast the gales appear to me to be at certain seasons of an equally cyclonic character. And Mr. Tebbutt quite co-incides in opinion with me as to the nature of those gales, as resulting from the combined forces of polar aerial currents and the set of the warm ocean current from the N.E., which has, I am persuaded, a great deal to do with the rains which have so often fallen upon our shores,—and especially during the late terrible season of floods.

I watched the state of the ocean during several of our late gales. It was everywhere, within reach of my sight, smoking with fog which, drifting in with the rain from the surface of the ocean current, caused that superabundant moisture which was twice observed on smooth walls and metallic surfaces that streamed with it, owing to the sudden condensation of the warm vapour. The high thermometer and the increase of Ozone which is characteristic of *sea* winds, both show how much those periods were affected by the influence of equatorial currents.

A storm of striking features, in February, 1863, was noticed by Mr. Tebbutt and registered in the *Empire*, which showed a progression to southwards.

Very little was wanting to the collected data, to give a complete history of that storm. Fortunately, I was at the time in a position to supplement Mr. Tebbutt's observations. I was then to the westward of the Bell River,—about 260 or 270 miles W. by N. of Windsor, and about 25 miles from the head of the Bogan. Having a barometer and thermometer with me, I was enabled to notice what took place; and one remarkable fact preceding the gale was, that we had the regular sea breeze on the evening before, which in all probability came in through a distance of 300 miles from the neighbourhood of Port Macquarie. I have frequently felt the sea breeze under the Liverpool Range. As there is no land much higher than 4000 feet between the two points, the sea breeze must at least have had about the same vertical thickness. In Maneero I have found it generally not more than that. As I was observing the western edge of the gale, the diameter of it must have been at least about 300 miles.

Another gale—that of April and May, 1864—is noticed by Mr. Tebbutt; and by the periods of minimum barometrical pressure and changes of wind, this was a gale from the northward.

Now, I would call attention to a fact I alluded to when I began, the wide area over which ordinarily the atmospherical phenomena are persistent.

When my late friend Mr. Kennedy was exploring the Barcoo and desert country about it and the Warrego, I carried on at St. Leonard's simultaneous observations, as I did when he was in York Peninsula. On the former occasion there was the most marked agreement with my own observations and those made by Mr. Kennedy. Eight hundred miles to the N.W.—especially on 28th–31st August, 1847—Kennedy had strong E. and N.E. winds on the desert of the Barcoo; whilst on the 26–27–28th, a heavy gale was blowing along the coast of Tasmania, and strong N.E. to N. winds blew at Sydney. The winds shifted from N.E. to S. in the latter part of September, 1847, both at Brisbane and on the Barcoo.

Again on 13th October, squalls and thunderstorms occurred simultaneously at Sydney and on the lower part of the Barcoo.

Such coincidences as these are, however, not always due to progressing gales. I suspect, from having made hundreds of similar observations, that separate storms often occur simultaneously, or nearly so, over wide regions, as if the moving causes were some kinds of electric shock propagated from a distance and successively charging (at minute intervals) areas of atmosphere in a similar condition. If Admiral Fitz Roy's dictum is true, that one storm cannot maintain itself for more than four days, it is impossible to account for the facts often observed of weeks of stormy weather without coming to some such conclusion as I long ago adopted, and which I am glad to see strengthened by Admiral Fitz Roy's opinion.

During thundery weather, I have frequently noticed the fact that thunderstorms are simultaneous, or nearly so, at Bathurst and Sydney; and if these storms be so propagated or connected, why not other kinds of storms, such as gales of wind and cyclones?

I will not now dwell further on this, but state distinctly that in my humble opinion Mr. Tebbutt rightly infers, not alone from the storms of 1861 cited by him, that such storms are occasioned by two currents.

I state unreservedly, and I can show it by phenomena of storms noted down, as in the example I now produce, that there are always two winds at work in all great derangements of the atmosphere in Australia.

A heavy thunderstorm from S.W. is always preceded by a N.E. wind, and if such a wind in summer blows fresh after sundown, in 9 times out of 10 the next day will exhibit thunder.

So, preceding the gales of 6th and 9th August, 1861, I noticed the upper clouds progressing from the westward, and the surface wind from westward also,—when, quietly at first, a body of clouds which had formed in the east began to move westwardly, and the east wind wedged itself in between the two westerly strata, and after a struggle of about 3 hours obtained the mastery.

A similar phenomenon was observed by me before the cyclone of 11-12th June last, and that of June, 1857. So constant is the struggle between the polar and equatorial winds, that I have never missed it when I have looked for it, at the commencement and close of a hot wind. The hot wind frequently *commences at Sydney from seaward at N.E., and ends at S.W. or S.;* clouds, for hours preceding the change, gathering in S.W. by condensation of the vapour suspended by the N.W. wind through the contact with the S. wind. The N.E. wind *hot* is the hot N.W. current deflected by the N.E.

Furthermore, I have stood out in a furious hot wind for hours watching the wind vane, which is then oscillating between S.W. and N.W.; and if any one will but place an aneroid on his table, under his eye, during one of our summer thunderstorms, he will observe the index oscillating to and fro, as the pressures occasioned by the two winds engaged in conflict alter according as they gain or lose strength by turns.

Taking then all these facts into consideration, I consider it demonstrated that there are always two winds engaged in all our storms.

Now, to utilise the observations we have by forecasting coming storms, seems to be the object of Mr. Tebbutt's paper. I agree with him, that to do this we must have more observers, and perhaps more correct ones than we have at present.

Many of the published notes in the daily papers are useless, from occasional typographical errors,—and errors of observation. I have been in the habit of checking the figures given by the observers, which, when the heights of the places of observation are known, is the easiest thing possible. If the readings are correct, the difference calculated between any two places ought to agree within a few feet. I have occasionally found 50 and 60 feet of difference on different days, which shows that there must be errors in reading or recording the observations. But if we had fresh troops of observers, where shall we place them?

If our East coast storms come in from the N.E. or S.E., they must hit the coast at some point or other, and it does not at all follow that they must necessarily travel upwards or downwards. Sometimes they hit the coast after *recurving*, and get doubled up by recoil from the mountains, and then, after a short struggle, in which the wind backs (and of course blows) as it did in the heavy gale of the 1st July last, return after the fashion of circles made by a stone thrown into water, which circles run contrary when they impinge on an obstacle.

At other times, the whole coast, as during the late season, from Cape York to Cape Howe, is similarly affected in succession or contemporaneously, and in such a case, Coast stations might give warning. But, it is very doubtful whether S.W. gales running up the back of the Cordillera, could be so watched and turned to account.

Nevertheless, as information would be obtained, which, if to be relied on, is always valuable, the establishment of fresh stations for observation would be desirable.

But, I think a more desirable object would be the passing of *a law* by the legislature, *rendering it imperative on masters of ships arriving from abroad, or belonging to our coasting marine, to place copies of their logs in the hands of the Astronomer.* We often read of *hurricanes* off our coasts, such being the character assigned by masters of small craft to a blow of wind which a ship of 1000 tons would consider as nothing. On the other hand, we should obtain data in connection with N.E. gales, by vessels coming from the Islands, and with E. gales, by passages to and from New Zealand, which would be invaluable to persons engaged in deciphering the elements of Australasian storms, and in turning them to account.

On the Cave Temples of India,
By Dr. Berncastle.

BEFORE proceeding to a description of the different cave temples I have visited in India, a brief account of the supposed religious origin, uses, and classification of those temples generally, will serve to elucidate the subject, and explain the names I shall have to apply to them throughout.

The old temples of India have long claimed from the antiquary a large share of attention, not only on account of the peculiarity of their construction, but also because the period of their erection appears in almost every case to be involved in the deepest obscurity. The hypogæa, or subterraneous cavern structures, concerning which I have at present to speak, are perhaps the most remarkable monuments of human labour and perseverance to be met with in Asia. Many of them contain statues of colossal dimensions, and their walls are covered over with elaborate embellishments of the most fanciful description. The ancient chronologers of India have not assisted us in revealing the antiquity of these wonderful mountain cave temples, but their statements and writings only serve yet further to perplex the confused accounts that have been handed down from past ages, and to make our conjectures more uncertain and unsatisfactory. It may appear, at first sight, singular that a people so skilful in the fine arts as the inhabitants of Hindostan, should have selected such lonely and uncouth places for the site of their idol temples. Islands, subterraneous caves, and almost inaccessible mountains appear to have been their favourite localities for the erection of buildings which, as we cannot doubt, were intended as places for the daily celebration of their peculiar worship. It is, however, to be considered that, from time immemorial, India has been a prey to marauding chiefs and lawless usurpers, who robbed, desolated, and destroyed almost every important place which they visited in their frequently-recurring predatory excursions. Many of the idols set up in these temples during the hours of devotion were thought to be of great value, and it is not uncommon even now to see them formed of gold or silver, having for eyes diamonds and other precious stones. I saw an instance of this in visiting the hill temple of Parbutty, near Poona, held in high veneration by the natives, and supported by the Government from motives of policy. A blind Brahmin in charge opened with his key the iron doors of the corner pagodas, each one containing a god in white marble. I was not allowed to approach the middle temple, but a light was procured and held against the door to enable me to see inside the group of the god Seva, in solid silver, Gunputty his wife, and Parbutty the child, both in solid gold. Their eyes are made of diamonds and rubies of great price, which I saw sparkling in the dark. They are robed in white dresses, put on by Brahmins, who are the only persons allowed ever to enter their sanctuary. The three idols are valued at 60,000 rupees. Twenty-five Brahmin priests of high caste are paid by the Company a sum of 18,000 rupees a year to live in the temple and perform the rites. A guard of sepoys is furnished by the Government for the protection of these idols. As these idols offered great temptations to the plunderer, it was necessary, therefore, in order to carry on the ceremonies inculcated in the sacred Vedoo, and at the same time to preserve the riches of the temple from the spoiler's hand, that these buildings should be erected in places presenting great natural advantages in the way of security. The officiating priests resided upon the spot, in rooms set apart for their accommodation; and the deluded worshippers who came, often laden with offerings, to pray, cared little for distance, or for the difficulties of the road; seeing that the more dangers they encountered in these their pious journeyings, the more acceptable they believed their service to be. Of the licentious character of the rites celebrated in these Pagan temples, it is needless here to speak. They have passed away.

It has been remarked by travellers in ancient and modern Egypt, that there is a striking resemblance known to subsist between the usages, the superstitions, the arts, and the mythology of the ancient inhabitants of Western India, to those of the first settlers on the Upper Nile. The temples of Nubia, for example, exhibit the same features, whether as to style of architecture or the form of worship to which they were devoted, with the similar buildings which have recently been examined in the neighbourhood of Bombay.

In both cases they consist of vast excavations hewn out in the solid body of a hill or mountain, and are decorated with huge figures which indicate the same powers of nature, or serve as emblems to denote the same qualities in the ruling spirits of the universe. As a further proof of this hypothesis, we are informed that the Sepoys who joined the British army in Egypt, under Lord Hutchinson, imagined that they found their own temples in the ruin of Dendera, and were greatly exasperated at the natives for their neglect of the ancient deities whose images are still preserved. So strongly indeed were they impressed with this identity, that they proceeded to perform their devotions with all the ceremonies practiced in their land. There is a resemblance, too, in the minor instruments of their superstition—the lotus, the lingam, and the serpent—which can hardly be regarded as accidental; but it is no doubt in the immense extent, the gigantic plan, the vast conception which appears in all their sacred buildings, that we most readily discover the influence of the same lofty genius, and the endeavour to accomplish the same mighty object. The excavated temples of Guerfeh Hassan, for instance, remind every traveller of the cave of Elephanta. The resemblance, indeed, is singularly striking, as are, in fact, all the leading principles of Egyptian architecture, and that of the Hindoos. By whom and by what means these wonderful efforts have been accomplished is a mystery sunk too deep in the abyss of time ever to be revealed.

Mr. Fergusson, who has devoted more time to their investigation than most travellers or antiquarians, with the exception of Mr. Prinsep and Dr. Bird, has arrived at the following conclusions with regard to the antiquity of the monuments; that the oldest relics of whose existence he is aware are the Laths, bearing inscriptions of Asoka, dating from the middle of the third century B.C., and that he is not aware of the existence of any cave anterior to, or even coeval with these, nor of any structural building whose date can reach so high as the first centuries of our era. He also states that it appears quite evident that the Buddhists were the earliest cave-diggers, and that it is not difficult to trace the connection of the whole series from " the earliest abode of Buddha ascetics " at Nagarjuni, to the Kylas at Ellora. As far as our knowledge of the cave temples of India extends, the whole may be classified under the following heads :—

First,—Vihara, or Monastery Caves.—1st, The first subdivision of this class consists of natural caverns, or caves, slightly improved by art; they are, as might be assumed, the most ancient, and are only found appropriated to religious purposes in the older series of Behar and Cuttack ; and though some are found among the western caves, their existence there appears to be quite accidental.

The second subdivision consists of a verandah opening behind into cells for the abode of the priests, but without sanctuaries or images of any sort.

In the third subdivision of Vihara caves, the last arrangement is further extended by the enlargement of the hall, and the consequent necessity of its centre being supported by pillars ; and in this division, besides the cells that surround the hall, there is always a deep recess facing the entrance, in which is generally placed a statue of Buddha, with his usual attendants—thus fitting the cave to become not only an abode for the priests, but also a place of worship.

To this division belong by far the greatest number of Buddhist excavations. The most splendid of these are those of Ajunta, though the Dherwarra, at Ellora, is also fine ; and there are also some good specimens at Salsette and Junir.

The second class consists of Buddhist Chaitya Caves. These are the temples, or, if I may use the expression, the churches of the series, and one or more of them is attached to every set of caves in the west of India, though none exist in the eastern side.

Unlike the Viharas, the plan and arrangement of all these caves is exactly the same ; and, though the details and sculpture vary with the age in which they were executed, some strong religious feeling seems to have attached the Buddhists to one particular form for their places of worship.

In the Viharas we can trace the progress from the simple cavern to the perfect monastery; but these Chaitya caves seem at once to have sprung to perfection, and the Karli cave, which is the most perfect, is also considered the oldest in India.

All these caves consist of an external porch, or music gallery, an internal gallery over the entrance, a centre aisle, which I will call the nave (from its resemblance to what bears that name in our churches), which is always at least twice the length of its breadth, and is roofed with a plain waggon-vault; to this is added a semi-dome, terminating the nave, under the centre of which always stands a Dagoba, or chaitya.

A narrow aisle always surrounds the whole interior, separated from the nave by a range of massive columns. The aisle is generally flat roofed, though sometimes, in the earlier examples, it is covered by a semi-vault.

In the oldest temples the Dagoba consists of a plain circular drum, surmounted by a hemispherical dome crowned by a Tee, which supported the umbrella of state. In the earlier examples this was in wood, and as a general rule, it may be asserted, that in these all the parts that would be constructed in wood in a structural building, are in wood in the caves; but in the more modern caves all those parts, such as the music gallery outside, the ribs of the roof, the ornaments of the Dagoba, the umbrella of state, &c., are repeated in the rock, though the same forms are preserved. These two classes comprehend all the Buddhist caves in India.

The third class consists of Brahminical caves, properly so called. In form, many of them are copies of, and all a good deal resemble the Buddhist Vihara, so much so as at first sight to lead to the supposition that they are appropriations of Buddhist caves to Brahminical purposes. On a more intimate acquaintance, however, with them, many points of distinction are observed. The arrangement of the pillars, and the position of the sanctuary, is in no instance the same as in a Vihara. They are never surrounded by cells, as all Viharas are, and their walls are invariably covered, or meant to be, with sculpture; while the Viharas are almost as invariably decorated by painting, except the sanctuary. The subjects of the sculpture, of course, always set the question at rest.

The finest specimens of this class are at Ellora and Elephanta; also on the island of Salsette. These two last I have visited and described. I have also described the Buddhist temple of Karli, and was the first writer who gave a description of the cave temple of Bambourda, near Poona, which, although differing from any other I have seen, I believe should be classed amongst the third, or Brahminical order. Dr. Bird told me that they were first described by a Danish traveller, in the transactions of the Asiatic Society, in 1853; but he was not aware that my account was published in my work in 1850.

I shall now attempt to describe the rock-cut temples in the order in which I visited them, beginning with the most celebrated—those of Elephanta, next Kannari, then Karli, and lastly, Bambourda. Elephanta, called by the natives Gara-pori, is an island seven miles from Bombay and five from the Mahratta shore. It is six miles in circumference, and is composed of two hills, with a valley between, at the foot of which, as you land, you see just above the shore on your right an elephant coarsely cut out in stone, of the natural size and colour, standing on a platform of stones, which has given the name to the island.

Ascending an easy slant, about half way up the hill, you come to the opening or portal of a large cavern, hewn out of a solid rock, into a magnificent temple; for such it may well be termed, considering the immense labour involved in such an excavation, an attempt that appears far more bold than that of the pyramids of Egypt. There is a fair entrance into this subterraneous temple, which is an oblong square, in length 135 feet by 120 broad. The floor not being level, the height varies from fifteen to eighteen feet. The roof was supported by twenty-six pillars and eight pilasters, disposed in four rows; but several of the pillars are broken. Each column stands upon a square pedestal, and is fluted; but instead of being cylindrical, is gradually enlarged towards the middle.

Above the tops of the columns a kind of ridge has been cut, to resemble a beam about twelve inches square, and this is richly carved. Along the sides of the temple are cut between forty and fifty colossal figures, in height from twelve to fifteen feet, none of them being entirely detached from the wall. Some of these figures have on their heads a kind of helmet; others wear crowns, with rich devices; and others again are without any other covering than curled and flowing hair. Some of them have four, and others six hands, holding sceptres, shields, symbols of justice, ensigns of religion, weapons of war, and trophies of peace. On the South side, facing the entrance, is an enormous bust with three faces, representing the triple deity, the Hindoo Trimurti or Trinity of "Brahma, Vishnu, and Siva." Brahma, the creator, occupies the centre position. This face measures five feet in length, the width from the ear to the middle of the nose is three feet, the width of the whole figure is near twenty feet. On the right is the preserver, Vishnu, holding a Lotus; and Siva, the destroyer, is on the left, having in his hand a cobra capella, or hooded snake, and on his cap a human skull. To the left of this bust, amid a group of uncouth figures, is one, a female form, to which the name of Amazon has been given, from the fact of its being without the right breast. This figure has four arms. The right fore-arm rests upon the head of a bull; the left fore-arm hangs down, and once contained something which is now mutilated and undistinguishable. The hand of the right arm grasps a cobra capella, and that of the hinder left arm holds a shield.

At the east end is a passage, about eighteen feet long, terminating in an open space that admits the light through a sort of shaft-hole in the rock, and containing a delicious spring of the finest water to be found in this part of India. As Bombay has long been proverbial for the badness of its water, the table of the Governor is supplied from this spring, and many who are about to sail from the country lay in a few dozens of it for the voyage, as it keeps well. The approach to this place is guarded by four figures, fourteen feet high, beautifully executed, and more perfect than any to be found in this temple.

At the west end, and almost opposite the passage that leads to the well, is a room or recess of about twenty feet square, having in the centre of it an altar, upon which are placed symbols of a worship "offensive to European notions of delicacy." The entrance to this recess is also guarded by eight naked figures, each fourteen feet high, sculptured in a manner which shows that the people by whom they were executed must have made considerable progress in the statuary's art. The whole of this portion of the excavation is in a very ruinous condition, and the roof appears to be fast sinking in. The rains being permitted to lodge within the whole of the temples four months out of the twelve does much to hasten the destruction of those interesting monuments. When the Portuguese became masters of this part of India and visited this island, they were so horrified by the character of this heathen temple that they ordered a piece of heavily loaded cannon to be planted opposite the entrance, with the hope of destroying the principal pillars that support the roof, and burying the cave in the ruins of the mountain above it.

Still further to the right, is the entrance to a subterraneous passage, with deep clear water. A friend of mine, prompted by curiosity, once swam some hundred feet up this passage with a lighted candle, but could not see to the end of the excavation. Snakes and other reptiles are often met with in some of these dark recesses, and the cavern itself is not visitable after the rains, until the ground has had time to dry into complete hardness. Different writers, according to their general notions on the subject of Indian antiquities, have adopted very different opinions relative to the age of this magnificent excavation; some referring it to the most remote age; others attributing it to a much more recent period. Mr. Fergusson alludes to the general similarity of these caves to those of Ellora, with which he has no doubt they are contemporary; indeed there is a degree of similarity between the two series, which is singular in structures so distant, and which can only be accounted for by their being undertaken at the same time, and probably under the same direction.

Colonel Tod considers that the noblest remains of sacred architecture, throughout Western India, are of Boodh or Jain origin, and assigns to the first temple of Dwarka, now sacred to Krishna, an antiquity of 1200 years before Christ.

The cave temples of Kanari, in the island of Salsette, are twenty-two miles from Bombay, and four beyond the village of Vehar; from which village, proceeding through a thick jungle, along the edge of deep gullies, you reach the village of Tulsi, in the immediate vicinity of the caves.

The Kanari Caves are excavated on the west and north faces of a round hill connected with the principal ranges, in the midst of wild and most picturesque scenery. They consist of one large Chaitya cave, and numerous small Viharas, all temples of Buddha. The largest is very like the temple of Karli in form, but smaller and not so highly finished. The portico in front contains two gigantic figures of a male and female, 25 feet high, and the walls are covered with smaller statues and inscriptions, similar to those of Karli. There have been ribs of teak to support the arched roof, of which few now remain. On each side of the nave is a row of fifteen octagonal pillars, each being surmounted by a group of two elephants carrying a male and a female, in rather a dilapidated state. At the end of the temple is a large stone Dagoba, or altar, which appears once to have been crowned with the teak-made umbrella that is now missing. The umbrella is peculiar to all the temples of Buddhist worship, and supposed to cover relics of Buddha. This cave is 90 feet long by 40 in breadth, and about the same height. Clusters of large bats are seen hanging from the roof, which is covered with them. I shot one for the purpose of examining it, and found it to be similar to the species called flying foxes.

The smaller caves are situated in the hill behind the large one, forming six stories, one above the other, giving the hill almost the appearance of a honeycomb. At the entrance of each cave is a deep stone cistern, containing beautiful clear water, and on each side of the walls is a carving of a sort of hieroglyphic figure, an inch deep, and about two feet long.

Descending southwards from this elevation are several deep pits, built up with burnt bricks, probably the burial-places of those who inhabited the caves.

Dr. Bird, in speaking of Kanari, says:—" The large excavation is further distinguished by having in front of it, on a ledge of the mountain, several small *mounds*, or burying-places of the '*rahats*,' or saints, who were tenants of the caves. One of them I opened in 1839, and found two copper urns containing human ashes. In one of the urns was a small gold box, containing fragments of white cotton rag, with a pearl, a ruby, and some small pieces of gold; in the other was a silver box with ashes."

"It is not only the numerous caves," observes Lord Valentine, "that give an idea of what the population of this barren rock must once have been, but the tanks, the terraces, and the flights of steps which lead from one part to another. Yet now, not a human footstep is to be heard, except when the curiosity of a traveller leads him to pay a hasty visit to the ruined habitations of those whose very name has passed away, and whose cultivated fields are become an almost impassable jungle, the haunt of tigers, and the seat of pestilence and desolation."

One thing that struck me as most singular, is the extraordinary manner in which the inscriptions on these temples is preserved, the characters being as distinct as if they were quite recently engraved.

The next inscription, over a water reservoir of one of the small caves of Kanari, has been rendered thus by the *savants* in Oriental antiquities :—"This tank is the pious work of Sulisadata (in obedience to) the word of the radical golden originator of all things, the prophet of friendship."

The inscriptions on these temples, they say, are in a language neither pure Pali nor Sanscrit, though approaching sufficiently near either to be intelligible through their medium. The character in which it is written differs but little from that of inscriptions on Asoka pillars, which was in use we know during the third century B.C. ; to this class belong Karli, Kanari, Aurungabad, Nassik, Junir, Ellora.

About half way between Poona and Bombay, in the Ghaut mountains, on the right-hand side of the valley as you proceed towards the sea, and a mile from the village of Karli, is situated the great cave temple of Karli, without exception the largest and finest Chaitya cave in India, and fortunately also the best preserved. It is the finest specimen of a Buddha cathedral which can be met with. It is excavated in "Amygdaloid trap," and is vaulted. As you ascend the hill by a steep tortuous path over rocks and through jungle, the entrance to the temple (impossible to find without a guide,) bursts suddenly upon the sight. Passing under a gateway, over which is erected a square stone room containing drums, trumpets, gongs, and bells, for the performance of sacred music during festivals, a dozen men being paid by the company for that purpose; you have on the right a pagoda, in which I saw an old faqueer, who had lost all his fingers from disease. In front of this is a lofty portico, supported at the entrance by two high octagonal pillars. The walls are all covered with sculptures of men and women, as large as life; and on each side project the trunks, heads, and fore-legs of three elephants, of great size, and well executed, carved, like all the rest, out of the solid rock; two of the trunks only remain entire. Several inscriptions in character and language unknown, one of which I copied on the spot, appear on the pillars, and on different parts of the portico; they are as legible as if done a few years ago. From the portico, a small door leads at once into the grand cave, which at first appears almost like magic, and surpasses anything I had ever imagined. Elephanta and Kanari cannot compare with it, and probably only those of Ellora may be superior.

The general outline resembles an old Gothic cathedral. On each side is a row of eighteen pillars, supporting an arched roof, lined with ribs of teak wood. The pillars are octagonal, with round bases. The first fifteen are surmounted by two elephants, each having on his back a male and female figure, with their arms entwined. On the other side of the Elephant, out of sight, are two horses couchant, which would have escaped my observation, had not a native called me behind the pillar, where it is almost dark, to point them out. The height of the temple is about fifty feet, its length 120, and extreme breadth forty-eight feet. The nave between each row of pillars is just twenty-four feet, leaving twelve feet for the aisles on either side, the passage along which is very dark. At the farther extremity is a large solid stone structure, round, and the upper part shaped like a dome, the circumference of which is forty feet. This dome is surmounted with a pedestal, narrow at the base, and becoming gradually broader like an inverted pyramid. In this is fixed a large open umbrella, made of strong teak wood, reaching very nearly to the roof. This sort of altar is called a "Dagoba," and is found in most all the cave temples of Buddhist origin. Innumerable large bats are hanging from the roof, or flying about, and a species of squirrel, with vertical black and grey stripes, is continually running along the walls, producing a very lively effect. This place being excavated out of the solid rock, from which also are formed the pillars, sculptures, and dagoba, the whole temple may be considered as one single solid structure, with the exception of the teak umbrella.

. A few yards to the left of the portico are some wells of clear water, one of which runs under a subterraneous passage, and near them are large square excavations like rooms, one above the other, an old ladder being the only means of ascending to the upper one. In each of these are about twenty little dark rooms placed all around, each having a stone seat. These appear to have been the separate chambers of the priests belonging to the temple. Here everything is plain, without sculpture or inscription. This is the Vihara, or monastery caves that appear to be attached as at Kanari to the cathedral-like excavation of Buddha worship.

Passing through Karli, on my return from Poona I paid a second visit to the caves to take a few sketches, and was not a little astonished to find them filled with swarms of people, large families being encamped in every corner, and outside all around, where stalls for the sale of fruit and sweetmeats were erected, giving the spot the appearance of a great fair. I found on enquiry that all this concourse of people was assembled to celebrate the Hindoo fetes of Jattera, which last a fortnight from the 6th of April, full moon, and that they were principally of the Coolie tribe who came there on an annual pilgrimage from all parts of the Concan, Canari, and the Malabar coast. Upwards of 1500 sheep had been killed in the caves the day before, as a sacrifice to the gods, which accounted for the number of fresh raw sheepskins I saw drying on the rocks and surrounding trees in all directions. On hearing this I congratulated myself on being able to obtain a meal of fresh mutton at the bungalow, but was informed by the Portuguese butler that not for any consideration could a slice be had from the natives, this being a religious ceremony that entitled none but themselves to partake of the sacrificial viands.

A sirdar of the Rajah of Sattara having favoured me with the loan of an elephant, I rode out on it to the cave temple of Bambourda, a mile from Poona, and had a very narrow chance of not discovering it. I was close to the spot, surrounded by natives, but they could not understand what I wanted. At last a young lad guessed it, and in a few minutes, after crossing some rocky ground, he led me to the entrance of the cave, which is below the surface of the earth, and might easily be passed by as a small gravel pit. It has not long been discovered, and never described until this account was written. It differs entirely from any other cave I have seen, and I should think is of much less antiquity than the other ones. In an open space in front is a large dome, supported by twelve square pillars, without any carvings, having in the middle four pillars, covered by a square top. The entrance to the temple is between two large lions couchant, of granite, which are the only evidences of sculpture of any sort contained in it. The roof is quite flat and low, supported by five rows of eight plain square pillars in each. At the end an opening leads into two separate rooms, in the middle of which are stone Dagobas. I saw no well nor cistern here, but on the right at the entrance is a deep square hole, which seems to have contained water.

My guide said that this cave extended several miles underground by a subterraneous passage, having another entrance on a hill three miles off and directly opposite, whch he pointed out; that it had been blocked up and reduced to its present size to keep out tigers and other wild beasts, to which it afforded a safe retreat. I found at the extreme end a modern wall, plastered over, that seemed to bear out what he said, and had it not been late, would have gone across to the opposite hill to verify the fact: Few people at Poona had seen this cave or were aware of its existence.

My desire for exploring cave temples having become known in camp, Captain Jacob, well informed on Indian antiquities, told me before I started from Poona, that if at Kurkala, five miles beyond Worgaum, I took the road to the left, I should reach the caves of Birsa, five miles off, but in the direction of the fort of Lohagurh, which I intended to visit on my return. All the villagers assembled around me at Kurkala assured me that it was on the right hand side, instead of the left as I had been told, pointing to a hill some miles distant, which I reached with great difficulty, across a country covered with rocks, and my suspicions were too well confirmed, when, after toiling for hours under a burning sun, I entered on the top of the hill, a small square pagoda filled with bells and peacock's feathers, such as I had passed on the road every day.

This mistake arose from my not knowing the Mahratta word for CAVE TEMPLE, and therefore the impossibility of making the simple-minded natives dream of what I was seeking with so much labour and, in this case, useless toil and disappointment.

I have since ascertained, beyond doubt, that these caves exist where Captain Jacob pointed them out, to the left of the main road—mention being made of them in " Grant Duff's History of the Mahrattas."

On Snake-bites and their Antidotes,

By DR. BERNCASTLE.

A few general remarks on the various Snakes of Australia will, I presume, be interesting to those who are exposed to the danger of them, and may also be a guide to the person bitten, as to the urgency of the case, and necessity for more or less active treatment.

The Snakes of Australia may, for our purpose, be divided into two distinct classes, the venomous and the non-venomous. The venomous most often met with are here named and classed in the order of their SUPPOSED virulence :—

The Deaf Adder.
The brown-banded Snake with yellow belly.
The brown Snake.
The black Snake.

The whip Snake.
The lead-coloured Snake.
Various other Snakes, according to particular locality.
Nearly all varieties of Sea-Snakes.

The non-venomous are:—

The carpet Snake.
The diamond Snake.
The green Tree-Snake.
The brown Tree-Snake, &c.

These are quite harmless, and like the Boa-Constrictor, capture their prey alive, and gradually devour it. The two first are nocturnal in their habits, and so is the prey they live upon. The pupil of the eye is linear, like a cat's, and having no poison fangs, their bite cannot be dangerous, so that no further observations on them will be required.

As a general rule, all snakes of a dirty, livid colour, with the fissure of the jaws straight, instead of curved, and flat head, may be looked upon as poisonous, and in a greater degree as these features are more or less present—the Deaf Adder and brown-banded Snake being very good illustrations of this rule, as they answer in a high degree to the above leading features, and are, as is well known, the most deadly of all our snakes. There are however many bright-coloured Snakes in this and other countries highly dangerous, as well as the livid ones. The real proof, however, of a venomous snake, consists in the poison fangs, one of which is situated on each side of the upper jaw, hidden in the fold of the gum, and can be seen when the animal is irritated, like a very sharp-pointed tooth, slightly curved backwards; it is traversed by a grooved canal in the tooth, leading from a gland placed under the eye, where the poison is constantly secreted for use; and when the snake intends to bite, the poison glands, compressed by muscular action, impel the poison into the excretory canal, which conducts it through the fangs, from which it is instilled into the punctured wounds they have made. The longer the snake retains his hold, the more dangerous will the bite prove, as he has been able by continued compression of the apparatus, to squeeze more poison into the wound than by a superficial sudden bite; there may also be found only one puncture instead of two, if the bite has been given sideways, one fang only having entered the part, which might lessen the danger.

One great peculiarity in all the Australian Snakes is, as compared with the venomous Snakes of other countries, the remarkably small size and shortness of their poison fangs, seldom exceeding one-sixth of an inch, and often much less, with proportionate small calibre; which fact being well borne in mind will assist materially in diminishing the danger, and simplifying the treatment as regards the excision of the bitten part, which, being never deep, does not require those frightful mutilations we often hear of in the country, with the addition of gunpowder set alight on the wound, fingers chopped off, and other useless acts, which a knowledge of the anatomy of the apparatus will prove at once to be quite uncalled for, as the cutting out of a piece of flesh as large as a sixpence, well raised up with the forceps, will necessarily include any part that the fangs could have reached.

It is widely different with the Snakes of tropical countries, whose fangs are often much thicker and longer; for instance, the Puff-Adder of South Africa, of which I have seen the fangs half an inch long, and thick in proportion. The Rattle-Snake, and Cobra di Capello, have much larger fangs than the Australian Snakes, their bite being also much more fatal. The Deaf-Adder is peculiar in having larger fangs than any other Australian Snake, and has something at the end of its tail like a sting, about a quarter of an inch long, similar to a thorn, which it can erect at will. There is a popular error very prevalent that when it bites it stings simultaneously with its tail, which it appears to do by its wriggling motion, but this caudal termination has been examined by the microscope and found to be imperforate; it only occurs in the old males, and, in spite of the terrors it has been invested with, must be considered as a harmless appendage of this otherwise most deadly reptile.

Sea Snakes are known by their flattened tail, and are found in abundance in the Eastern Seas, near the shore. I caught one on the Malabar coast, with which the sea was swarming, about ten miles from land: it was rather like the brown-banded Snake, with yellow belly, three feet long, with flat tail; the poison fangs were distinct, and I pronounced it venomous to those who were handling it incautiously. Persons in ships having often an idea that they are something like eels, have, more than once, paid the penalty of such a mistake with their life. I knew of two instances in India occurring, one to a surgeon of a man-of-war at Madras, and one to a major returning home.

The fangs of all snakes, when extracted or broken off, rendering them harmless for the time, are re-produced to any extent after a few weeks, each reptile being provided with a number of rudimentary fangs, ready to re-place the lost ones.

The ignorance of this fact has been fatal to snake-charmers in India, who exhibit the Cobra in the streets without any danger, and have all at once died from its bite, when least suspecting it. Underwood, of Melbourne, probably made the same mistake. In the present state of our knowledge, there is no such thing as a distinct certain antidote for a snake bite, but there may be included under the head of antidotes, a system of medical and surgical treatment, which, if promptly and carefully applied, will, I have no hesitation in saying, be found equal to overcome any symptoms arising from the poisonous reptiles of this country.

I shall proceed at once to point out the treatment which has the general sanction of the medical profession in various parts of the world, and which has been found to succeed in desperate cases where no particular antidote could have been of any avail.

TREATMENT:—The person bitten should immediately suck the wound well; and if he cannot reach the part, cause it to be sucked by somebody, as it extracts a large portion of the poison, which is thus prevented entering into the system, and the danger becomes less in proportion. This practice is of high antiquity, and is known to be harmless to the person doing it, who may wash his mouth out with salt and water afterwards. A ligature should, at the same time, be applied, rather tight, about half an inch above the wound, between it and the heart, which should be left on for some time, as it stops the circulation, and prevents the poison being conveyed by the absorbents into the system. The part bitten should be raised up well with the forceps, and a piece cut out not larger than a sixpence, which will include the whole depth of the puncture, and the bleeding should be promoted by warm water. There is no fear of cutting any of the veins or arteries if the flesh is well pulled up by the person cutting it; and if the bleeding is unusual, continued pressure on the part with lint or a handkerchief will stop it. When the bleeding has ceased, the ipecacuanha poultice may be applied to the part as a matter of further precaution. The surgical part of the treatment, which is the first to be carried out, will thus consist in the sucking, the ligature, the excision, and applying the ipecacuanha poultice. I do not recommend to enlarge the puncture, or scarify the part—which promotes absorption—but I should prefer it to be sucked well, undisturbed by any interference, until it is cut out with the knife or scissors.

I should not object to the part being touched with the actual cautery or red hot iron, if such be at hand immediately, which would prevent excision being required; but I think it is more painful, and inferior in efficacy, as it is not followed by a flow of blood which is so useful. The patient ought not to be dragged about as is the custom, but may sit in an easy chair, in the open air, his state being something similar to a person in a fainting fit, who requires all his strength to rally against the state of collapse; and for that purpose experience has proved that there is no remedy so certain in counteracting the effects of the poison and the excessive prostration of the entire nervous system, as a large quantity of brandy, whiskey, or any other spirits taken pure, or mixed with water, at the option of the patient, and in quantity a pint or more, according to the urgency of the symptoms. All· this should be taken as soon as possible after the bite; no intoxication will take place, and if the symptoms of it appear, no more should be given. This large amount of spirits, that under ordinary circumstances might of itself be fatal, will be found completely to overcome the poison by suddenly rousing the prostrate nervous system to regain its equilibrium, and thus become the real ANTIDOTE, and the only one that can actually be depended on in any dangerous case of Snake bite. A child will be able to take it by the wine glassful, with equal part of water, and the tolerance of pure spirits in such cases is wonderful. I believe this important remedy was found out in America, where the Rattle-Snake is so common, and where old Indians would allow themselves to be bitten for a pint of pure whiskey, which they drank off at once, and found no symptoms of poisoning from the bite, or of intoxication from the whiskey. This fact being once established, its application has spread far and wide, but not so generally in this country as it should have done, considering its well acknowledged successful results.

As the patient rallies, and urgent symptoms disappear, the antidotes can be withheld, and if immediately after the accident, this plan of treatment has been actively carried out, a few hours would, in most instances, place him out of danger.

The efficacy of these rules is only equalled by their extreme simplicity, which will enable any person to proceed at once with the treatment without the loss of a minute, as every minute's delay increases the danger. For the use of people living in the country, out of reach of immediate medical assistance, I have completed a small box, containing spirits to begin with, and all instruments, appliances, and antidotes required for curing any snake-bite, with printed directions how to use them effectively.

I will conclude by observing that the blacks of this country, who must have great experience in snake-bites, use, in their rude, untutored way, the same surgical treatment as is here advised, with the addition of immersing the patient in cold water: repeated cold water affusion to the face might be used with advantage instead of immersion. The bites of centipedes, scorpions, tarantulas, and other venomous insects, are best treated with ammonia applied to the part and taken internally. The same surgical treatment as applied to men should be used for all animals bitten by poisonous reptiles.

On the Wambeyan Caves,
By Dr. James Cox.

[Read 9th July, 1862.]

It is not so easy in Australia as in Europe, to plan at short notice a tour suitable for the brief periods of relaxation we are able to rescue from the pressure of Sydney work. So, when I was the other day casting about for some expedition in which to spend a week's holiday with satisfaction, I found myself rather puzzled to hit on any new line of country, having already explored most of our own vicinity. My friend, the Rev. Mr. Hassall, jun., relieved me of my difficulty by suggesting a visit to the "Wambeyan Caves;" but so ignorant was I—and I do not find that I am an exception—of their whereabouts, or their qualities, that I had to ask what part of the colony they were in. The answer I received was, that they were a day's ride from Berrima. Others were soon induced to join our expedition, but many refused because they had not heard them spoken of, and because I could not inform them how long our visit would take. As I can now, however, answer that question, I should advise any man who has a week to spare, and loves this kind of pleasure, to visit the Wambeyan Caves.

On Wednesday, 12th March, at twelve o'clock, eleven of us started from Bendooly, Mr. Cordeaux's residence, four miles on this side of Berrima, on horseback, leading two packhorses with the necessary amount of provisions.

From the back premises of Bendooly we went away due west, and made for Wanganderry, a sheep station of Mr. Cordeaux's, about twelve miles distant. We reached this about two o'clock; thence we made for Bullio, a second station of Cordeaux's, still going west. From Bullio we made for Bowman's Hill, the descent to the Wollondilly River, which we crossed about six o'clock, and camped on the Horse Flat about half a mile down the river bank : in all about twenty miles from Berrima. The country passed through to this point is for the most part extremely monotonous, the only thing striking my attention as peculiar, being the great variety of *Epacris*, and a peculiar shrub, called there the bitter willow *(Daviesia)*; although this is as intensely bitter as quassia, the cattle are very fond of it; but unfortunately, in districts where it is eaten, so strong a bitter is communicated to the milk and butter that they are unfit for use. By diverging to the right, before reaching Bowman's Hill, to the edge of the cliffs, a grand panorama can be obtained of the valley of Burragorang and Coolong.

I should advise any one taking this trip in future to follow our example and camp on the Horse Flat, as it is well adapted for it; and in the morning, you are more prepared to meet the great difficulty—the ascent of the Telegang mountain.

At daylight we started for the caves, a distance of ten miles. The road is difficult to find, but fortunately we had an excellent guide in our friend Mr. Henry Oxley. Ascending the river for about half a mile, you cross it, ride along the opposite bank for another quarter of a mile, and again cross it to a small creek. Still steering west, you ascend the creek for a few hundred yards, which brings you to the foot of the Telegang mountain.

This magnificent hill is about a mile and a quarter up, and its characters represent the whole surrounding country, which for miles round, as far as the eye can reach, is composed of a succession of such hills on a minor scale. The hill itself is essentially trap (not in large masses on the surface, but lying in the form of small loose broken pieces), very steep and pointed, thinly wooded with gum, box, and stringy bark, and richly grassed with a soft tufty grass resembling the kangaroo grass, which seems excellent for grazing, as at the top of every little pinch is a cattle camp. We ascended the crest of the hill, but I should advise any one intending to ascend it to do so gradually round the right side, as the footing for the horses is much more secure. The view from the top of the various windings of the Wollondilly in the distance is very magnificent. Here also is to be seen a peculiar species of *Casuarina* (native oak). The sexes of the trees are separated—the female bears a fine cone-looking seed vessel, but the male flower resembles the common acorn.

Following the path which takes to the right, you again steer west, and about a mile from the top of the hill good water is to be found.

Ascending this creek for about a mile, the path turns sharply to the left, on to the crest of the ridge. Special attention should be paid to this point, as from not observing it on our return, but continuing straight on, some of us were benighted, and found ourselves in difficulties. The path from this turn is plain for about three miles, when another creek is made, which bears well away to the left, leading you to an old sheep station, called Telegang station. Continuing a westerly course across the cleared patch of land, you take the path which leads from the angle formed by the right bank of the watercourse on which the station is situated and the line of cleared ground, bearing well to the right for about three miles; the character of the country and vegetation then altogether alters, almost by a line of demarcation: you have, in fact, reached a limestone country, thinly covered with low stunted box and cooraman. An exquisitely clear stream of water is reached, with a bed of white marble pebbles, which is the Wambeyan Creek. About half a mile further a rocky barricade, some two hundred feet high, obstructs your further progress. The stream of water runs into a large archway, which is the mouth of the Wambeyan Caves. The Wambeyan Creek, after a course of about two miles further, falls into Marrs Forest Creek which falls into the Guinecor Creek, a branch of the Wollondilly. The limestone rocks in this district do not occur as a few thick beds of limestone with subordinate layers of calcareous shale, but in one bold reef-like mass of some hundreds of feet thick, separated in places by a few layers of impure limestone, and deeply intersected by perpendicular divisional planes through which the water percolates to form the caverns. The running stream, as above mentioned, if followed to this solid barrier of rocks, runs into an archway, which is the real mouth of the caves, and through it you enter the first of a succession of caverns. This special one is called the "Wambeyan Church." I presume from its arched cathedral-like roof; and from an absurd looking rock, accurately resembling a "parson in his pulpit," with his book, bibs, and scarf—the remains of an enormous stalagmite. This cavern attracts special attention, as it is fortunately lighted from both ends—the opposite end having fallen in and opened the end of the cave, from one of those peculiar funnel-shaped holes seen in most limestone countries and very common here. The height of this cave is, I believe, about one hundred and twenty feet; and it is about 400 feet long. The floor, on the left side of which the stream of water continues its course, is covered with large broken masses of stone; which I believe have rolled in from the far end, in some places covered with a green *conferva*, in others with a pink kind of lichen. The roof, which is also tinged with this peculiar lichen, I believe only since daylight has been so fully admitted, has suspended from it long delicate stalactites, varying in form and beauty, some of immense length, and the walls are studded with fluted columns, between which are also hung delicate pieces resembling tapestry and fringe.

Between these columns are seen the openings of smaller caverns, the haunts and homes of the Wallaby and the Bat. The stream of water, when it enters the cave, is fully six feet wide, but if followed to the right hand corner of the distant end it is found to have dwindled away to a stream not six inches wide, and now enters a dark gallery. In following out this gallery it is necessary to use lights, and to prepare yourself for a wet and slippery scramble, as deep pools of water now and then stop your progress. I should advise any one wishing to see these caves to advantage to take with them a good supply of wax candles, a couple of dozen of blue lights, and a pole to feel your way among the pools of water, which, however, in a dark subterranean passage always appear more formidable than they really are.

The first thing to attract your attention is the intense cold; and secondly, if well lighted, the magnificent effect of the lights on the snow-white crystalline marble; and thirdly, the difficulty of finding the right way, for on all sides of this main gallery, galleries of less size turn off, some of which have the appearance of being the main course. However, if you advance in a straight direction with the first cave for about 100 yards, the beauties of the place increase, and here we had first displayed to us the effects of our blue lights on the pure white crystalline stalactities which hung round on all sides. This passage then bends to the right, and about another 100 yards on becomes much expanded when to the left is seen another large opening, of which we will speak again.

Here all appearance of the stream ceased, but pools of water were occasionally met with. It became evident, however, that we were in the main channel of the creek, and that during floods this passage was full of water, from the bunches of rubbish perched high up on the ledges of the marble rocks. Our course now for the next hundred yards was easy and dry (all traces of water having disappeared), until we again found daylight. We had in fact reached the opposite side of the rocky barrier across the creek, for undoubtedly it was the main creek we had again reached, commencing from a marble arch in the bluff rocks, but differing in there not being the sign of a drop of water, which from its marks we could see to have been there during floods, nor as far as we could see down this creek, which had very steep banks, could we perceive where the running stream made its escape. To the right of this exit several very interesting channels lead off, suspended from the side of one of which is, what is called the sounding-board, a remarkable thin sheet of marble, and from it Mr. Oxley brought forth sounds of sweet melody, which reverberated on all sides.

To all appearance this was the end of the cave. But what had become of the water ?

Looking down the creek, from the mouth at this end, about a hundred yards up the bank to the left, is seen a native fig tree, at the base of which is a small unattractive-looking opening, the only known entrance from the surface, but I doubt if it is the only means of entering what are termed the "Fig Tree Caves." At this mouth we found some fine specimens of the dog-tooth spar.

On entering here lights became necessary at once, as the footing is very dangerous, deep crevices occurring on all sides, till the cavern suddenly expands to an unknown extent. After feeling our way carefully to the left, and having got on a firm footing, a blue light revealed to us its magnificence. The grandeur of the natural sculpture is here very great, and the thickness and length of the stalactities and stalagmites wonderful, but they are not so purely white as those before seen. The floor of this cave is in some places almost knee-deep with a dark brown-coloured, light, dry amorphous powder, which at the time I took to be dry pulverised dung of wallabies, as they were seen in great numbers; but, on examining a small sample that I brought back with me, I found it contained almost no vegetable matter. The ledge of rocks on which we stood suddenly ended in an abrupt precipice, at the bottom of which we conjectured the water ran, but on lowering a light no trace of it was seen. Branching off to the right, this precipice became less steep, and a few of us descended, though with difficulty, as we now undoubtedly heard sounds like falling water; but, after wandering and scrambling about for some time, we could discover no more than a number of vast dry caverns. Having ascended again, we took more to the right; after having explored several beautiful galleries leading off, the sounds of distant falling water still becoming more distinct.

As you proceed to the right, the footing is both dangerous and difficult, while the floor seems made of masses of rock which have slipped from the mouth we entered by, and filling up what must have been once a large and deep cavern. Here also the noise of water was distinct, and a few of us determined, if possible, to descend and see it—an undertaking which proved to be one of great difficulty and danger, owing to the loose and slippery state of the rocks, the uncertainty of the right way, and the deep and narrow crevices we had to descend. After descending a shaft some fifty feet, the rocks lost the dirty brown appearance they had above, and began to get white and crystalline, as in the tunnel before described; in fact, it was evident we had entered a tunnel of a minor kind, still running in a westerly direction, which at last ended in a shaft so narrow that we were obliged to descend it on our hands and knees.

Having reached the bottom, we were, however, rewarded by finding the object of our search—a broad running stream—in the midst of summer as cold as ice—about 200 feet below the surface of the ground, and having for its bed a solid block of white marble. This channel was, as a general rule, about ten feet high, running in a downward and westerly direction. Attempts were made to follow the stream up and down, but the water became in places so deep that it was impossible to do so.

Having ascended again with the object of ascertaining where this stream made its exit, we descended the dry Wambeyan Creek for about a mile and a-half. At about this distance the banks became very high, and to our delight we discovered the water spouting out of what looked like a solid bluff of rock, in two different places, about one hundred yards apart, and pouring the water again into the Wambeyan Creek through narrow fissures.

From the top of the cliffs a good view can be had of the surrounding country, and the different forms of vegetation map out with accuracy the extent of the limestone, which is very limited.

I must now return to the tunnel leading from the left of the main tunnel from the "Church." You are obliged to climb some rocks to enter it, and having entered and followed it up for about thirty yards, it becomes very contracted, and ends in a hole just large enough to allow a man to drag his body through. You now enter by far the finest part of these caves, consisting of a series of small chambers, all connected by archways, which seem as if they had been excavated out of a mass of solid white marble —the floor being remarkably crystalline and pure, as if it had been formed by pouring over the surface the material of the surrounding rocks, in a fluid state, which had then been allowed to crystallise ; and, in reality, it is in this way that it has been formed. The water, impregnated with carbonic acid, dissolves the rocks, forming with them a soluble bi-carbonate of lime which, on being again exposed to the atmosphere, allows one atom of the carbonic acid to escape, leaving a deposit of the insoluble carbonate on the spot. It is on the same principle that all stalactites and stalagmites are formed.

These chambers have been called the "Organ Gallery," from the great length and regularity of the stalactites and stalagmites which, in many cases, have met and form one continuation, giving the appearance of the pipes of an organ. So thick are they in some places, that it is impossible to get between them, and so sharp in others that you require to avoid them with care. As you proceed to the right, one chamber after another, each seeming more beautiful than the preceding, succeeds ; the splendour and magnificence of which, in my opinion, can only be appreciated by a personal visit. You are at last prevented from proceeding to the left by coming to the brink of a deep precipice, which we were unable to descend. I am inclined to think that this is the continuation of the watercourse we were unable to follow up, for although we could not hear the sound of water running, still, on throwing down stones it was evident by the splash that there was a deep pool of water. It may, however, be a succession of other caves.

On following out these chambers to the right we were conducted to a cavern of enormous extent, far larger than the "Church," and from a small opening in a distant corner daylight was seen. We had a magnificent view of this cavern by means of the blue lights, and from what I saw from the distance, I was inclined to believe that this cavern we were looking into was the cave we had visited from the Fig-tree opening, and that, in fact, we were standing beneath the precipice which obstructed our course to the left.

One peculiarity in this cave is, that the floor of it in some parts is so deeply covered with the peculiar dark powder before mentioned, as literally to prevent your being able to wade through it.

On the Fibre Plants of New South Wales,
By CHARLES MOORE, ESQ.

[Read 5th October, 1864.]

THE character of the vegetation of this Colony, in many respects so remarkable, is, as regards its economic value, but little understood. From it neither commerce, science, nor the arts have as yet been benefited to any appreciable extent. With the exception of a few trees, the timber of which is used for building and fencing purposes, scarcely any importance has been attached to any qualities of our indigenous plants, many of which I feel convinced contain valuable properties which only require to be made known. It was generally expected that the vegetable products sent from this Colony to the Paris and London Great

Exhibitions would have been the means of ascertaining their commercial interest ; but beyond testing the strength of some of the woods, and pronouncing the White Ironbark of Illawarra to be the strongest in the world, the authorities connected with these exhibitions have not furnished us with any further information, although various vegetable substances, supposed to have medicinal, dyeing, and textile properties, were forwarded from this colony on both occasions. We have been in fact thrown on our own resources, and every effort should be made by all persons interested in this matter, to ascertain by investigation whatever commercial value our plants may possess before it is too late. Already extensive tracts of country have been cleared, which formerly bore the richest and most varied vegetation. The brush forests to which I allude, so general along our coast, are fast disappearing before the axe of the settler. To judge of the future by the past and present, a few years more and these will have ceased to exist. I have been induced, therefore, to draw attention to a few plants which yield a strong and durable fibre suitable for a variety of purposes, as it is in such forests as those referred to that the fibre producing plants which I shall now proceed to bring under notice are principally found :—

The first in importance is the Gigantic Nettle—*Urtica gigas* —a remarkable tree abounding on rich alluvial soils, from Illawarra to the extreme north ; in the Clarence and Richmond districts it almost exclusively covers vast spaces of ground, and many of the trees attain a height over 100 feet, and are 40 feet in circumference. The bark, which is very thick in both the young and old state, furnishes a strong and durable fibre much used by the Aborigines for making their dilly bags, nets, &c. It is easily prepared by crushing or beating the bark until nearly dry; by this means all extraneous substances are sufficiently removed to make it fit for exportation or for other uses. It must on no account be steeped in water, as this has the effect of rotting it. The Aborigines prepare it by chewing the bark. The prepared fibre, as Mr. Lardner of Grafton states, may be obtained at from 3d to 4d per pound.

In the Northern districts another species of arborescent Nettle—*Urtica photiniophylla*, called the small-leaved nettle, furnishes by its bark a similar fibre to the last, but of a finer description, and admirably suited, it is supposed, for Paper-making. The fibre of this tree is prepared in the same manner as the former, and may be obtained at as cheap a rate and in unlimited quantities, and I would here remark, that although stripping these trees of their bark will destroy the main stem, yet the root is not seriously affected by the process, as the destruction of the stem causes innumerable shoots to spring from its base, which would annually yield a supply of young fibres perhaps better suited for general purposes than that from older growth.

I shall now refer to the fibres known as Kurrajong, an aboriginal name, I believe for fibre, and not, as is commonly supposed, applied to any one plant—at all events Colonists know several plants under this name. The Kurrajong of Sir Thomas Mitchell is "*Sterculia heterophylla*," a tree not uncommon in many parts of the Colony, particularly in the Western districts. The aborigines in the interior, almost exclusively employ the fibre from the bark of this tree in manufacturing their nets, fishing-lines, dilly-bags, &c. It is of a strong and durable character, but of little commercial value, as the expense of collecting it and the carriage would be more than it is worth. The Kurrajong: from which the district beyond Richmond is named, is *Hibiscus heterophyllus*, a plant of very frequent occurrence in all thickly wooded places within the coast range; the fibre from this is exceedingly tough, and perhaps more generally used by the natives, than that of any other. Very large quantities of this bark might be obtained and at a comparatively trifling cost. Another, but smaller plant than the preceding, the *Pimelea hypericifolia*, also bears the name of Kurrajong; this yields an excellent fibre, and as it grows in the greatest profusion in various places from Illawarra to Twofold Bay on the coast, and from Berrima to Araluen inland, no difficulty would be experienced in procuring a supply of its bark, which, in its raw state, is often used by settlers for purposes as a substitute for twine. Again, in the Northern brush forests, particularly on the banks of rivers, one of the most common plants to be found, is called by settlers Brown Kurrajong—*Commersonia echinata*, the fibre of which is more valued by the natives for its strength and durability, than any other kind; of this these people make their fishing-nets and lines, and it does not, it would appear, easily rot. It is not however so easily prepared as that from the Green Kurrajong—*Hibiscus heterophyllus*. Concerning this plant, Mr. Lardner, of Grafton, who is well acquainted with the mode of preparing its fibre for use, remarks, "Both the wood and bark are hard, and a good deal of crushing is required to get the fibre." The bark contains a very large quantity of strong mucilaginous matter, which no washing will entirely remove. The fibre is very long, and not interlaced as in the nettle, it is very strong when moist, but becomes hard and brittle if much of the glutinous substance is allowed to remain in it.

Having thus adverted to the plants—known as Kurrajong—I shall now proceed to notice a tree, the inner bark of which furnishes a coarse but valuable fibre, which has been long known and used by the settlers on the Clarence and Richmond, in which districts it is most common, and where it usually attains a very large size. This tree was described by me from a dried specimen furnished by the late Dr. Stephenson, being then unknown to botanists, as a new species of *Brachychiton*. The dried flowers had a dull brownish colour, which I then supposed was something of the natural colour when fresh. I therefore called it *B. luridum*. Since that time I have had many opportunities of seeing this fine tree in flower, and no name could have been more appropriate than that of *luridum*,—a name adopted on my authority by Dr. Müller in his Fragmenta, and by Mr. Bentham in the Flora of Australia. Instead of being lurid, the flowers, which are large, somewhat bell-shaped, are of a beautiful rose colour, and as these appear before the new leaves—the tree being almost deciduous—no finer sight could be imagined than a large tree in full flower. It is called in the districts referred to, "Sycamore," and its bark may be got under that name in any quantity, at a very moderate rate. The only other indigenous plants to which I shall invite attention as fibre bearing kinds, are an aroidaceous plant, called by settlers Traveller's Grass, and the Gigantic Lily; the first of these *Gymnostachys anceps* is well known, and abounds in all thickly wooded situations along the coast line, having an inland range of about 50 miles. It bears a leaf similar to the flag or Iris, and attains a height of six feet and upwards; a strip of the leaf ⅛ of an inch in width, drawn over a fire so as to soften the fibre, or even without this preparation, is strong enough to resist the efforts of a man to break it. I fancy therefore, that if the properties of this invaluable plant, at least to the bush traveller, were properly tested, it would be found to yield a fibrous material of considerable commercial advantage. The last but most important fibre bearing plant is the Gimmeah of the natives; the Gigantic Lily of the settlers, and the *Doryanthes excelsa* of botanists. It is closely allied to the American Agave, commonly called Aloe, but it is not a true lily. In the year 1850, at the first meeting of the Australian Society, the late Sir Thomas Mitchell read a most able and interesting paper on the resources of the County of Cumberland. I am not aware whether that paper was published or not, nor can I learn whether it or any copy of it is in existence, but I have a perfect recollection that in that paper Sir Thomas laid particular stress on the value of the *Doryanthes* fibre, which he thought was equal if not superior to the New Zealand Flax *Phormium tenax*, with which it was compared, and by way of proof he had a specimen of the flax prepared, which was submitted to the inspection of those who were present when the paper was read, and was pronounced to be equal in length, colour, fineness, and strength to any other kind known. I was then comparatively a young Colonist, and my knowledge of the country but limited—of the principal localities where this plant is found, I knew little or nothing. Being therefore under the impression that it was not to be found in any great quantities, that it was in fact, sparingly distributed over the Country, I ventured in discussing the merits of the paper at the Meeting, to give expression to my belief, and to add that as it was known to grow slowly after being cut down, no regular supply of its leaves would be obtainable. This opinion, a most erroneous one, has been quoted since by more than one person as being correct, but I now know from personal acquaintance with the habits of this plant, that it grows in such abundance in various places, as to furnish an unlimited supply of material for any purpose for which it may be required. It is found in the greatest profusion on both banks of the Woronora River, all over Mr. Holt's ground at

South Botany, extending southwards from this to the hills above Illawarra. But it is in that vast and wretchedly poor country lying between the Hawkesbury River and the Wollombi Ranges, that this plant flourishes in its greatest splendour. In this inhospitable region, it is not only abundant, but it is the only plant to be met with that is either particularly attractive, or useful to the traveller. I know of no finer sight than to pass through this country during the flowering season of *Doryanthes*. The very parched-like vegetation with which it is surrounded, and the poor arid soil from which it grows seem by contrast to add additional freshness and lustre to its rich red wax-like flowers. Port Stephens is also another locality in which this plant grows in equal abundance, and as all the places mentioned, are within an easy distance of water carriage, a constant supply of the leaves might readily be procured at small expense.

I have thus enumerated the plants which, I am aware, furnish a really excellent fibrous material; in doing so, I claim no credit for having supplied any information which was not known to many persons before; the only object I had in view was to draw attention to these plants in a condensed and collected form, in the hope that those who may be interested in the manufacture of fibre, or may desire to bring such material into use, may know, not only the plants which will supply it, but where such plants are to be found. There are other indigenous plants which the natives employ in making their nets, bags, &c., among which are several grasses and reeds, but with them I am not sufficiently acquainted to speak with confidence. Possibly, what has been stated may elicit from others information regarding these. I shall conclude by remarking that in addition to the indigenous plants referred to, there are several introduced kinds which yield a valuable fibre, such as the *Sida retusa*, originally sent from the Mauritius and the West Indies, but now an acclimatised plant in this and the adjoining Colony of Queensland; it has, in fact, become everywhere a troublesome weed. The American Aloe, and all the kinds of Plantain and Banana, are most valuable for their fibre, and to all such plants I would venture to direct the attention of Colonists in general, and particularly the Managers of the new Paper Company now commencing its operations in the neighbourhood of Sydney.

On Osmium and Iridium, obtained from New South Wales Gold,

By A. LEIBIUS, Ph. D.,

Assayer to the Sydney Branch of the Royal Mint.

[Read Nov. 2nd, 1864.]

ACCOMPANYING the Platinum in its crude state as Platinum ore, such as is chiefly found in Russia and South America, a series of rare metals is found, which latter are known to chemists under the collective name of "Platinum-metals," and comprise the metals known as Rhodium, Ruthenium, Palladium, Osmium and Iridium. Palladium and Rhodium were discovered in Platinum ore by Wollaston, in 1803; the Ruthenium in 1844, by Clauss, to whose researches we owe almost all that is known about this metal, whilst Tennant found in 1804, that the alloy of Osmiridium, which was shortly previous found in the insoluble residue of Platinum ores, and considered as *one* substance, consisted of two distinct metals, to which he gave the names of Osmium and Iridium.

These two metals, although they are sometimes found by themselves, generally occur as a natural alloy of osmiridium of different composition, namely, Ir. Os., which Berzelius found composed of 49·34 Os., 46·77 Ir., 3·15 Rhod., and 0·74 Fe., and Ir. Os_3 which Berzelius found to contain 25 o/o Irid., and 75 o/o Osmium, and which latter some mineralogists call Irid-Osmium.

This Osmium-Iridium, or Osmiridium, of which I intend to bring a short account before your notice, does not only occur in Platinum ore, but is also found in company with Gold, and especially in Californian Gold. The Gold from New South Wales brought to the Mint is also alloyed with a sometimes not inconsiderable quantity of this Osmiridium.

At a heat at which Gold fuses freely the Osmiridium is totally infusible, and its high specific gravity, which ranges from about 19 to 21 (according to the preponderance of the Osmium over Irid.), causes the same to sink to the bottom of the melting pot, where it is easily separated from the Gold. It is through this process that the Sydney Mint has collected, in its crude state, the Osmiridium, which, since its establishment, has amounted to about 3 lbs.

There are several methods for extracting pure Osmium and pure Iridium out of this impure Osmiridium. The method adopted by me was the one given by Woehler, and which, for working on a small scale, at all events, is the most convenient. I will shortly describe it:—

The quantity of Osmiridium taken under operation was 8 ounces, which were powdered in a steel mortar, and mixed with an equal quantity of fused Salt (Na. Cl.), the mixture introduced into a glass tube, such as used for analyses, and heated in a gas furnace, whilst moist chlorine gas was allowed to pass slowly for about 3 hours over the mixture, heated to a dull red heat. By this means a double salt of Chloride of Sodium with Chloride of Iridium is formed, as well as a double salt of Chloride of Sodium with Chloride of Osmium. But a great part of the Chloride of Osmium formed is again decomposed by the water of the moist chlorine gas into osmic acid, (which escapes, and is collected in a balloon which is in connection with the glass tube) and into metallic Osmium and Hydrochloric Acid. But the metallic Osmium gets again formed into Chloride of Osmium, and combines to a double salt. $2 \text{ Aeq. Os Cl}_2 + 4 \text{ HO} = \text{Os O}, \text{Os}, 4 \text{ HCl}$. The contents of the glass tube, which at the end of the operation contain the double Chlorides of Iridium and Osmium with Sodium, are dissolved in water which leaves titaniferous Iron and other impurities of the Osmiridium undissolved, whilst the double chlorides just mentioned are readily soluble. But only about 30 % of the weight of Osmiridium employed are brought in solution by this process. A repetition of the same with the dried residue extracts a little more, so that after three operations I got about 50 % in solution.

This solution, which is dark red-brown, is distilled with strong nitric acid in a glass retort, to convert the Chloride of Osmium into Osmic Acid, which distills over and collects in dilute Ammonia. The residue in the retort is poured, whilst still hot, into a strong solution of Sal ammoniac, when the greatest part of the Iridium falls down as a blackish crystalline powder, having a dark red streak, and which is a double salt of Chloride of Ammonium with Chloride of Iridium or Irid-Salmiak.

The liquid, which is filtered off from the Irid-Salmiak, is evaporated with soda to dryness, gently heated in an earthen crucible, and then boiled out with water, which leaves Oxide of Iridium behind as a blackish powder, which is dried and reduced to Iridium by Hydrogen gas.

The purest Iridium is obtained by heating the Irid-Salmiak, just mentioned, to a strong red heat, when pure Iridium is left behind if the Irid-Salmiak employed has been once or twice recrystallized. In this way I obtained the Iridium here produced. It is a black powder. Subjected to strong pressure whilst somewhat moist in a suitable apparatus, and then to a strong white heat, the Iridium is obtained in a compact, though very brittle mass, which allows of polish. I endeavoured to obtain a little in this way; its colour is that of polished steel. (Specimen shown.)

This Iridium, which obtained its name from the Greek word Ἶρις, because it forms different salts, the solutions of which possess almost all colours of the rainbow, is extremely difficult of fusion. At a heat by which platinum is fused, it merely contracts a little and gets silver white. Of late Messrs. Deville and Debray, in Paris, who have occupied themselves very largely with the extraction of platinum and platinum metals have been especially successful in the construction of furnaces for obtaining the highest degrees of heat. These furnaces are constructed of lime, and heated with a mixture of either coal gas and oxygen, or oxygen and hydrogen, in the proportion of 1 oxygen to 2 hydrogen. In this furnace they have been able to melt about 400 grains of pure Iridium in one operation, whilst the same furnaces fused about 25 lbs. of platinum in one operation. The Iridium thus fused is pure white and similar to polished steel, but brittle from its crystalline structure within. Its specific gravity is the same as Platinum, namely, 21·15; it alloys with Zinc and Tin. The Iridium as obtained as black powder, is used as the best black colour for porcelain painting. But its most important application appears to have been discovered but quite lately, through Deville and Debray, since it forms a fusible alloy with platinum, which, when it contains 25—30 % of Iridium, resists every acid. Vessels of such an alloy are already manufactured by Desmontis in Paris, and whilst the technical application of Iridium, which hitherto has been but very limited, has thus been brought into a new phase, the Russian Government has given especial instructions with regard to the development of their vast resources of platinum ores, from which not only the valuable platinum, but also the no longer valueless Iridium are obtained.

Although the Australian Gold does not contain anything like a sufficient quantity of Iridium to become one of the resources for obtaining the latter for technical purposes, I thought that the importance which this interesting metal seems destined to have, would sufficiently warrant my drawing your attention to the same by giving you this short outline, and exhibiting a few specimens of the metals and its compounds, as well as its usual companion, the metal Osmium, of which I shall speak presently.

With regard to the different compounds into which Iridium is capable of entering, I need not trouble you. The solutions of the different salts represent, as already mentioned, almost all the colours of the rainbow, but unfortunately they do not keep long, but decompose under change of colour.

The most important Iridium Salt, namely the Irid-Salmiak, already mentioned, I have here. This dissolves in 20 parts of water, but colours distinctly yellow even 40,000 parts.

On heating it to red heat, pure Iridium remains behind.

OSMIUM.

I will now shortly describe the companion of the Iridium—the Osmium. It is very difficult to get Iridium quite free from Osmium, of which traces adhere with great pertinacity. The operation for preparing Osmium out of Osmiridium falls in with the preparation of Iridium by chlorine gas, as before described.

The Osmium which is collected during the preparation of Iridium, partly as osmic acid, in a balloon attached to the tube in which the mixture of Osmiridium and Salt was heated, and partly as Chloride and Bichloride of Osmium, is dissolved in dilute

Ammonia, and the yellow solution which soon gets brown from further decomposition, is evaporated until all Ammonia is driven off, when a compound of Ammonia—Sesquioxide of Osmium falls down as a black powder. (Sample shown.)

When this substance is heated after being dried, it decomposes with a hissing noise, Nitrogen and aqueous vapours being evolved and the Osmium becomes reduced to the metallic state with great violence. An admixture of $\frac{1}{3}$ Sal ammoniac assists in making this decomposition less violent. (Ammonia—Sesquioxide of Osmium, as well as pure Osmium shown.)

This metal Osmium, which received its name from the Greek 'Οσμή (smell) in consequence of the strong and peculiar smell of its highest oxide, the osmic acid, has only of late been more closely investigated through the researches of Deville and Debray. They found its properties essentially different from former observers. The specific gravity ranges from 21·3 to 21·4, is therefore heavier than Iridium or Platinum (21·15.) It is not fusible, but at a very high temperature, by which Iridium fuses and Platinum volatilizes, it is evaporated as osmic acid without showing any fusion. If Osmium is heated in a graphite pot with 7 to 8 parts Tin to strong red heat, it dissolves in the Tin and separates on cooling as a crystalline powder of great hardness, which can be obtained after dissolving out the Tin with hydrochloric acid. The Osmium in its character very much resembles Arsenic. It enters into combination with chlorine, as already stated, forming protochloride and bichloride of Osmium, the first having an olive green, the latter a red-brown colour. The solutions of these salts very rapidly decompose under separation of Osmium and formation of H. Cl.

The most interesting compound of Osmium is the Osmic acid $Os\,O_4$. It is obtained when metallic osmium is heated in the bulb of a glass tube, whilst oxygen gas passes slowly over it; the osmic acid thus produced is condensed in fine white needles in the next glass bulb, which has to be kept well cooled, (apparatus shown.) In this way I have prepared this specimen, (osmic acid shown.)

This Osmic acid fuses more easily than wax into an oily liquid. It has an insupportably pungent odour, and its vapours attack the lungs strongly, and excite a burning pain in the eyes. To give you a faint idea of its smell, I produce here a very dilute solution of osmic acid, by decomposing a solution of osmate of potash with Hydrochloric acid. The smell thus produced, is not at all dangerous. Osmic acid is reduced by the alcohol flame; if therefore a granule of osmium be placed on the edge of a piece of platinum foil, and held in the flame of a spirit lamp in such a manner as to allow part of the flame to rise freely into the air, this part becomes brightly luminous, because the osmic acid formed by the combustion of osmium mounts upwards, and is again reduced by the flame to metallic osmium, which thus mixes with the flame as a finely divided solid body, and thereby increases the luminosity.

Osmic acid attacks the skin and every organic substance.

Osmium and its compounds have at present only a scientific interest. It was my intention to prepare an extensive series of Iridium and Osmium compounds to lay before this Meeting, but I must defer doing so till I am enabled to work upon a larger scale than I have done hitherto, and for which purpose I require several chemicals and apparatus, which cannot be procured in this Colony.

On the Prospects of the Civil Service under the Superannuation Act of 1864,

By LIEUTENANT-COLONEL WARD.

[Read December 7th, 1864.]

I SUBMIT, in this paper, the conclusions at which I have arrived after examining, as a Commissioner appointed under the Act, the financial provisions of the Superannuation Act of 1864.

The sum paid, either as a single or annual premium, for an annuity to commence at a certain age not yet attained, and to continue during the remainder of a life, should be sufficient, if invested at compound interest at the current rate, to produce at the death of the annuitant (if his life has been of average duration) a sum equivalent to the value of the annuity he will by that time have received.

In calculating the premium to be thus paid, the following chances are taken into account:—

1. The probability of the purchaser of the annuity surviving to receive it.

2. The number of years he will probably live to enjoy it, should he so survive.

These probabilities are usually deduced from the Carlisle tables of mortality; and the value of a deferred annuity, corrected by these probabilities, is that which the purchaser should pay to compensate the fund out of which the annuity is to be paid.

It is essential, however, in order that the fund may be thus compensated, that the premium paid should be invested, and the interest thus obtained re-invested immediately, at the current rate. Neither principal nor interest can be applied to any other purpose without detriment to the fund, and therefore risk to the purchaser's annuity. If a portion of the premium paid by A, or of the interest which has accrued from its investment, be applied to paying an annuity assigned to B, it is probable that the fund will be unable to meet A's claim at maturity, but it is absolutely certain that an unendowed fund so managed, will ultimately become insolvent. All that B is entitled to receive *from the fund* is the equivalent of the contributions he has paid, determined in the manner before explained. He may on other grounds be entitled to a larger annuity, but this difference cannot be paid to him out of moneys which have accrued from the subscriptions of other expectants, without injury to the latter.

In testing the financial provisions of the Superannuation Act of 1864 by these principles, it will not be necessary to examine critically every condition under which an officer can retire. It will be sufficient for my purpose if I can show that, even under circumstances favourable to the fund, it is impossible to carry out, for any lengthened period, the obvious intentions of the Act.

Let the test be applied to the following conditions embraced in the Act:—

1. A public officer of sixty years of age and thirty years service may retire on a pension equal to his full pay.

2. Every public officer not specially exempted by the Act may be required to pay to the fund, until he retire or die, an annual sum not exceeding four per cent. on his salary. Provided that any one awarded a pension before the expiration of ten years from the date of his first contribution will be required to continue his annual contribution until the ten years have expired.

3. The above to apply to all officers in the public service at the passing of the Act.

The following table, calculated on the principle before explained, shows—(1) the pure premium which officers of ages between twenty and sixty should pay annually to secure from an unendowed fund at the age of sixty, should they live so long, a retiring allowance of £100 a year; (2) the present value of the sum they would thus pay; (3) the present value of the sum the law requires them to pay; (4) the difference between the two latter values, or the endowment which should be granted at once from other sources if these officers are to be paid, without injury to others, the retiring allowance which the Act prescribes. In these calculations, the duration of life assumed is that given in the Carlisle tables of mortality, and the rate of interest 5 per cent.

AGE.	1. Pure Premium in £'s to be paid until the age of sixty to secure £100 per annum for life on attaining that age.	2. Present value of No. 1.	3. Present value of contribution which can be levied under Act, i.e. 4 per cent., until the age of sixty, or for ten yrs.	4. Endowment required at once.
20	5	£76	£60	£16
25	7	100	57	43
30	10 nearly	134	54	80
35	14½	179	49	130
40	22	242	44	198
45	35½	331	37	294
50	64 nearly	455	29	426
51	..	484	28	456
52	..	515	28	487
53	..	550	28	522
54	..	587	28	559
55	..	627	27	600
56	..	670	27	643
57	..	717	27	690
58	..	769	26	743
59	..	827	26	801
60	..	894	26	868

This table shows— (1) That a person now of the age of twenty, who desires to obtain at the age of sixty, should he live so long, a pension of £100 a year for the remainder of his life, should pay £5 per annum until he attains that age ; (2) that the present value of such payments is £76 ; (3) that the present value of the utmost which the law can require of him is £60 ; (4) and that the difference, or £16, must (if he is to receive at sixty years of age that which the law prescribes) be obtained from some other source. Again, as a contrast, the table shows that a person now of the age of fifty, who desires to obtain at the age of sixty, a pension of £100 a year for the remainder of his life, should pay, until he attains that age nearly £64 per annum. The present value of such payments being £455, and that of the utmost the law requires being £29, the remainder, or £426, should be supplied at once from some other source.

For pensions of greater value, the sums which should be paid, can be demanded, and must be obtained from other sources, vary of course in exact proportion to the rate of pension, and can be readily calculated from the table.

From column three can be ascertained the present value of the utmost which any officer can be called on to pay, but not that which probably he will pay. Take, for instance, the case of an officer who enters the service at the age of twenty at a salary of £100 a year, and retires at sixty at a salary of £600. To enable him to receive from an unendowed fund at the latter age a retiring pension of £600 per annum, he should, as the table shows, pay from the first, £30 per annum, *i.e.*, 5 per cent. on £600, his ultimate salary, which is equivalent to 30 per cent. on his salary on entering the service. The law only requires that he should pay 4 per cent. on the salary he may at the time be receiving. Therefore, the present value of the sum which such an officer will be required to pay cannot be correctly ascertained from column three of the table ; and the insufficiency of his payments to yield the sum he is entitled to receive at sixty, is not correctly represented by column four, which only indicates the actual insufficiency in the improbable case of an officer entering the public service, and remaining in it until sixty years of age, without an increase of salary. I draw attention to this, to remark that the examples I have taken do not sufficiently expose the inadequacy of the provisions of the Superannuation Act.

From the data furnished in the Blue Book of the Colony, it may be roughly estimated that the amount of retiring allowances on full pay liable to be claimed during the next ten years on the conditions under examination are—

At a distance of 1 year from the present date £2250
„ 2 years „ 700
„ 3 „ „ 1525
„ 4 „ „ 1500
„ 5 „ „ 1400
„ 6 „ „ 1175
„ 7 „ „ 1000
„ 8 „ „ 450
„ 9 „ „ 1260
„ 10 „ „ ... ... Nil.

The immediate endowment required to prevent these pensions being paid out of the contributions of other subscribers to the fund is by the above table—

For those who may retire in

The 1st year ... ... 2250 x 8·01 = £17023
2nd „ ... ... 700 x 7·43 = 5201
3rd „ ... ... 1525 x 6·90 = 10522
4th „ ... ... 1500 x 6·43 = 9645
5th „ ... ... 1400 x 6·00 = 8400
6th „ ... ... 1175 x 5·59 = 6568
7th „ ... 1000 x 5·22 = 5220
8th „ ... ... 450 x 4·87 = 2191
9th „ ... ... 1260 x 4·56 = 5746

Total ... ... £70516 .

Say £70,000.

The same endowment would be necessary to meet claims accruing at the moderate rate of £1500 per annum for the first four years, and £1000 per annum for the following six years.

The pensions which have already been granted under the Act may be classified as follows:—

	£	s.	d.
To one of the age of 49 a net pension for remainder of his life of	350	0	0
To one of the age of 55	433	6	8
To one of the age of 57	504	0	0
To four of the age of 60 in all	1696	6	8
To one of the age of 68	192	0	0
Total	£3175	13	1

The present value of these pensions, ascertained by means of the usual tables, exceeds £30,000; and as they have been granted to persons who have contributed little or nothing to the fund, they also, in fairness, should be charged against such endowment as the fund may receive.

Now the endowments which, under the provisions of the Act, are available, or supposed to be so, during the next ten years are,

1. The sum of £10,000, paid out of the Consolidated Fund, in accordance with clause 16 of the Superannuation Act.

This, however, has been diminished by a claim of £1470, on account of a recent death, and is now but £8530.

2. The contributions of officers who may leave the service at their own wish before they have become entitled to any payment from the fund, or who may be dismissed.

By comparing the Blue Book of 1860 with that of 1863, it has been ascertained that during these three years, salaries in the aggregate amounting to about £30,000, have from the above causes been surrendered by officers whose average service has been seven years.

On the assumption that retirements in future will be at this rate, the following sums may be carried to the credit of endowment:—

	£	s.	d.
At the end of the first year, the contributions of those who have subscribed one year only,—4 per cent. on £10,000	400	0	0
At the end of the second year, the contributions of those who have subscribed one and two years	600	0	0

At the end of the third year, the contributions of those who have subscribed one, two, and three years... £800 0 0 and so on, making, in ten years, an aggregate amount, of which the present value is about £9500.

The subscriptions of the entire public service to the Superannuation Fund amount to about £10,000 per annum, and the present value of such an income for ten years, at 5 per cent. interest, is £77,215.

From these results it will be seen that the endowments already received, and those to be expected during the next ten years, are not equal in value to the pensions which have been already granted; also, that at the end of ten years from the present time, the fund will probably have received from two sources an endowment equal in the aggregate, and at the present time, to about £18,000, and that it will have become liable for payments not fairly chargeable to it, of which the present value is about £100,000. The difference, or about £82,000, is the present value of the extra charge which will, by that time, have been imposed on the fund, and which the united subscriptions of the whole of the public service, up to that period, will be found barely sufficient to meet.

In the calculations I have submitted, no consideration has been given to the following claims to which the Superannuation Fund is liable, and which are sufficient to absorb one half of the fund created by the Act:—

1. An Officer under sixty years of age can obtain a pension equal to half his salary after fifteen years' service, on submitting a medical certificate of incapacity; and for every additional year of service an additional pension equal to one-thirtieth of his salary.

2. If above sixty years of age he can obtain the same pension, for the same service, without medical certificate.

3. If of a shorter service than fifteen years, he can obtain a pension varying from one month's pay for a year's service to two months' pay for three years' service.

4. If an Officer die in the service, his relatives of any degree become entitled to receive a month's pay for each year of his service.

Under these circumstances, the prospects of the Civil Service under the Superannuation Act of 1864 may be considered to be hopefully stated in the following words:—Every person now in the Public Service who is a subscriber to the fund created by the Act, and who may remain in the service for ten years from this date, will then find that he had the satisfaction of contributing to the pensions of those who have retired before him, but that there is nothing available for pensions which may then be due, or afterwards become so.

The question which I have thus brought under the notice of the Society is of interest to every contributor to and every recipient from the Fund. I apprehend that when the Fund becomes insolvent as, unless further endowed, it assuredly must in about ten years, those who may then be pensioners will have to submit to a reduction of their retiring allowances, in order that others entitled to be placed on the pension list may share with them, according to their claims, the available income. All contributors to the Fund have a claim to be pensioned from it. The Act does not appear to make the claim of any one superior to that of another; and as it cautiously provides that the pension or gratuity granted shall be paid out of the Fund, so far as the same shall be adequate to discharge it, the fact of a pension having been granted to one would hardly justify his being paid in full to the prejudice of another, though a later claimant. If it be clearly understood that, when the period of insolvency shall have set in, those entitled to pensions will be allowed to divide the annual income between them in proportion to their claims, there is perhaps no necessity for immediate action. In that case, those who may get first on the pension list, and have contributed the least to the fund, will receive the most, whilst those who may be placed on it in ten years time will, perhaps, receive a half-pay retirement. This, however, is, comparatively speaking, a bright prospect. But, if the pensions are to be paid in full, on the principle of "first come first served," it behoves those who cannot expect to qualify themselves for retirement during the next ten years to consider their prospects, and to take steps for the improvement of their position. To give the Fund, with its present liabilities, a prospect of continued vitality, it should at once be further endowed with the sum of £80,000. If this cannot be obtained, the pensions granted should be limited to the capability of the Fund, which I have shown to be considerably less than the Act presumes.

On the Distribution of Profits in Mutual Insurance Societies,

By M. B. PELL, Esq.

[Read December 7th, 1864.]

THERE is no part of the subject of Life Insurance which has occasioned so much difficulty, and given rise to so much diversity of opinion and of practice, as that of the distribution of profits. The methods which have been adopted are very various, and very few of them seem founded upon any intelligible principle.

Many attempts have been made of late years to form an exact theory on this subject, and to deduce systematic rules; but it cannot, I think, be yet said that there is any method which is generally recognised as theoretically correct, and capable of application in all cases.

In order to form correct rules for the distribution of profits, it is necessary, in the first place, to lay down some fundamental principle, depending upon the nature of the contract of insurance, upon which the method of distribution must be based, and in the next to express the principle by means of formulæ capable of practical application. Writers upon this subject have generally assumed, without comment or controversy, that the fundamental principle is the following. If at any time, upon investigating the affairs of a Mutual Insurance Society, a surplus is found to exist, there should be returned to each member of the society that portion of the surplus which he contributed. A sum being reserved sufficient to cover all the liabilities, the surplus, if any, is considered not as the property of the society, and not strictly speaking as profit, but as the property of certain members held in trust, to be returned to them according to the proportions in which they contributed to it. If it turn out at any investigation that the members have been paying too much in the form of premium, or that the sum reserved at the preceding investigation was more than the event has shewn to have been necessary, then the surplus is to be regarded as a separate fund from which each member is to be repaid in proportion to his contribution. When the amount of the surplus has been ascertained, nothing remains then but to determine how much each member contributed towards it. But, with the greatest respect for those eminent writers who have made this principle the foundation of their investigations, there are many consideration which have driven me to the conclusion that it is in reality fallacious, and in many cases is, and necessarily must be, ignored. I shall endeavour to show that where there is no antecedent agreement as to the mode of distribution of profits, the adoption of the principle against which I am contending involves a violation of some of the rules which are universally recognised and adopted in settling mutual contracts, and in regulating the affairs of monetary and commercial associations. I cannot see that there is anything so entirely peculiar in the mutual contract of life assurance as to take it out of all ordinary rules, and to require or justify successive revisions and amendments according to circumstances as they arise.

In stating my objections to this principle, I shall endeavour to show (1) that it cannot possibly be fully carried out; (2) that if in regulating the affairs of any society it could be pushed to all its legitimate conclusions, it would be found that the society was not in reality an insurance but an investment society ; (3) that the principle must be fallacious, for if consistently applied, it would, under some circumstances, lead to results, the justice, or even the legality, of which could not be maintained.

In a paper by Mr. Sheppard Homans, actuary of the Mutual Life Insurance Company of New York, published in the London Assurance Magazine in October, 1863, a most elaborate method is given of estimating the contributions of the several members to the surplus fund. "It appears," he says, "that the contributions or over-payments of policies during a bonus period may in general be found thus :—*Credit* each policy-holder (1st) with the amount actually reserved at the last preceding distribution of surplus as the then present value or re-insurance of the policy ; and (2nd) with the *effective* (or *full*) premiums paid since that time, both sums being accumulated at the actual current rate of interest, to the date of the present distribution ; and charge him (1st) with the actual cost of the risk to which the company has been exposed, during the interval, determined by means of a table representing the rates of mortality and interest actually experienced ; and then (2nd) with the amount now reserved as the present value of the policy. The difference between the sum of his credits and the sum of his debits determines the overpayment or contribution from the policy proper."

This is perhaps the clearest statement that has been made upon this subject, and amounts to this. The premiums were originally settled according to a certain rate of interest, and a certain table of mortality, with a margin or loading added to cover expenses and contingencies. At the former investigation a sum equal to the liability upon each policy was calculated upon the same basis and reserved to the credit of the policy. At the present investigation it is found that during the interval the rates of interest and of mortality have been more favourable than those assumed, and a new scale of premiums is calculated upon the experienced rates, being the scale according to which the members should have paid if those rates could have been foreseen. To each member there is returned the difference between what he has paid and what it is supposed that he ought to have paid, together with the superfluous accumulations of interest upon the sum reserved to his credit at the former investigation. But even this elaborate method is very far from attaining to that mathematical equity which is intended, for it must be remembered that the sums to the credit of the policies at the former investigation would have differed, not only in amount, but in proportion, if the events of the succeeding bonus period could have been foreseen ; and, therefore, to carry out the principle fully, those sums should be revised, which would greatly alter the results, and would lead to further, and practically interminable, complications.

By the effective premiums Mr. Homans explains that he means the actual premiums with a certain per centage upon the amount insured deducted to cover expenses. This mode of apportioning the expenses is correct as far as it goes—there is no reason why a policy upon an older life should be charged more for expenses of management than one upon a younger, the amounts assured being the same. But it falls far short of settling the question of the apportionment of expenses so fully, as the strict mathematical equity which the system proposes to carry out seems to require. It would probably be found, upon a careful examination, that the actual expense to the society occasioned by any policy has little, if any, dependence upon the amount assured; but that the expense is pretty nearly the same upon one policy as upon another. Excepting, perhaps, in very large societies, where the expenses are relatively light, it would in many cases be found that if the policies for small amounts were charged with the expenses which they had really occasioned, there would be nothing of profit left to them, although a considerable general surplus might exist. It might and probably would appear in some cases, that such policies had been an actual loss to the society. In seeking to determine the real contributions to surplus by the several members, there is no reason why these considerations should be neglected, and their omission seems to render the results obtained of no practical value.

To carry out the method explained by Mr. Homans, it would be necessary at an investigation to form a new table of mortality, upon the actual experience of the Society since the former investigation. It is difficult to see how, in so short a time and with so limited a number of lives, any table could be framed of any value whatever; but without such a table it would be impossible to apportion the actual losses or cost of insurance during the interval, in accordance with the assumed principle. The losses might be apportioned in the same proportion as if the assumed rates of mortality had been actually experienced; and this would seem the only practicable method in any case where the number of members is too small to form the basis of a new mortality table; but it is to some extent arbitrary, and very imperfectly in accordance with the principle upon which the system rests.

There is another consideration which cannot be consistently neglected, if a really accurate estimate is to be formed of the contributions of the several members of a society to the surplus fund. It is well known that it is much easier to find safe and good investments for smaller sums than for larger ones, and that as the funds of a society increase, there is an increasing difficulty in finding safe and profitable investments. It may happen, and indeed has happened, that a portion of the contributions of the earlier members of a society are more profitably invested than the funds received from those who come after them. If, then, a member is considered to retain any special property in the money which he has paid to the society, the earlier members might well contend that they are entitled to the full benefit of the higher rate of interest at which their funds were invested, and it might even perhaps be allowed that as the older investments expire, the earlier members are entitled to have their funds reinvested in the most profitable securities which the society can find. The justice of this claim can hardly, I think, be disputed if the principle against which I am contending be allowed. The newer members, whose funds are necessarily invested at a lower rate of interest, can hardly be said to have contributed to any surplus which may exist, according to any higher rate of interest, than what those funds have actually yielded. In England, where the rate of interest upon money invested in good securities is tolerably uniform, these considerations would not perhaps be of much importance, but the case is very different in this colony.

To take account of the various rates of interest in calculating the contributions to surplus, would involve difficulties, which would probably be found to be insuperable, but their neglect would render the results of no practical value.

If the principle is once admitted that the original contract of assurance is to be varied, to the extent that every member is entitled to claim as his own, anything which he has paid in excess of what experience has proved to have been requisite, we shall be driven to conclusions totally inconsistent with the nature of insurance. If there has been a proportionally lower rate of mortality among the younger lives than amongst the older, then the younger lives should be charged with the losses upon their own class only. The member who insured at the age of thirty should be charged with no losses except those upon policies taken out at that age. To push the principle a little further, those who insured at the age of thirty, five years ago, should not be charged with losses upon policies dated ten years back; and so on by successive subdivisions, until we should come at last to the conclusion that no member can be equitably charged with any losses, except those upon his own policy ; which would amount to this, that upon the death of a member there should be paid back to his representatives the exact sums which he paid in, with interest added and expenses deducted.

Suppose, again, that the members of the society live in two towns, and that experience proves that the rates of mortality are more favourable in one town than in the other. If any account is to be taken of the proportion in which the members have contributed to surplus during any period, it cannot be denied that those who live in the healthier town should be charged with losses according to their own more favourable rates of mortality. On the same principle, the towns should be divided into sections, the members residing in which should be charged with their own losses only. For similar reasons we should go on to subdivide into streets, and then into houses, and finally into single policies, arriving thus at the same conclusion as before ; which is, indeed, the final conclusion to which the assumed principle must necessarily lead, and the only perfectly equitable solution of the whole difficulty.

I shall now endeavour to show that the fundamental principle which has been so commonly assumed, that any surplus which may accumulate during any period is not really the property of the society, but is merely held in trust to be returned to the members, is inconsistent with the nature of the mutual contract of insurance usually entered upon ; and not only is not, but in many cases could not reasonably or even legally, be adhered to.

If during any period a surplus is accumulated on account of higher rates of interest or low rates of mortality, or excess of loading, then according to the assumed principle, this is the property of some or all of the members in a certain proportion ; and this proportion, it must be observed, is quite accidental, depending upon a variety of circumstances, which cannot in any case be foreseen. Now, suppose that upon the eve of the day upon which the investigation is to take place, a loss exactly equal in amount to this surplus which has accrued, is incurred through some accidental cause, as the failure of a bank. There could be no possible doubt, I conceive, that the surplus should be appropriated to make good this loss. To the justice and legality of such an appropriation, no objection could possibly be made. But according to the assumed principle, such an appropriation would be grossly unjust, being an application of the private property of certain members, to make good a partnership loss. If there had been no surplus, then all the members must have borne the loss, in a certain proportion. The fact that there happens to be in the hands of the society a fund, the private property of the members, cannot alter the proportion in which the loss should be borne, and to apply this fund to cover the loss would be clearly unjust, unless the proportion were the same, which could only happen by the merest accident. According to the principle, the fallacy of which I am endeavouring to prove, the only proper course would be, to apportion the loss, and to apportion the surplus separately, and so to balance the accounts. This would lead us to the absurd conclusion, that some of the members would have to bear a certain loss, or abate somewhat of their claims according to the original contract, although the society on the whole was in a perfectly solvent state, whilst to apply the surplus to cover the loss, would be at once to affirm that the surplus fund is, and that it is not the common property of the society—common property to pay losses, but not common property to be distributed as profit.

Again it might be found upon investigation, that by reason of high rates of interest, a certain profit had accrued, but that in consequence of a high rate of mortality, a loss had been incurred. To follow the obvious and necessary course of applying the profit to cover the loss would involve similar contradictions.

The word *equitable* has been much used by writers upon this subject, and it seems always to have been assumed that equity consists in returning to every member so much as he may have paid in excess of what has in fact proved to be sufficient; or, in other words, to reform the original contract by the light of new experience. I think that I have sufficiently shown that this principle of equity, if carried out to its full extent, and I cannot see that there is any particular point at which we can stop short in its application, is inconsistent with the existence of any contract of insurance at all. My idea of equity, as applied to this subject, is that the original contract should be rigidly adhered to, without reference to subsequent events. A member contracts to pay an annual premium calculated upon the basis of certain rates of interest and mortality. If on the whole the rates of interest and mortality prove favourable, a surplus will accumulate, and will be the common property of the society, independently of the sources from which it may have been derived, and should be dealt with in the same manner as if it had been caused by a rise in the value of securities, or otherwise accidently.

The observed rates of interest and mortality, and calculations respecting the expense of management, may afford very useful data for the formation of new societies, or for determining the conditions upon which new members should be admitted, but I cannot see that they have any relevancy whatever in estimating the proportion in which an existing surplus is to be divided.

I will endeavour by an illustration to make my meaning more clear. Suppose that a number of persons should combine together to form a society for the purpose of cultivating land, so as to provide themselves with such quantities of wheat, maize, and hay as they might require, each member agreeing to take so much of each commodity at a certain fixed price, to be paid annually in advance,—the agreement to continue in force during a certain time, and the profits, if any, to be divided equitably at fixed intervals.

If the profits were to be divided according to the principle attempted to be applied to life insurance societies, it would be necessary when a surplus had accumulated to make an accurate estimate of the cost of producing each commodity, and to charge each member accordingly, so as to ascertain how much each had contributed to the surplus. If wheat were found to have cost much less than had been anticipated, then the member who had agreed to take wheat only, would receive a large share of the profit. If the cost of hay agreed exactly with the estimated price, then the man who took hay only would receive no profit. If there was a loss upon the maize, then those who took maize should, on the same principle, instead of sharing in the profit, be required to make good the loss. It would be contrary to the principle to appropriate the contributions from the wheat consumers to pay the losses occasioned by the maize consumers, for every man's contribution should be regarded as his own. I think it will be conceded that this mode of apportioning the profits would be directly at variance with our most commonly received motions of equity, and that the principle involved would, if fully carried out, render mutual contracts to be performed in future practically of no effect.

An estimate of the actual cost of the several commodities produced would furnish useful data in forming a new society for similar purposes; and the calculations of how much each member contributed to surplus might afford an interesting arithmetical exercise; but in determining how the profit in hand should be divided such estimates and calculations would be wholly irrelevant.

I will now endeavour to explain what I consider to be the true principle upon which profits should be distributed in Mutual Life Insurance Societies.

Suppose that a number of persons mutually insure their lives. Each member contracts to pay a fixed sum annually during his lifetime, and the society contracts to pay a certain sum upon his death. At the end of five years, suppose a fund will have accumulated in the hands of the society, and at the same time each policy will have acquired a certain value. Suppose now that it were determined to wind up the Society, and to divide the fund. Each member should in the first place of course receive the present value of his policy, or the value of his claim against the society. If the payment of these sums should exhaust the fund, there would be an end of the matter: the Society would have proved exactly solvent and no more, and no one would have lost or gained anything by it.

The present value of the policy on the life of any member is his share of the fund, being precisely what he would lose if the fund were annihilated, and what he would receive if the Society were wound up. It is, in fact, the sum which he has invested and risked in the concern. It is not, of course, so great as the full amount of the premiums which he has paid, with interest added, for a portion has gone to pay for losses by deaths during the five years, and for this he has received an equivalent, viz., the security which he has enjoyed during the five years, that in case of his death a certain sum would be paid to those for whom it was his intention to provide.

It is not my object in this paper to consider how the present value of a policy should be determined, but in a merely business like point of view, it should be such a sum as would enable a member, in case his own society was wound up, to compound with another similar society to insure his life at the same premium which he had hitherto paid, although his age was greater by five years.

If upon winding up a society it were found that the funds were not sufficient to pay back to each member the present value of his policy, it is quite clear that each must abate proportionally. Whatever per centage is wanting on the whole, the same per centage must be deducted from each. I cannot see that there would be any other just or legal way of apportioning the loss, and it appears to me equally clear that if, instead of a deficiency, there were a surplus, it should be distributed in the same proportion; that is, in proportion to the present value of the policies or to the sums invested and risked in the Society by the several members. This is precisely in accordance with universal practice in all cases where several persons are jointly interested in any undertaking. Profits are always divided in the same proportion in which losses, if incurred, would be apportioned. It may be urged, as an objection to this method, that, under certain circumstances, some of the members would receive a larger share of the surplus than they had contributed; but it would always be found in such cases that if a loss had been incurred, the same members would necessarily have borne the larger share of the loss, and in the same proportion.

In a purely proprietary company, under proper management, the insured incur no appreciable risk, and receive no share of the profit. The shareholders take all the surplus, to which they have contributed nothing. They are simply paid for the risk which they have incurred, small though it be. The insured enjoys a security for which he pays, and the shareholder undertakes a certain risk for which he is paid. To say that this is inequitable, because the shareholder had contributed nothing to the surplus, would not be more absurd than it would be to condemn as inequitable a system, under which a member of a Mutual Life Insurance Society might, under certain circumstances, receive a larger share of the profits than he had himself contributed. When a man becomes a member of a Mutual Insurance Society, he not only insures his life, but, to a certain extent, he engages in the business of life insurance; he is at once insurer and insured, and as insurer he may be considered at any time to have invested in the business a sum equal to the present value of his policy, and is entitled to a proportional share of the profits in the same way and for the same reason that a shareholder in a proprietary company is so entitled.

This present value is small at first, and increases with the duration of the policy, but where the premium is paid in a single sum, the policy has at once a considerable value. In estimating the present values of the policies at any investigation, it is necessary of course to take into account any previous bonus additions which may have been made, every such addition amounting in reality to a new paid-up policy.

Any system of distribution which depends upon the assumption that the loading is the principal source of profit, the "bonus producing power" of the policy, as it has been called, is quite inapplicable in this colony. In England the rates of interest upon good securities are tolerably uniform, and the probability of any great fluctuation very remote, so that it is safe to calculate upon a rate of interest a very little less than what may actually be obtained. But here, although a comparatively high rate of interest may be obtained, its continuance cannot safely be depended upon, so that there is necessarily a wide difference between the assumed and the experienced rates. This has been, and will no doubt continue to be for many years, one of the largest sources of profit to Life Insurance Societies in this colony.

By a method explained by Mr. Meikle in a paper recently published in the *Assurance Magazine*, the contributions from interest alone by the several members of a Society may be calculated with exactness upon the supposition that the members die according to the assumed rates of mortality. By a similar method some general results may be obtained as to the effects of more favourable rates, and of loading. I cannot within the limits of this paper enter fully into this part of the subject, but can only state some results in a very general form. The contributions to surplus from a very high rate of interest are larger in proportion to present values from older and from paid up policies, than from ordinary policies of short duration. The reverse is the case with respect to profits arising from loading and from low rates of mortality; the contributions from these sources from policies of very short duration, being larger in proportion to their present values, than from older or from paid up policies. The losses which might be occasioned by high rates of mortality would be in the same proportion. There is a greater proportional profit on the newer policies, but, at the same time, there is a greater risk. According to the method of distribution which I propose, the younger policies would under such favourable circumstances receive less, and the older ones more, than they had contributed; and the general effect would be that, until a member attained to the average age, his bonus additions would be less than an equivalent for his contributions to surplus; but afterwards the balance would be in his favour. This would be the case in an old society with policies existing of all ordinary durations.

None of these results respecting contributions, according to my view of the matter, afford any argument for or against the method of distribution which I advocate. I have stated them merely for the purpose of explaining the reason of certain effects, which that method produced at the recent investigation of the Australian Mutual Provident Society. The circumstances of that Society are wholly exceptional, and I believe unprecedented. The rates of mortality during the past five years have been unusually low, and the profit from this source upon policies of short duration, although not very considerable, is large in proportion to their present values. The method, therefore, of dividing the surplus in proportion to present values, has in this case operated favourably to the older and more valuable policies. Under ordinary circumstances, where there is the usual proportion of old and of new policies, this would not have produced any very marked effect. The business of the Australian Mutual Provident

Society, however, has increased so enormously during the last few years, and the preponderance of very new policies, is so excessive, that a policy of six years standing may be regarded as an old policy, and one of ten years as very old.

On account of the favourable rates of mortality which the Society has experienced, this new business has proved very remunerative, and of the profits from this source, the policies of longer duration have in some cases received a larger share than what they actually contributed. Those who think there is anything really inequitable in this, should remember that those who have received the larger share of the profits have also incurred the larger share of the risk. The accumulated capital, the property of the earlier members of the Society, was the guarantee fund, without the security of which the greater number of the newer members would never have insured their lives in the Society at all; and upon this fund, if any loss had been incurred through a high rate of mortality, the larger share of the loss must have fallen. Any such loss must have been made good, if possible, out of the surplus arising from high rates of interest, to which the newer members have contributed comparatively little. The larger share of such losses would unavoidably have fallen upon the earlier members, and, therefore, they are entitled to participate in profits in proportion to the sums which they have invested in the society and exposed to such risks. It would be very unjust that the newer members should share fully in the profits arising from favourable rates of mortality, whilst they are to a great extent secured against losses by the funds already accumulated.

Even supposing that the real contributions to surplus from every policy could be estimated, it would be inequitable to divide profits in that proportion, unless there was an understanding that losses—in any way incurred—should be separately estimated and similarly apportioned. If the surplus from one source, or from all sources, is merely held by the society in trust to be returned to the members in certain proportions, then clearly if a loss be incurred through rates of mortality in excess of the assumed rates, or otherwise, this loss must be the private debt of the members, to be paid by them in certain proportions, independently of any surplus which may have arisen from other sources. Such a system would be inconsistent with what seems one of the fundamental principles of insurance, viz., that all losses shall be borne in common and paid for out of the common fund; and could not reasonably or even legally be carried out except under a distinct antecedent agreement.

On the Agricultural Statistics of New South Wales,

By C. ROLLESTON, ESQ.

[Read December 7th, 1864.]

I BEG to lay on the table of the Society three sets of tables, setting forth respectively as follows, viz. :—

Table 1.—1st the imports of wheat and flour, the estimated value thereof, and the value per head of the population. 2nd the colonial produce, with the average price per bushel of wheat, estimated value, and value per head of the population. 3rd the exports of wheat and flour, estimated value thereof, and value per head of the population.

Table 2.—The second table shows the quantities, in tons, imported, produced in the colony, and exported, with the net quantity left for consumption, and the proportion to every 100 of the population.

Table 3.—The third table exhibits the proportion of land under tillage in the *principal crops*, and the produce per acre.

The three sets of tables embrace the quinquennial period from 1859 to 1863, both inclusive.

It has seemed to me to be of some importance at the present juncture, that we should arrive at as near an approximation, as the information before us will admit, as to the results of our colonial husbandry during the last few years.

I take this means of giving publicity to the subject, since owing to the lateness of the period when the returns for 1863 were received, no time was afforded me for analysing them prior to their publication, and the usual official channel is now closed to me.

If any one will take the trouble to refer to the "Statistical Register" for 1858, he will find a set of tables similar to those now before you, extending over the period from 1854 to 1858, both inclusive. He will find the following results plainly brought out, and stated at pages 12, 13, and 14 of the prefatory report, viz., that the average annual value of our imports of wheat and flour for the five years was no less than £368,473; that was at the annual rate of £1 5s. 3d. per head of the population.

The total sum sent out of the colony during this period for wheat and flour, was £1,842,365; this was for the five years, 1854 to 1858. Well, what did we produce during this period? The statistics of agriculture show us that on the average of the five years, our wheat crops yielded 1,346,052 bushels per annum (an average of rather more than 15 bushels per acre.) The price of wheat during these five years ranged from 7s. 4d. up to 16s. 5d. per bushel, the average being 11s. 4d.; this gave an annual value to our wheat crop of £762,312, or at the rate of £2 12s. 3d. per head of the population.

The annual value of our imports and home produce together, was £1,120,785, or at the rate of £3 17s. 6d. per head of the population; but from this we must deduct an export at the rate of £86,356, or 6s. 4d. per head annually, which leaves £3 11s. 2d. as the annual average value of the consumption of breadstuffs per head of the population. Including wheat for seed, the net quantity of wheat and flour left for consumption, after deducting exports, averaged 44,361 tons annually, that is at the rate of 14·9 tons to every 100 of the population, equal to very nearly 300 lbs. to every man, woman, and child in the colony.

I have referred back to these results of a previous investigation, in order to institute a comparison with the figures I have now to treat of, which have reference to the later quinquennial period, 1859 to 1863.

The average annual value of wheat and flour imported during this period was £354,826, equal to 19s. 9d. per head of the population; and the total sum sent out of the Colony for breadstuffs was £1,774,133.

We will put the results of the two quinquennial periods together, viz. :—

	Value, Annual Average.	Value per Head.	Aggregate Value.
1854 to 1858	£368,473	£1 5 3	£1,842,365
1859 to 1863	354,826	0 19 9	1,774,133
Difference	£13,647	£0 5 6	£68,232

I am comparing now the declared values of our importations,—quantity I will come to presently. It appears then, that the value of the importations in the five years, 1859 to 1863, did not reach the average of the previous five years by £13,647, or 5s. 6d. per head.

If we look, however, to the quantities imported, we shall find the figures reversed; for whereas the annual average of the first five years was 17,141 tons, the average of the last five years was 23,499 tons—that is an excess at the rate of 6,358 tons annually.

Our home produce of wheat, from 1859 to 1863 inclusive, averaged 1,331,371 bushels annually, or rather over 11 bushels per acre, being a smaller average by 15,281 bushels than the yield of the previous five years; the prices of wheat ranged from 6s. 6d. to 8s. 6d. per bushel—the average being 7s. 3d., which gave an annual value to our wheat crop of £493,801, or at the rate of £1 7s. 11d. per head of the population.

The comparison stands thus, viz. :—

	Average Acreage. Acres.	Bushels.	Price.	Value.
1854 to 1858	87,906	1,346,652	£0 11 4	£762,312
1859 to 1863	116,061	1,331,371	0 7 3	493,801

The computed value of our imports and home produce together was at the annual rate of £2 7s. 8d. per head of the population, against £3 7s. 6d., during the previous five years.

The difference in the rate is attributable not (as has been shown) to deficiency of quantity, but to the higher value during the earlier quinquennial period.

Including wheat for seed, the net quantity of wheat and flour left for consumption, after deducting exports, averaged 47,919 tons, that is, at the rate of 134 tons to every 100 of the population—equal to about 260 lbs. to every man, woman, and child in the colony, that is, about 40 lbs. less per head per annum than we found to be the consumption of the previous quinquennial period.

It is reasonable to attribute the higher rate of consumption of the first five years to the comparative extravagance of the period following the gold discovery. We know that waste and extravagance marked that era, not in food only, but in drink, in dress, and in necessaries of all kinds. The sobering process of the last five years has had the effect of introducing habits of economy into every household, as herein exemplified.

What are the results then of this branch of our inquiry? They are these:—First, we imported during the decade—1854 to 1863, inclusive—wheat and flour to the value of £3,616,498, we exported to the value of £888,238, leaving a sum of £2,728,260 against the colony for breadstuffs, exclusive of rye, oats, barley, rice, &c.

Secondly, that whilst the extent of land sown in wheat has increased by 32 per cent. over the average of the first five years, the average yield of our own crops has not kept pace with this increase, nor with the increase of the population. This result is owing, for the most part, to the disasters of the last two years. Excepting the year 1854 the crop of last season was far below any year of the decade. The largest yield was in 1856, viz.—1,756,964 bushels off 106,124 acres; the smallest was in 1863, 808,919 bushels, off 103,962 acres, equal to 95 lbs. of flour per head of the population, without deducting wheat for seed, or about one third the quantity required for consumption.

In the first quinquennial period we imported 36·0 per cent., and we produced 64·0 per cent. of the wheat and flour provided for consumption. In the second quinquennial period we imported 44·0 per cent., and produced 56·0 per cent.

In the first five years the average acreage sown in wheat was 49·4 per cent. of the land under tillage. In the second five years it was 41·4 per cent. only—a falling off of 8 per cent. And here I should like to point attention to the remarkable decrease in wheat cultivation, and to the corresponding increase in the cultivation of maize, which is observable in the years 1862 and 1863. You will observe in table 3 that whilst in 1860 we had 49 per cent. of our cultivated land under wheat, and 19 per cent. only in maize, in 1863 we had 33 per cent. only under wheat, and 31 per cent. in maize.

There is another striking feature in the table of produce which goes to prove the greater certainty attending the cultivation of maize. It will be seen that the years fraught with disaster to the wheat crop, were rather favourable to the growth of maize, for in 1862, we had $33\frac{1}{2}$ bushels of maize per acre, and only $9\frac{1}{2}$ of wheat; and in 1863, we had $30\frac{1}{2}$ bushels of maize to only $7\frac{1}{2}$ of wheat.

The expediency of substituting maize-flour for wheaten-flour—or, rather, of using the two together—is a question of deep moment. It involves a saving to the country of something like £300,000 a-year; and Mr. Mort has placed us under great obligations for having brought the matter so prominently before the public, and for setting so good an example. No other colony can compete with us in growing maize, whilst all (excepting Queensland) can beat us in the growth of wheat.

But I must not dilate at greater length on this topic. The paper is already longer than I intended, and yet there is one practical conclusion at which I should like to arrive before closing my remarks. It is to determine from the data before us, what remuneration the agriculturist may expect, on the average of years, for his labour and expenditure in the cultivation of wheat.

We have seen that the average yield of the five years—1854 to 1858—was fifteen bushels per acre, and that the average price (let it be observed that this was a period of comparatively high prices, owing to the effects of the gold discovery) was 11s. 4d. per bushel. The result is, that the farmer, during these years, reaped a return of £8 10s. per acre as the reward of his toil. But his seed wheat has to come out of this, at the rate of $1\frac{1}{2}$ bushels per acre, and this reduces his profits by 17s., leaving him only £7 13s. per acre.

This, however, is the result of five years of higher prices than have ruled since. Let us see then how much the farmer has made by wheat-growing on the average of the last five years—1859 to 1863.

We have seen that the average yield was only 11·3 bushels per acre, whilst the average price was 7s. 3d. per bushel. Now suppose, after deducting wheat for seed, the farmer had a clear 10 bushels of wheat for sale to the acre, the average remuneration for his expenditure of time and labour would amount to £3 12s. 6d. per acre. If now we take the mean of the two quinquennial periods, we get the result of £5 12s. 9d. per acre as the cash return to the farmer. But this is a more favourable view than it would be wise for him to make the basis of his calculations; because, on turning back to earlier statistics, I find that during the four years previous to the decade I am speaking of, namely, from '49 to '53, the average price of wheat was barely 6s. per bushel.

The South Australian farmer is content to get his 3s. 6d. per bushel on the ground, and his average produce may be stated at about 12 bushels to the acre, that is about 42s. per acre, whilst our average return per acre is more than double. And yet what are the facts? Why, that the cultivation of wheat was in 1862 at the rate af $2\frac{1}{2}$ acres to each person in South Australia, whilst in New South Wales there was not half an acre. If this is so, the South Australian farmer may calculate on a remunerative market for his breadstuffs in Sydney for many years to come, if we do not bestir ourselves. We can also readily understand how it is that we received from that colony in 1863 over 400,000 bushels of wheat and over 12,000 tons of flour of the aggregate value of £270,717.

In disparagement of the results arrived at in this paper,

doubts may be thrown upon the perfect accuracy of our returns of agriculture. All that I can say in answer to this is, that they have been complied with the greatest care, and that every possible precaution has been taken to ensure accuracy in their collection. To say that errors may be possible is only to say that all human efforts are fallible ; but there are no more reasonable grounds for rejecting the conclusions at which we have arrived in this matter than for rejecting the results of any other inquiry into the social condition of the people, or into the comparative progress of the colony in any other branch of industry.

Seeing the great importance of the subject, it would be well that means were taken to render the enquiry into our agricultural resources less open to question, and to publish the information obtained in more minute detail and with greater promptitude.

I must, however, take leave to deprecate the idea that the duty of collecting the returns is performed in a perfunctory manner. It is true with regard to the boundaries of districts, that, taking one year with the other, uniformity has not in all cases been observed; but in the aggregate it is only proper to say that the most careful scrutiny, from year to year, has disclosed no seriously appreciable error.

(YEARS 1859 TO 1863, INCLUSIVE.)

1. TABLE shewing—1st, the Imports of Wheat and Flour, the Estimated Value, and the Quantity and Rate per head of the Population.

   2nd, the Colonial Produce of Wheat in bushels, the Average Price per Bushel, and the Number of Bushels, and Rate per head of Population.

   3rd, the Export of Wheat and Flour, the Estimated Value, and the Quantity and Rate per head of Population.

Imports.

Year.	Population.	Wheat.	Flour and Bread.	Estimated Value.	Value of Imports per Head of Population.
		Bushels.	Tons.	£.	£ s. d.
1859	336,572	289,370	3,302	188,199	0 11 2
1860	348,546	763,563	10,393	461,993	1 6 6
1861	358,278	577,314	15,118	434,838	1 4 3
1862	367,495	446,640	14,673	339,318	0 18 5
1863	378,934	612,366	14,249	349,785	0 18 5
Average of 5 years..		537,850	11,547	354,826	0 19 9

Colonial Produce.

Year.	Population.	Wheat.	Average price p. bu. through-out the Colony.	Estimated Value.	Value of Colonial produce per Head of Population.	Value of Imports and Colonial Produce per Head of Population.
		Bushels.	s. d.	£	£ s. d.	£ s. d.
1859	336,572	1,605,353	8 6	682,275	2 0 6	2 11 8
1860	348,546	1,581,597	8 0	632,638	1 16 3	3 2 9
1861	358,278	1,606,034	6 6	521,961	1 9 1	2 13 4
1862	367,495	1,054,954	7 0	369,234	1 0 1	1 18 6
1863	378,934	808,919	6 6	262,898	0 13 10	1 12 3
Average of 5 years		1,331,371	7 3	493,801	1 7 11	2 7 8

Exports.

Year.	Population.	Wheat.	Flour and Bread.	Estimated Value.	Value of Exports per Head of Population.
		Bushels.	Tons.	£	s. d.
1859	336,572	23,339	1,889	53,813	3 2
1860	348,546	16,170	4,269	94,156	5 4
1861	358,278	23,297	4,447	102,132	5 8
1862	367,495	15,541	5,964	95,068	5 2
1863	378,934	9,461	7,318	111,285	5 10
Average of 5 years..		17,561	4,777	91,291	5 0

2. TABLE shewing the quantities of Breadstuffs Imported, Produced in the Colony, and Exported during the years 1859, 1860, 1861, 1862, and 1863; also the Proportion per 100 of Population.

Year.	Population	Import of Breadstuffs (in Flour).	Colonial Produce (in Flour).	Total.	Export of Breadstuffs (in Flour).	Net Quantity for Home Consumption.	Proportion per 100 of Population.
		Tons.	Tons.	Tons.	Tons.	Tons.	Tons.
1859..	336,572	9,732	35,674	45,406	2,407	42,999	12·7
1860..	348,546	27,361	35,146	62,507	4,628	57,879	16·6
1861..	358,278	27,947	35,689	63,636	4,964	58,672	16·3
1862..	367,495	24,598	23,443	48,041	6,309	41,732	11·3
1863..	378,934	27,857	17,976	45,833	7,528	38,305	10·1
Average of 5 yrs		23,499	29,585	53,084	5,167	*47,919	13·4

* Wheat for Seed is included in this quantity.

3. PROPORTION of the Cultivated Land under the Principal Crops, during the years 1859, 1860, 1861, 1862, and 1863.

Name of Crop.	ACRES PER CENT.					Mean of 5 Years.
	1859.	1860.	1861.	1862.	1863.	
Wheat.....	46·8	49·3	41·4	35·7	33·8	41·4
Maize......	19·9	19·7	19·4	25·1	31·1	23·0
Barley.....	1·7	1·0	0·9	0·8	1·3	1·1
Oats.......	2·3	2·5	2·4	3·3	4·2	2·9
Potatoes....	3·5	3·5	3·3	3·0	3·7	3·4
Hay........	18·5	17·8	15·1	17·4	15·7	16·9

PRODUCE per Acre of each of the Principal Crops, during the years 1859, 1860, 1861, 1862, and 1863.

Nature of Produce.	ACRES PER CENT.					Mean of 5 Years.
	1859.	1860.	1861.	1862.	1863.	
Wheat bhls.	13·8	12·2	13·0	9·7	7·7	11·3
Maize do.	32·3	28·8	29·8	33·6	30·5	31·0
Barley do.	14·9	13·9	14·0	12·0	16·3	14·2
Oats do.	15·4	15·1	21·1	20·1	14·4	17·2
Potatoes tns.	2·3	3·0	3·0	2·6	2·7	2·7
Hay do.	1·3	1·0	1·2	1·4	1·4	1·2

On the Defences of Port Jackson,

By G. A. MORELL, ESQ., C.E.

[Read September 6th, 1865.]

IT is generally admitted that the effectual defence of Port Jackson presents many difficulties. Not one of the several projects that have been proposed at different times seems to fulfil entirely and satisfactorily the object in view, viz., the possibility of preventing an enemy from entering Port Jackson, or the certainty of having such advantage over him from our batteries, as to oblige him to surrender or retreat if we permit him to enter the Harbour. These difficulties arise chiefly from the extent of Coast to be fortified, which encloses an area of about ten square miles, and has no less than twenty Points, Headlands, or Islands, and twenty Bays or Coves to be commanded or covered, and also from the enormous expense required to complete extensive and effective works, and to maintain a large military force to man them.

Any complete system of defence for Port Jackson, if extended from Sydney to the Heads, would be too costly for the Colony at present; but batteries might be commenced to afford temporary defence, with a view to their being afterwards converted into works of such power as to render them efficient and secure.

The probability of being obliged to strengthen our defensive works in a co-relative proportion to the advance of Military science, was overlooked in the construction of our present batteries, and in our future works we must not forget the rapid improvements that are made daily in the heavy artillery and vessels of war likely to be brought against us.

It must be admitted that whether we have or have not the co-operation of English Men-of-War or of a Colonial Navy, batteries and forts are indispensible for the defence of our Harbour.

It is therefore requisite :

I. To consider carefully the strategical field of Port Jackson with regard to Defensive and Offensive operations, and to make a topographical examination of all the positions to be commanded or covered.

II. To fix upon the best positions for our forts and batteries strategically, and with regard to communication with headquarters.

III. To determine the number and strength of our batteries, so that they may command every place where a vessel could lay to, to shell the city, taking into consideration the amount of Military Forces at our disposal, the assistance we may derive from Ships of Her Majesty's Navy, and the outlay necessary for the completion of the works.

IV. To determine the construction necessary for our forts and batteries, in order to make them of sufficient strength and power to resist any attack made upon them by sea or by land, considering the improved ordnance likely to be used against us, and to make these works as extensive as may be required by their particular positions to enable a sufficient number of soldiers to manœuvre within them, in order to secure effective defence and to keep up a rapid and regular fire against an attacking enemy.

V. To determine the quantity and power of the ordnance required for the works proposed, considering the improvements made in vessels of war, the sides of which are now made sufficiently strong to resist the penetration of projectiles fired from old cast iron guns, and also the long ranges at which we shall have to attack the ships of an enemy, and the uncertainty of firing at moving objects.

I shall explain my views upon each of these points separately.

I.

1. On looking over the Echiquier General of Port Jackson, with regard to defensive and offensive operations, we find that the elevation of the North Head (353 feet) renders it a tempting position to an enemy, as it would defilade works on Middle Head, George Head, Inner South Head, Green Point, Shark Point,

Bradley Head, Shark Island, Clark Island, Point Piper, and Darling Point, and would command North Harbour, Middle Harbour, the Sound, the Channels, Watsons Bay, Taylor Bay, Rose Bay, Double Bay, and as far as Rushcutters Bay, besides the whole of the approaches to the Harbour by sea; but this formidable position could easily be rendered inaccessible by a battery on Middle Head, except on the ocean side, where a landing could be prevented.

North Head is too distant and too isolated to be permanently occupied, and Works erected thereon could only be advantageous to us in the event of our being able to spare many of our troops.

2. Middle Head is one of the best positions in Port Jackson, but unless strongly fortified at the gorge by a ditch and wall about 400 yards long, enclosing an area of nearly 15 acres, it would prove insecure, as an enemy could bring boats at night into Hunter Bay and Obelisk Bay to land large bodies of troops to attack the batteries of Middle Head in the rear, and by preventing our re-enforcements reaching other positions from the attacked point, facilitate the tactics of his fleet. Vessels steaming 5 knots per hour, on entering by the East Channel, would not be exposed to the fire of Middle Head batteries more than six (6) minutes within a range of 2000 yards, and would keep during that time more than 1000 yards from these batteries; on entering by the West Channel vessels would be exposed twenty (20) minutes at a less range than 2000 yards, but as soon as they had rounded George Head they would have no more to fear from the batteries of Middle Head, and in the case of landing parties attacking these batteries, they might prevent re-enforcements from reaching in time other positions attacked by a fleet. If reliance could be placed on obstructions across the Channel to prevent the ingress of ships, Middle Head strongly fortified might prove the best position in Port Jackson; but as permanent obstructions that would keep out our own vessels as well as an enemy's are out of the question, Middle Head cannot be considered strategically the best position for Head-quarters on the North Shore.

3. George Head, if we have temporary obstructions is of more importance. The height of its crest in close communication with roads, the impossibility of an enemy surrounding it, from

the approaches being so extensive and well commanded, safe retreat being secured in case of a reverse, the practicability of affording re-enforcements to other positions, if needed, by land or by water, together with the fitness of the ground to contain Shell-proof works and barracks, and to command every battery we might have from Darling Point to the entrance of the Harbour, indicate it as the best position on the North Shore for Headquarters for the number of troops to be permanently kept in readiness against the attacks of an enemy. Vessels steaming 5 knots per hour must be exposed to the full fire of batteries on George Head for 25 minutes, at a less range than 2000 yards, and within that same range, the guns of George Head will cross fire with those of every battery as far as Point Piper. Vessels forcing a passage through obstructions thrown across the channels would be followed by the guns of George Head until past Bradley Head.

4. On examination of the ground from Inner South Head Lighthouse to the Gap, we find that the first point north of the Gap Bluff is decidedly the best for a battery. There is no intervening ground to interfere with the fire of guns as at each of the other plateaux towards the Lighthouse. This position might be of value with long range guns. Vessels entering by the East Channel would be exposed to the fire of the guns of a battery on Inner South Head for 28 minutes, within a range of 2000 yards, but only for 4 minutes within a range of 1000 yards. Engaging vessels at sea, which could easily keep out of 1000 yards range, would prove almost a waste of ammunition, as the elevation of the guns would vary at every shot. At night this battery would be nearly useless. It is too far from Watsons Bay for tactical operations, although it is invaluable as a look-out from which to transmit information by Electric Telegraph to other batteries.

5. Green Point is strategically a very good position; a battery there is necessary. Vessels entering by the East Channel would be raked fore and aft by its guns nearly point blank, being fully exposed to their fire for 12 minutes within a range of 1000 yards, and for 20 minutes within 2000 yards; entering by the West Channel vessels would lie 16 minutes only within the same range, but a low ricochetting fire from Green Point would be

almost certain to disable them. The proximity of Watsons Bay (for communication by water), renders this position most valuable in a logistical point of view. In time of war it will also afford a powerful support to vessels seeking shelter in Watsons Bay.

6. Shark Point is another good position. Vessels would be exposed 24 minutes within a range of 2000 yards to the fire of guns placed there, but their speed may be increased and the time of their exposure lessened. Guns at that position would cover Taylor Bay and Rose Bay where vessels could lay to to shell the city. It is easy of access and ought to be occupied.

7. Bradley Point is a most important position with any system of Defence we may adopt. With obstructions in the Channels, it is as important as Shark Point, although further from them, and without obstructions, it is strategically the best position in Port Jackson. Within a range of 2000 yards, it commands almost every place where a vessel could lay to to shell the City. Heavy Guns placed at Bradley Point would bear constantly on an enemy for three-quarters of an hour, from the time of his entering Port Jackson until he had reached Darling Harbour, being nearly all the time raked fore and aft. Bradley Head, might, however, like Middle Head, prove an insecure position unless strongly fortified at the gorge on the higher ground, to prevent an enemy from attacking its batteries in the rear.

8. With obstructions in the Channels, Point Piper, Darling Point, Garden Island, and Careening Point need only have subsidiary batteries, where guns may be taken if wanted; but without obstructions, these positions require powerful batteries for guns to cross fire with other works within a range of 2000 yards upon vessels attempting to shell the city and shipping.

9. Shark Island and Clark Island would be very good positions if we could spare many troops to occupy permanently strong forts erected thereon, otherwise they are too liable to be surrounded by a fleet and attacked by landing parties, without the chance of assistance or re-enforcements reaching them. Strong Forts numerously garrisoned on these Islands would be too costly to build and to maintain.

10. Although the present batteries at Fort Denison, Lady Macquarie's Point, Fort Macquarie, Kiribili Point, and Dawes

Point, and the dismantled battery on Bradley Point are frequently depreciated, and are no doubt defective in some details of construction, their situation is in accordance with the rules of Defence at the time they were designed, which could not possibly foresee or provide for the consequences of the recent wonderful developement of the mechanical appliances of war. With our experience, the same mistakes are not likely to occur in new works, and the old ones may be modified so as to render them efficient batteries.

11. The inner positions of the Harbour as far as our Powder Magazine must be protected by batteries on Fort Phillip, Goat Island, Ball's Head, or Long Nose Point, to prevent vessels under shelter in some of the Bays, from shelling the City. The new Powder Magazine at Spectacle Island ought without delay to be made shot and shell proof.

12. If obstructions were placed across the "Sow and Pigs" Shoal, a strong Tower on the rock there would be necessary to fire point blank on either side at vessels attempting to force a passage, but without obstructions, there seems no necessity for such a work.

II. AND III.

The extent and number of our Batteries require much consideration.

We may be exposed to receive a hostile visit from a single frigate, but it is more likely that not less than a squadron would dare to venture into Port Jackson, with the probability of being received by British men-of-war; if we trust to the latter to defend us, they may be overpowered by a stronger force if not well supported by land batteries. It is more prudent to depend chiefly on our batteries, regarding the powerful assistance of H.M. Ships, if at Sydney, as an additional advantage.

Two systems of Defence seem practicable.

The first consists in the strength and power of our batteries and forts and upon their extent, to cover every point where an enemy could attempt a landing, or lay to to shell the city and shipping. The strongest work of such a system should be at Bradley Head as a centre of operation, the batteries at the Heads being subsidiary; the heaviest of guns would be required at every work, with a large number of men and good military roads to every position.

This system is the most rational, and the only one in accordance with the laws of Defence and Attack, but it is too costly to be entertained at present by the Colony. I find from a rough estimate that it would not cost less than a quarter of a million sterling before its completion, and not less than £60,000 annually for the maintenance of the necessary troops and for repairs.

The second system of defence consists in obstructing the Channels at the entrance of the Harbour, and in concentrating round these obstructions, where vessels may be expected to be delayed, our strongest works, making provision, however, for the possibility of vessels taking us by surprise or for their forcing a passage, by constructing subsidiary works within the obstructions.

Movable obstructions beyond booming a narrow channel or canal are not generally considered as means of defence, but we are obliged to take into consideration the small number of troops at our command and the cost of Defensive Works. If mechanical contrivances could be relied on, a small opening might be left in the obstructions of the channels to be closed at a short notice on the appearance of suspicious craft. Any obstructions must be made of as permanent a character as possible to prevent boats intended to land troops from passing over them or blowing them up partly, to effect a *coup de main* on our batteries.

The cost of the construction of this second system of defence would not be half that of the first, and the expense for maintenance would be within our means; but its efficiency would also be proportionately diminished, as so much depends upon obstructions which a powerful and ingenious enemy might succeed in clearing away.

I have carefully considered this second system consisting of obstructions and batteries to protect them, and I shall now refer to it more particularly.

The best position for booms is necessarily where obstructions already exist. The "Sow and Pigs" Shoal leaving two narrow channels, one on each side, presents greater facilities for placing obstructions than any other position.

If booms are only floated or laid the whole distance from the Sow and Pigs Rock to the shores, large vessels at full speed would most likely pass over them *by forcing them down;* they could undoubtedly accomplish this by sending boats over night to prepare a gap in the booms by attaching bags of shot or other weights to them to diminish their buoyancy, or by blowing them partly away with torpedoes. Such booms could not prevent boats passing across or over them at night for the purpose of landing large bodies of troops within the obstructions for a *coup de main* on our batteries.

If to remove these objections we make our obstructions in the form of dykes, leaving only a small opening in each channel for navigation, the scheme becomes more feasible, as it must be self-evident that it is easier to boom and to command a narrow channel of from 300 to 400 yards than 1700 or 1800 yards, the whole distance from shore to shore. Engineers differ in opinion with regard to the probable results that dykes constructed across the Sow and Pigs Shoal might produce in Port Jackson, and it certainly is a most interesting subject for discussion. Booming small openings is merely a matter of engineering detail; a plan could be devised for obstructing these channels temporarily in time of war.

Booms would require powerful batteries to protect them, and the best positions for these batteries would be at point blank ranges from the obstructions.

George Head and Green Point are preferable to Middle Head and Inner South Head for Head-quarters and batteries, for if booms are to detain an enemy, it is better to engage vessels at short ranges in narrow passages where turning and manœuvring is impossible, and where every one of our shots would tell from our knowing by previous target practice the exact range and elevation for every point in the channels, than to engage them partly at sea where the costly ammunition of our heavy guns would be mostly wasted. It is hardly probable that an enemy would venture to force a passage under the fire of strong batteries, with heavy guns at George Head and Green Point, supported by others on Middle Head and Inner South Head. Vessels would be raked fore and aft by two batteries in whatever position they should occupy, and a rapid and accurate fire from heavy guns would soon oblige them to surrender or drive them on the shoal in their attempt to retreat. The firing of the enemy could not do much damage to strong works constructed at a proper elevation to resist shot and shell, whereas the enemy would be exposed to the fire of our batteries, from which every shot would tell with unerring precision.

In order to be prepared in case of surprise we ought to have two strong batteries within the obstructions, one on Shark Point and the other on Bradley Point; a strong iron fort on the "Sow and Pigs" rock, with the heaviest guns procurable, would prove the most formidable of all our works, for every shot from these guns at such short ranges could sink a vessel. Subsidiary Works on Point Piper, Darling Point, and Careening Point would also be required, to be furnished with guns from Head-quarters when necessary. The lower part of the Harbour below Dawes Point must likewise be protected by similar works on Fort Phillip, Goat Island, and Long Nose Point.

The comparative economy of the second system of defence was my reason for proposing it to the Select Committee of the Legislative Assembly on Harbour Defences.

The plan I then proposed consists of:

A Tower, on the "Sow and Pigs" rock, covered with 6-inch armour plates, backed with timber and Iron frames, armed with one 600-pounder Armstrong rifled shunt gun, mounted under a cupola (non-revolving), and with two 300-pounder Armstrong rifled shunt guns mounted on traversing platforms and turn-tables; the guns to fire through embrasures.

Four Dykes partly closing the entrance of the Harbour at the "Sow and Pigs" Shoal, and leaving two openings for navigation of 400 yards each, one in the Western Channel and one in the Eastern.

Movable booms to be stretched across the channel between the dykes, or removed on each side of them when the passages are open.

A Fort on George Head to be used as Head-quarters on the North Shore, with secure shot and shell proof barracks for 150 men, stores and magazine, towards Chowder Bay. The offensive and defensive work to consist of one 600-pounder Armstrong rifled shunt gun, under a non-revolving cupola, placed on the extreme height, the rock being sloped for depression.

Two 300-pounder Armstrong rifled shunt guns in an iron "batterie blindée," about 50 feet below the crest, and four 150-pounder Armstrong rifled shunt guns below the last, in four connected wells, with iron-plated shields and roofs. All these works are to be connected by covered ways and surrounded by a ditch and loop-hole wall.

A Fort on Green Point, consisting of a "batterie blindée" for two 150-pounder Armstrong rifled shunt guns, surmounted by a cupola (non-revolving) for one 300-pounder Armstrong rifled shunt gun.

Within a bastionette adjoining, on the Watsons Bay side, shot and shell proof barracks for 50 men to be constructed so as to render this work a secondary head-quarters.

A "batterie blindée" on Middle Head, situate on the extreme height, between the "Hut" and the north point of Middle Head. This battery to hold one or two 150-pounders, brought from George Head when necessary to engage an enemy. Proper sling waggons to be provided. Turn-tables, traversing platforms, and gun carriages, to remain in the battery. The guns to be kept mounted in this work in war-time only, in charge of a detachment from head-quarters on George Head.

Modifying the unfinished battery on Middle Head, so as to mount one or two heavy guns (up to 7 tons) taken there when necessary. The details of the works are similar to those for Point Piper, explained below.

A "batterie blindée" on the highest point of South Head, between Gap Bluff and the Inner South Head lighthouse. This battery to contain one 150-pounder, to be taken there by a detachment from Green Point in time of war, and in other respects to be similar to the "batterie blindée" on Middle Head.

A "batterie blindée" for two guns on Shark Point, similar to that on Inner South Head.

A "batterie blindée" on Bradley Head for one 300-pounder

Armstrong rifled shunt gun, and one 150-pounder to be brought from George Head when necessary. This battery to be similar to the above-mentioned " batteries bliudées."

NOTE.

Ordnance of the above proposed Works to consist of—
Two 600-pounder Armstrong rifled shunt guns.
Five 300-pounder ditto ditto
Twelve 150-pounder ditto ditto
The 150-pounders only would be movable, and distributed over the works as circumstances require.

A sunken barbette battery on Point Piper, to consist of a well for a heavy gun (up to 7 tons), brought there when necessary, and two platforms for field pieces.

All the guns to fire "en barbette," and the heavy piece to be mounted on a traversing platform with a double bed, raised or lowered at will, to fire over the parapet, by means of hydraulic machinery, or Morell's conical screw lift, which will not (like the hydraulic lift) require constant attention in time of peace, in order to secure its acting when wanted.

A similar battery on Darling Point to that proposed for Point Piper.

Similar batteries to the last mentioned on Goat Island and Long Nose Point.

A well for a heavy gun at Fort Phillip.

Modifications of our present batteries, so as to secure their efficient co-operation with the proposed scheme.

The construction of good roads to connect the positions referred to.

Stabling at George Head for twenty-four horses, and at Green Point for sixteen horses. Twenty horses to be kept always trained to move the heavy guns and ammunition to the different positions.

Telegraphic communication to be established between the head-quarters and Sydney, to avoid delays, and to obtain troops or volunteers at the shortest notice ; many accessories to be provided to ensure the regular performance of the duties required of our troops and volunteers, so as to lighten the hardships they must necessarily endure in actual engagement, and afford them security when off duty.

The formation of a corps of Volunteer Engineers, to act in connection with the Naval Brigade and Volunteer Artillery, to throw up earthworks at any place if required, as an additional security against the landing of an enemy.

The erection of a sunken barbette battery at Botany, for one heavy gun, and two heavy field guns brought there when required.

IV.

The laws of attack and defence, although modified to meet the requirements of improved artillery, remain nearly the same for coast defences, for if we have long range guns and more penetrating projectiles, these will be opposed by vessels coated with armour plates.

The question is whether it is necessary for us to oppose iron-coated forts to the artillery of an enemy?

The ordnance now carried by the vessels of foreign navies (of which I shall speak presently) would justify such constructions even if the superiority of iron forts to masonry had not been admitted by every nation.

Other considerations also induced me to propose the construction of iron batteries. I rejected Earthworks on account of the thickness of parapet that would be required to resist new artillery. The firing through embrasures would be too limited, and the accuracy of our opponents' rifled guns would render these embrasures mere shell traps. If our guns were mounted "en barbette," the direct or ricochetting fire of an enemy would soon silence them.

Sand batteries present nearly the same objections. We are aware that the bomb-proof sandworks of Fort Wagner, on Morris Island, were captured after being breached by rifled artillery at ranges of from 1300 yards to 2000 yards.

Brickwork batteries and towers require too many guns on account of the difficulty of obtaining a lateral range for them, and the embrasures weaken the walls considerably. Thus Fort Sumter, in South Carolina, a brickwork containing 135 guns, succumbed to an attack of seven batteries of 8 in., 10 in., and

100 pounder Parrott rifled guns, with two 80 pounder Whitworths. From General Gillmore's Report it appears that a breach 80 yards long by 12 feet deep was made from August 17th to August 23rd, 1863, (six days) by 5009 projectiles thrown from the 17 guns forming the 7 batteries, at an average range of 3881 yards; not over one half of the projectiles fired struck the masonry, and only 1668 helped to form the breach. More than two years before, in April, 1861, we find again from the official reports of General Gillmore, that Fort Pulaski surrendered in less than 48 hours! This Fort was a pentagonal brickwork casemated on all sides, the walls being $7\frac{1}{2}$ feet thick and 25 feet high, with one tier of guns in embrasures and one tier "en barbette." It contained 48 guns, 20 of which bore on the attacking batteries; these were five 10 in. and five 8 in. Columbiads, four 32 pounders (smooth bore), one 24 pounder Blakely rifled gun, and two 12 in., and three 10 in. sea coast mortars. The breaching guns which did the work were four 8 in. and 10 in. Columbiads for shot and shell, two 84 pounders, two 64 pounders, and one 48 pounder, rifled with flat grooves from old unhooped 42, 32, and 24 pounders, to fire James' shot and shell, and also five 30 pounder Parrott rifled guns. The range from 1650 to 3100 yards, and the number of shots fired in three half-days 3543.

The experiments of 1860 and 1861, proved the uselessness of masonry to resist the attack of rifled ordnance, and we find from the Report of the Ordnance Committee on Breaching experiments against Martello Towers (dated January 25th, 1861), that brick towers 40 feet diameter at top, 46 feet at base, and 36 feet high, with a least thickness of 7 feet 3 inches at foot, and 5 feet 6 inches at the springing of the arches, can be practically demolished by very few shots; the 158 Armstrong projectiles, which took effect against Tower No. 71, fired from one 80 pounder, one 40 pounder, and one 7 in. howitzer (Armstrong), having removed 2168 cubic feet of masonry at a range of 1032 yards, or 13.72 cubic feet per shot.

But the most convincing experiments were made in October, 1864, in the Bexhill bombardment, to test the comparative power of the 70 pounder Armstrong shunt gun, and 70 pounder Whitworth. Both the shunt and Whitworth guns passed their solid shot through the 7 feet brickwork, and their shells penetrated 5 feet in a 9 feet brickwork before bursting. [The Shunt gun caused more damage than the Whitworth, on account of the larger area of the shot and the greater charge of powder contained in the shell.]

The effect of Artillery against good rubble masonry was tested as far back as 1834 at Metz, in France, and it was found that at 1094 yards, a 36 lbs. projectile fired with 12 lbs. of powder produced a mean penetration of 18.2 inches.

As heavy rifled artillery has a proportionately greater effect than the old smooth bore guns, it would be unsafe to trust to masonry for our batteries, and at least that portion of our works likely to be exposed to the fire of heavy rifled ordnance ought to be covered with armour plates, and the best section of iron wall for us to adopt must be determined by comparing the experiments on the different iron targets.

As a notice of the relative merits of the various targets tested in England and other countries would alone suffice to fill a very long paper, I shall only mention a few experiments shewing the results of the trials of the best targets in connexion with the ordnance used against them. I have illustrated many of the target experiments by drawings on which I have also compiled tables shewing the effect produced upon them by the several kinds of ordnance.

The construction I have suggested for our exposed forts and batteries is calculated to offer the greatest amount of resistance to heavy shot with the least possible thickness of iron wall. With the rigidity of the backing and framing, I combine the resistance of solid plates 6 in. thick, and provide the bolts with a peculiar compression washer. The external openings of my embrasures, are hardly larger than the internal openings, and are to be fitted with folding shutters of $6\frac{1}{2}$ in. forged plates.

I provide for any re-inforcements that may be required at any position by making my batteries large enough to have a heavy gun placed in each embrasure if necessary. The expense of plating the exposed sides of a large circular or oval Fort is not very considerable, compared with the advantages to be derived from being able to use additional guns safely in the batteries. The difficulty of procuring heavy rifled guns now, and their great cost render such provision necessary ; and if good roads are made between the different works, the heaviest guns might be moved from one battery to another in a few hours, if needed to dislodge an enemy from any position he might occupy.

The forts on George Head and Green Point and the batteries of Middle Head and Inner South Head being fully armed with the 16 heavy guns I propose for them, could sustain any attack even from iron-clads, and probably oblige them to retreat with great loss.

I propose to mount the guns on traversing platforms and turn-tables in order to move them from one embrasure to another so as to obtain with each gun as much lateral range as if they were mounted "en barbette." I recommend this arrangement in preference to revolving cupolas, for with fixed forts, damage to the iron walls will not affect the working of the guns, the battery may be strengthened with more guns if necessary, firing may be kept up in the same direction or on totally different points at the same time, and accommodation can be provided for a sufficient number of troops to repel the attacks of assaulting parties without interfering with the artillerymen at their guns, whereas with revolving cupolas, the artillerymen must neglect their fire to repulse assailants, and when receiving the fire of several vessels from different points simultaneously, they can only respond to one at a time, thereby being exposed to have their iron wall and machinery so damaged as to render the guns almost useless except in the direction of their last shot. The expense also of constructing and maintaining revolving cupolas with all their machinery is greater than for fixed batteries with guns of the same calibre.

With a complete system of defence, iron forts or batteries would be required at every position, but with obstructions in the channels, the subsidiary works within the obstructions, intended to receive guns only in the event of one or two vessels effecting an entrance by surprise, could be masked batteries without armour plates.

I propose to make these works "barbette batteries" sunken in pits, where the guns after firing would be lowered to be re-loaded. They would have to be built on the highest point of the position to avoid their being taken "en defilade"; their parapet could be of any thickness and surrounded by a small ditch and glacis beyond. These works would be entirely masked, the only indication of their position to an enemy being the appearance of the guns for one or two minutes at a time whilst firing. Their cost would not exceed much the expense of the excavations, the alterations to the traversing platforms and a few accessories.

Foreign navies carry much heavier ordnance now than formerly:

The armament of French ships of war consists principally of the 100-pounder "Canons rayés," to which 300-pounder Armstrongs, besides numerous heavy guns cast and built up at the Imperial Factories, will be added shortly. French vessels are afloat and in course of construction to carry 600-pounder guns.

The Russians are known to possess in their navy large bore and rifled American guns, besides Armstrong and Mackay guns; they have also ordered a large number of steel and other hooped guns from Captain Blakely, part of which are already in the service; they are also beginning to supply their navy with steel guns from their new Imperial Factory. They have moreover many guns of Krupp's homogeneous steel made purposely for their navy. Their order given last year to the Essen Gun Factory consisted principally of fifty 9 in., and a large number of 6 in., 8 in., 11 in. and 15 inch guns.

The Americans are known to have in their Navy, guns of almost incredible calibre, such as Blakelys up to 900-pounders, Parrotts rifled guns from West Point Foundry, Cold Spring, N.Y., principally 6.4 in., 8 in., and 10 inch guns used in turretted ships, and carrying respectively shots of 100 lbs., 200 lbs., and 300 lbs. weight. They have also many Rodman and Dahlgren hollow cast iron guns (principally cast at Fort Pitt Works) of 9 in., 10 in., 11 in., 13 in., 15 in., and 20 inch bore, capable of throwing shot and shell from 100 lbs. to 1000 lbs. weight. At Fort Pitt alone over two thousand cannon have been cast during the late war, among which are more than one hundred 15 in. guns now in use in their army and navy.

Almost every nation has some of the guns I have mentioned as well as their own new guns.

I have illustrated and made sections in my drawings of nearly all the new naval guns used by England, France, America, Russia, and other powers, and it will be remarked after careful examination of the sections and official tables of experiments, that the British rifled guns, the Armstrongs, up to 600-pounders, have proved superior to any of the same calibre.

V.

More than ten years ago, in 1855, during the Russian war, three French floating batteries "Devastation," "Tonnante," and "Lave," covered with $4\frac{1}{2}$ in. armour plates received the fire of the Russian smooth bore guns at Fort Kinburn without injury at the ranges of 600 and 700 yards. This success and also the favorable results of experiments on $4\frac{1}{2}$ inch armour plates at Portsmouth and at Vincennes the year before, in 1854, led to the construction of heavier and more powerful guns.

Plated vessels to resist this new ordnance were begun in France and every naval power followed her example. Thus within the last six years the building of wooden ships of war may be said to have been discontinued and only iron-clads built.

In 1862 the "Normandie" an iron-clad of 36 100-pounder rifled guns, and 5800 tons burden, carrying 840 tons of armour plates on her sides, crossed the ocean, going from France to Mexico. We have since heard of the cruise of the French iron-clad squadron, in 1863, and of the Russian iron-clad squadron in 1864, and more recently of the contemplated cruise of the combined squadron of English and French armour-plated vessels.

It is a well-known fact that the proportion of the American iron-clads to British is as 6 to 1 in regard to number, and that their new Monitors and turretted ships were designed with the view of being rendered sea-worthy by raising their sides with ordinary plates, so as to fit them for crossing the ocean. [It is not probable, however, that these vessels would come to Australia.]

The necessity of having good sea going armour plated vessels with small draught of water, has long been felt, and new vessels are specially designed for this object, such as the "Lord Warden" and "Lord Clyde" in England, and the "Valeureuse" and "Magicienne" in France, which carry a sufficient thickness of armour plate to enable them to resist the penetration of the heaviest shots at ordinary ranges.

Improvements in plating vessels of war may soon enable them to put on their armour at will, and to store it away partly for distant voyages. Thus, within a few years, a squadron visiting this port may apparently consist of wooden ships, yet turn out afterwards to be sufficiently plated to resist the penetration of shell, even at short ranges.

The possibility of disabling even ordinary steamers moving at ordinary speed is not to be relied on with only a small number of guns and men. Major Owen in his "Essay on the Motion of Projectiles," says: "As a steam vessel can constantly change her position and move very rapidly, it is often extremely difficult when firing from a land battery, even to hit her, except when she is obliged to advance in a certain direction or has arrived within a very short range." He remarks upon the difficulty of judging distances for laying a gun upon an object at a long range, from the difficulty of observing the effect of the fire and the disturbing influence of the wind, and recommends that "the ranges over the water in front of the battery should be known to the gunners in the battery."

General Taylor, Inspector of Artillery, and late Commandant at Shoeburyness, has also remarked: "It holds to the common sense opinion that permanent fortifications to be effective at the proper moment must be held by men who know exactly where every shot will fall."

If it be assumed that one or two experimental shots fired at a vessel will determine the range, can the argument be sustained for Port Jackson where every shot will have to be experimental as the range will vary every moment with the motion of the steamer? Besides, it is on record that floating targets at long ranges and also at comparatively short ones are not often hit with the shots of the best rifled guns, even by the most practiced gunners at Shoeburyness.

These few remarks shew the great importance of target practice at every one of our batteries and the necessity of having guns fit to do the required work accurately at long or short ranges.

I subjoin an official table of the comparative amount of work done at 1000 yards by the smooth bore 68-pounder gun (95 cwt.) and by the 150-pounder rifled gun, where it is seen that the 150-pounder gun can do 5.24 times the same work as the 68-pounder with only $2\frac{1}{2}$ times the same charge of powder, and $2\frac{1}{4}$ times the weight of shot, or the former will do $2\frac{1}{2}$ times more work at 1000 yards than the 68-pounder will do at 200 yards. If the 150-pounder is made the same bore as the 68-pounder (8 in.), it is also found that the rifled gun has greater accuracy than the smooth bore with spherical projectiles.

The greater point blank range of rifled guns over the smooth bore is well known, and I have given only a few tables of ranges and deviations of the heaviest guns up to 600 pounders.

At sea, vessels will fight at the distance their guns will carry; but in our Defences we must use rifled guns, because we must have power and accuracy in order to reach the enemy.

I have calculated the strength of the iron walls of the forts and batteries I proposed in my plan of defence, considering weight and cost, to give the greatest resisting power obtainable against racking or punching projectiles, whether ponderous shots fired at a low velocity or rifled bolts fired with the highest possible velocity, so as to distribute their effects over the whole structure. The same calculations are made in designing iron-clad vessels, so that our superiority over an enemy must depend chiefly on the power of our guns to do the work required of them, at from 1000 to 4000 yards. The short time vessels may be exposed to the fire of our batteries renders it necessary to have guns that will send their shot through armour plates, otherwise we should require more guns and men than we can procure for the purpose of racking vessels, and perhaps we should not have the chance of shattering their sides with shells afterwards.

Commander Scott, R.N., says in a paper he read before the Royal United Service Institution, in June 1863, " The size of the gun is of vast importance, more than is generally assigned to it, and for this reason, 20 guns, each a one-pounder, are fired at a target of Iron $1\frac{1}{2}$ in. thick, and produce no effect. One gun, a 20 pounder, is fired and smashes it. The velocity in both cases being equal, in both cases the same amount of metal is

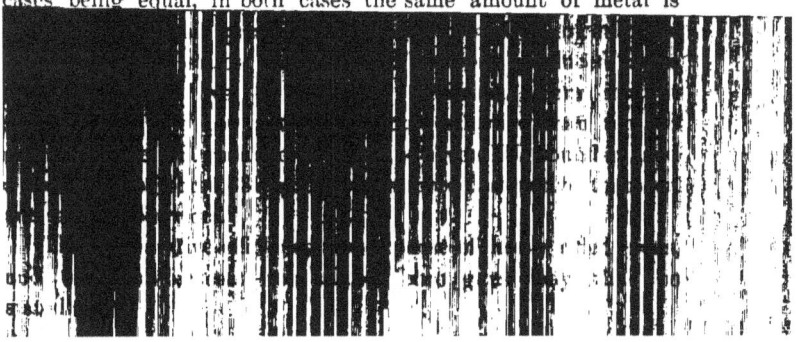

Total Weight and Cost for one Round per piece of the Ordnance I propose.

Ordnance.	Weight of Guns.		Cost of Guns, Carriages, Slides, and Accessories.		Weight of		Cost of Powder and Shot.
	together.	separately.	together.	separately.	Powder.	Shot.	
			£ s. d.	£ s. d.			£ s. d.
Two 600-Pounders	46 Tons	23 Tons	9,411 10 0	4,705 15 0	130 lbs.	1200 lbs.	14 0 0
Five 300-Pounders	60 Tons	12 Tons	11,384 5 0	2,276 17 0	200 lbs.	1500 lbs.	17 0 0
Twelve 150-Pounders	84 Tons	7 Tons	16,355 16 0	1,363 1 4	300 lbs.	1800 lbs.	18 12 0
Total	190 Tons		£37,152 11 0		630 lbs.	4500 lbs.	£49 12 0

Total Cost for one Round per piece of the 68-Pounder, 95 cwt., Cast Iron Guns.

1st.—For the same weight of Metal as with the proposed Rifled Ordnance (66 being required).
2nd.—For the same amount of work done (140 guns being required). [*See Note below*].

			£ s. d.	£ s. d.			£ s. d.
1st.—66 68-Pounders	303¾ Tons	4¾ Tons	16,500 0 0	250 0 0	556 lbs.	4488 lbs.	46 4 0
2nd.—140 68-Pounders	666½ Tons	4¾ Tons	35,000 0 0	250 0 0	2240 lbs.	9520 lbs.	98 0 0

NOTE.—From the latest experiments, the work performed at 1000 yards by the 600-pounder may be estimated at three times that of one 150-pounder, and the work done by the 150-pounder, half that performed by a 300-pounder; and taking the efficiency of the 150-pounder equal only to five 68-pounders, the above results are obtained.

Comparing the number of men required in each case we have for the rifled guns—

Two 600-pounders	40 men
Five 300 ditto	80 ,,
Twelve 150 ditto	120 ,,
Total	240 men

And for the one hundred and forty (140) 68-pounders we shall have to employ 1120 men, even by reducing the detachment for each piece from 10 to 8 men.

It must be remarked also that beyond 1000 yards this equivalent number of 68-pounder guns would be useless with solid shot, whereas the rifled guns could still send their shells through armour-plates.

The cost of maintaining 1120 efficient artillerymen instead of 240 would be more than four times as great, and supposing that half of the 1120 men were volunteers, a saving of more than £20,000 annually would still be made in troops alone, by using heavy rifled guns instead of the ordinary smooth bore.

The weight of shot used with these rifled guns is not more than one-half of that used with the 68-pounders to do the same work, and not over one-fourth of the quantity of powder is required. The expense of a general discharge of one round with the rifled guns is less than half the cost of the same discharge with the 68-pounders.

The original outlay, taking into consideration the cost of ammunition per piece, would also be considerably less for rifled guns.

I do not wish to say that 68-pounder guns are useless, on the contrary, I admit that at 200 or 300 yards they are very formidable, particularly if in large number, but they would not answer for long range guns (2000 yards or more for instance) against ships protected with some kind of armour.

One 68-pounder from our highest work would probably fire more than 100 rounds before sending one shot through the deck of a moving vessel, for according to the latest experiments, the best rifled guns would at 2000 yards have a mean difference of range of 30 yards for every five rounds.

I do not wish to enter into a dissertation upon the merits of the different rifled guns; it would be impossible in this paper to treat of the best materials to be employed in their manufacture, of the best method of rifling, or of all the details of their construction. I have illustrated the rifling and projectiles of the different heavy guns that have attracted public attention. Armstrong built up guns have not yet been surpassed; their safety against bursting and the improvement recently introduced in their rifling and projectiles, their accuracy and endurance, and their perfect adaptability to fire spherical shot as well as cylindrical bolts with or without studs recommend them for casemate guns. The shunt rifling is also better than any other except Scott's rifling. The principle of both is the same, and if Scott's rifling should prove the best, the Armstrong guns could be rifled with the Scott groove. There would be no difficulty in doing so, as the Ordnance Factories in their circulars require particularly "that the form of rifling and the number of grooves should be specified." The Armstrong rifled guns could be re-tubed at any time when the grooves are worn out, and any new rifling that may have been found superior can then be introduced.

Having to depend principally upon the Royal Artillery for working our guns, it is better to place the Armstrong in their hands than a strange weapon not adopted in the service.

I cannot help expressing my admiration of the Whitworth homogeneous iron guns, and particularly of the Mackay steel guns, but neither the Hexagonal bore nor the Windage Adaptation Ordnance have been proved to offer greater advantages than the Armstrong.

The expense of carrying out a complete system of defence probably guided the Select Committee on Harbour Defences in their recommendation of few heavy guns and their selection of 68-pounder cast iron guns. They wished probably to provide for the immediate defence of Port Jackson, but it is doubtful whether the 68-pounders would silence the guns of an iron-plated frigate. It is easy to foresee that if the armaments of foreign powers be not reduced, small armour-plated vessels with heavy guns will soon be sent to foreign stations.

On the Transmutation of Rocks in Australasia.

By the Rev. W. B. Clarke, M.A., F.G.S., F.R.G.S., &c.

[Read 10th May, 1865.]

Before the particular examples which it is one object of the following remarks to illustrate, are introduced to the notice of the Society, it may be advisable to preface them by a brief general consideration of the doctrine of Transmutation, or, as it is otherwise called, the Metamorphism of rocks.

It is not my intention to enter at any great length upon it; but the subject is of such great importance and interest to geologists, that a more close and careful inquiry might well engage our attention. It has been treated of by at least one hundred authors of eminence, and their works, either in memoirs and addresses, or in volumes of considerable size, are in themselves a library. It will be understood from this, that it would be difficult to condense their remarks into any applicable compact abstract. Nor have I the intention of doing so. I shall, however, refer to several of them in the course of this memoir, and borrow from them only what is absolutely indispensable. Yet, I am anxious to guard my own conclusions by such coincidences as may be appropriate; though it is no part of my intention to enter deeply into any questions raised by their discussions. As I speak in the presence of chemical and metallurgical analysts, whatever bears upon their peculiar province will, no doubt, attract sufficient attention to invite elucidation, if any difficulty is presented within the range of their researches, and if my own explanation of certain phenomena known to them as well as to myself be not satisfactory, I shall be very grateful should they take up the question where I may leave it, and treat it more to the purpose. Professor Smith, Mr. Hunt and Mr. Miller of the

Mint, Mr. Stephens and Mr. Krefft, have all at some time or other studied on the spot the examples I propose to dwell on from our own vicinity.

I must not, however, confine myself to them alone, for if they are to be explained, it can only be by comparison with other instances of like kind in other countries.

The terms Transmutation and Transmuted are equivalents of Metamorphism and Metamorphic; but I incline to the Latin rather than to the Greek derivatives, because it seems to me they are more expressive of what is intended. They occur very often in geological treatises, and one class of ancient formations is especially called "metamorphic," because they are exposed over wide areas, and exhibit everywhere the evidence of the transmutations they have undergone in deep recesses of the earth's surface before they were brought up and visibly exposed. It is not of these formations that I propose to treat, except in a passing way, on this occasion. But on other instances of change induced in rocks of other formations under circumstances and conditions which appear explanatory of the causes of change, I may dwell longer.

It may seem a strange thing to some, to have it propounded that there is nothing really stable in the solid structure of the earth's surface.

Observation shows that in rocks of all ages there have been external and internal changes, either of composition or of texture, which must have gone on in some of them from the beginning, and, therefore, it is reasonable to infer in all; and these changes can also be proved in some instances to be now in progress. I am not speaking of rocks in the act of formation, though Transmutation may be contemporaneous with deposits from the very first; but I assume that the deposits have taken place, and that the transmutations of them have been of subsequent date.

It has been observed in numerous localities that at the contact of two rock formations, both of them have undergone a change of material or of composition or of texture. This is most frequently the case where one formation belongs to sedimentary or aqueous rocks, and the other to what are called igneous.

In some instances, the alteration seems to be induced by what

Daubrée calls *imbibition*, i.e., when a rock is in a condition to be compared with a sponge, so that mineralised salts or fluids can permeate it. Other changes take place by the more direct agency of chemical, galvanic, electric, or other mysterious forces, among which *heat* plays an important part, but not to the extent which is generally imagined. Pressure also acts powerfully and entirely alters the condition of rocks. It is not surprising that hasty observations should have led some geologists to attribute effects to heat, which we may see, perhaps, by and by, it is hardly capable of effecting alone. Thus trappean rocks have oftentimes been charged with causing great elevations and disruptions when they have been incapable of producing any such effects, so far as inquiry shows them to have merely flowed through fissures caused by other agency, and to have produced effects somewhat different from those attributed to them.

When two masses of different kinds of rock, or of different composition, structure, origin and age, are in contact, there is often noticed a mutual change near the planes of contact; this transmutation *Delesse* calls *normal metamorphism*. When these changes are evidently traceable to adventitious causes, such as irruptions of heated matter, the transmutations are denominated special or *abnormal*. In one or other of these ways large masses of strata are changed; and although the ancient slates and associated rocks known as *metamorphic*, betray a transmutation on the largest scale, the phenomena of such change are widely apparent in the Tertiary, Cretaceous, and Jurassic formations of the Pyrenees, the Alps, the Carpathians, Turkey, the Caucasus, Armenia, and Himalaya; and, what is remarkable, in the greater mountain chains the transmutations are more striking than in the smaller ranges of the same age, as is evidenced in the Hartz, Wurtemburg, the Jura, Aragon, New Castille, and in other mountains where the natural features are on a smaller scale. D'Archiac shrewdly points out that these variations are not necessarily due to the presence of igneous rocks, because transmutation has gone on in the greater chains oftentimes far from such igneous matter.

It appears, nevertheless, certain that where transmutation

has occurred, there has been a contact of the changed with the transmuting agent.

Naturally it will occur to the mind, that in order to determine accurately how such transmutations have taken place, we require a careful analysis of the rocks for some distance beyond the planes of alteration, with a distinct understanding of the way in which physical forces of determinate character act upon materials of the kinds in question, whether considered under a mere mineral or a metallurgical aspect.

Some facts are so constant under certain conditions that they may be considered as established. If, for instance, an eruptive rock is in contact with a sedimentary rock, both will be changed. And Fournet calls that of the former *exomórphism*, and of the other *endomorphism*.

As these are the most commonly observed, and as they apply to the examples from this neighbourhood, it may be as well to dwell particularly on such as are abnormal, or special kinds of transmutation; and we may confine ourselves chiefly to the endomorphic or transmuted sedimentary rocks. But all in due order.

Generally, igneous rocks of different characters produce different kinds of transmutation; and deposits of calcareous, aluminous, or siliceous composition, will, of course, be affected differently by the same kind of transmuting agent.

Thus it is found that granitic rocks, trappean rocks, and lavas, all produce varying changes when in contact with rocks of the same name.

I propose not to dwell upon rocks of great antiquity. But I may mention one remarkable fact in Victoria which I noticed, in company with Messrs. Selwyn and Aplin, where the granite of Mount Alexander is in contact with the gold-bearing, quartziferous, Silurian schists of Specimen Gully, near Castlemaine.

Not only do all the quartz lodes cease as lodes at the contact with the granite, proving the probable fact that the granite is younger than the slates; but at the junction there are numerous striking variations in the slates themselves, together with the occurrence of small amounts of minerals and metals.

Iron is often in this way discovered in abundance, as in the

Isle of Elba, where that rich habitat of iron is in close proximity with granite, and in this colony about the Dromedary Mountain and from it to Maneroo.

In contact with granite rocks, coal is often converted into Anthracite and Graphite.

In New South Wales I have often found Pegmatite or graphic granite at the points of intrusion of ordinary granite, and in some instances corroded. In certain cases in some countries, corroded pegmatites are very metalliferous. Again, granites are frequently found in a decomposing state, called rotten granite. In such cases the rotten granite is traversed oftentimes by porphyritic elvans or by quartz veins. Such may be seen on the descent from Bowenfells to the river Cox, on the Bathurst line; it is an instance of transmutation effected, perhaps, by silicated vapours which have resulted in quartz veins: and it was in one of those very spots I first found Australian gold in 1841.

I must anticipate here the mention of a fact connected with granite, which is curious,—that rock which is enveloped in or entangled with granite, is very seldom if ever prismatised or altered into columns—the columnar structure being extremely common in rocks that are in contact with trap. The conclusion to be drawn from such a fact is, that the granite could not be as hot as the trap, and therefore the *plasticity* of granite is not due to simple fusion.

On the other hand, where granite has been itself enveloped in igneous matter—lava for instance,—it undergoes a change.

Witness this specimen from an extinct volcano in Auvergne.

Granite produces a singular change on certain arenaceous rocks, as in this fragment broken off at the junction of a granitic intrusion with "green sand." It is silicified.

Silicification is a very common product of the contact of granite with calcareous rocks. Limestones thus affected exhibit their fossils frequently silicified, and the unsilicified limestone is changed to a saccharoidal marble, the colours passing away, and the marble becoming white.

Occasionally, however, similar changes in limestone have been produced without contact with granite; and the transmutation is to be attributed to slowly acting molecular and galvanic forces, or to lateral pressure and contact of beds.

The soft chalk of the Isle of Wight and Ballard Down, near Poole, in Dorsetshire, has thus been converted into a hard limestone close to the fault which traverses that range of country, and near to which upheaval has taken place.

These specimens I collected from Ballard Head in 1835. There is no granite or other igneous rock within many miles of that vicinity.

One of the most remarkable changes I have ever noticed in the neighbourhood of granite, occurs a little south of Bathurst in this colony.

At what is called the Great Western Copper Mine, some of the slates are converted into Mica schist and Griesen; and limestones associated with them are changed into white saccharoidal marble, whilst in the slates Tremolite in layers and sulphuret of copper with lead abound.

So completely is the original structure masked in some of the beds, that I was taken to what was called a limekiln, a considerable distance from the marble. A good deal of whitish granular rock had been collected and had been subjected to fire, but in vain, and this whitish granular rock turned out to be Griesen. It was, nevertheless, an altered rock, and I believe altered by granite. Near Bathurst the granite is frequently found decomposed with elvans passing through the decomposed portions.

In another part of the country, full ninety miles west of Bathurst, the granite of the Sappa Bulgas, or Harvey's Range, has converted ordinary sandstone, very much of the age of our rocks near Sydney, into a vitrified rock such as is here exhibited. The same granite has, further to the west, converted slate into pitchstone and jasper.

In some countries garnet is a common product of granitic transmutation, and in New Zealand and New Caledonia garnet rock is of common occurrence in the districts where great physical forces have been in operation. The specimen before us is from the north part of the latter island.

On the eastern flank of the great Maneroo plateau I noticed

epidote as a very common mineral under similar circumstances of transmutation. Epidote is included by Delesse in the same division of minerals formed in rocks by transformation, as garnet. Most of these minerals when found in calcareous rocks, have been silicated. Chiastolite also occurs in slates over granite on Jejedzric Hill in Maneero.

When sandstones come in contact with granite rocks, they are frequently converted into quartzite, producing metallisation, silicification and vitrification. A true *quartzite* may according to Delesse always be distinguished by the occurrence in it of *mica*.

It can scarcely be doubted that the silica has often been administered by silicated waters or springs, under the action of transmutation by Imbibition which has gradually produced the observed changes.

In some instances these springs may be almost proved to have been poured forth on the ancient sea margins; for, in certain places a number of marine shells that belong to shallow water, have been found silicified wholly or in part, as is noticeable in some of the Jurassic formations, but notwithstanding this, no one, it seems, has found a silicified Ammonite; though occasionally Ammonites and Belemnites occur unsilicified amidst silicified shells. The explanation is, that the Cephalopods being inhabitants of deep water were not exposed to the influence of the silica so freely administered near the shore; and after mineralisation in another way, may have drifted to the shallower depths. Perhaps, however, some fossils have been silicified under a more perfect power of assimilation than others; for, in various Spirifers I have found what must have been a tendency to resist or to accept silicification in some parts of their organization more than in others. Thus, frequently the spiral appendages have been silicified, whilst the rest of the animal was transmuted by calcareous agency.

Respecting Granite itself, it appears to undergo a transmuting action. I am one of those who deny the occurrence of what is termed *primitive* granite. If such exists, I believe no human eye ever beheld it. The researches of Virlet and Scherer demonstrate, that the crystalline structure of certain granites surpasses altogether the limits of granite, *i. e.* the facts which belong to the different materials are such as frequently to contradict all conceivable notions of such a rock having been formed simply by igneous fusion, and that, therefore, water must have been an agent of considerable importance.

About nineteen or twenty years ago a controversy took place between some continental geologists as to the origin of the beautiful marbles of Italy. Near the Lake of Como exist certain rocks that have been denominated Gneiss, and this has been adduced as a proof that such gneiss and the marbles also, are the result of the transmuting power of granite. Now, in the Italian peninsula, no sedimentary formations are known to exist of older epochs than those of the Jurassic and Cretaceous and Upper Tertiary.

M. Boubée asserted that older rocks did exist concealed under the deposits named, and that *M. de Collegno* and others who took the same view as he did were wrong. He maintained that heat could not permeate so as to change by igneous transmutation any rock thicker than 6 or 7 feet; and that, therefore, masses from 100 to 1000 feet thick could not be so changed. He concluded, then, that the Jurassic limestones (which belong to the same category as those of Greece), were altered by slowly-acting, long-continued, electric and chemical molecular forces. But I must say, that M. Boubée does admit occasional examples of transmutation by heat alone, and that is, I presume, all that the advocates of that doctrine require. They do not, and they cannot ignore other agencies.

The fact that the impressions of fossil plants occur often in highly silicified beds, proves that a change by imbibition of silica may occur, set free by heated waters or vapour.

No one could pretend that any plant could leave a cast in such hardened rock as this in which a cast of a Lepidodendron from Sofala appears, or of this in altered shale from Canoona. It is absurd to suppose that the silicated rock was in a plastic state when the plant became enveloped in it.

On the other hand, it cannot be denied that lime, iron, and other metals have occasionally made their appearance in veins by direct igneous emanations impregnating and coating solid rocks of other kinds. And the only source that can be supposed for silica so developed is from granitic rock. Silicated water at a temperature of 212 degrees Fahrenheit, is, I believe, quite capable of producing, in time, much of the changes observed.

The more direct agency of heat will be dealt with when we enter upon the subject of Trappean Transmutations.

It must, however, be borne in mind, that although siliceous rocks in contact with granite are transmuted, it is not always so.

The influence in all cases must be in proportion to proximity; and there are instances in which granite does not appear to be the direct cause at all, for it is of a totally different origin—since it occurs sometimes where no granite exists.

In the case of our great Hawkesbury rocks, so common about and under Sydney, the ground may be seen full of bright sparkling crystalline particles, which it is difficult to understand as belonging to a sandstone formed by drift and deposition alone, unless we suppose, what is probably the case, that the original granitic and quartz detritus, of which much of the rock is composed, has, since its formation, undergone a transmutation which has produced the crystalline particles and facets that stud the whole of the strata, and betray no kind of abrasion whatever. They may have been formed by secretion from a silicified menstruum in which the deposits took place.

I have washed away by water and acid the coloured and cementing matter of most of our sandstones, and also of the red sands of the interior desert, and have then found when under the microscope, that the particles are generally only crystallised in part, seldom assuming more than a rude resemblance to hexagonal crystals, except where they have formed as druses in small cavities.

Whilst alluding to this change, I may mention, that, although quartz veins have certainly resulted from intrusion of silica into fissures, frequently veins of quartz in quartzite and other silicated rocks are the product of secretion from the rock itself, the quartz having filled up cracks produced after the rock was formed. Australia abounds with examples. Here is one from N.W. Australia,—Brecknock Harbour.

Mr. Sorby has examined the crystals of quartz and other constituents of granite, and has discovered in them the presence of visible water sometimes in cavities otherwise filled with air.

Taking this fact in common with the different degrees of fusibility of quartz, mica, and felspar, which are the elements of normal granite, it is quite clear that igneous fusion alone cannot have been concerned.

The fusion point of Silica may be taken at 2800° C. (or 5072° F.). According to Fournet, quartz in a state of fusion may cool down from 1300° to 1800° (*i. e.*, from 2171° to 3292° F.) below its fusion point, without consolidation. The other minerals fuse at a much lower temperature than quartz, and yet, if you examine granite, you will perceive that quartz very often occurs enveloped in felspar and mica also; how is this fact to be understood, if no change has taken place in the granitic mass since its formation? The granite must originally have been in a very different condition from a single mass merely fused by igneous action; and if we admit this and other considerations which we cannot now stay to speak of, then it follows, that whether or not the granite has undergone in itself any transmutation, it is highly probable that the chemical and mineralogical action and the presence of vapours would certainly influence any mass of sedimentary matter in contact with it, and, therefore be a source of what we have seen called *exomorphism*, altering, where the vapours and heat and mineral matters have had fair play, the surfaces at least of the external substances. And we shall see how hydrated agencies could exist if we recollect what has been demonstrated, that there must have been originally from 1 to 50 per cent. of water in granite.

It is well known that the vapour of water under pressure at a high temperature is capable of dissolving silica, and, therefore, granite, under the influences stated, may silicify a rock capable of receiving the change, or of producing even veins of quartz in fissures; and thus we may explain many of the phenomena with which we are familiar, and which are exhibited where sedimentary rocks are in contact with granite, as in the instances illustrated by specimens, and cited from this colony.

In the same way argillaceous rocks become silicated into siliceous slates and some kinds of gneiss. And thus we have by the presence of water in plastic or heated granite, a true origin for many of the phenomena we designate Transmuted or Metamorphic. We learn, also, in this way, how certain granites themselves, which are really schistose in structure, and might be even termed stratified, have resulted from the transmutation of ordinary schists.

Such I have described, in one of my reports to the Government, as having been met with by me in the neighbourhood of the Murrumbidgee River.

I have already mentioned the alterations which shales and sandstones have undergone in connection with the granite mass of the Sappa Bulgas or Harvey's Range, west of Molong.

Now, I have ascertained from inquiry and examination of the rocks, that all along the western frontier of New South Wales, as on the Darling River, and between it and the Barcoo, there is an enormous development of silicified and vitrified sandstones.

As the phenomena extend over so vast an area, it can hardly be attributed to anything short of a normal transmutation ; and, therefore, in all probability it may be to the action of granite rather than of any real trappean rocks. There is, I think I may safely say, no range of any considerable elevation or extent in the low region along the Darling, which does not betray the clearest proof of transmutation. And in some parts of the country, far beyond, near the Lower Barcoo (or Cooper's Creek), Mr. A. C. Gregory found the rocks altered in a remarkable degree.

The late Sir T. L. Mitchell made a similar observation, but he merely mentions the fact without attempting to account for it. Both he and Captain Sturt were struck by the polygonal forms and hardened nature of many loose fragments on the summits of the groups of hills, such as D'Urban's, Dunlop's, Greenough's, &c. In the hills which lie along the river channels of the Narran and Bokara, 150 miles further north, pebbles of such transmuted rocks occur in abundance. The collection here present was made from the ridges of that neighbourhood near Curawallinghi, on the Ballandoon River. The conclusion from them must be, that great denudation, of which these are the spoils, has taken place, and that formerly the insulated groups of hills were connected in one grand plateau, the less hardened masses having been removed.

As we pass onwards to the Balonne and along the Maranoa,

in Queensland, similar phenomena are presented; but in some instances the alteration there may have been due to trappean rather than to granitic rocks, as in the case of the flanks of Red Cap and other hills on the Cogoon.

No mention has yet been made of Porphyry or other varieties of granite rocks; but it may be concisely stated that there are instances of slate rocks converted to porphyry, of porphyry passing to granite, and of porphyry which has undergone a crystalline tendency. Here is a rude octohedron of porphyry from near Harvey's Range. At Port Stephens I visited a Cone Hill, on the summit of which there is a most remarkable assemblage of prismatic columns, of almost equal interest with those described by Humboldt as occurring in the Andes.

Many of the Porphyries in New South Wales, where they have been silicated, exhibit beautiful double hexahedral prisms, a variety, no doubt, due to transmutation, and which is generally considered to belong to the Devonian epoch of Europe. Such porphyry occurs on the Hunter, and at Arthursleigh, near the Wollondilly, in Argyle.

It would take up too much time to dwell on the jasperised rocks, which are another result of granitic transmutation. I can only say that they are extremely common in parts of this colony, and also in the northern part of New Holland generally. I have examined huge examples of this change not far from the granite of the Peel River and Hanging Rock districts; and I have little doubt that the jaspers so common in certain beds of our coal-fields have been derived from the destruction and abrasion, and driftings and deposition of the fractured rocks of an earlier age, allied to that to which the example above quoted clearly belongs.

Here, again, we are on the limits of equal change produced by Granite and Trap.

The trappean rocks include basalt, dolerite, greenstone, diorite, and various others, in which the felspar is hydrated and allied to lime felspar. In the granitic rocks, the felspar is an orthoclase or potash felspar.

Trap rocks are assumed to have been formed under water, and to have been subjected to great pressure; but when they come near to day, they become vesicular, puffing off their steam or associated gaseous vapours, as bread does in an oven, and so becoming in a subaerial position very like some lavas. Filtration, secretion, or other allied operations, fill the cavities afterwards with minerals which are observed not to be confused, but to be deposited one over another. In this state they become what is called amygdaloidal.

Much of such cellular basaltic lava distinguishes the trappean overflows in Victoria; and it is also common in parts of New South Wales. It certainly forms the youngest basalt of the gold-fields. Indeed, so recent is it that grasses, reeds and other vegetables are found under the basalt scarcely altered, only scorched and not burned. How is this to be accounted for, if the transmutations by basalt are really effected by intense heat? In all probability the traps act frequently like granite; but there are differences also.

The most striking instances of the slightly changed character of vegetable matter in contact with trap are to be found near Daylesford, in Victoria, where leaves and plants only partly altered, or mineralised in sulphuret of iron, are embedded in fissile clay beneath the basalt, and when examined present in fact almost a recent appearance. Whatever may have been the actual cause of such change, it is impossible to believe that the basalt was at fusion heat, when it overflowed. At Wentworth Gold Field, New South Wales, similar facts are noticed.

In this colony, the presence of trap and basalt has produced numerous and greater changes at the contact with coal beds and with calcareous and silicated formations. The instances are too numerous to be quoted on this occasion. But all must not be passed over.

In order to deal with the coal beds, we have first to consider what are the actual effects of heat on combustible substances.

The effects in the laboratory are well known to Professor Smith and other gentlemen present; and the artificial manufacture of coke is known to produce results which imitate the phenomena observed in nature.

Combustibles may be classed as turf, lignite, bituminous coal, and anthracite or stone coal. These form a series which advances to graphite or plumbago commonly called black lead.

Now, in order to ascertain under what temperatures such substances become transmuted, M. Delesse employed M. Jacequelaine to subject them to distillation, and from the notes made by the latter (which I will abridge) we shall see how transmutation may be produced at a lower temperature than is generally believed. We find, then, the following results :—

Turf threw off its odour at from 220° to 230° C., and distilled at 260°, = 516° F.

Lignite became empyreumatic at 220°, and distilled at from 260° to 285°.

Coal from St. Etienne threw off its odour at 150°, that from Dresden at 205°, and English coal at 295°, distilling at 400°, which was also the point of distillation of Swansea anthracite, though it became odorous at 310°.

We may therefore take the point of distillation of bituminous matters in such combustibles as, respectively, 260°, 300°, and 400° = 752° F. This is far below red heat.

Now, taking the scale of temperature of the earth at 1° F. for fifty feet vertical, the above temperature will correspond to a little more than seven English miles, so that a basalt or trap coming up from that depth would be sufficiently hot to convert coal into coke. And inasmuch as at a little more than a quarter of the temperature mentioned, or about 212° Fahrenheit, the water in the combustible would pass off, it is certain that a basaltic outburst coming from a depth of little more than two miles would be quite sufficient to produce considerable change.

M. Jacequelaine says that other processes besides that of heat can volatilise combustibles.

Thus heated alkaline solutions percolating to a great depth may dissolve the bitumen and increase the proportion of carbon, and so we have one explanation of the cause why the deepest and oldest coals are richest in carbon ; and we may also thus understand why dissolution and not dry distillation may be supposed capable of producing the change from lignite to graphite.

Whilst on this topic it is only natural to express an opinion on the occurrence of the Mineral Oil so abundant in America, and in various parts of Europe and Asia.

That it may originate in a natural distillation of combustible matter there can be no doubt. And some geologists have ventured on the haphazard conclusion, that it will be found under almost all large areas of bog or turf. We already know, that the bogs of Ireland have supplied materials for candles, and there are minerals also in New South Wales, such as Bog-butter, which have resulted from decomposition of vegetable matter in peat.

A mineral of this kind, belonging to the waxy and resinous species, I showed some time ago to Professor Smith. It came from the neighbourhood of Twofold Bay. A mineral of a like character has more recently been discovered at Wettin, in Germany, in the Royal Coal Mine, in association with much rock oil.

In the volume for 1863 of "Good Words," a very useful periodical edited by Dr. Macleod, there is an excellent paper by Professor G. Rogers, of Glasgow, on Coal and Petroleum; in it he supposes the rock oil to be produced by coal seams affected by pressure and internal heat, the lowest coals nearest the igneous source being converted into anthracite. He thinks the distillation has caused the oil to accumulate in deep fissures and subterranean reservoirs below the coal formation, and even as low as the Silurian rocks, and that it is poured out from those reservoirs by the same mode of action as produces Artesian springs.

Another author has supposed it to be an exudation from coral reefs, a proposition which originated in a mistake and which requires little refutation. A French geologist of eminence to whom I have already alluded—M. Virlet d'Aoust—arguing against another opinion (that, because some of the oils have a peculiar character they are allied to animal matter, which appears to be the case with oil distilled from the Cannel coal under Mount York, in New South Wales), has put before us some facts which cannot be set aside by mere conjecture.* He even controverts the idea of an origin in coal, which two distinguished chemists of Germany, Messrs. Turner and Reichenbach, have held

---

* Nevertheless, we must not overlook what Sir R. I. Murchison says in his "Siluria" (3rd ed. pp. 282-3 and 560-1) of fossil-fish-bearing beds producing bitumen at Caithness, and of the fish-bearing beds of the High Alps from which oil has been distilled. See, also, his paper in *Proc. Geol. Soc.* I. 139. [3rd April, 1829.]

in common with Prof. Rogers, and declares that if coal is the sole origin of the oil (call it by what name you like) then such a hypothesis involves conclusions so extraordinary, that it must be abandoned.

He takes for his test the Isle of Zante, where petroleum has been known for more than 2300 years, and which must have furnished an annual supply of 22,643 avoirdupois tons English (23,000,000 kil.). Reichenbach acknowledges that in every quintal there are twenty ounces of oil, and therefore there must be at least 368,000,000 of quintals (each being equal to 1 cwt. 3 qrs. 25 lbs. E.) to produce the petroleum of Zante alone.

Herodotus is the first person who mentions it, and from his time to this, the quantity of petroleum has been sufficiently great to require more coal than the whole of England could have supplied if obtained for the purpose.

This, however, is but the $\frac{1}{25}$th of the supply of naptha from Rangoon, which, according to Mr. Coxe, produces 92,781 tuns a year.

The author then refers to Trinidad, and to the "rivers of oil" flowing up along the Alleghanies and in Pennsylvania, and in Ohio. This calculation, he rightly assumes to overbear all theory and hypothesis.

M. Virlet, in his work (*Dictionnaire Pittoresque des Sciences Naturelles*), says the origin of bitumen in general is not due to the transmutation of organic debris, but to eruptions by emanations, which in penetrating sandstones, shales and limestones, of all countries, has modified them in its own way.

Whatever may be the real origin of these fluids they are certainly of different kinds in composition. This is also certain, that the brown Cannels of Scotland do produce oil by distillation, and we have here near Hartley a brown cannel allied to but not exactly identical with the Bog-head Scotch cannel, which, though of true Carboniferous age, contains a high percentage of mineral oil. I believe the oil will be found to exist in cells. I have, elsewhere,* very recently shown that I was the first

---

* The reference is to a paper "*On the Coal Fields*," in the *Catalogue of Natural and Industrial Products of New South Wales, exhibited by the*

person in this country to suggest the existence of cannel containing oil, and therefore, I will not now say more on that subject.

There are oil-bearing shales or carbonaceous deposits behind Mount Kembla, in the Illawarra, from which I selected specimens in the year 1849, and I believe such will be found to exist elsewhere. These shales do not produce so much oil as the cannel coals, and when used up in the retort appear to be of the character of charcoal. They are, therefore, not so much transmuted as the cannel. At Stony Creek, near Maitland, such cannel also occurs. At Brisbane Water there is a very heavy coal which is *supposed* to be capable of producing oil, but it appears to contain too much ash. Similarly in the Illawarra, in Tasmania, and in New Caledonia, there are deposits which come nearer than the shales of American Creek to graphite, but have not actually attained to it completely. I have specimens here from all these localities.

During the geological survey of Trinidad by Mr. Wall and my friend Mr. Sawkins, they concluded that the bitumen of that island is distilled from vegetable bog matter by the mere heat of the sun.

In Auvergne, however, amidst the extinct craters, bitumen exudes from the soil and concretes the particles of sand sticking to the feet; this is a specimen of it. In the Danubian province of Roumania, bitumen, solid and liquid, occurs together with rock-oil. In this colony there is a spot where bitumen also appears. It may be useful to examine this selection of specimens from Trinidad, sent to me by Mr. Sawkins during the survey.

Combustibles may, in some instances, be transmuted without being burnt. The coal seams about Mount Wingan on the Page River have been burning for years, and we see them, as well as some in England, where they have long been on fire, exhibiting similar appearances to coal seams transmuted by trap. In

---

International Exhibition Commissioners at Sydney in 1861. P. 86. The examples quoted were the Cannel (allied to the Bog-head coal) of Mount York, and of Loders' Creek in the Liverpool Range. This is further treated of in a paper by the Author, "*On the Oil-bearing Deposits of New South Wales*," read before the Geological Society of London, February 1866, in which other localities are mentioned.

various parts of the Hunter River basin, porcellanite containing impressions of ferns of the coal epoch occur, and even at Khanterintee (which name, I think, implies action of fire), above the beach near Newcastle, there are similar appearances. In the Illawarra the coal is sometimes converted into coke and prismatised. The specimen now on the table came from the mine at Bellambi. I saw the spot in the mine whence it came, and doubt not it was affected by the trap dyke which traverses the beds.

At Rive de Gier, in France, near Lyons, there is a mountain called St. Genis-Terre-Noire, where all the changes by coal on fire are well exhibited. First, there is *irisation;* then the coal becomes cellular and full of cavities; then harder and more brilliant; lastly, it passes to a coke with metallic lustre. The coal is thus affected through several feet of thickness.

Now, if we examine the coal seam in Nobby's Island at the mouth of the Hunter, altered by the greenstone dyke that passes through it, we shall see a similar transmutation.

I obtained, several years ago, examples of *irisated* coal and half-burnt shale from an old pit on the ascent to Mount Keera; and here you perceive the irisation. The same feature distinguishes the transmuted coal of New Caledonia, as shown by the specimens before us, which I lately received from my correspondent there, M. Garnier, the French Government Geologist. I am not sure about the transmuting rock in that island; but in Illawarra it is basalt. Similarly, the coal-beds on the Nattai, near the Fitzroy mine, have been affected by igneous rocks; and one variety is full of minute concretions of ferruginous matter which look like seeds.

I have already shown that in Illawarra the coal in one place is prismatised. It is so in Spitzbergen, in the Arctic Ocean; but though it was supposed from certain fossil shells very like some in our Australian lower Carboniferous beds, that the Spitzbergen coal was of that age, recent examination by Professor de Koninck, of Liége, shows it to be of Permian age.

Coal prismatised in this way passes sometimes from Coke to Anthracite and Graphite. The whole of these sometimes occur together, the graphite being nearest to the trap.

M. Delesse mentions coal in Algeria, which was transmuted from lignite by trap, but not coked, though enveloped by the igneous rock which could not, therefore, have had very great heat.

In England there are numerous localities where coal beds are altered just in the same way. In 1838 I visited a spot in Radnorshire, where such was the case, and here is a portion of the transmuting basalt. In the Isle of Anglesea the coal also is coked and becomes incombustible when near Dolerite.

Various minerals are introduced into coal by transmuting agents, oftentimes by water impregnated by earths and salts.

Thus iron, sulphur, lime, manganese, magnesia, alumina, and even quartz itself are found in abundance, sometimes crystallised.

Mr. Gould found a particle of gold in coal in Tasmania, and in this specimen of coal from New Caledonia you can perceive the crystals of quartz studding the laminæ. Sir R. Murchison has mentioned a similar occurrence in the coal of Barrow Hill, near Dudley. (Sil. Syst. p. 497.)

In fact, minerals of all kinds are found in some Coals, natural Cokes, Anthracites and Graphites.

That this latter is an evidence of the influence of igneous action may be acknowledged, when we consider that the great plumbago mine of Borrowdale, in English Cumberland, is in the midst of a trappean mass passing through Silurian slates. Another instance of the alteration of coal beds in contact with trap passing to basalt, occurs at Dudley, where the shales are converted into jasperoid porcellanite (as in Trinidad, and on the Hunter). There is especial mention of this in Murchison's "Siluria," where the author compares the altered shales to the "brand-erde" of the Germans.

With two or three further remarks I will dismiss this part of the subject.

I have previously given my reasons for believing that the Hawkesbury rocks near Sydney had been subjected to transmutation, arguing from the crystalline particles. I see also an additional argument in the fact that these rocks are full of little bits of graphite, which are so perfect, that in my explorations I have sometimes picked them out with a knife to serve for a pencil when I happened to have no better one at hand.

T

Lignite, one of the lowest forms of combustible, sometimes becomes prismatised, at other times it is only found in the form of charcoal—which occurs in all coal seams more or less; just as it is found in lava from Madeira, where wood of a recent tertiary epoch is entangled.

At Andernach, and in other places visited by me on the Rhine, I saw trunks of trees and leaves only partially carbonised in a hydrated volcanic tuff. In lava near Neûwied, carbonised trees in an upright position just as they grew, may be seen.

In a volcanic tuff, or ash bed, at Kœnigswinter, under Drachenfels, I found stems of trees converted into semiopal, just such as occurs in Tasmania. Here are specimens for comparison.

At Herculaneum, a beam has been found in the volcanic tuff which covered that city, preserving its woody character; and, according to Delesse, Pelouze found in it 50 per cent. of carbon.

With respect to the prismatising of coal, we must not be led into errors from the fact that similar effects occur from artificial heat in the *chemise* or lining of a furnace, for simple desiccation will prismatise some combustibles; and it is stated, on authority of careful experiments, that such prismatised combustibles are never at a red heat. In fact, prismatisation is a minor transmutation than that of coking.

This is well illustrated by the oil-bearing Cannel of Mount York. Though full of oil, it has undergone transmutation in a perceptible degree; its laminæ are obliterated, the strata lines are merely *stripes*, whilst the blocks into which it is separable are distinctly, though rudely, prismatic. It is difficult to separate it in planes which present unbroken its distinctive impressions of Glossopteris, a fossil plant which marks its epoch. A further proof of transmutation is exhibited over it, where a silicate of alumina occurs full of bright crystals of pyrites, which mineral has thus resulted from the removal of the sulphur from the cannel.

One proof that water must be present in these changes, is the occurrence of zeolitic minerals (which are not common near granitic contacts where the water is less), and also by hydroxydes of iron and alumina. This element has been already mentioned in relation to granite; but heat must also be occasionally widely diffused, for anthracite occurs in the European Alps where there is no direct contact with igneous rocks, and such heat, therefore, was probably due to the inherent temperature brought up from below when the Alps were elevated.

There is one character assumed by granitic and trappean rocks, and also by coal and other transmuted deposits, which ought to be mentioned. I mean the spheroidal form.

Basalte en boules is a common geological expression; the concentric layers exfoliate like the coats of an onion, as in this specimen from Launceston, in Tasmania. The same structure occurs in certain coals at Newcastle and in India.

It also occurs in sandstones, as at Five Dock, near Sydney, where a hard concretion is surrounded by successive layers of softer rock.

It is transmutation allied to prismatisation, and in fact columns of basalt are explained as originating from the juxtaposition and mutual pressure of spheroidal masses.

In this colony and in Tasmania I have found this structure very common in the middle and lower Carboniferous rocks. At Woollamboola Lagoon, Jervis Bay, and about Wollongong and to the north of it, the beach rocks which are full of fossils are studded with round balls of calcareous matter often containing a shell or coral.

On the Hunter, as near Glendon, these spheroids are of immense size and line the left bank of the river for some distance. In the Jervis Bay district, as you will see by these examples, shells have been twisted out of their proper bedding and now appear outside the ball. Similar instances occur in the white limestone of Balme in France, where siliceous balls with silicified Terabratulæ occur.

Chemouset adopts the same view as myself, viz., that when the Terabratulæ were deposited, the balls did not exist.

Other kinds of transmutation occur. Thus the coal near Swansea, in Glamorganshire, has in one place been formed through the agency of a vein of sulphuret of iron, or in common with its occurrence, not in columns or spheroids, but in a series of cones or conical sections of a spheroid.

In some parts of the lower Carboniferous formation of New

South Wales—as at Worregee on the Shoalhaven, near Singleton on the Hunter, and at Coyeo on the Page River—there occur many curious concretions of carbonate of lime simulating crystals of selenite, but attached to each other in radiating forms of very considerable size and thickness. In one instance the substance is a marble, the molecular atoms having united in the same way as in Carara or Pentelic marble. I found similar concretions in the Carboniferous beds at Spring Hill in Tasmania, not far from trap.

No doubt these peculiar concretions have been formed under some such agency as that which produces flints in beds of Chalk; but they are all examples of transmutation; and as just such spheroids as I have before mentioned are common in argillaceous rocks in contact with trap, a low temperature may have assisted in forming the lime concretions of the Carboniferous rocks.

In the coal shale of the valley of D'All, in the Thuringerwald, and in the upper Green sand of Cave Hill near Belfast, in Ireland, are similar spheroids where the rock is in contact with trap. But in the latter case the argillaceous odour remains with 8 per cent. of water. Delesse figures an instance of felspathic rock in the Vosges Mountains, which has been changed into parallellopipedons which in the interior are perfect concentric spheroids.

It is not surprising, then, that in other localities a true prismatic structure should have been induced in argillaceous and calcareous deposits, as in the beautiful columns of the South Tyrol country.

I would point out that in many of our Australian deposits we find a tendency in the thinner portions to break off into geometric forms having columnar divisions, with occasionally convex upper surfaces; and that at Point Puer, in Tasmania, in various parts of Victoria, and about Wollongong and elsewhere, the rocks are often jointed so as to produce a tesselated structure or miniature representation of a "giant's causeway." In fact it is the prismatic structure, the joints being lined with ferruginous emanations or deposits.

Spheroidal forms appear to be common not only on earth but in air and water. Vapour is suspended in spheroids held up by electric agency, and owing to the same structure in the perspiration of the human hand it may be passed safely through molten metal.

The laundress spits upon her iron, and the saliva runs off in globules—and water in a spheroidal form remains unevaporated in a red-hot crucible or pan—so that where heat is concerned the same form is assumed, as where it appears to be absent.

All physical things seem to have a tendency to take this particular structure, and heat administered in gentle doses, together with infinitesimal draughts of gases and mineral vapour during long periods of time, superintended by the administrative aid of chemical, galvanic, and other natural forces, has a mission in the final renovation of the constitution of the world.

Little has been said of metallic combinations or changes; but no person can spend a day among our Hawkesbury rocks and not be struck by the fact that iron, at least, has been introduced by means of imbibition, and through fissures into our common sandstone, and the colouring of these rocks brought out by oxidation, presenting most remarkable forms and varying outlines, betrays the influence of iron in a striking way. .

One of the most common of all exhibitions of iron is that of Pyrites. It belongs to all ages, and has been produced in all kinds of rock. It is a great enemy to some mining operations, such as the production of gold, and much wealth is lost because it is difficult to separate it from the precious metal.

Now, this mineral, owing to its combination with sulphur, is a pure product of transmutation, and in turn it becomes an agent thereof. The sulphuration of the springs of Greece has been traced to the decomposition of this mineral. And what is more curious, from pyrites have resulted huge deposits of hydrated iron. In the Cevennes mountains, in Languedoc, pyritous emanations or eruptions have produced a mass of the mineral near Alais, of great thickness, and on the opposite side of the valley in which the quarries are situate, there is a great mass of hydrated iron, which is proved to result from the decomposition or transmutation of the pyrites.

M. Virlet, who first called attention to this curious spot, exhibited to the Geological Society of France, in August, 1814, a specimen which created some surprise. In it the pyrites occupied the centre of the mass, whilst the outside had entirely been changed into hydrated ore.

I am now able to exhibit an equally interesting proof of similar transmutation. This specimen was brought down with many others from the Harding River, De Witt's Land, and sent to me by the Hon. F. P. Barlee, Colonial Secretary of Western Australia. This example is doubly striking from the fact that the iron retains its crystalline form. The gangue of this mineral is an altered rock associated with trap. M. Virlet says, that at whatever period the Jurassic rock of the Cevennes was intruded into by the pyrites, the change spoken of still goes on, and he believes it to be electro-chemical.

With respect to minerals in general, it may be remarked, that they may be deposited at a temperature much lower than is necessary to fuse them.

Below, or not higher than 104° F., products characteristic of metalliferous veins may be formed.

On the authority of M. Julier, it is stated by Daubrée, that an old brass cock of ancient Roman origin was found at the baths of Plombières, under a mass of masonry, and that it was covered with crystals of sulphuret of copper absolutely identical with Cornish sulphuret in aspect, form and properties. The water there also deposits quartz crystals, holding alkaline silicate in solution.

From Somma (Vesuvius), limestone has been ejected untouched, and granite also in Auvergne. The former was covered by minerals such as occur in the open air. Therefore, similar phenomena take place far below, as well as near or at the earth's surface.

The temperature of springs seldom goes beyond 212° F., and under three-fourths of the earth's surface, springs have to support an ocean of 200 atmospheres; rocks, therefore, may be altered at great depths by pressure, and by imbibition of gases bringing up from greater depths minerals and metallic emanations which, when a fissure has been formed, may rush to the surface, producing mineral veins in convenient places.

Thus, Daubrée considers the gold and tin deposits of Saxony, Bohemia and Brazil have been formed; but if so, why not those of California and Australia?

Those who adhere to what I believe to be a fiction, viz., the origin of gold deposits from fusion, may be startled by a fact reported recently by Mr. Blake of California, that he found a crystal of calcite (Calc spar) having through it a *wire* of native gold.

In the last edition of Lyell's Elements of Geology, published in January last (and which I received after I had prepared the materials for this paper), I am glad to find that he quotes some of the same facts which I have quoted to-night. One passage from this new edition of an important work, will show more fully how much the author of it coincides in the views I have just expressed : viz., that from the bottom of p. 733 to middle of p. 734.

Referring to the prismatic structure of rocks, I must now exhibit a singular column from the lower Carboniferous formation at Colo Colo, on the Paterson River, transmuted in this way by porphyry. Fossils occur outside this prism as on the outside of the balls from Jervis Bay.

Here is, however, a far more striking instance of this structure in another specimen of fossiliferous calcareous grit, of Secondary age, from Bramston Range, on the Flinders River, which was brought away by Mr. James Atkinson, of Oldbury, near Berrima.

I saw another about six weeks ago at the house of his *compagnon de voyage*, Mr. Burke, at Mittagong. In each instance the sides of the columns, which are separated or united by calcareous spar, exhibit the fossils of the formation in good preservation, but assuredly under circumstances which could not have existed when the rock was first deposited.

I may now approach the subject of transmutations in our own vicinity.

The upper beds of rock in the counties of Cumberland and Camden consist of a series which I long ago denominated the Wianamatta beds, and this designation is now adopted by the geologists of Europe. They consist of shales, calcareous grit and sandstone, with carbonaceous layers and casts of wood and a good deal of iron. These beds are frequently traversed by dykes and bosses of basalt, which have passed through the underlying

Hawkesbury rocks at the junction of the two series, and have hardened and altered both at the points of contact.

On Razorback, northern ascent, the plant-bearing calcareous grits have in one instance become completely spheroidal near a trap dyke and in its line of direction.

On the south side of Razorback, near Picton, there is a deposit of very curiously structured carbonate of iron, a yellow cone-in-cone ore, an effect of transmutation, and satisfactory enough as to my views of the age of the deposits in which it occurs. I have specimens of identically the same ore from the Maranoa and Flinders Rivers, in Queensland.

At Prospect Hill, an old dioritic summit has been surrounded by the Wianamatta deposits, so that it rises through them like an island. Portions of disintegrated and regenerated sedimentary dioritic matter form some of the beds, which contain casts of plants. Through these and the other beds, basalt full of chrysolite has subsequently risen and formed a coulée with columnar structure, on the north-east extremity, and this has transmuted the Wianamatta shales in some places into a greenish jaspery substance.

On the east of Paramatta, about half way to Sydney, a mass of columnar basalt has risen through the lower Wianamatta beds, and from this Sydney is supplied with road metal. About twenty-five years ago there was visible on the flanks of this mass a series of parti-coloured aluminous beds, inclined to the basalt, which have been destroyed in the process of excavation; but I was fortunate enough to make a coloured sketch of them whilst they were in existence. The prismatic structure here is partly curvilinear and partly vertical. Between the prisms occur lumps and strings of calcareous spar, and the outside of them is covered with a greenish talcose-looking substance, of a fibrous texture, so much resembling woody fibre, that it has deceived even botanists in that respect. Now this substance, in fact a mixture of the ordinary basalt with lime, is, I conceive, an effect of transmutation. It is by no means unusual to find such products of basalt. Whether the lime has been derived from the calcareous matter in the Wianamatta beds, or comes from an independent source, it is perfectly in accordance with numerous examples in other parts of the world. For instance, at the Giant's Causeway, in Ireland, where basalt has overflowed chalk, there are deposits of lime; and between the basalt and a bed of rounded quartz and clay which had covered the chalk before the outburst, crystals of quartz and calc-spar occur in the cavities of the bed; and a thin layer of carbonate of lime is also formed. This carbonate of lime is fibrous, just as the specimens are from the Pennant Hills quarry. It fills in the interstices between the basaltic matter just as it does in the latter place.

In the neighbourhood of Camden, in some excavations made for me many years ago in the presence of, and by the direction of Sir W. Macarthur, I recognised a very much greater change than this is at the junction of basalt with the Wianamatta calcareous beds. Similarly at Burwood, near to the Railway station, there is a fan-shaped mass of columnar basalt, which has transmuted the soft shales of the Wianamatta series. There are other places in Cumberland where basalt has risen and has produced numerous examples of transmutation, just as under the Mittagong Range the Wianamatta and underlying Hawkesbury rocks have been changed.

These latter deposits with which the remainder of my remarks will be directly connected, underlie the Wianamatta beds, and rise round them in a basin-formed trough between the sloping edge of the coast district of Cumberland and the vertical escarpment of the eastern edge of the Blue Mountain plateau.

Denudation of a considerable extent had taken place before the Wianamatta deposits began; and, therefore, the basalts that have altered both series must have been erupted more recently than the latter.

At points of junction of the two series, as on the west of Prospect, I have come upon several instances in which the Hawkesbury beds have been changed as much as the Wianamatta beds, affording an exact parallel with the changes under the Mittagong.

In one of the specimens of the latter, you will observe that the most siliceous rock has been partly vitrified, and is very nearly allied in this state to some of the rocks from the Narran, Darling, and Maranoa districts.

It is not, therefore, surprising to find similar transmutations in the heart of the Hawkesbury rocks. We have, indeed, near Sydney some of the most remarkable transmutations which have ever been submitted to the inspection of a geologist.

There is a mass of white rock seen from the North Shore of Port Jackson, on the top of the cliffs north of Bondi Bay, which offers one of the most striking examples. This is finely depicted in the photographs on the table. Again, near Botany North Head, on the cliff near the old station, there is another example. At Five dock is a third; near Pyrmont there is a fourth; on Lane Cove a fifth; and at Waverley there are traces of a sixth. Others exist in the same formation on the Hawkesbury rocks, as at the head of Cowan Creek, which I visited many years ago.

In all these places the sandstones have undergone a great change, and have become prismatised.

The occurrence of prismatic sandstone has appeared to some persons an anomaly. But it is not an uncommon feature in sandstone countries of a geological age not widely distant from the age of our Hawkesbury rocks.

I have brought hither for comparison two prismatic examples from the Hartz, from my own collection, and some others from other countries. Nevertheless, this kind of structure is not generally observable in the purest sandstones, and the prismatic action is, therefore due, perhaps, to a molecular alterations as well as to the element itself which holds the siliceous particles together having been affected by heat.

In some spots no trace exists visibly of the existence of basalt or other trappean rock. But in others there is open to inspection a clear contact between them. Thus, below the cliff near Bondi, which is a little north of that commonly known as "Ben Buckler," (but which Mr. Hill tells me is a corruption of a native word, "Baalbuckaléa,") viz., at Meriberi, a mass of basalt appears at the sea level and for a considerable height above; so that it is an intrusive dyke which only forms a boss in that vicinity. Again, at the Sugar Loaf Hill near the Bargo River, the boss of trap which forms that conical summit amidst the bush is yet partially covered by transmuted sandstone in situ, the relics of the masses that have been swept away.

There, all the changes are easily traceable from unaltered to highly vitrified compact beds; the basalt itself having in all its features, especially the calcareous portions, the closest resemblance to the Pennant Hill rock.

Again, at the lately boasted-of gold diggings on a branch of the Nepean River, a few miles from Mittagong village, I found the whole of the drift in which the few particles of gold dug there were found, composed of most highly transmuted fragments of true Hawkesbury sandstone. I broke with my hammer a very great number of these pebbles accumulated in heaps, and I am quite sure, that no other drift than that exists, and in one of the creeks near by I picked up basalt.

Another example of a similar kind to that of Bargo exists about a quarter of a mile west of the lock-up on the Berrima Road, near the Little Forest, where a mass of basalt stands in the midst of a denuded area, the sides and summit bearing altered fragments of the same Hawkesbury rocks. Most beautiful dendritic oxidations of manganese occur on some of the faces of rough basaltic blocks. Most of our Hawkesbury rocks, especially near to Sydney, are poikilitic, *i.e.*, they are variously coloured by the oxidation of iron, the hues of which have changed from the usual ferruginous colour of rust, to yellow, reddish, and grey, not always giving an agreeable tint to our public buildings. Take the Exchange, for instance, and other edifices in Sydney, where dull-coloured dark grey and yellowish toned stones occur in no definite arrangement with the rest. Again, most extraordinary forms are occasionally represented by the distribution of the iron in some blocks of stone; and it appears that whilst the sand was moist or friable enough to allow ferruginous impregnations to pass downwards in successive layers, or after all these were deposited, another series of white laminæ not at all disarranging the former, have crossed them apparently at about equal consecutive intervals of time. Any one who will go about the city and inspect the walls of houses and other buildings, will find plenty of good examples. Occasionally, the forms referred to take the character of a landscape, resulting from a combination of lines and colours. Witness the stone fairly representing a hilly island, over the main entrance of the Custom House. One of the most ordinary forms is a nodular, or concretionary arrangement, and these concretions have sometimes a diameter of forty feet.

Now, I class these changes and appearances among the phenomena of transmutation.

But, when prismatic action occurs *colours* on the external surfaces of the stone are *generally absent*. The coloured portions occur in the interior in patches or blotches; and in the case of the Five Dock quarry the columnar portions have a centre, generally of rectilineal sides, in which the ferruginous matter has been attracted, as it were, to that centre, or left when the rock became jointed and gases passed upwards, deoxidising the iron. The surfaces of these prisms are, however, speckled with portions of a white and, where wet, pasty substance which has evidently resulted from an external agent, and which puts on the character of a transmutation. It is probable, therefore, that the internal assemblage of ferruginous matters is occasioned by a transmutation which has removed the colouring matter from the surrounding parts. And yet we must bear in mind that, as the silica is pure and generally transparent, and the silicate of alumina, which varies sometimes in excess of one or other of the ingredients, is also white, it is not always to transmuting agency we must refer the whiter portions of sandstone in the Hawkesbury series.

In various parts of the country I have noticed white bands for some distance on each side of a crack in coloured sandstone, and often there, where wide enough, the fissure is filled in with silicate of alumina which thus forms apparently independent dykes; such as are near the east end of the wall of the Victoria Barracks.

The occurrence of silicate of alumina is a by no means rare phenomenon in sandstone rocks. M. Etallon, in a short paper on the soil of the Gres Bigarré, near Luxeuil, in the department of the Haute Saone, in France (and published there), describes the association of alumina with silica and iron. The clay is a characteristic feature of this lower member of the Trias. But frequently silica has been introduced subsequently to the deposit, and he suggests its origin in mineral springs. He mentions also the occurrence of ferruginous patches cemented by silicic acid; these occasionally form veins or concentric curves. There is so much in this account parallel with what may be seen in this colony, and especially on Mount Victoria, where just such veins occur in the sandstone, that it is a useful illustration of what we find in Australia.

Silicification has also produced kidney-shaped concretions of jaspery quartz; but sometimes, though rarely, there occur *little columns in the rock*, slightly granular, of a white substance, pulverulent, and having all the characters of *alumina*. These prisms, which are quite distinct from the rock itself, are about 0.01. m. through, and 0.03 m. high.

Springs are mentioned which are felspathised, and probably rise from granitic rock below the sandstone.

In many cases near Sydney, the cracks or fissures are, on the contrary, lined with ferruginous matter, forming sometimes thick casings, and, as on various points of the beach rock about Port Jackson, on the coast to the north of Manly Beach and elsewhere in the inner region, presenting dykes of ironstone which are not always continuous for long distances, but which swell up into bosses or irregular masses, as on the North Shore; the entrance of Middle Harbour; head of Cowan Creek; the Long Reef near Narrabeen, &c.

Other masses of hydrated oxide of iron occur at Brisbane Water, at Fitzroy near the Nattai, and other places.

The conclusions I have come to from a somewhat careful examination of the whole of the localities mentioned and numerous others, is that the Fitzroy iron ore is a product of transmutation.

The west end of the Mittagong is composed of a trachytic rock, full of little crystals of specular iron. On it rest unaltered the Hawkesbury beds. But these beds have been affected by an after irruption of basalt, which there forms a considerable portion of the range, and has produced a transmutation of the sandstones and other rocks at the surfaces of contact.

Springs have burst out at the junction of the formations, and have brought up the iron and other minerals which are associated with it, so that beds and stalactitical masses of the iron, originally derived from the trachyte, or from a source common to both, have resulted since, or during the formation of the Hawkesbury beds. It is possible, that the basalt may have had something to do with the iron, for, on descending about six weeks ago from the summit of the basaltic portion, near the head of the Gibraltar Creek, I found the sandstone in contact with the basalt hardened into a ferruginous conglomerate like " cement " of the gold-fields, and traces of hydrated oxide of iron exactly resembling that which forms the Fitzroy mine. Nodular lumps of carbonate of iron occur in the Wianamatta beds and in the Hawkesbury rocks, with patches of coal; but the great masses of hydrated ore occur in beds as in the places named, and at Soldier's Pinch near Mount Victoria, and in other localities in that region.

Returning now to the fissures near Sydney. About a year and a-half ago, I found at the end of a peninsulated mass of sandstone, on the North Shore between Greenwich Bay and Ball's Head, a dyke of brownish rock, at the sea level, which was highly ferruginous and clayey, and on each side of which for some distance the beds of sandstone were tilted away from it and extremely hardened. Breaking it up, I found the interior on one side of the cliff putting on the appearance of an amygdaloidal trap, and this being in connection with the hardening of the sandstones, there is good ground for believing that the supposition of its origin is not chimerical. Yet this dyke appears from the analysis of Professor Smith to be principally a silicate of alumina, though highly ferruginous.

Having the impression on my mind that this is a true igneous dyke, I began to trace out its further relations, and I have now traced it distinctly from the mouth of Lane Cove, through the Greenwich isthmus, on the one side, through Ball's Head isthmus on the other side, and so into a dyke of similar character at Point Piper and into the sea very near to the occurrence of the Meriberi columnar sandstone and dyke of basalt, a distance of six geographical miles.

Of course continuous tracing is impossible, for the waters of the several bays of the main harbour intervene between the points where the dyke is visible; but as the general bearing E. 20° S. is persistent, I have no doubt that it is a dyke formed when the whole mass of the harbour was filled in with continuous deposits of sandstone, and, therefore, of far greater antiquity than the present features of the land. Generally it can only be most distinctly made out where the land is lowest; but at Greenwich the existence of the dyke is traceable to a height of full 200 feet above the sea level, and on the water edge at one side of the isthmus the sandstone has been prismatised, though not to the same extent as in the localities photographed.

There are abundance of specimens here assembled to illustrate this dyke.

The occurrence and phenomena of the iron dykes, such as those near the Racecourse at Randwick, and on the North Shore will be fully treated of hereafter by Mr. Miller, to whom I leave the further details of the examples cited ; but I may mention that he has discovered gold in very minute proportion not only in the masses of iron ore, but in this very dyke of silicate of alumina, as well as in other patches of North Shore iron.

At the sea extremity of this dyke near Meriberi, the occurrence of silicate of alumina and various intermediate changes of the sandstone, which is there cemented by it, are particularly striking ; a more extraordinary locality than that between the north head of Bondi Bay and the main coast line towards the South Head of Sydney nowhere is met with; for the fissured character of the cliffs and the transmutations of the rocks are most remarkable.

No doubt hundreds of other localities exist along the coast, which have not received yet, but which deserve examination. At any rate, with the present remarks as a guide, it is possible many of the open dykes on our harbour will, by close attention, be found to be of the same character as those which occur on the beach at Newcastle and at Wollongong, and at intermediate places, and which are, undoubtedly, open dykes from which the trappean matter has been removed. It is probable that in these, and many others in the Carboniferous formation, the igneous action may be made visible, and that as we ascend to the Hawkesbury and Wianamatta beds, which are so much above the coal beds, the igneous products may themselves be found to have been altered and so decomposed into these silicated ferruginous clay dykes.

It is clear that the prismatic structure induced on the sandstones must have been effected by the trap in a very different condition of these beds. Now, if we examine the prismatic sandstone, we shall find that it is sometimes very absorbent, and does not justify the opinion once formed of its durability. At Meriberi, and at Five Dock it has been extensively used for the roads. Being consulted about it some years ago by a surveyor, I undertook an examination of it for his guidance; and the result was, that it was far from answering the expectation formed of it. Some of it had a higher Specific gravity than portions of unaltered sandstone, but of some the density was lower. In 1864, Professor Smith obtained S.G. of some unaltered rock, 2·41 and 2·44, and of the altered rock 2·47. In 1859, I obtained S.G. of other portions of white columns 2·37. The compact hard sandstone of Blackwattle Swamp gave me 2·45; but at Pyrmont the Specific gravity of the harder rock came out 3·01, and the softer 2·31. In general the Specific gravity of transmuted sandstone is higher than the nominal value. Thus, an altered red sandstone near Belfast underlying a dolerite has a polyhedral structure, and its Specific gravity nearly 7 per cent. (6·43 per cent.) higher than the unaltered. At Comber, in the county of Down, the Specific gravity increased from 2·522 to 2·545.

On the contrary, a white prismatic sandstone at Wildenstein, very like the Meriberi prisms, having a light greyish blue tint, was found by M. Delesse, to whom I am indebted for this example, to have a lower Specific gravity than the unaltered rock which is red, though the difference is not very great. The explanation is, that the quartz was slightly vitrified, for the density of the sandstone fused artificially came out 2·081 instead of 2·342. It would lead me away from my present purpose to discuss the question of vitrification.

Respecting the transmuted rocks at Meriberi, near Bondi, their white colour arises partly from the silicate of alumina with which the grains are cemented. There is no vitrification of the mass, only the prisms are generally clean, the joints cutting through the larger pebbles of quartz in the coarser varieties. It is such a change as might be anticipated from the action of heat administered in water.

The loss of colour is like that of the rocks at Wildenstein, and the strata lines, which are distinctly marked at Meriberi, have a zig-zag course, and the prisms on the south side cut them obliquely at angles of 62°, 68°, 73°, dipping N.N.W. The height of the rock above the sea at the quarry is 207 feet on the north side, and 214 feet on the south side. The opening strikes S., 70° W., and the breadth is 50 paces. I give these measurements to show that an ample space has been cleared to exhibit fully all the phenomena. That the prisms have probably been formed, as is usual in such cases, at right angles to the intruding basalt, and as in numerous cases quoted by Delesse, is shown by the way in which they dip. Near St. Catherine's School, the imperfect prisms also have a partially fan-shaped arrangement in a dome-like mass. At Meriberi the vertical portion is removed, but on the height south of the opening, the summits of prisms occupy some space. The unaltered rock contains casts of stems of plants; but none of these are seen in the altered rock. They have been probably all obliterated by partial fusion of the silica, for it is well known that silicification destroys very often the delicate parts of organic structures so transmuted, as Dr. Duncan has recently found in examining the silicified fossil corals of the West Indies.

As the quartz pebbles are only slightly altered, it is clear that the heat radiating from the trap never was so great as to completely fuse the silica, or dissolve it entirely. And I, therefore, believe that the heat was hydrous, as all such changes must be at first. An examination of the unaltered rock is necessary to understand the amount of change. I submitted 619 grains of a column from Meriberi to absorption, and the weight gained was three grains. Some of our Hawkesbury sandstones are so incoherent, that when the blocks from the Railway cutting on Darling Causeway, at the head of the Grose River, are thrown over the embankment, many of them crumble to powder. The sandstone near Meriberi is not quite so loose as this; but some of it consists merely of particles of semicrystalline quartz, without any visible cement, which of course are easily separable. This explains why the summits of the fractured cliffs, themselves huge quadrilateral columns, to the south of the quarry are strewn with quartz pebbles, the relics of destroyed beds of loosely aggregated grit and sandstone. At this locality no doubt can exist that the transmuting cause has been the dyke of basalt below, and that the eruption was to some degree violent. We may infer this from the fact, that between the dyke and the sides of the cliff, there intervenes, besides the aluminous matters, a bed of hard fractured sandstone pebbles. Much of the clay that there exists takes the character of *bole*, and that is often a clear indication of the presence of trap—as at the Giant's Causeway, where it exists among the basalt, and from which the specimen was collected which is now before us.

I have dwelt on the features of this Bondi locality, because it illustrates more clearly than others all the principal characteristics of such phenomena as are illustrated by it.

At Botany Head, where the prismatisation has been intense, the presence of igneous matter is not so clear. I have frequently examined the cliffs to seaward very closely, but I have not found any dyke.

But, if we turn to Five Dock (which I have visited in company of Professor Smith and Mr. Hunt) we have as it were an intermediate example. There the sides of the quarry are about twenty to twenty-five feet high in the deepest parts. The lower members of the strata are all partially hardened, and the laminæ of deposit are apparent with layers of silicated alumina between them; yet soft as they comparatively are, they form well defined polyhedral prisms by means of clean joints cutting through them, of which the sides vary from nine to thirteen inches, and the dip apparently fan-like, is on one side to N.W., on the other to S. 30° W.

The beds on the north side themselves undulate in a sweep inclining 5° E. and 8° W.; the upper ten feet consisting of thin beds of tile-stone, white clay and blue shale, with much reddish clay, all of which have been greatly disturbed and probably crushed during the partial upheaval and depression which these rocks have undergone.

One feature in this quarry is strongly marked. There is much ferruginous matter in the normal rock; but in the calcareous rock the whole of that red coloured stone is in the *interior* of the prisms, as before mentioned.

Now, though there can be no doubt that this quarry marks

the site of trappean influence, the transmuting agent is concealed. But, as the upper portions mark the coming in of the Wianamatta beds which near by are well developed, and as the basaltic trap of Burwood is but two miles distant to S.W., the conclusion we must naturally come to is, that that trap has extensive ramifications under the surface and has produced the transmutation at Five Dock.

It is, therefore, only reasonable to consider, that where similar changes have been noticed, a similar cause for them exists ; and as the processes connected with excavations of the soil go on, these dykes may be hereafter discovered.

There are, however, other visible demonstrations of igneous rock than those mentioned ; as near Canterbury, and along the old Liverpool road, where, in one part, probably connected with the Prospect and Bull's Hill district, blocks of porphyritic diorite lie by the way side.

How far these eruptions may have been contemporaneous with the peculiar formation of the country near Sydney, it is impossible to say. But the broken and fragmentary, insulated or peninsulated masses of sandstone, with cliffs and ledges apparently successional, and the peculiar parallelism which exists in the direction of the outlines of the harbour coasts, all point to a series of prolonged changes by which the deposited and once more highly elevated Hawkesbury rocks were subsequently depressed, cracked and broken down along certain lines of joints. thus allowing the intermediate masses to be swept away, leaving only such landmarks as Spectacle Island, Cockatoo, Snake Island, Garden Island, Pinchgut, Clarke's Island, Shark Island, the patch off Grey Cliff and some other minor features. These point to a once general extension of rocks over the whole harbour, of which these small islands were summits ; whilst the coast is marked by the larger and more striking islands, now peninsulated by sandy beaches, of the South Head, North Head, and other masses of like kind, both north and south of these.

When we look to these features and observe the agency of igneous forces we may naturally conclude that the irruption of basalt and other rocks of like kind may have been the result of the depression of the country along the sea line, in turn producing the effects on the rocks which we have been considering.

We must now look a little closer to the condition of these transmuted sandstones.

I have mentioned under the head of granitic rocks the alterations near the Sappa Bulgas, and the extension of a line of transmuted sandstones along the Darling, Narran, and so on into Queensland. I am now able to state that, from information obtained in October last, from the journal of Mr. Arthur Bloxam, and from Mr. M'Hattie more recently, that these altered sandstones extend as far as Paroo River and beyond,—and it is remarkable that at a very short distance from them exists a development of basalt, leaving us in no doubt that that rock has had something to do, as well as granite, with the transmutations to the westward. The locality reached by Mr. Bloxam was about 29° S., and between 144° and 145° E., or 130 miles to the N.N.W. of Oxley's Table Land. He mentions in one part of that country a sudden chasm, implying depression of a portion of a sandstone country, and the occurrence of springs similar to those which appear to rise along the line of transmuted country, from the Warrego to the north of South Australia.

The transmutation must have been very considerable also in the Peak Downs and Mackenzie River districts, for, about 23° S., and 148° E., many of the creeks are filled with altered sandstones and shales like those already described.

A similar remark may be made respecting portions of country in N.W. Australia.

The sandstones of the Glenelg River, and of Brecknock and Camden Harbours, and in patches all through Tasman's Land and De Witt's Land, are in similar condition, as the specimens before us prove.

Mr. F. T. Gregory found semi-columnar sandstone in conjunction with trap on the Sherlock River, in 21° 29' 10" S., and 118° 42' E. Springs were common in that region.

The connection of springs with transmuted rocks and lines of fissure is beautifully illustrated in a recent paper in the "Comptes Rendus," by Messrs. Martin and Garrigou, under the head of "*Physique du Globe*," on the mineral springs of Ax and Luchon. The authors show how granites have been changed and formed also out of neighbouring materials, where springs have traversed the rocks.

Mr. Stutchbury has given a description of the transmutations of Sandstone near the Sappa Bulgas, to which it may be well to refer. The following is an abstract of a part of his Report of 1st July, 1852 :—

"Near Dewembang the sandstone is contorted and prismatised, The columns are not so compact in the interior as on the outside. which is distinctly defined by a double boundary. The strata lines are visible.

" At Gundi, on the Little River, the sandstone is arched in synclinal and anticlinal curves ; and on Cockabroo Plains it is jasperised and porphyritic, becoming full of nodular concretions of iron ore as near Geary. Five miles from Murrumbidgeree the ground is covered by pebbles of compact hæmatite, extending for more than a mile. At Cumbogle Combang the sandstone is again prismatised."

This description does not, however, convey the whole of the facts. The sandstones have been converted into a homogeneous flint or chert by the fusion of the pebbles and sand into one compact mass. All kinds of suppositions have been adduced to account for similar changes in the coal-fields, and in such fused conglomerates as exist at Merton, on the Hunter,—and boiling water has been called in to explain them.

Now, in Tasmania the identical changes have been produced in sandstone similar to that which occurs on Cooper's Creek, at the Sappa Bulgas, and elsewhere ; and there is no doubt whatever, that in the localities about Green Ponds, which I have most carefully studied, the cause of change is to be traced to greenstone and basalt.

Not only at Green Ponds, but at Picton, and still further to the north, near Spring Hill, the igneous rock is in direct contact with the transmuted semi-vitrified sandstone ; and if the specimens here present from the Sappa Bulgas and Picton be compared, no absolute difference can be discovered. I have selected portions of transmuted rocks which show in each a border of the unchanged rock. The rock is prismatised as well as vitrified, and it is capable of such clean cleavage that it might be chipped into the form of the arrow heads and flint instruments used by the aborigines of Europe, just as similar spear heads are used by the Australian aborigines.

The only difference which I think may occur in rocks, transmuted by basalt and granite or greenstone, is the presence in the latter of an alkali derived from the greater proportion of felspar in the transmuting agent. Both Mr. Miller and Mr. Ulrich of the Victorian Geological Survey undertook for me the delicate analysis of the Cooper's Creek and Sappa Bulgas rock for alkali, and a minute proportion was detected by each of them.

I do not know whether any alkali has been traced in these transmuted sandstones near Sydney. I am myself unable to determine it.

Certainly, we have no such complete vitrifications near Sydney as at Green Ponds, in Tasmania; but, on the other hand, though I found imperfect prisms near Lovely Banks, in the same district, in contact with trap, I have never seen such perfect columns as those we can find in this neighbourhood. Tasmania may yet produce them; but I did not see any in the course of a very careful survey of the valley of the Jordan, and at Jericho, where contacts are common.

There are, however, other changes produced on the south of Green Ponds (near Bagdad, and about Constitution Hill) on beds of the Carboniferous formation which are worthy of notice. These portions of shale, containing casts of plants, are filled with chalcedonic veins. I broke them from masses in contact with the igneous rock now exhibited.

The facts which I have now endeavoured to illustrate are, that there is an intimate relationship between prismatised rock, ferruginous deposits, silicate of alumina, and basaltic and trappean outbursts. This will be further strengthened if we consider that silicate of alumina abounds in certain trappean rocks; and that various clays are constantly found in association with them.

I have also endeavoured to point out not only the probable connection of the physical features of our own vicinity with the causes of igneous action beneath us, but that there is proof abundant to show that the solid rocks, whether sedimentary or intrusive, are still undergoing constant change, and that no part of the earth's crust is stable, in consequence of the continual motion of the mineral particles. I must now draw upon your patience in order to make a few further practical remarks.

It might be supposed that most of the phenomena mentioned in this paper have died out, and that no actual instability, such as changes of level, are now going on.

If it did not carry me out of my present field altogether, I could easily prove that there are undoubted evidences of considerable changes of level of a quasi-permanent character about Moreton Bay, and in the southern part of this territory, and in Victoria, as well as in South and in West Australia.

But there are other such changes going on nearer our own homes—changes which, however inappreciable by the eye of a common observer, are yet capable of being measured by the delicate contrivances of our colleague, the Government astronomer. He can tell you that there are invisible forces at work which betray their existence by effects that derange his close calculations and defy his grasp. And whether those are all external, as produced by expansion of the rocks by solar heat or contraction by cold, or by the action of rain water filtering through fissures, and so introducing or removing extraneous matter, or whether there is still an expansion or contraction under such normal transmutation as was mentioned when I began, this is undoubted, that the Astronomer does not know at what horizon he can fix his level of the foundation for his instruments, nor does he know whether to-morrow it will be where it was this morning.

No doubt this is not confined to Sydney Observatory, but is common to others, proving that the fact itself belongs to a general and not to a local law—one which is, of course, modified in its application by the peculiar structure, texture, and conditions of the rocks of each locality.

I do not doubt that my first views on this question are sustainable, and that, although there may be general causes at work, there are also local circumstances that render the present site of the Observatory an unfortunate one.

In the days of the late Captain Stanley and Admiral King, I united with those officers in urging the necessity of placing the Observatory upon a wider base of rock, such as the North Shore affords; and I have since accompanied my friend Mr. Smalley to a spot which Captain Stanley and myself examined together and which he approved.

Whether in the progress of ages any such transmutation as has been discussed to-night, will be detected in the Flagstaff-hill, and which we have seen to exist elsewhere, no one can foresee. But if the views now expressed of the processes by which the transmutation of rocks is produced, viz., *slowly acting forces and moderate temperatures during long periods of time*, be correct, we shall come to the conclusion to which we are brought by many other independent lines of reasoning, and which close observers have not failed to enunciate, that, though the epochs during which the earth has existed is but a moment compared with the eternity of its Creator, it is still, in comparison with the past period of man's existence, of inconceivable antiquity.

P.S.—Such persons as feel an interest in the subject discussed in the preceding remarks, will be amply gratified by studying the researches of M. Delesse, in his "*Etudes sur le Métamorphisme des Roches (Paris*, 1858,)" a work full of instructive details.

In the "*Bulletin de la Société Géologique de France*," 2nde *Série, Tomes* i, iii, iv, vi, will be found much valuable matter on the same and allied topics in papers and notes by MM. Virlet d' Aoust, Nérée Boubée, Durocher, and others. M. le Vicomte d' Archiac has also some useful observations (see Tom. v. p. 3) in his admirable work "*Histoire des Progrès de la Géologie* (1853.)" These are the principal authorities, with the exception of Herr Scheerer, to whom I have looked for foreign facts on which to base a comparison of my Australian examples. The circumstances under which this paper has been committed to the press, have hindered more particular references in place.

W. B. C.

St. Leonard's,
    11th April, 1866.

UNIV. OF
CALIFORNIA

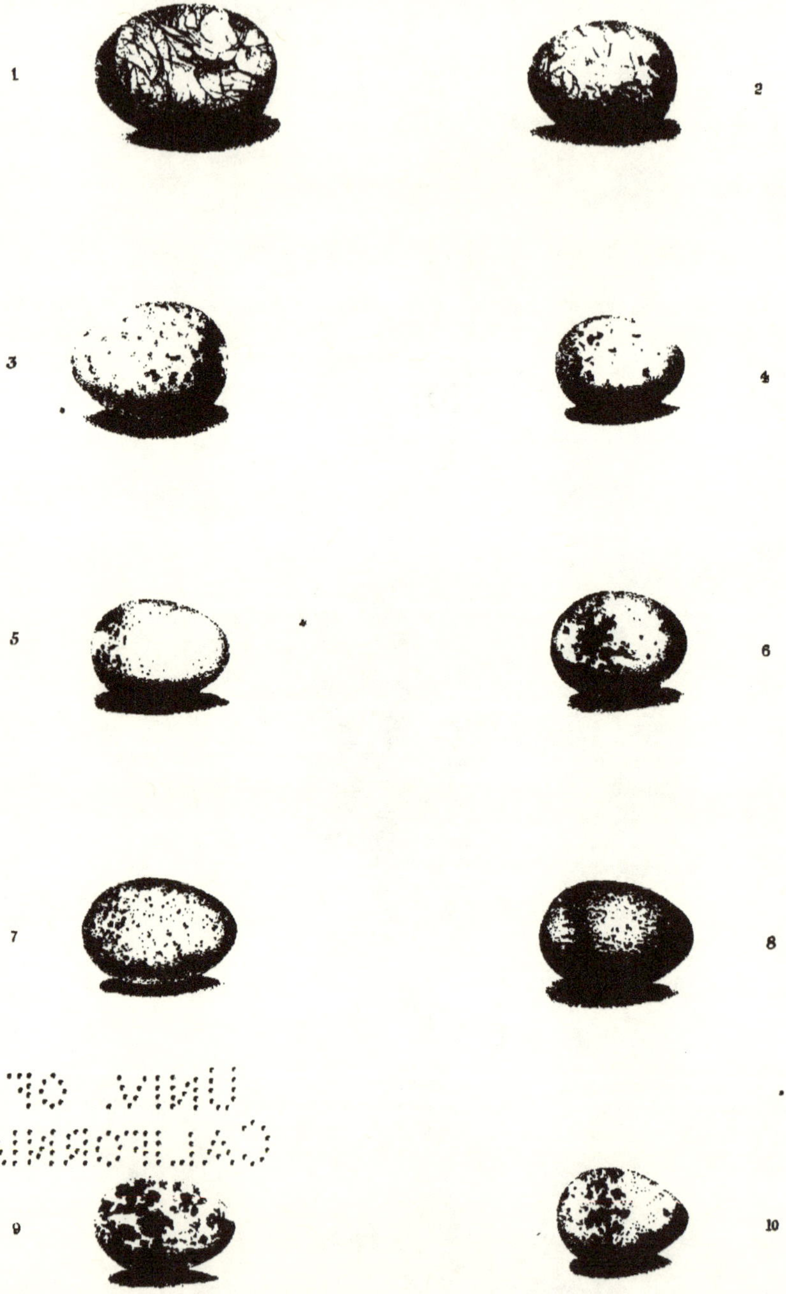

AUSTRALIAN OOLOGY. Plate. I.

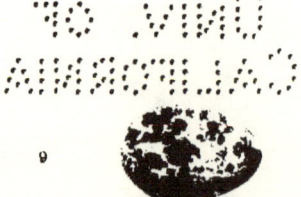

Helena Scott, del. E.P.R. dirext De Gruchy & Leigh, imp.

On the Oology of Australia,

By E. P. RAMSAY, ESQ.

[Read 5th July, 1865.]

BEFORE Mr. Gould entered upon his magnificent work, there seems to have been very little done in Australian Ornithology.

In fact, the subject, although one of the greatest interest, was, as a whole, almost entirely neglected. In Dr. Shaw's "Zoology of New Holland," only a few plates are devoted to the subject, which were taken from specimens in collections made by Sir Joseph Banks, during Captain Cook's first voyage.

Some figures again have been given in the "early voyages of Phillip, White, Collins, and King; and Lewin's "*Birds of New Holland*" contain only about 25 or 30 plates."

Vigors and Horsfield commenced a work upon the Birds of Australia in the collection of the Linnean Society, the largest collection then existing, but unfortunately they did not proceed beyond the true Honey-eaters. (*Meliphagidæ*.)

Descriptions of Australian species have also appeared in the works of various authors, such as Cuvier, Latham, Shaw, and Vieillot, but many of these are meagre, and in some instances incorrect.

Thus, no general or reliable history of this portion of our Fauna had been undertaken before May 1838, when Mr. Gould left England for Australia, there, personally, to investigate the manners and habits of our birds in their native state. And we see with what great success his efforts have been crowned; exceeding even his own most sanguine expectations, for at the close of his magnificent work, we find that through his instrumentality, no less than upwards of 360 *new* species have been discovered and figured, (thereby raising the number to 650 species.)

Among which, he states, "are comprised many forms remarkable for their novelty, the anomalous character of their structure, and the singularity of their habits, such as the Bower-birds (*Ptilonorhynchi* and *Chlamyderæ*,) and the mound raising birds, (*Leipoa, Talegalla,* and *Megapodius,*)" errors concerning which have been all rectified in his work.

No part of Australia is better suited for bird-life than New South Wales, and from the brushes, scrubs, and belts of luxuriant vegetation found all along the coast, between the mountains and the sea, one would naturally expect to find New South Wales tenanted by a fauna peculiar to itself. This is really the case: New South Wales is inhabited by a greater number of species than any other part of Australia, although the species *strictly peculiar* to it are less in number than those *peculiar* to Northern Australia. Upon examining Gould's table of the distribution of species, we find that 385 are known to inhabit New South Wales; 289 South Australia; 243 Western Australia; 230 Northern Australia; and 181 are found in Van Dieman's Land. Of these 88 are peculiar to New South Wales; 76 to South Australia; 36 to Western Australia; 105 to Northern Australia; and 32 are peculiar to Van Dieman's Land; 33 being found in all parts of Australia.

By the term *peculiar* Mr. Gould does not imply that such species are strictly confined to their respective countries, but, that *as far as is yet* known, they have not been found elsewhere. As the character of the soil differs and varies considerably, so each dissimilar district is clothed with a different style of vegetation, and each has, as it were, a Zoology of its own. For instance, the lofty *Eucalypti* are tenanted by the honey-loving Parakeets (*Trichoglossi*) and some *Ptiloti*. The *Banksiæ* swarm at various seasons of the year with the true honey-eaters, (*Meliphagidæ*.) The Fig trees are resorted to by the Regent and Satin-birds, and the *Ptilinopi*. The Palms by the large fruit-eating Pigeons (*Carpophagæ*), and the beautiful *Lopholaimus*. In the dense scrubs we find the Brush Turkey and *Leipoa*, and on the grassy slopes and plains, the Ground Parrots and terrestrial Doves, while the densely wooded spurs of the mountains and gullies, are traversed by Lyre-birds and the *Orthonyx*.

Most of the Old World birds are beautifully represented with us: The Merlin and Kestrel of Europe, by our *Falco frontatus* and *Tinnunculus cenchroïdes*. The European Osprey, by *Pandion leucocephalus*; the sparrow-hawk, *(Accipiter nisus)* by our bird of the same genus, *Accipiter torquatus*, which is found throughout the whole of Australia. We also have our Plovers, and Dottrells, one Avocet, and one stilted Plover. Among the Water-birds, the Grebes and Cormorants of Europe are also well represented by *Phalacrocorax carboides, Podiceps gularis,* and *P. Australis.*

In addition to having most of the European genera represented with us, few countries can boast of so many distinct genera peculiar to itself as Australia, such, for instance, as *Ægotheles, Pardalotus, Strepera, Gymnorhina, Grallina, Pteropodocys, Pachycephala, Colluricincla, Falcunculus, Oreöica, Menura, Psophodes, Origma, Malurus, Pyrrholæmus, Struthidea, Ptilonorhynchus, Chlamydera, Licmetis, Calyptorhynchus, Platycercus, Euphema, Nymphicus, Scythrops, Myzantha, Anthochæra, Entomyza, Sittella, Climacteris, Leipoa, Pedionomus, Talegalla, Tribonyx, Cereopsis, Anseranas,* and *Biziura,* &c., &c.

Some species are universally dispersed over the whole country, from North and Western Australia to Van Dieman's Land, as *Corvus Coronoides, Ichthyaetus leucogaster, Milvus affinis, Chelidon arborea, Phaps chalcoptera.* The Emu, *(Dromaius Novæ Hollandiæ)* and the Bronze cuckoo, *(Chalcits lucidus,)* a migratory species, which also pays an annual visit to New Zealand. Others again are, as far as is yet known, confined to particular parts.

In New South Wales we have *Aquila? Morphnöides, Podargus humeralis, Erythrodryas rosea, Eöpsaltria australis, Menura superba, Psophodes crepitans, Malurus Lamberti, Epthianura tricolor Origma rubricata, Polytelis barrabandi,* &c. In South Australia, *Malurus melanotus, Ptilotis cratitia, Xerophila leucopsis,* and both Western Australia and North Australia have also birds peculiar to those parts.

In taking a general view of the Australian Fauna, we find a very marked deficiency in the Raptores or birds of prey. The whole of these, including the hawks and owls both nocturnal and diurnal, comprise only 37 species, among which we find only one of the restricted genus *Aquila* or True eagles; no vulture of any kind, and only two kites, *Milvus affinis* and *M. issurus*. Among the nocturnal owls, however, those belonging to the genus *Strix*, are more numerous than in any other country, comprising no less than four species, whereas other countries are provided with only one species of this useful genus.

Among the perchers, the insectivora are greatly in excess; of the *Podargi* there are 6 species, the Honey-eaters (*Meliphagidæ*) include more than 20 genera and 63 species, while of the *Maluridæ*, which are among the most beautiful and brilliantly colored of our Australian birds, there are 13 species.

The *Fringillidæ* (finches) are found in great numbers; and the *Psittacidæ* extremely numerous, more so than in any other country. They form four great groups, the *Calyptorynchi*, *Cacatuæ*, *Trichoglossi*, and ground Parrots.

The *Calyptorhynchi* procure the greater part of their food from the *Banksiæ* and *Casuarinæ*, the small branches of which may frequently be found torn open by these birds in search of Lepidopterous and other Larvæ; nor are even the woody nuts of the *Banksiæ* proof against their immensely powerful jaws, but are split open and the white kernel eagerly devoured. Of Calyptorhynchus there are at least 7 species known, and all, I believe, inhabit Australia.

The *Cacatuæ* number six species. The *Trichoglossi* subsist chiefly upon the honey procured from the flower-cups of the *Eucalypti*, and the Ground parrots, which include the genera, *Euphema*, *Platycercus*, *Psephotus*, *Melopsittacus*, *Nymphicus*, and *Pezoporus*, are all peculiar to Australia. The united groups of these comprise 60 species.

While the *Gallinacea* are few, being only represented by two genera of which jointly there are only 5 species; the Pigeons and *Hemipodes* are very numerous, and many of the former, such as the *Carpophagæ* and the *Ptilinopi* are very beautiful. The *Procellaridæ* which are found visiting the whole of our coast, are also in species more numerous than in any other part of the world.

The matter forming the preceding paragraphs has been for the most part extracted from Gould's "Birds of Australia." I have, however, thought it desirable to introduce them here in order to afford a general view of the character of Australian Ornithology.

Now, while so much has been said about the birds themselves, I find that their habits and economy *as connected with their nidification*, are but imperfectly understood, and that the nests and eggs even of many of our most common species, remain still undescribed.

It is this part of our Ornithology then, viz.: The "*Oology* of our Australian Birds," to which I intend paying particular attention, for indeed there is little or no hope of finding new species within a considerable distance of Sydney. I have frequently heard it regretted that collections of Australian birds' eggs are not more numerous ; and that those which are occasionally made, seldom contain more than fifty or sixty species. Most of our birds have the credit of only laying two eggs at a sitting; though even if such were the case, they make up for this shortcoming by having two or three broods in the year. I find, however, that three eggs, are upon the average, laid by our birds. The Honey-eaters lay two or three ; the *Acanthizæ*, *Maluri*, and *Chthonicola* three or four; Larks three. The Quails are great layers ; the Parrots also, often lay from eight to ten eggs ; most of the King-fishers lay four or five ; and the Finches six or eight.

Many of the nests of our birds are most beautiful, and as well worth collecting as the eggs. Nothing can surpass the neatness, warmth, and at the same time, the strength of the nests of some of our *Acanthizæ*. And it is not less interesting to observe the peculiar structure and material used in the formation of those of the White-winged chough, (*Corcorax leucopterus*) and of the *Grallina*, which are composed of mud with grass to strengthen them, a compost which will harden in time to an almost incredible degree, when exposed to the rays of the sun. Upon one occasion, I threw one of the large basin-shaped nests of the Chough to the ground from a height of more than thirty feet without its breaking.

Besides the Chough and *Grallina*, we have another bird which builds its nest of mud, upon a horizontal bough; this is the *Struthidea cinerea*, a bird not found in this district, its habitat being the South Eastern portion of the interior. Mr. Gould quoting from Mr. Gilbert's journal, states that the nests of the *Struthidea* are similar to those of the *Grallina*, and placed in like situations upon a horizontal bough; those found by Mr. Gilbert had a thick lining of grass, more than is usually found in the nests of the *Grallina*, and one of them contained four eggs, "the medium length of which was one inch and a quarter by seven-eighths of an inch in breadth; their colour was white, with blotches, principally at the larger end, of reddish brown, purplish gray, and greenish gray, some of the blotches appearing as if they had been laid on with a soft brush."

I might mention many other nests equally curious and beautiful, but will proceed to those more immediately connected with our plate. It may be imagined that the figures are too highly coloured, but those who have taken eggs themselves, will know how greatly the specimens fade. The bloom of the more brightly tinted goes off in a few days, while some even lose their original colour altogether, and turn as in the case of the Pied robin, (*Petroica? bicolor*) from green to a dull brown; I might cite numerous other instances, for nearly all the eggs fade considerably, even when kept from the light in close boxes. I have tried various means to remedy this, but without success. Gum, if laid on thickly, causes some to keep their colour, but imparts an unnatural gloss, which does not improve their appearance at all. The best way, upon the whole, is to empty them carefully, and if possible, without using water; when an egg is once wet, it immediately loses its bloom: *sucking* has this in its favour, that the contents may be withdrawn through almost an invisible hole. Many people use a complete set of instruments for egg-blowing, but these, although useful and handy, may very well be dispensed with.

The paintings from which the figures on Plate I. were lithographed and colored, have been executed by Mrs. Edward Forde, and were, with the exception of the three first, (Nos. 1, 2, and 3) painted from specimens at most only three or four days from the nests, so that by these means I have secured correct and unfaded colors. As far as I am aware, none of these have been figured before in any publication; and even if they have, we know that the descriptions and coloring must have been taken from faded specimens, unless the author has taken the same precaution and had them painted within a few days after they were laid.

Some of our species breed very early, commencing in July, and often continue until December. The early breeding birds, such as some of the *Acanthizæ* and *Eöpsaltriæ*, and many of the Fly-catchers, have their second brood in October, and very often a third in December. So that if the eggs of our Australian birds are few in number, they certainly make up for it in the number of broods which they have; I have been informed by some of my old school-fellows, that they have taken no less than eight nests from one pair of birds during the season, as soon as one nest was taken, the birds constructing another, and so on, until the birds had built eight separate nests, and laid fifteen eggs. And I have myself, in the case of what we considered rare birds, taken four or five nests from the same pair. A curious fact relating to some species, is, that they are found breeding before their plumage reaches the colour of the adult birds. Whether these are the young in their first year, or whether these species take two or three years before arriving at the plumage of the adult, I have not yet determined; from the plumage alone, one would judge them to be the young in their first year. I am not alluding to such birds as the males of the Satin and Regent birds, &c., which we well know take two or three years before appearing in the livery of the adult, but to certain species of the genera *Acanthiza* and *Melithreptus*, the generality of which obtain their livery at the end of the first year, but which I have found breeding while yet in the first year's plumage.

Much perplexity has arisen on account of naturalists finding young birds breeding while in first year's plumage, supposing, naturally enough, that they were adult birds, and consequently considering them as new species.

POMATORHINUS TEMPORALIS,

The Temporal Pomatorhinus.—(Gould, B. Austr., Vol. IV., pl. 20.)

Pl. I., Fig. 1.

The genus *Pomatorhinus* is well represented in Australia, but the great 'strong hold of this tribe is the south-eastern portion of Asia, and the Islands throughout, to the North of Australia. From what I can learn from the notes of various authors, upon the Asiatic members of this genus, I find that our Australian species seem to form a separate and distinct group, differing in their habits and nidification, and chiefly in the curious markings of their eggs, in which all our species closely resemble each other. From these facts alone they quite merit their separation into another genus.

Four species of *Pomatorhinus* are found inhabiting Australia: *P. superciliosus*, *P. ruficeps*, and *P. temporalis*, the eastern and southern parts; and *P. ruberculus* the northern portion, where it takes the place of *P. temporalis* of New South Wales. *P. superciliosus* enjoys an extensive range of habitat, being found equally plentiful in Western Australia. *P. ruficeps* was discovered by a German Emigrant in South Australia; its habitat is chiefly the borders of the Darling and Murray Rivers.

The *Pomatorhini* have been placed by most authors among the Honey-eaters (*Meliphagidæ*); but Mr. Gould informs us (after a careful study of habitats and economy) that they have no affinity to that tribe whatever,—he has therefore placed them in a separate family, between the *Corvidæ* and *Meliphagidæ*, and I can myself testify that as far as our Australian *Pomatorhini* are concerned, they neither assimilate in their habits, actions, or nidification, to any of the numerous genera of Honey-eaters, for which Australia is so famous.

In Fig 1, is a very good representation of the eggs of *P. temporalis*. I found this, which is about the largest species, very plentiful on the Bell River, also in the districts of Wellington, and the Lachlan. They are usually met with in small troops, and not unfrequently on the ground, over which they hop and run with surprising agility and ease, and where they procure the greater part of their food. They are very pleasing and active in their movements, but very garrulous and noisy, especially when disturbed. Sometimes a troop may be seen gently feeding upon the ground, hopping over it with a quick and easy motion, until some more watchful individual will give the alarm by a hoarse guttural cry, which is immediately taken up by the rest, as they fly off, emitting a garrulous croaking noise, to the nearest tree, settling upon the slanting trunks, hopping upwards by degrees and chasing each other to the ends of the highest boughs, from which they will often fly off, one after the other, to repeat the same actions elsewhere.

They breed chiefly in September, October, and November, making a large coarse nest of twigs slightly interwoven; the lower part is much rounded, the upper rather elongated, and sometimes drawn into a neck, the back twigs being brought forward so as almost completely to hide the small opening, which has, as it were, a thatch of twigs over its entrance. Very often too the twigs from the lower side project upwards, rendering it (seemingly) almost impossible for the bird to enter without disarranging them.

It is lined with a great quantity of grass or stringy bark, with which the eggs are frequently covered when the birds leave their nests. The top of some bushy tree, or the end of some thickly branched bough are the sites chosen for the nests, which, when in the former situations, are placed nearly upright, but when in the latter, upon their sides, being built of course to suit the boughs in which they are placed.

Several nests may be found within a few yards of each other in the same clump of trees, with birds sitting in each of them. The number of the eggs found in a nest varies from 5 to 10. My brother, Mr. James Ramsay, informs me that he has taken no less than fourteen from one nest, and in these cases believes them to be the joint property of several birds; the usual number, however, is 5, which are either much elongated or rounded in form, and not unfrequently have the ends of equal thickness; the medium size is one inch in length, by 9 lines in breadth. The ground colour is brownish, yellowish, or purplish-buff, covered with a most peculiar network of veins and hair lines, running in various directions, both across and round the surface; these lines are of a dark purplish brown. The colouring matter has the peculiarity of being easily rubbed off.

Mr. Gould remarks:—"The markings of the eggs may be more easily imagined, by supposing a hair or hairs to have been carelessly drawn over them after having been dipped in ink."

POMATORHINUS SUPERCILIOSUS.

The White-eyebrowed Pomatorhinus.—(Gould, B. Austr., Vol. IV., pl. 22.)

Pl. I., Fig. 2.

All that I have said with respect to the habits and actions of the former species, may equally well be applied to this. It is not, however, such a noisy species, nor found in such large troops. The nest is similar to that of *P. temporalis*, but smaller; and has the entrance more completely covered by a thatch of twigs. The eggs are three or five in number; their usual length is $10\frac{1}{2}$ or 11 lines, by $7\frac{1}{2}$ to 8 lines in breadth; some are rounded in form, others more elongated. The ground color is of a brownish gray tinged with olive, clouded with purplish brown and greyish olive, and sparingly veined with dark bistre. Some specimens are of a uniform dull greyish olive brown, clouded with a deeper hue, and without veins, and have a clouded band round the centre. Like the foregoing species, this is frequently found upon the ground, hopping about with the greatest agility under the trees, especially during the early part of the day; when flushed they fly off to the nearest tree, and commence to ascend it by a series of hops and jumps until they reach the end of the boughs, from which they fly off in a string. They are very sprightly and quick in their movements, and have the peculiarity of drawing their heads in and puffing out their feathers as they ascend the branches, looking like a number of brown balls bouncing among the limbs.

This species has a wide range of habitat, being found equally common on the Darling, Lachlan, Bell, and Murray Rivers, as well as over the whole southern portion of the country, and in Western Australia. Upon the Bell River, and near the Lachlan, I found them very plentiful in company with the *P. temporalis*, and have frequently found several nests of both species built in the same clump of trees, for which purpose they show preference to the thick bushy tops of a species of *Acacia*, allied to the "Myall."

Mr. G. Krefft informs me that the nest and eggs of the *P. ruficeps* so closely resemble those of the *P. superciliosus*, that the one description will answer for both species. The eggs of the *P. ruficeps* have, however, more commonly a clouded band round the centre, which is also visible in some specimens of the eggs of *P. superciliosus*.

Specimens sent to me from the Darling River, as the eggs of *P. ruficeps*, are somewhat larger than one would expect from the size of the bird, and are lighter in colour, clouded with a purple brown, with a very few streaks of a darker hue, in length 10 lines by 7½. The eggs of *P. rubeculus* I have not yet seen. This species is confined to the northern portion of Australia, where it takes the place of the *P. temporalis* of New South Wales. *P. temporalis* is the oldest known species, and was described by Latham under the name of *Turdus frivolus*.

XANTHOMYZA PHRYGIA.

The Wart-faced Honey-eater.—(Gould, B. Austr., Vol. IV., pl. 41.)
Pl. I., Fig. 3.

Although this species was at one time plentiful in our neighbourhood, it has of late years become rare, and can now only be looked upon as an occasional visitor. I found a few specimens feeding in the *Eucalyptus* trees the year before last (1863), but had not previously seen any since June, 1859, when they arrived in great numbers, and literally swarmed in the swamp-mahogany trees, *Eucalyptus sp.*, which were then in bloom, their bright yellow and black plumage contrasting beautifully with the green foliage and still greener plumage of the various Parakeets, with which the tree was crowded. *

---

* Since these notes were written, this species has again visited us in immense numbers, and many pairs have remained and bred in the neighbourhood of Sydney, their stay lasting from August to December, 1865.

I met with numerous flocks of this species last year near Braidwood, traversing the bush from one blossom tree to another, squabbling and fighting with almost every Soldier Bird they came across, for they are rather inclined to be pugnacious, and will often indulge their propensity, particularly upon the smaller Honey-eaters, which manfully attack them in return.

They are usually very plentiful in the neighbourhood of the Bogan River. During my last visit to those parts I succeeded in finding several nests, and was not long in procuring their eggs also. As I expected, upon climbing up to the nests, I was immediately attacked by not only the parent birds but also by several of their feathered friends, attracted by the cries of their mates,—all gallantly keeping up the attack until I had reached the ground again, snapping their bills so close to my face that I stood no small chance of having my ears pecked off, and always flying at me from behind.

The nest is a neat cup-shaped structure composed of stringy bark, and lined with finer shreds of the same material. It is $2\frac{1}{2}$ inches across inside, by $1\frac{1}{2}$ inch deep, and placed between the upright forks of some tall sapling, or upon a horizontal bough. They breed during November and December, or perhaps earlier in some localities, and lay two or three eggs—10 to $11\frac{1}{4}$ lines long, by $8\frac{1}{4}$ to 9 lines in breadth. These, when freshly taken, are certainly among the most beautiful I have ever met with; but unfortunately, as in most bird's eggs, the bloom goes off, and the bright tint soon fades.

From my note book, I find that when first taken from the nest they are of a deep saturnine buff, spotted with irregular markings of a deeper hue, in some, evenly distributed over their surface, in others, more crowded at the larger end; there are also a few indistinct dots of greyish lilac dispersed over the surface; but these lilac dots are not visible in all specimens. I have one, however, in which greyish lilac spots predominate. The specimen from which the figure on our plate (Pl. I., Fig. 3) has been taken, is the largest and finest of its species that I have ever seen; all, however, are not of this form, some being more lengthened and less rounded.

This species of Honey-eater was one of the first known, and was described under various names, and placed in several genera by as many different authors; but as its habits and economy became more perfectly understood, and ornithologists began to classify their birds more from their habits, &c., this species was finally placed among the Honey-eaters, and a new genus formed for its reception, viz:—that of *Xanthomyza*, of which, at present, it is the only species known. The curious miniature wart-like excrescences round the eyes and ears, have gained it the colonial name of the *Wart-faced Honey-eater*, while from its black and yellow plumage, it is called also the *Mock Regent-bird.*

PTILOTIS FUSCA.

The Fuscous Honey-eater.—(Gould, B. Austr., Vol. IV., pl. 44.

Pl. I., Fig. 4.

Of the genus *Ptilotis*, there are at present 16 species known, being the most numerous group of the Australian *Meliphagidæ*. " Nearly all the species (says Mr. Gould) are prettily marked about the face, or have the ear-coverts largely developed, and characterized by a coloring different from that of the other part of the plumage."

Although the members of this genus are among the most brilliantly coloured of the tribe, this species has nothing in its plumage to recommend it, which may account for its being somewhat overlooked. I find little or no mention of its habits or economy, and nothing of its nidification, even in Mr. Gould's magnificent work; although it is one of the most common species of our Sydney birds.

The fuscous Honey-eater breeds in September and the three following months, making a neat cup-shaped nest of stringy-bark, strengthened by the addition of a great quantity of cobweb; it is lined with fine shreds of bark, hair, and sometimes the silky down from the seed-vessels of the wild cotton, (*Gomphocarpus fruticosus.*) It is usually placed among the twigs at the end of some horizontal bough, or among the bushy tops of the young *Eucalypti.* The Turpentine trees, (*Syncarpia*) also afford favorite sites for their nests, which are $2\frac{1}{4}$ inches across by 2 inches deep. The eggs are two in number, from $8\frac{1}{2}$ to 10 lines long, by

6 to 7 lines in breadth; the ground color is of a deep yellowish buff, with spots of a deeper and more reddish hue, and a few of faint lilac, in some sprinkled equally over the whole surface, in others crowded, or forming a cone at the larger end.

In painting these eggs, as well as those of *Xanthomyza phrygia*, the true tint of color is only to be obtained by using light Saturnine red. The ground color of the eggs of *Ptilotis fusca*, upon fading, becomes flesh-yellow, and the markings yellowish or reddish brown, the lilac almost disappearing.

These Honey-eaters are usually found during the winter months, in small groups of from 5 to 10 in number; it is not a migratory species, but remains with us all the year round, and is one of the numerous birds which frequent gardens; it may be found in the orchards, either when the trees are in full bloom, flying round the blossoms in search of insects, or when the fruit is ripe. They seem to have a decided preference for the sweet juice of pears. This species of Honey-eater is, I believe, strictly confined to New South Wales.

PTILOTIS AURICOMIS.

The Yellow-tufted Honey-eater.—(Gould, B. Austr., Vol. IV., pl. 37.)

Pl. I., Fig. 5.

This beautiful Honey-eater is one of our most common species, and found very abundantly in the neighbourhood of Ashfield and Parramatta. It shows a decided preference for the more open parts of the bush clothed with underwood of *Acacia* and young *Eucalypti*, rather than the thick scrubby parts nearer Sydney.

Like most of the genus, the yellow-tufted Honey-eaters are very partial to fruit, and during the season, they resort to the gardens in great numbers, accompanied by many other species, and may often be seen squabbling over the over-ripe pears and oranges. They are very fond of exercising their pugnacious propensity upon the larger birds, Hawks, Owls, and even the sleepy-looking Goat-suckers are quickly attacked as soon as perceived; even their own species, when wounded, and crying out, come in for a share of their dislike. Often a dozen or more may be seen clustering upon a bough huddling up together, pecking at, and fighting with, each other, or screeching, as if holding a jubilee over some common enemy.

This is not a migratory species, but is always to be found throughout the whole year, and breeds much earlier than the generality of the tribe. We have eggs taken in the early part of June, and others found in October, November, and December. They have two, and sometimes three broods during the year; August and September being their favorite months for breeding.

With respect to its nidification (I will quote what I have already said upon the subject in vol. vi. of the " Ibis " page 244,) " I find upon referring to my note-book, that we captured two young, well able to fly, on July 18th, 1863 ; but during some seasons birds breed much earlier than in others.

The nest is a neat but somewhat bulky structure, open above, and composed of strips of stringy bark, lined with finer shreds of the same material, and the silky down from the wild cotton (*Gomphocarpus*.)

The site selected is usually some low bushy shrub, among the thick tufts of the *Blechnum*, (*B. Cartilaginum*) or carefully hidden in the thick rich clusters of the beautiful *Tecoma Australis*. The ferns and *Tecoma* seem their favorite places for nestling ; among the clumps of the former, we have frequently found 3 or 4 nests within a few yards of each other, fastened to the stems and leaves of the ferns : sometimes they will place their nests among the dead leafy tops of a fallen *Eucalyptus*, or in gardens among the prickly branches of the orange trees ; they may be also found, not unfrequently, suspended in a fork of the bough of a small bushy forest oak.

The total lengths of the nests are generally 3 or 4 inches by $3\frac{1}{2}$ in diameter, being inside 2 inches deep by $1\frac{1}{2}$ or 2 wide. The eggs, which are usually two in number, are of a pale flesh-pink tinged with yellowish buff, deeper at the thick end where they are spotted or blotched with markings much deeper in hue, and of a reddish-brown tint. In some, the markings form a zone near the larger end, in others, an irregular patch, with a few dots sprinkled over the rest of the surface ; when freshly taken they have a beautiful flush of pink; some specimens are almost without marking of any kind, and like the eggs of most of our Australian birds, vary considerably in form. The usual length is from 9 to 11 lines by $7\frac{1}{2}$ to 8 lines in breadth.

In the nests of this Honey-eater, we occasionally find the eggs of a Cuckoo, (*Cuculus inornatus*) which closely resemble those of the Honey-eater, they may be distinguished however, by being of a uniform pale flesh-color or of a yellowish-buff, and seldom having spots or markings of any kind. We have one specimen of this egg, which has a very few dots of deep blackish and reddish brown; in length they are $11\frac{1}{2}$ lines by $8\frac{1}{4}$ in breadth. A few days after the young Cuckoo is hatched, it commences to grow very rapidly, and soon fills up the greater part of the nest, unceremoniously treading on its foster brethren, and eagerly swallowing the greater share of the food which the parent-birds bring them, until the unfortunate rightful owners of the nest are either starved to death, or smothered by the weight of its body, and as soon as dead, are thrown out by the parent-birds, which seem to be quite proud of their foster nestling. This species of Cuckoo will sometimes deposit an egg in the nest of other Honey-eaters, as we have found them in those of *Melithreptus linulatus, Ptilotis chrysops*, and *P. fusca*. And upon one occasion an egg was found in the nest of *Zosterops dorsalis*.

On the 30th January, 1864, I shot a very beautiful variety of the yellow tufted Honey-eater, of a pale yellow color above and below, having the ear-coverts and tufts, front and sides of the head, the throat, outer webs of the tail, and wing-feathers brighter and of a deeper yellow, the shafts of all the feathers white, bill and claws brownish horn color, irides dull slate blue, feet and legs bluish lead color. This was not the only specimen, there were two others about the garden at the same time, but not in company with it. They seemed to be much scouted by the rest of their species, feeding quietly by themselves and not crying out at all. Several times, while I was about to shoot one of these Albinos, a yellow-breasted Robin, (*Eöpsaltria Australis*) perched close beside it, took an inquisitive look in its face, and then, with a harsh squeak flew off again, as if quite disgusted with such a "freak of nature."

SEISURA INQUIETA.

The Restless Fly-catcher.—(Gould, B., Austr., Vol. II., pl. 181.)

Pl. I., Fig. 6.

This pretty Fly-catcher which is distributed over the whole of the South-eastern and Western portion of Australia, is one of our most interesting and lively species; among most school-boys it.is known in New South Wales under the name of the Land-Wagtail, in contradistinction, I suppose, to the Water-Wagtail, (*Rhipidura Motacilloides*) to which it closely assimilates in plumage, nidification, and habits; and indeed, the name is not altogether inappropriate, inasmuch as the present species prefers to build its nest far away from the water, and not unfrequently high up among the branches of the trees, whereas that of the Water-Wagtail, is nearly always found in the vicinity of some creek or river, very often on a bough overhanging the water and within a few inches of its surface.

The restless Fly-catcher, is not a migratory species. During the winter months it frequents the gardens and orchards, and becomes exceedingly tame; it is often seen around the out-houses and yards, and not unfrequently hopping over the backs of the cattle and horses, doubtless in search of flies; it is always on the move, and well merits its name; runs lightly and quickly over the ground, wagging its long tail from side to side as it goes along.

Its note is loud and clear, but it also indulges in a guttural sort of squeak, uttered when flying, or settling on a bough, in addition to this, it has also a peculiar habit of poising itself in the air a few feet from the ground, and during this operation, emits a sort of gurgling sound not unlike the sharpening of an instrument on a grind-stone, on account of which, it has obtained the name of "The Grinder." This ceremony finishes by the bird darting down to the ground, seizing some worm or caterpillar, and flying off, uttering a loud squeak of satisfaction. Whether this is a sort of jubilation over some fine fat worm which it has espied lurking in the grass, I leave to others who understand the language of birds to decide.

The nest of this Fly-catcher, like those of most of the tribe, is round and cup-shaped, 2½ to 3 inches across by 1¼ deep, and placed upon a horizontal bough over a fork, or by the side of an upright twig, it is chiefly composed of bark and grass, neatly interwoven; the lining is of grass, hair, or roots, and the edges often ornamented with lichen, fastened on by cobweb. It is usually placed at a considerable distance from the ground, and often at the end of some dead bough.

The eggs are two or three in number, from 9 to 10½ lines·in length, by 7½ in breadth, rather rounded in form, having the ground color of a dull white, stained with spots and blotches of dull chestnut-brown and greyish lilac, the latter appearing as if beneath the surface. In most of the specimens, the spots form only a distinct zone nearer the larger end, but in some, are sprinkled over the whole surface. The birds are for the most part found breeding in October, November, and December, but sometimes earlier or later, as they feel inclined. They have two broods in the year.

Eöpsaltria Australis.

The Yellow-breasted Robin.—(Gould, B., Austr., Vol. III., pl. 11.)

Pl. I., Figs. 7 and 8.

The nest of this species much resembles in form, those of the true Australian Robins of the genus *Petroica*, to which the birds also closely assimilate in their movements and habits, with the exception that the *Eöpsaltriæ* are lovers of the more unfrequented parts of the bush, while nearly all the members of the genus *Petroica* prefer the open and half cleared patches of land.

The nests of the yellow-breasted Robin are either placed in the upright fork of some small tree, or built upon some horizontal bough, often within two or three feet of the ground. It is a beautifully round and cup-shaped structure, 3 inches high by 2 inches across and 1½ deep, composed of strips of bark, and lined, most frequently, with the narrow thread like leaves of the native oak, (*Casuarina*) and a few dry leaves of the *Eucalypti*. The edges and parts of the outside are studded with small pieces of the mouse-ear lichen, and hanging from the sides, are long chips of bark, some of them 4 inches or more in length and $\frac{1}{2}$ an inch wide, fastened on one above the other with cobweb, the lowest of them reaching several inches below the bottom of the nest.

The eggs, which are two or three in number, are of an apple green, or light greenish-blue color, spotted, blotched, or minutely dotted with deep brownish-red, yellow-brown, and obsolete spots of faint lilac. Some are thickly speckled all over so as almost to hide the ground color, and in these the yellowish-brown markings predominate; others are distinctly spotted, or have a zone of dots, or one large blotch at the thicker end without any other markings. They are in length $10\frac{1}{2}$ to 11 lines by 7 to $7\frac{1}{2}$ in breadth, and are usually found in September and the three following months.

Mr. Gould, in his "Birds of Australia," figures four species of *Eopsaltria*, two from Western Australia, but the other two, *E. capito*, and the one at present under consideration, *(E. Australis,)* are confined to the Eastern portion of our continent.

The yellow-breasted Robin is very common in the neighbourhood of Sydney, it prefers the thickly wooded parts of the bush, although it is sometimes found in the gardens and orchards. Its flight is short and rapid, and seems to be scarcely brought into use more than is necessary to flit from one tree to another. It is seldom seen among the higher branches of the trees, keeping near the ground where it obtains the greater part of its food. It is an extremely tame bird, scarcely troubling itself to get out of your way. If there is any "clearing" going on in the bush, or a woodman splitting timber, there also will be found our yellow-breasted friend perched transversely against the upright stem of the nearest tree, waiting for any grub or caterpiller that may be knocked out of the wood, and darting down, almost under the blade of the axe to seize its prey. Its usual cry consists in the continuation of a clear shrill piping note, kept up in the same tone and key often for the full space of a minute or more without the slightest variation, its tail sometimes bobbing up and down at each interval as if keeping time. When suddenly disturbed, it often utters a sort of squeak, and upon perching, jerks its tail up after the manner of the true Robins.

MICRÆCA MACROPTERA.

The Brown Fly-catcher.—(Gould, B., Austr. Vol. III., pl. ii.)

Pl. I., Figs. 9 and 10.

This bird, although one of our most common, and sombre-colored, is one of our sweetest songsters. At day-break it may be seen perched upon the dead top of some lofty *Eucalyptus*, pouring forth a song of the most cheerful and pleasing strain: its notes are varied, and may be heard at a considerable distance. Mr. Gould remarks that they resemble those of the Chaffinch (*Fringilla cœlebs*). They have a decided preference for perching while singing upon the very topmost boughs of the most lofty trees, from whence they will dart off to capture some insect on the wing, and then return to complete their song. They are very tame, and fearless of man: and will frequently come and perch beside you when walking in the fields or bush; wagging their tails from side to side— as if perfectly sure that they were either privileged birds, or, on account of their dull plumage, not worth shooting.

This the so-called "Tit-lark" of Australia, which is a general favorite, is both a summer and winter resident. They are constantly found about the fences and rails, and are not unfrequently seen on the roofs of houses, always in pairs, and occasionally seeking for spiders under the eaves, which they eagerly devour; and, if building at the time, will carry off the web to cement the nest. Last year a pair took possession of a large Oak-tree, near our dwelling-house, at Dobroyde, and afforded us much amusement in watching them: seeking for spiders and cobweb under the eaves and corners of the stables. One day, by watching one carry off a large piece of cobweb, my brother discovered its nest, placed in a fork near the end of a horizontal bough. While adding the cobweb, the bird sat in the nest, and, pushing itself round and round, stuck the web on the edges. The nest is small, but very neat and compact—$1\frac{3}{4}$ inch across, by $\frac{1}{2}$ inch deep — composed of grasses sunk in the fork of a horizontal bough; the edge is even with, or slightly raised above, the branches, and ornamented with small scales of bark, securely fastened on with cobweb, and rendered so like the bark of the tree, that it is no easy task, for one who is unacquainted with its habits, to discover it. The eggs are two in number; but I remember two instances in which we found three in a nest: this, however, is very rarely the case. In length, they are from $8\frac{1}{2}$ to 10 lines by 6 to $7\frac{1}{4}$ lines in breadth. They vary considerably in colour, some being of a beautiful bluish-green, with a zone of brownish-purple and greyish-lilac blotches round the centre, and a few dots over the rest of the surface; in others the spots are dispersed equally over the whole. . As the eggs fade, the ground colour becomes very pale, and the markings turn to dull reddish-brown. This species has two, and sometimes three broods in the year. The peculiar instinct which birds have, of ornamenting the outside of their nests with small scales of bark and lichen which grow upon the same trees, is beautifully illustrated in not only the nest of the present species, but also in those of many other Australian birds: as in that of the Yellow-breasted Robin (*E. australis*), and more particularly in those of the Nut-hatch (*Sittella chrysoptera*), which are not only ornamented on the outside with scales of bark, from the same or similar branches, to which they are fastened, but the inside is carefully lined with small pieces of the mouse-eared lichen so arranged as to bear a very close resemblance to the eggs. The shortest and easiest way of finding the nest of either the Titlark or Nuthatch is to watch the birds. Any one accustomed to birds'-nesting can tell in a very short time, whether the birds have a nest or not, and when this fact is settled, nothing is easier than to watch the birds until they go to it.

The Theory of Encke's Comet.
By G. R. Smalley, Esq.

[Read August 2nd, 1865.]

Before entering upon the subject of my present paper, I must express my hope that you have not prepared yourselves for any brilliant discovery, or the advancement of any new theory. It is not intended to enter upon any speculation as to the Physical Structure of Comets generally—a subject, beyond all others, deficient in data. My object on the present occasion is to find out by an examination of certain familiar facts, "What is the use of Encke's Comet, rather than what it is made of."

Encke's Comet, though bearing the name of that eminent Astronomer, is also known as "Pons' Comet," from Pons, who discovered it in 1805, and again in 1819; but there is no doubt that this same Comet had been previously seen in 1786, and again in 1795. Encke indeed, though he always refers to it as Pons' Comet, pointed out the identity of the object observed on these four occasions; made it his intense study, and predicted its return in 1822. It was true to its appointment, and, which makes it an object of some local interest, its re-appearance was observed in that year by Rumker, at Sir Thomas Brisbane's Observatory, at Paramatta. Justly then has it acquired its usual title from Professor Encke, who devoted twelve years of arduous labour to its discussion, and not only predicted its future appearances, but established the important proposition to which I shall draw your attention this evening.

These "Hairy Stars," as they have been termed—wandering vapours, it may be—that appear in our system for a brief period, when most of them launch into the immensity of space, and "no man sees them more," were, in the darker ages, objects of superstitious veneration: and even in more enlightened times they appear to excite in many minds, not only a romantic interest, but an undue disposition to connect them with certain terrestrial events.

These ephemeral bodies, of which probably there are a vast number which we never see, follow the same rule as that observed in all other Planetary bodies, that is, they move in the geometrical curve which we call a conic section. This is a mere problem in geometry, for when we have obtained by observation, the co-ordinates of a body's path—generally from the right ascension and declination—we can lay down the form of that path, and identify it, much in the same sort of way as we may lay down upon a map and identify the track of a traveller, from his observed latitudes and longitudes. Of these curves, some of the Comets select the ellipse, or oval, more or less elongated, in which case the return may be predicted. Some few have been suspected—though with no degree of certainty—of moving in hyperbolic paths; whilst the greater number appear to move in parabolas (the path of the common projectile), a curve which forms a sort of connecting link between the ellipse on one side, and the hyperbola on the other; in such cases as the two last, the return of the Comet cannot be anticipated.

Now, without pausing to comment upon the remarkable circumstance of nature selecting for her operations those curves which are exhibited by dividing a cone in different directions, I will merely remind you how Newton demonstrated that, if a body be projected in space, and acted upon continually by a force which varies inversely as the square of the distance, and resides in a fixed centre, that body will describe one of "the Conic Sections," the centre of force being in the focus. Conversely, if we find from Geometrical considerations, that a body describes one of the conic sections about a centre of force situated in the focus, we are sure that the Law of Force is that of the inverse square of the distance.

Now, observation shows that Comets do move in conic sections, and that the Sun resides in the focus. Hence it follows that Comets necessarily follow the Law of Gravitation. Moreover, there must be a certain amount of substance about them, however attenuated that substance may be—otherwise they could not be subjected to the Laws of Gravitation. Again, admitting the previous statements, we find that the nature of the orbit described by a body, is dependent upon the proportion which the projectile force bears to the central force. With the *initial* velocity of projection we have, I think, no concern—for it is far beyond our comprehension—but we may fairly enquire whether any subsequent cause, can be assigned for the diversity of orbits which manifest themselves in the case of comets. Arguing from the elliptical, or nearly circular form of the orbits of all the permanent bodies of our system, we should be disposed to expect that other bodies following the same general laws, would run their races in similar courses: undoubtedly this is merely an argument from analogy, as there is no "*à priori*" argument against a body having been originally projected under such circumstances that it should describe an hyperbola or a parabola, instead of an ellipse: but it leads me to a question which I shall have occasion to dwell upon—namely, "what are the causes which may deflect a moving body from its original path?"

Starting from our own immediate system, we know that the combined action of the sun and planets produces perturbations in the orbits of the latter, though their mean paths remain undisturbed. We see a most interesting illustration of this in the discovery of the Planet Neptune, which was due to the Mathematical Investigations of Adams and Leverrier, who had previously demonstrated that certain irregularities in the orbit of Uranus could only be accounted for by perturbations caused by another exterior planet: this planet was looked for and discovered in the position indicated.

Now here we are considering bodies whose masses have to each other some considerable proportion, and although it is a consequence of the Law of Universal Gravitation that each of two bodies should attract each other in direct proportion to their masses; yet whilst a larger produces perceptible perturbations in the orbit of a smaller body; these perturbations are not significant—and there is no permanent derangement—in the case of the solar system. But far different is it in the case of a comet. Here we have a body of such extreme tenuity that its mass is not comparable with even the smallest of the members of our own system. How easy then is it to conceive that, whatever may have been the original path of a comet, that path might be completely changed by the disturbing action of one or more bodies within whose influence it happened to pass: and although it must still continue to describe *one* of the conic sections, yet the nature of the curve may be entirely altered in consequence of the change of velocity produced by the disturbing planet. Hence we are prepared to reconcile the apparent anomaly of the parabolic or hyperbolic paths of comets, with our pre-conceived notions of the superior and refined simplicity of the elliptic orbit. We may fairly consider it by no means improbable that comets were originally impressed with a motion which would cause them to describe ellipses, and that the orbits they subsequently moved in were the effects of perturbation, rather than original design.

Strangely enough, Jupiter and his Satellites seem continually to have been "stopping the way" of comets. On two or three occasions comets have threaded their way through Jupiter's system, and whilst on the one hand none of the Satellites have been in any degree affected, it has been plainly proved that the comets have been considerably deflected from their previous course.

Without, however, troubling ourselves to enquire what may have been the nature of a comet's path *originally*, it is sufficient for our purpose to know that they are liable to be disturbed when they come within the influence of our own system.

It was such considerations as these that made the comet which bears the name of Encke, so eminently his own. I have already remarked that it was detected by Pons in 1819, but that Encke proved its identity with one that had been observed on three previous occasions. And this he did by calculating backwards the planetary perturbations to the respective times of observation. With most indefatigable labour he successfully performed this self-imposed task—a work requiring high mathematical genius—extreme accuracy in computation—sound judgment and nice discrimination. The result was as he had anticipated; he found that the disturbing effects of the planets would have been just such as to verify the correctness of the assumption, that the comet which had been observed on the four occasions in question, must have been one and the same body. He now proceeded to carry his calculations forward, and again taking into consideration the attraction of the planets, he predicted its re-appearance and perihelion passage on the 24th of May, 1822. As it was not seen in Europe on that occasion, this opportunity of verifying the correctness of Encke's calculations must probably have been lost but for the Parramatta Observatory, when it was observed by Rumker, on the 2nd of June, and on subsequent occasions. From the observations then made, it would appear that the comet passed its Perihelion on May 23rd, at 23h. 7m.—that is to say, just 53 minutes before the beginning of May 24th.

With the improved data now before him, Encke was enabled to correct his elements, and predict with still greater accuracy, the Comet's re-appearance at intervals of *about* 1210 days. Since then, its name has been down as one of this World's regular visitors, and it never forgets to leave its card at the appointed time.

I have endeavoured to give some idea of the form and dimensions of this comet's orbit, by a diagram, constructed on scale from the elements computed for the year 1865; and I will just compare a few of Encke's elements for 1832 with the corresponding ones for the present year, merely observing that, for the sake of simplicity in numbers, the Earth's mean distance from the Sun is taken for unity, and that the quantities are set down sufficiently approximate for our purpose. They are as follows:—

	1832.	1865.	Diff.
Major Axis	4·445	4·436	— 0·009
Minor Axis	2·374	2·363	— 0·011
Perihelion Distance	0·344	0·341	— 0·003
Periodic Time	1210 Days	1206 Days	— 4

These results are not intended to bear a very close investigation, but they serve to illustrate, in a general manner, the fact that the axis, and, therefore also, the periodic times of the elliptic orbit of Encke's Comet, are continually diminishing; and Encke attributes this phenomenon to "the existence of an ætherial medium which pervades all space."

There is nothing inconceivable in the idea that there is an invisible, almost imponderable æther pervading all parts of space —on the contrary, assured as we are, that "Nature abhors a vaccuum," we may fairly think that no part of space is absolutely void, though we can well understand that such ætherial medium would, by gravitation, be condensed in the immediate vicinity of substantial bodies.

It remains, however, for us to examine whether this supposition of Encke's about the "Ætherial medium," does account for the fact, that the comet which bears his name has been continually decreasing the size of its orbit and its period of revolution from the time of its first appearance up to the present time.

Now I have already remarked that, however attenuated the *material* of a comet may be, it *must* still be subject to the Laws of Universal Gravitation; and, though I may be treading on familiar ground, yet I will just observe that when a body moves in an ellipse under the action of a force tending towards a fixed centre, any diminution in its velocity, from whatever cause it may arise, will have the effect of diminishing the dimensions of the ellipse, and therefore of diminishing the time of revolution. But this is just the effect that would be produced by an ætherial medium, and I venture for a few moments to draw attention to a principle, well known as it may be, upon which this fact depends.

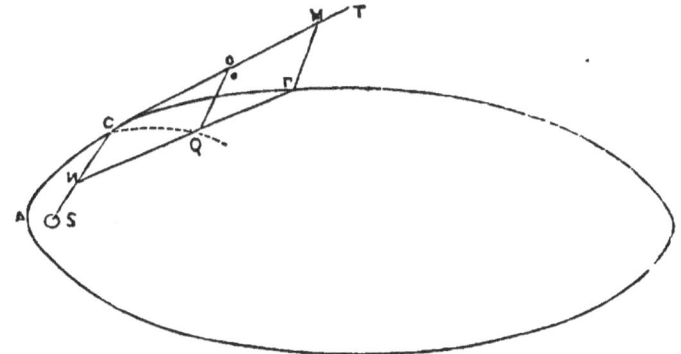

It will not affect the question if we suppose the resistance offered by this assumed ætherial medium to act at any instant, and at any place in the ellipse, as at C, when the direction of the comet's motion is that of the tangent CT. The Comet is under the influence of two forces, viz., the centrifugal force (as it is commonly, though incorrectly, called), in direction CT, and the sun's attraction in direction CS, towards the focus of the ellipse. Consider any portion of time, however small, and let Cn represent the space through which the comet would be pulled in that time by the sun. Also let Cm represent the space through which it would move in the same time in consequence of the velocity it had at C.—supposing it to have remained unchanged in magnitude and direction. Then if we complete the parallelogram $Cm\ Pn$, according to the Second Law of Motion, P will be the place of the comet at the end of the supposed time. But now suppose that a resistance is created by the ætherial medium in a direction contrary to that of the comet's motion when at C, so that Co will represent the space described in the same small time—Cn as before, representing that due to the sun's attraction—then completing the parallelogram $CoQn$, as before, Q will be the place of the comet—a point evidently nearer to the sun than P, and the ellipse will be deflected from CP to CQ. Now this is true, however small the supposed interval of time may be. Make it therefore infinitessimally small, and suppose the medium to be continually acting, then it is clear that the boundary of the ellipse is being contracted continually, and that although the orbit answers the elliptic condition at any particular time, yet the path of the Comet is, in reality, a spiral terminating in the sun, into which body the comet must eventually fall, unless some very unforseen circumstances should cause it to deviate from its present course.

It must be remembered that Encke arrived at this theory only after a most careful and elaborate calculation of the planetary perturbations. These disturbances are duly allowed for, so that any influence they might possess in changing the comet's orbit, must be altogether excluded from the question.

But before finally accepting Encke's solution, simple as it is, we are bound to enquire whether there is any other that can be offered, and if so, what are their respective merits.

There is another theory propounded. From observations of Halley's Comet especially, it is supposed that comets possess the property of throwing off and leaving behind them, in a vaporous state, some portion of their matter, which is repelled by the sun; whilst the remaining portion is still attracted by the sun, and proceeds under the usual law of gravitation. This theory would certainly explain the phenomenon of Encke's Comet—for if some portion of the mass were entirely disposed of, the remainder, having less mass than before, would be more subject to the sun's attraction : consequently, the orbit would be diminished, and therefore the periodic time continually decreased. Now without pausing to reflect upon the complicated nature of the theory thus offered, we may observe that the phenomena on which it in a great measure depends, have not been witnessed in many comets, nor do the vaporous effusions, even in Halley's Comet, appear to have been *always* in the direction where it would meet with least resistance. When two theories, equally probable, are proposed for our acceptance, we are naturally prepared to receive the more simple. Of the simplicity of Encke's theory compared with the latter, there can be, I imagine, but little question. Again, are they both equally possible? The second may indeed be quite possible, so far as we know, but I am not aware of any evidence that renders such a conclusion decisive; and with regard to Encke's theory, it is so easily reducible to ordinary dynamical principles, that one question only can be raised, and that is, " the probable existence of an etherial medium."

There are independent proofs of this, and it renders Encke's theory in the highest degree probable.

Formerly, light was supposed to be emitted from self-luminous bodies, in extremely minute particles, travelling with enormous velocity, and impinging on the retina. This " Theory of Emanations " sufficiently accounted for most optical phenomena.

It failed, however, to explain the experiment of Newton's Rings, in which, if a lens of ever so slight a curvature be pressed upon a piece of plate glass, concentric rings of different colours are observed, separated by dark intervals.

But this singular phenomenon is fully accounted for by "The Undulatory Theory of Light"—a theory whose truth has been so severely tested, that it has now obtained universal acceptance. It is, perhaps, needless to remind you that it supposes light to be propagated from a luminous body, which excites a series of successive undulations in a highly elastic ætherial medium. Such a medium must then exist—otherwise the light of the sun could not be transmitted to us—if, as we infer, undulations are the mode of doing so.

Then we may fairly conclude that there is an ætherial medium pervading all space, dense indeed in the vicinity of substantial bodies, but dwindling away in space—into extreme rarity. There is then no obstacle to Encke's theory, which unites great simplicity with all reasonable probability. And we cannot avoid being struck with the beautiful manner in which it assists the Undulatory Theory of Light; the one helps to establish the theory of the other, and we are forcibly reminded of the truth of Bacon's observation, that "no natural phenomenon can be adequately studied in itself alone, but to be understood; it must be considered as it stands connected with all nature."

On certain possible relations between Geological Changes and Astronomical Observations.

By G. R. SMALLEY, ESQ.

[Read October 11th, 1865.]

IT is, I confess, somewhat doubtful, whether the title of the present paper sufficiently expresses the purport of my remarks this evening. It has been selected for want of a better; but the real object that I have in view is to show that certain localities may be undergoing some slow geological changes of a most singular and unexpected character,—changes imperceptible to any ordinary observations, but capable of detection by delicate and refined observations made with instruments of the highest class by the practised astronomical observer.

Though previously aware that some suspicions had been at different times entertained that the changes of azimuth, as observed with the transit instruments employed in the observatories of Greenwich, Edinburgh, and Trivandrum, were periodic; yet my attention was especially drawn to the subject by the singular fluctuations in the errors of level and azimuth, which I have remarked since the Sydney Observatory came under my direction. Now I am compelled to admit, that although I think I have detected something like a periodicity in these fluctuations, yet they are not sufficiently regular to draw any decided conclusions from them taken by themselves. And we cannot be surprised at this when we consider the position of the present observatory. Bounded, as it is, on three sides by precipitous rocks, at distances varying from one to three hundred feet long; and the hill itself composed of material which peculiarly unfits it for an Observatory; so that there are continual displacements of the component parts, of such magnitude as to prevent the detection of those subtle changes which result from the regular laws of nature. Moreover, since the erection of the observatory, the stability of the hill has been still further endangered by the excavation of stone from the sides; and on such occasions sudden and irregular instrumental changes have been observed, which could be accounted for on no other supposition.

Still impressed with the conviction that such periodic changes do occur as must be traced to regular Geological laws, and not to accidental circumstances, I selected for my investigations the Royal Observatory of Greenwich, and I need hardly comment upon the importance of such selection. Situated upon a well selected soil in the midst of Greenwich Park, and kept free, by legal enactment, from any disturbances such as roads or railways—or indeed anything which might produce the slightest vibration; with the ."Astronomer Royal" for England as its Director, and a large and highly efficient staff; with instruments, the best that art and money could procure, we may be satisfied that even the shadow of doubt cannot rest upon the observations made and reduced there.

The results employed by me in my present investigation, were obtained from the published Greenwich Observations for the years 1858, 1859, 1860, and 1861. But, before I proceed, I will briefly draw your attention to the mode of obtaining those results.

In a public observatory, the principle astronomical work consists in observations of stars, as they are in the act of passing across the meridian of the observatory. For this purpose an instrument, called a Transit Circle, is employed, the application of which, is sufficiently illustrated by the common theodolite, bearing in mind that the axis is supported by solid stone piers, sunk several feet into the ground, and that the telescope itself, is not supposed to have any motion, except in a vertical plane coinciding with the meridian of the place. Now if the instrument were put in complete adjustment, and could be so retained, the axis would be perfectly horizontal, and the line of collimation of the telescope would always move in the meridian of the place; but as from mechanical defects and other causes, it is practically impossible to ensure these conditions for any length of time, it is usual, after the instrument has once fairly settled down, to bring the errors of level and azimuth, as they are termed, within moderate limits, and to determine, by very delicate observations made every evening, if possible, their actual amounts at the time, and to apply the results thus obtained as corrections to the ordinary star observations; at the present time it is the error of azimuth, with which we are principally concerned.

If there were any fixed star situated exactly in the prolongation of the earth's axis, we should have nothing to do but to turn the telescope upon that star; and if, after perfect adjustment in other respects, this star appeared upon a vertical wire in the focus of the object glass, we should know that there was no error of azimuth. And even if there is not this coincidence, the error of azimuth, which ought always to continue small in a good instrument, can be readily determined by means of a micrometer.

It is true that in neither Hemisphere is there a star exactly coinciding with the corresponding Pole; but in the Northern Hemisphere there are two stars—" Polaris, of the second Magnitude, and λ ursæ minoris of the fifth Magnitude—neither of whose angular distances from the Pole much exceed a degree; and in the Southern Hemisphere we have σ Octantis, a star of the sixth Magnitude, whose angular distance from the Pole is about ¾ of a degree; and by the application of Observations made upon one of these stars, in a manner familiar to the astronomer, we are enabled to determine the azimuthal error of the meridian instrument with as much essential accuracy as if we strictly had a Pole star to guide us.

This error being now determined, it is easy to erect a fixed azimuth mark so far distant from the observatory that any small accidental change in its position be imperceptible. Such a mark is of great importance to enable the astronomer to determine the position of his instrument at times where he is prevented from observing his azimuth stars. It is usual to have this mark constructed of stone or masonry with a fine distinct mark engraved upon a plate embedded into the upper part. Near St. Leonard's Church, on the North Shore, there is a tree in the last stage of rottenness, having attached to one of its branches an iron ring with two cross wires—this constitutes the azimuth mark of the Sydney Observatory! *

Let me now proceed to consider the circumstances of the Royal Observatory at Greenwich.

The constitution of Greenwich Hill, is, I believe, gravel with a substratum of clay. The Observatory itself is about 150 feet above the mean level of the Thames, and the direct distance from the river is about half a mile. It stands, speaking roughly, about 100 feet from the edge of the north side of the hill, where it slopes rapidly down towards the Thames; at about the same distance also, there is a considerable slope towards the west; and at the distance of a mile or thereabouts on the south and south-west lie the vallies of Blackheath and Lewisham: towards the east there is little or no fall for about three miles. I speak roughly from memory, but I do not think I am far wrong in my descriptions of the locality—the height of the Observatory I have given accurately.

---

* Since this paper was written, I have succeeded in re-placing the tree by a substantial stone column. G. R. S.

I have already observed that the transit circle is of the hightest order. It was erected in 1850, and its entire weight is, in round numbers, about 17 cwt., with its axis supported by two granite piers of immense strength and thickness, sunk several feet below the surface.

I have dwelt upon these details because it is necessary to premise that the observations upon which the present enquiry is founded, have been made under the most favourable circumstances, and with the greatest possible care and accuracy.

As pictures give a clearer and more impressive view of events than any verbal or written description, so I think curves represent more conspicuously than figures, such periodic changes as those which I am about to discuss.

In these diagrams, one side of each of the squares represents one second of arc for azimuthal deviation—the blank line being the meridian—and another side perpendicular to it represents an interval of three days. In Fig. I., every observation for the determination of error of azimuth is set down, and the points corresponding to such observations jointed by lines. Hence the curves thus described represent the actual deviations to the east or west of the instrument itself, or of the ground upon which the instrument stands. In Fig. II., the curves are described "libera manu" through the mean positions of the deviations. Now, on examining these diagrams, we cannot fail to be struck with the remarkable similarity of the general outline of the curves. You will perceive that in each of the four years they appear to indicate a maximum elevation towards the east about the vernal equinox, and a minimum deviation towards the west, about the autumnal equinox. Carried over four consecutive years, we can hardly suppose such a phenomenon to be accidental. No doubt you will remark many irregularities in these curves, but I am rather glad to see them than otherwise, because in spite of errors of observation and mechanical defects, it brings out the laws of nature in greater relief.

I have already endeavoured to explain how these azimuthal changes are obtained, and it now remains for us to examine how this apparent periodic regularity may be accounted for. Astronomical causes are out of the question, so that I know of no other alternatives, except instrumental changes due to tempera-

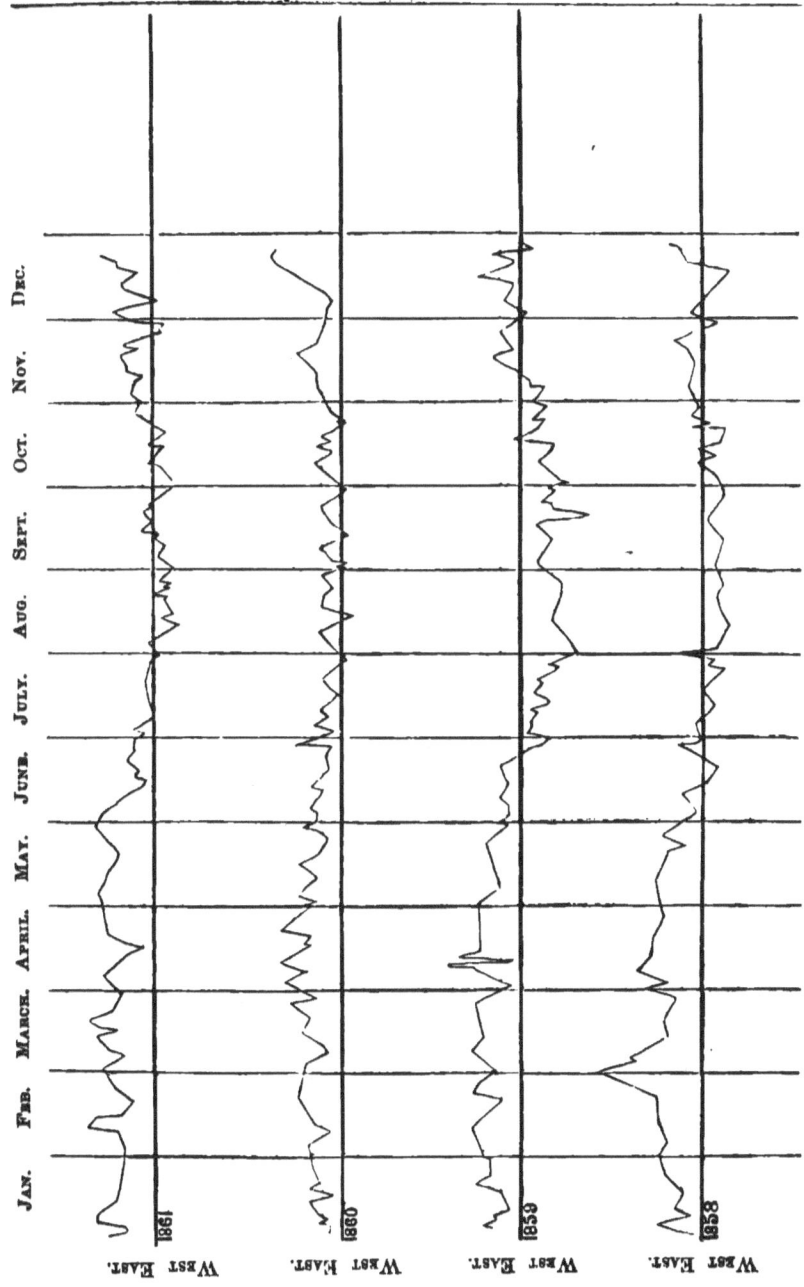

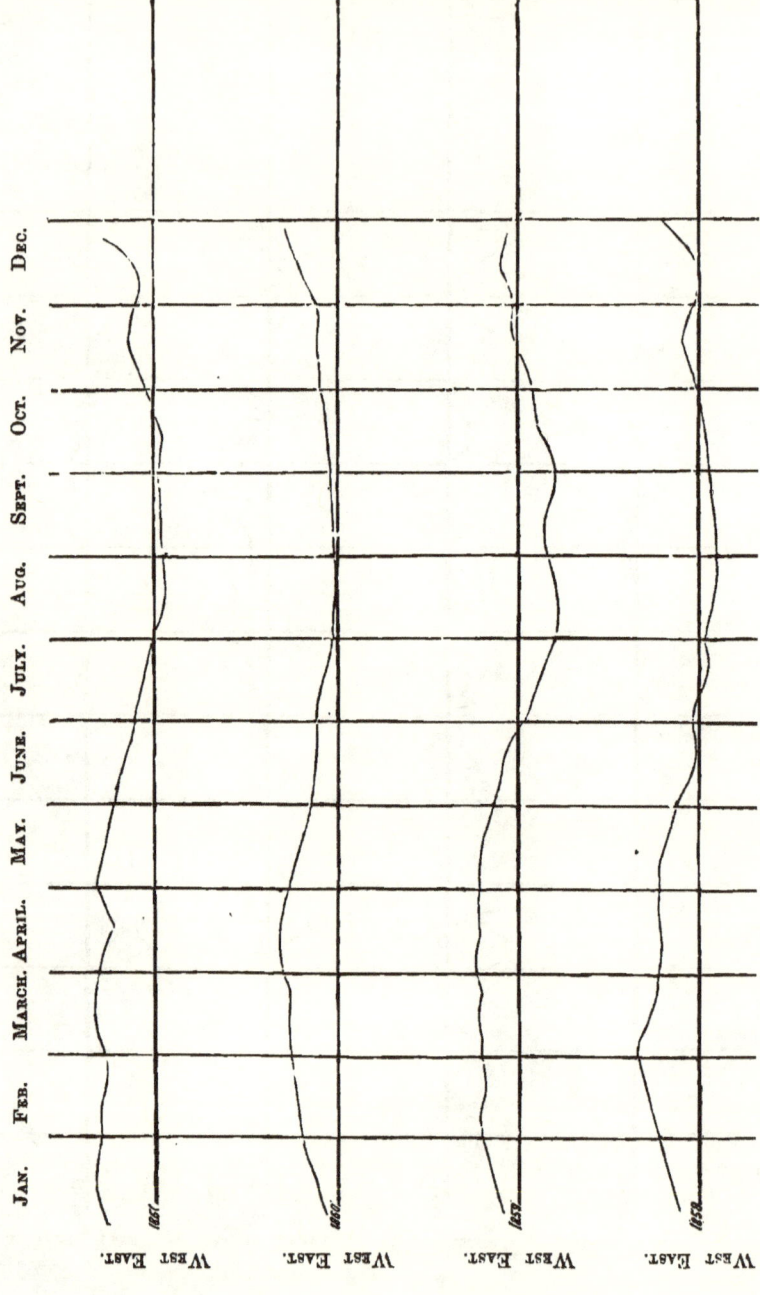

ture or actual periodic changes in the position of the ground upon which the instrument rests.

Now it is hardly to be conceived that the expansion and contraction of the different parts of this complicated instrument—the transit circle—should follow such regular laws as those which appear to obtain in the case before us. And even if it were so, we should expect that the extremes of azimuthal deviation would correspond to the extremes of external temperature—but this is contrary to observation. Can we then do otherwise than conclude that these remarkable periodic variations are due to an actual twisting—if I may use the expression—of the hill or ground upon which the Observatory is established?

It will naturally be enquired whether such a phenomenon is confined to elevated spots. I am inclined to think it is. I think I have traced it at Sydney—it has been suspected at Edinburgh and Trivandrum—and I have endeavoured to verify it in the case of Greenwich: all these are elevations of some magnitude. On the other hand, I have carefully examined the observations made at the Observatories of Oxford and Cambridge—both of which are situated on comparatively low and gently rising elevations,—and I find, not only that the azimuthal changes are very small, but no regular law of periodicity can be detected.

In order to contrast the irregularities which arise from instrumental or accidental causes with those which appear to follow some law of nature, let me again direct your attention to the first diagram in which every observation of azimuth is exhibited. You will perceive two very remarkable and sudden deflections amongst several others—one on the 15th of April, 1859, and the other on the 20th of September in the same year; yet on both these occasions I find recorded in the Greenwich observations that the transit circle had been raised from its bearings on those days, and it was suspected that it had not quite recovered its natural position at the time the observations for azimuth were made. Compare these descrepancies with the general symmetry exhibited by the four curves, and we cannot help feeling that the laws of nature assert their superiority, notwithstanding accidental irregularities which are easily detected.

In order to connect, as far as possible, these changes—which

I now feel myself justified in calling geological—with thermal changes, I proceeded to examine the temperature results at the Royal Observatory of Greenwich. For this purpose I examined the readings:

1st, of Thermometers in the external atmosphere.
2nd, of those at a depth one inch below the surface.
3rd,   ditto   ditto 3·2 feet   ditto   ditto
4th,   ditto   ditto 6 ditto   ditto   ditto
5th,   ditto   ditto 12 ditto   ditto   ditto
6th,   ditto   ditto 26 ditto   ditto   ditto

Out of all these classes of observations none appeared to accord so well with the azimuthal changes as those made with thermometers whose bulbs were placed twelve feet below the surface of the ground. In this case the minimum temperature corresponded to about the end of March, and the maximum temperature to about the middle of September.

I do not at the present time pretend to offer any theory upon this intereresting subject, I merely state facts as I find them, with the full conviction that they will be found useful in future investigations.

Since the preparation of this paper I have found, what I was not previously aware of, that this subject had been, to a certain extent noticed by Mr. Ellis of the Greenwich Observatory, in the year 1859. His investigations are conducted somewhat differently from mine, and he devotes himself more to the periodic changes of level than of azimuth, and endeavours to combine the two elements. Whilst, however Mr. Ellis's results are more general than mine, yet they do not exhibit those very decided laws which I have endeavoured to establish, but it is satisfactory to find that his conclusions all tend to the same point. And it is singular that quite unintentionally I have commenced my investigations at the very point where he left off. Mr. Ellis examines the years 1850 to 1857 included, and I have confined myself to the four succeeding years, and this may perhaps account for the greater regularity observable in my results—the instrument and piers having had time to assume what may almost be called a permanent position.

The present state of "Astronomical, Magnetical, and Meteorological Science; and the practical bearings of those subjects."

By G. R. SMALLEY, ESQ.

[Read December 6th, 1865.]

IN the present paper I propose to examine "the relation which exists between Astronomy, Magnetism, and Meteorology, considered as subjects of scientific pursuits:" "their present state, and the improvements which have been arrived at in the means and methods of observing:" "the practical bearings of those subjects, whether connected or unconnected, and the best means of advancing their utility."

In commencing with the science of Astronomy, it becomes necessary to define with some accuracy what we mean by it; and here also we must draw a wide distinction between Astronomy *as it was*, and Astronomy *as it is*.

It is no uncommon an error, and it is certainly a very prejudicial one, to consider that the science of astronomy consists in what is familiarly expressed by the phrase "star gazing;" and that an astronomer, whether professional or otherwise, is likewise a mere "star gazer."

And here I must stop to inquire, "what do we mean by star gazing?" In reply, I say, that any one who has the means to purchase a tolerably good telescope, equatorially mounted, and who has the time at his disposal to examine objects of known interest, to verify predicted phenomena, or to seek for new objects by the process which is technically called "sweeping the heavens," is a "star gazer." But we must consider astronomy as a link in the chain of physical sciences, and the public astronomer ought perhaps more properly to be called the public observer. Astronomy cannot be properly pursued without mathematical aids, or without the assistance of optical and mechanical science. Again, although it is absurd with our present knowledge and calculus to predict meteorological changes in different parts of the world subject to different local influences, yet we must not hastily reject the notion that the moon as well as the sun may be capable of influencing our atmosphere as well as our tides and magnets.

Of all sciences none is so comprehensive and elaborate in detail—none offers so vast a field for speculation and discovery,—and none has attained to such perfection as that of astronomy. And yet with all its great antiquity—for it is said to have been studied by the Chaldeans 2,250 years before the Christian era—with all the refinements of the present instruments and methods of observing: and with all the increasing supply of astronomers, professional as well as amateur,—a supply which seems to increase with the demand—we find yet more to be done.

There are at the present time, in different parts of the world, no fewer than 70 public observatories; and in England alone there are 12 private observatories, where observations are systematically made and reduced.

No doubt many private observatories and observers may be found in every country, and it would be no easy matter to estimate the number of individuals so engaged. Assigning to Greenwich that pre-eminence amongst national observatories, to which it is justly entitled, we find that the Astronomer Royal has under his direction eight permanent assistants, and nine supernumeraries. In the principal observatory of the Southern Hemisphere—at the Cape of Good Hope—there are four permanent assistants, and four supernumeraries under the direction of the astronomer; and we should find a proportional staff in most other observatories of any long standing.

And yet with all this, how unfinished and uncertain do we find the principal and most important work of a fixed observatory, namely, the accurate determination of the positions of the fixed stars. To quote the language of Sir John Herschell, "every well determined star, from the moment its place is registered becomes to the astronomer, the geographer, the navigator, the surveyor, a point of departure which can never deceive or fail him—the same for ever and in all places—of a delicacy so extreme as to be a test for every instrument invented by man, yet equally adapted for the most ordinary purposes; as available for regulating a town clock as for conducting a navy to the Indies; as effective for mapping down the intricacies of a petty barony, as for adjusting the boundaries of transatlantic empires."

"When once its place has been thoroughly ascertained and carefully recorded, the brazen circle with which that useful work was done may moulder, the marble pillar totter on its base, and the astronomer himself survive only in the gratitude of posterity. But the record remains, and transfuses all its own exactness into every determination which takes it for a groundwork, giving to inferior instruments, nay, even to temporary contrivances and to the observations of a few weeks or days, all the precision attained originally at the cost of so much time, labour, and expense."

Such are the opinions so elegantly expressed by this great philosopher, in the introduction to the catalogue of 8377 fixed stars, published by the British Association, for the advancement of science. Yet, out of the countless number which optical improvements bring within our sphere of observation, 1500 only appear to be *accurately* recorded: of these, the catalogue just referred to, furnishes the most reliable portion. Perhaps, the number of those which have been determined with very great precision, does not exceed 2000, whilst of the fundamental stars—or those selected for the nautical almanac—there are 141. Hitherto, the fixed stars of the Southern Hemisphere do not appear to have received their due share of attention, and it is only now, that there seems to be some prospect of those observatories which possess first-class meridian circles, co-operating in forming a complete catalogue, of all stars up to the ninth magnitude, after the example of Argelander, in the Northern Hemisphere.

Among the improvements which have been made in astronomical instruments, none perhaps deserves more attention than the method now almost universally adopted for observing bodies on the meridian. Previous to 1850, it was usual to employ two instruments for the purpose. A transit instrument, by means of which the time of a star's passing the meridian, and hence the right ascension was obtained; and a mural circle which furnished the stars altitude when on the meridian. These two elements, which like the latitude and longitude of a place, are requisite for determining the position of a celestial object, could not be obtained at the same time except by the aid of two observers: and, moreover, the mural circle was open to objections from the mode in which it was usual to mount it.

Now, however, both these instruments are combined in one under the name of the Transit or Mendian Circle; so that complete observations of a body are made simultaueously by one observer, and both instruments receive an amount of strength and freedom from mechanical defects which could not be previously obtained. Even in this instrument an improvement is now made, and one which I have adopted with advantage in the small transit circle of the Sydney Observatory. Formerly it was necessary to raise the transit instrument entirely off its bearings, in order to obtain the error of collimation of the telescope. This was at all times a work of difficulty, and oftentimes of hazard; the necessity for this is now superseded by the simple expedient of having an aperture through the centre of the telescope, which is closed when not in use, and affords an uninterrupted view of one collimator from the other.

Time would fail to dwell upon the improvements which have been made in telescopes equatorically mounted, and the progress which has been made by opticians and mechanics in the construction of lenses, and that delicate apparatus for measuring small spaces, known as the micrometer. Professor Airy considers the screw of the micrometer attached to the telescope of the transit circle at Greenwich, the workmanship of Messrs. Troughton and Sims, to be almost perfect. But there is still room for improvement in the graduation of circles, and the construction of lenses. Both indeed have attained to a high degree of excellence: yet the most finely graduated circle is found to be somewhat imperfect, and the optician has not yet succeeded in producing a lens perfectly achromatic.

Hitherto I have been speaking of instruments especially adapted to the scientific work of an observatory, and in such a case there is probably a limit to improvement, for what is required is stability, clearness of definition, and accuracy in measurement: and these will be sacrificed if we attempt to obtain very high magnifying power, a result which is more favorable for the gratification of our curiosity than for purposes of scientific utility. And here, for scientific purposes, is the advantage of a refracting over a reflecting telescope. Perfect distinctness is the first essential, and this can be obtained in a high degree by a lens of moderate dimensions, but is most difficult to arrive at in a polished reflector of large dimensions—the very curvature of which is more or less irregular at first, and is always liable to alter by the flexure arising from its own weight. And, moreover, perfect distinctness being supposed, as the magnifying power is increased, the degree of illumination of the magnified object is diminished: hence what is gained by apparent enlargement is lost in detail. Amongst those who have been most successful in the construction of reflecting telescopes, we have the well-known names of Sir William and Sir John Herschel, Lassell, Delarue, Nasmyth, and Lord Rosse—the first of these commencing with a telescope of 7 feet focal length only, eventually succeeded in producing one of 40: and the last, at his own expense, with his own designs, under his own immediate direction, and with much of his own personal labour, completed in 1848 a reflector of no less than 53 feet focal length; one of the most interesting results that have been derived from telescopes of such high magnifying powers is the resolution of Nebulæ into clusters of stars of definite magnitude; but beyond this, however interesting they may be, it is questionable whether any important discoveries will ever be made by their means.

The most important feature of the present time is the division of labour in the different branches of astronomical science, especially amongst amateurs.

I have already alluded to the very comprehensive nature of observatory work, and were it not for the labour of private observers prompted by their love of knowledge, much would remain unknown, and still more would be left undone. Thus we find some devoting themselves to a careful examination and measurement of the solar spots; others to a similar examination of the mountains and depths which appear upon the surface of the moon; some applying the powers of photography to a minute delineation of those objects, and others passing sleepless nights in searching the heavens for new planets and comets, or the resolution of nebulæ, and the measurement of double stars.

Nor must we omit to mention, what is perhaps the greatest discovery of the day, " spectrum analysis." Well may we be filled with amazement, at the thought, that by comparing the spectra of the fixed stars, with that produced by known substances in a state of combustion, we may, at no very distant period, be enabled to determine the constituents of bodies, so remote from us that their distances cannot even be guessed at.

Such an investigation as this, even if there be no practical benefit to be derived from it, is obviously one of the deepest interest; it is as interesting to the chemist, as it is to the astronomer, and it is impossible to foresee what discovery it may lead to.

To carry on the enquiry, needs the command of a powerful telescope, and the most delicate contrivances of the optician—contrivances which can only become effective, by frequent experiments, and need to be in the hands of the experienced man of science. With such a view, it is satisfactory to know, that the Astronomer Royal at Greenwich, departing from his usual rule, not to employ the force at his command, in mere speculative investigations, yet takes so deep an interest in this question, that systematic observations are carried on, and improvements continually made in the apparatus for observing.*

I trust it may not be very long, before we may be in a position to pursue the same subject in the Southern Hemisphere.

The present state of magnetical and meteorological science bears an invidious comparison with that of astronomy. At the same time it need not surprise us, for the age of the latter sciences may be reckoned by days, whilst the former is reckoned by years. And again, astronomy is, to a certain extent, within everybody's reach, whilst magnetism requires in the observer considerable mathematical training, expensive and delicate instruments, and

---

* Since this paper was read, I have received a letter from the Astronomer Royal, in which he informs me that "he has *virtually* abandoned the spectrums analysis "—the expense and labour are such that he thinks it best left to amateurs. G. R. S.

most careful manipulation—it will, of course, be understood that I am speaking of terrestrial magnetism.

This subject was hardly entered upon previous to the year 1840, when magnetic expeditions were promoted, and temporary magnetic observatories established in different parts of the world, the objects of such observations being to determine the following elements. The "*intensity*" of the terrestrial magnetic force—the "*dip*" or inclination of the direction of such force to the horizon —and the "*declination*," or as navigator's call it, the *variation*, or angle which such direction makes with the astronomical meridian. Meteorological observations were necessarily combined with these, for the two subjects are evidently closely connected. But it must be admitted that we have not made any very great progress in either.

It is true we are able to conclude that the moon exercises an influence upon terrestrial magnetism, and that it is somehow connected with the solar spots; we are convinced that it is a function of heat, and that it is connected with electricity, if it be not the origin of those elements. We find that magnetic disturbances are coincident with great thermal changes, but not necessarily with electric storms. Again, most magnetic phenomena may be produced by electricity—not so the converse, unless we introduce the element *motion*. It is true we are able to trace something like a general law of the "Diurnal, Annual, and Secular" variations of the magnetic elements, as for example that the declination needle has two maximum deviations from its normal position, in the 24 hours, and likewise in the year. Also, that magnetic storms have their changes which extend over a period of about ten years,—which corresponds to the changes which occur in the number and magnitude of the solar spots,—and that it is most undoubtedly connected with the "Aurora."

Still, with all this, how little do we know of the source and laws of a power which may perchance prove to be the key to the universe itself.

But great improvements have been made in the means and methods of making magnetical observations. The apparatus now employed at the Kew observatory, under the direction of the

Royal Society of England, has attained a very high degree of perfection.

The application of photography to magnetism and meteorology, by means of the most minute changes in the position of a magnet, or in the height of the barometer and thermometer as at any time self recorded, is an indication of improvement and progress.

It is a matter of surprise, as well as of regret, that electrical observations are so much neglected. The importance of such observations in connection with magnetism and meteorology need not be enlarged upon, and I am not aware that in any observatory, excepting those of Greenwich and Kew, are systematic observations made of the electric condition of the atmosphere. I am happy to inform this Society that I am now making arrangements for carrying on electrical observations, at the Sydney Observatory, at the usual meteorological hours, and on occasions of unusual disturbance, with apparatus especially constructed for the purpose.

It would seem almost superfluous to comment upon the "practical bearings" of a Scientific Observatory, yet is the *cui bono* enquiry so frequently made, that it seems unavoidable to overlook it. Surely when we consider that every nation, whether old or young in the scale of importance, deems it expedient to have a national observatory, it would seem impossible to avoid the conviction that some practical benefit is to be derived from it, either as a means for promoting knowledge and refinement, or as the centre of operations whose utility is obvious. The general importance of practical astronomy to navigation is well known, and every available place for observation is called into requisition. At every important place on the earth's surface, ought the latitude and longitude to be determined by a long and careful series of observations, made with a superior class of instruments; each of such places becomes in its turn a centre, to which stations of secondary importance must be referred, and without which, geography is incomplete, and much of the surveyor's labour spent in vain.

The discovery of general meteorological laws is of the highest practical importance to navigation, agriculture, and public health:

and it is only by a long series of careful and systematic observations well reduced and collected, that such laws can be arrived at. I could wish, indeed, that every health-officer and medical practitioner, whether in his public or private capacity, might be persuaded to devote some attention to the presence of that agent which we call ozone for want of a better term; and also to the presence of humidity at any time, as indicated by the readings of the wet and dry bulb thermometers. Nor are magnetical observations of less practical importance. Their relations to meteorology have been already alluded to. They are of the utmost importance to the surveyor in the interior of a country: and still more so to the mariner along a rocky iron-bound coast.

It is to be hoped that the whole of this colony will be surveyed on a sound scientific basis, but according to the method hitherto adopted, some idea may be formed of the importance of magnetic operations, when I state that the boundary line of an estate, might, in the course of 60 years, be found to differ from the original determination by upwards of a degree, owing to the secular variation of the magnetic meridian.

The whole range of magnetic observations is called into active play in the determination of the error produced in the ship's compass by the attraction of the iron, in the several parts; for want of such determination there is reason to suppose that many a good and well found ship, has been cast away.

The advantages of a magnetic survey of this country I propose to discuss more fully upon a future occasion, at the present time I will confine myself to an illustration of some practical importance. In commencing this survey I determined to take such stations as were most convenient, at intervals of about 15 miles, and without any enquiries as to possible local imfluence. I decided thus, because I believe that most localities in this country have more or less local influence, and whilst it would be easy afterwards to reject from the magnetic chart suspected stations, yet it would be far from easy to determine from enquiries made before-hand, what localities were certainly free from causes which would influence the observations. Three of my stations, Nobby's at Newcastle, Musclebrook, and Wingen, (near what is called the Burning Mountain) exhibited singularly discordant results.

Wingen was especially remarkable. Taking for example the observations for the inclination of the needle, at Scone they were what I should have expected from its geographical position; not so at Musclebrook, which is about 15 miles on this side; whilst at Wingen, which is about 15 miles further north there was a difference of nearly a degree. To make certain, the observations at Wingen and Scone were repeated with the greatest possible care, and the same results obtained. I have since learned that large quantities of iron stone are known to abound at Wingen, and to a certain extent—though not so great perhaps—at Musclebrook and Nobby's. This is a most interesting subject, and is one which we can but lightly touch upon, on the present occasion. Even though the divining rod may no longer find believers in its power, yet we cannot refuse to acknowledge the indications of the magnet, and perhaps a practical importance may be claimed for it beyond what has hitherto been known or investigated.

The best assistance which can be rendered to science is by noting and recording remarkable phenomena, and communicating the same to some establishment where they will be examined and collated with others. A few important facts are better than large masses of ordinary observations. In England alone there are volumes of unreduced and unpublished magnetical and meteorological observations, which are thus rendered useless for want of the proper force to reduce and discuss them. Yet there must and will be progress—every one may assist in the advancement of science if he has but the will, and no one could fail to have the will did they but reflect that "Art is long and Time is short."

Reading and Wellbank, Printers, Bridge Street, Sydney.

On the Manners and Customs of the Aborigines of the Lower Murray and Darling, by

Gerard Krefft.

[Read 2nd August, 1865.]

It is much to be regretted that many of our fellow-colonists who have had ample opportunities for observing the aboriginal inhabitants of Australia, have never made an attempt to record the manners and habits of a people now without a doubt upon the verge of extinction: and as every observation—be it apparently ever so trifling—will become of greater interest from year to year, I may be held excused if I come before you to-day with some *bonâ-fide* notes relating to the Aborigines of the Lower Murray and Darling. Nearly eight years have passed since they were made, and many of the natives, then in the prime of life, have disappeared already, and but few of them will be remembered by the settlers who now occupy their hunting grounds.

Unlike the American Indian, who slowly retreated before the settler, the Australian clung to the soil upon which he was born, but he did not become civilised; he tried to eke out an existence, feeding upon his Kangaroos and Emus, and occasionally interfering with the squatters' stock: but finding that he could not do so with impunity, he came to terms, bartered his opossum rug for blankets; his game for flour, beef, or mutton; his services as a shepherd or stock-rider for other luxuries of civilised life; and at last he became dependent for almost everything upon the occupant of his own domain. The consequence of all this is obvious. A native once used to flour, tea, sugar, and tobacco, can hardly exist without them; hence very few independent tribes remain within the settled districts, and the younger members of them have almost forgotten the vegetables or the game upon which their fathers once feasted.

If these people did not retreat before the white man it was not their fault; they have only the alternative of making a compromise with the settler, or of fighting the next tribe they come in contact with; and generally they adopted the first—they remained upon the soil which had given them food for so many years, took to rum and tobacco, sacrificed their wives and daughters to the white man (if a free offer may be called a sacrifice), and at last, almost ceased to increase in numbers as the women became either barren or produced a weak half-caste offspring, who were not fit to endure the same privations, or obtain their food in the same ingenious manner as their black brethren.

The Aboriginal population of Victoria in 1847 amounted to about 5000; in 1858, shortly after these notes had been taken, their number had been reduced to 1768, men, women, and children; and if they have decreased at the same rate to the present day there will scarcely be a thousand souls left.

When I started from Melbourne, in October 1857, for the Lower Murray, I counted the number of natives who visited our camp at every station, and the following is the result, the average distance being about 25 or 30 miles from post to post. Between Melbourne and Spring Plains—about 70 miles—no native was observed.

Station	Count
Apple's Hotel	8
Campaspe River	15
Echuca	35
Maiden's Station	8
Gardiner's Station, (Gunbower Creek)	45
Gardiner's Out-Station	12
Campbell's Station	18
Loddon Junction	23
Reedy Lake	10
Lake Boga	6
Marrapit River	14
Swan Hill	18
Tintindyre	13
Coghill's Station	7
Hamilton's Station, and Murrumbidgee Junction	22

Lagoon, near Junction	12
M'Callum's, and Grant's Station	31
Euston (including native police)	40
Half-way Lagoon	29
Kilkine	11
M'Grath's Station	7
Jamieson's Station, (Milldura), and Williams's Station, (Gall Gall)	35
Darling Junction	35

which, in round numbers, would amount to about 400 souls.

Between Melbourne and the Campaspe, the natives have very much degenerated, they were, in fact, represented by a few old men and decrepit women, and two or three diseased wretched children; but, nearing the Murray, their condition appeared to improve, and at Gunbower Creek they were found in considerable numbers, most of the men fine stalwart fellows, some more than six feet and one nearly seven feet in height.

Fishes, crayfish, the eggs of tortoises, ducks, emus, the mallee hen, and the black swan, appeared to be their principal food at that time, they were therefore tolerably independent and remarkably lazy as I thought, though on consideration it appeared to me that their philosophy was quite correct; why should they exert themselves? They did not lay in stores, and many of their viands being of a perishable nature, and to be had almost every day, there was no reason why they should work like their civilised brethren; there are only two beings which appeared great fools in their eyes, namely a white man and a working bullock.

My stay at Gunbower Creek was not of sufficient duration to study the manners and habits of these people; the men all carried guns (some very queer looking fowling pieces), they were all tolerably good shots, but when trusted with ammunition would invariably come home empty handed, though their own camp fires seemed to be well supplied with a variety of game.

After a while, many of the smaller animals were bartered for tobacco and flour, but in not one instance could they be induced to kill a bat; they even asked, when I had captured one of these creatures alive in the tent, to let it go, as it was "brother belonging to blackfellow."

They told me that if it was killed, one of their lubras would be sure to die in consequence. They had their corobbories of a moonlight night, keeping our party awake with monotonous songs, and once they even had a sort of quarrel, and in consequence a fight—a woman, as usual, being at the bottom of it—but after all nobody was hurt, and I missed a good opportunity of observing their burial rites.

There were, however, a few graves in the neighbourhood of Mr. Gardiner's station, in a thick pine scrub, enclosed by a rude brush fence, and covered with large pieces of cork. They appeared neglected, and were much more rude in shape than the graves subsequently encountered farther down the river. The settlers treated the poor blacks invariably with great kindness, in return for which they would look after the squatters' property with a keen eye. They would never allow the men to destroy any old fences or huts for the sake of a few dry slabs or a piece of bark; and if no heed was taken of their remonstrances, would invariably report it at the next station. If their watchful eyes observed the tracks of a few stray sheep, they immediately altered their course, and took me miles out of my road to—as it appeared—no purpose whatever, until the stragglers were overtaken, and safely delivered at the head-station.

Like all the other tribes they would share their food with each other, and if out hunting, and having too many followers for the few pounds of flour and tea with which we started, it was frequently found necessary to starve part of the garrison, by making the natives who accompanied us, eat their rations before our eyes, so that the idle camp followers were compelled to look after opossums, and leave us alone.

Following the course of the Murray, I noticed about 18 or 20 natives encamped near Campbell's Station, one of them a remarkable character, being an aged woman in good condition, with a large white beard; the natives at this place appeared to subsist principally upon fish, of which 3 or 4 kinds including the Murray Cod *(Oligorus macquariensis)*, were roasting on their camp fires.

At the Loddon Junction more natives were observed, all armed with fishing spears, and freely offering their women for a small number of hooks and lines.

At Reedy Lake, about ten men and women were noticed, and at Lake Boga, six; the natives who visited the camp at Lake Boga were remarkable on account of their powers of mimickry, and the good English they spoke; all had been under the tuition of the Moravian Missionaries, and one appeared to make a livelihood by offering to preach like one of them; he had a way of his own of saying home truths, like "white-fellow always pray give it daily bread, but bail give it damper." It appears that the Moravian Missionaries had made an attempt to teach the natives agriculture, but I fear with little success. A few small plots of ground enclosed with a brush fence, and overgrown with weeds, were all that was left of these "native gardens," to which their owners pointed with considerable pride.

In this part of the country where extensive reed beds are of common occurrence, the natives live for several months during the year on "Typha roots," or Wongal *(Typha Shuttleworthii)*; at a certain period, I believe January or February to be the months, the women enter these swamps, take up the roots of these reeds, and carry them in large bundles to their camp; the roots thus collected are about a foot to eighteen inches in length, and they contain besides a small quantity of saccharine matter, a considerable quantity of fibre. The roots are roasted in a hollow made into the ground, and either consumed hot or taken as a sort of provision upon hunting excursions; they are at the best but a miserable apology for flour, and I almost believe that it was more on account of the tough fibre thus obtained that these roots are made an article of food.

As soon as a sufficient quantity of "Wongal" had been roasted, the whole tribes settled around the improvised oven, every body chewing the roots most vigorously; the lumps of rejected fibre were afterwards collected by the women, and spun into threads from which their fishing-nets and other domestic utensils were manufactured, these nets forming the staple article of barter between the tribes inhabiting the reed-beds and those parts where no Wongal was produced. If we take into consideration the large nets for catching water-fowl in use, it is indeed astonishing how great the perseverance of these people (and how sound their teeth) must have been, and it is not to be wondered at that the possession of one of these nets has always been considered to be a sort of fortune to its owner.

At the present time no more fishing-nets of Wongal fibre are manufactured, as the natives barter twine from the settlers instead.

Between Lake Boga and the Junction of the Murrumbidgee, some sixty or seventy natives were observed encamped in small lots near the river or lagoons, most of them occupied with fishing. We passed several graves, the last near Coghill's Station, of the simple form noticed at Gunbower Creek, whilst a little farther on a regular hut had been erected over the departed native; and at Hamilton's Station were two graves of this description, in a very good state of preservation. The form of these sepulchres changed again soon, being, instead of bark, covered with grass and reeds; a fishing net generally enclosing the whole fabric.

Nearly all the trees along the river-bank showed more or less traces of the presence at one time of a large number of natives: square pieces of bark for drying their opossum skins upon had been cut, often to the height of 20 feet above the ground; there were also many signs upon these trees where canoes of great dimensions had once been removed, whilst fresh cuttings of this kind rarely occurred.

It may be of interest to give a short description of the manner in which a canoe is manufactured:—

The tree selected is generally the species of Eucalyptus, known to the settlers as "*Flooded Gum*," by which the river banks from Swan Hill to the Darling Junction are invariably fringed; the trunk must be free from branches or knots, and, if possible, slightly bent; having found a suitable tree of this kind, a large forked branch is cut, and the tree being jammed between, it serves the native as a sort of ladder; he begins by making two incisions which at first run parallel to each other, and then closing more and more join at the ends, the whole having the form of an elongate shield. The outer bark is then removed sufficiently to permit the introduction of a number of flattened sticks of tough wood, each about a quarter of an inch thick; these sticks are wedged under the piece of bark, which is to form the canoe; they

bend easily, and soon loosen it from the trunk. With a couple
of grass-ropes around the bark, it is then allowed to slide down,
and is put upon the stocks in a regular way. Dry leaves, grass,
and small branches, having been collected and put into the still
flat piece of bark, they are fired, and the sides soon begin to turn
up; when sufficiently bent, 3 or 4 sticks are introduced, to
prevent the bark from curling any more; accidental cracks or
holes in the canoe are filled up with clay from the river-bank,
and the boat is ready for use.

These canoes are generally propelled with long elastic spears,
and considerable progress is made on smooth water, as lakes or
lagoons; but to steer the frail bark dead against the stream in
such a river as the Murray is almost impossible; when going up
stream, the natives keep close alongside the river banks, where
the current is less, but they never travel long distances up the
river, but frequently visit friendly tribes by going overland, and
having manufactured a canoe, they drift down the stream, back
to their own hunting grounds.

A supply of clay is always kept in these canoes, and often
when the bark is not of sufficient depth, a clay rim or dam is
raised on both ends, to prevent the water from coming in; being
all good swimmers, the natives appear very careless with their
frail craft, and if she sinks, which is however very seldom the
case, they quietly swim ashore and build another. To sit
perfectly quiet is the first rule, balance yourself well, keep
baling out any water which may run in, and trust to the native
who propels the boat; the least motion from one side to the
other suffices to fill and sink it, there being seldom more than
about an inch of board. Being at home in the water, like New-
foundland dogs, they appear to think that every white man who
trusts himself to their bark canoes, must necessarily be the same,
and if half-a-dozen men are willing to cross the river at once, the
natives have generally no opposition to offer, and would almost
as soon see some of their passengers drowned as cross the
river twice.

When out fishing at night, they have a small fire burning in
the bow of the canoe, which is for that purpose covered with
clay; some of the fishes are attracted hereby, and many of

them speared. A loop of grass-rope, or green hide, attached to the side of the canoe, through which the spear is run into the bottom of the river, answers the purpose of an anchor.

Passing farther down the Murray, the natives increased in numbers, and at a lagoon near Kilkine, we found some 50 or 60 of them assembled for the purpose of "making young men;" these wretched youths being passed through various ordeals, one of which was to mount the candidate upon the shoulders of the biggest man in the tribe, to run round the camp fires with him, all the rest following with hideous noises, and to deposit him without as much as a shirt on, in some part of the scrub. Five or six of them passed the night there, shivering and hungry, until released by the men the next morning, and introduced to the adults of the tribe as "men." I do not think that these ceremonies were gone through in the orthodox style, and the youths did not appear to believe in them at all; they assured me they only submitted because of their rights hereafter to take a lubra unto themselves.

Both men and women were well made, with highly intelligent countenances; but, except the young girls, none of them wore any covering whatever. When the men approached at the first interview, they wore two or three feathers of the White Cockatoo in their hair—a sign of their being messengers of peace,—and two of them who accompanied our party to the Darling Junction, never removed these feathers as long as they were upon the hunting grounds of another tribe.

On no occasion did I notice any of the natives to travel at night, and whenever noises were heard, for which they could not account, they were invariably put down to the credit of Devil-Devil, and no promise whatever could induce them to leave their fires.

A few miles from Milldura, at a place called Mondellemin by the natives, a permanent camp was established, and in a few days some twenty of them, including men, women, and children, were assembled near our huts; they could not at first understand what brought us there, but when we purchased some of the native animals captured by them, they ever after brought in a good supply and became our permanent huntsmen. The boys would go out to collect insects, the women to look for small mammals, and the men looking for the larger game; they would try their best to please, and obtain the reward offered for some of the more rare creatures, but not succeeding, they would as quickly try to pass off some common animal as the one which we were in want of.

Being very anxious to obtain Mitchell's tail-less Chœropus *(Choeropus ecaudatus)* high rewards were offered, though in vain; the cunning natives, not succeeding in finding the animal required, were in the habit of bringing any number of the common bandicoot, *(Perameles obesula)* with the tail screwed out.

Altogether they became very useful, and very much attached to us, (as long as our flour bags lasted, at least); but whenever the stock of flour diminished, they would break up their camps, and pay visits at the neighbouring stations; returning as quick as possible when they heard that a steamer had arrived with fresh supplies. At one time, when about fifty bags were in store, I observed two natives trying to count them; but, their numerals being limited to one and two, this became rather a difficult task; *rangul* means two, and *meta* one, so that *rangul, rangul, meta* is equivalent to five, and so on ad infinitum; of course, to count *fifty* in this fashion was too much for them, so informing the tribe that there were *thousands* of flour bags in the store, they returned shortly after, with a stick, into which they made a notch for every bag, keeping henceforth as good an account as the storeman. Nothing could keep them near the camp, or induce them to exert themselves in hunting, except seeing a good supply of flour on hand; and when some two months before our return to Melbourne, the stock became very low, and I feared to lose the natives, they were completely out-manœuvred; as I filled the empty bags with sand during the night, and piled them up with the rest.

Never did I behold such astonished faces as the natives showed on the next morning; they examined the ground for miles, looking for dray tracks, and as no steamer had passed, could not account for the flour thus arrived, and as usual, put it down to the agency of "Devil-Devil."

I have often tried to find out if they had any ideas of religion, but without success; I know that the younger children often learn to read and to write, and I believe that Mr. Goodwin, of Yelta, has had some very successful scholars, but I do not think that the adults ever understood the principles of Christianity.

Once I met old Jacob, a Darling chief, in Mr. Goodwin's house, intensely looking at a colored print, representing our Lord as the "Good Shepherd," with a lamb upon his shoulders. Jacob addressed me in his quaint way of—"make a light! name belonging to that one Shepherd?"

I tried to explain the meaning of the picture, but to no purpose, and all I got out of poor Jacob was:—"bail shepherd belonging to this country! never see him carry lamb on his shoulders, he always leave him along the bush." Taking the print literally, I do not think Jacob was far wrong.

The natives living near Mr. Goodwin's place were much more comfortable in many respects than any of the tribes seen before; they could always count upon a certain price in the shape of flour, tea, and sugar, for any work performed; they lived in closed sort of huts, which had somewhat of a permanent character; but I have reason to believe that all the good examples of Mr. Goodwin and his assistant, were counteracted by the presence of a lot of hard-drinking and hard-swearing bushmen at the Darling Junction public-house, opposite.

Here, at Yelta, or rather on the New South Wales side of the River, the natives had always assembled in large numbers for the purpose of feasting upon fish and bartering their famous Myall-spears for reeds, Wongal-twine, and nets the produce of other parts of the country; in olden times no doubt their stone hatchets were exchanged in a similar manner, as from Gunbower Creek to the Darling Junction there is not a stone to be met with the size of a man's fist. I have been told that the green stone, serpentine, or jade tomahawks used by the natives, were obtained at Mount Macedon, and that a certain locality on the side of the mount had been considered neutral ground by the neighbouring tribes, who went there for the purpose of obtaining suitable material for their weapons.

About this time of the year, in the month of July, a similar gathering had taken place; and one night I visited the camp, accompanied by Mr. Goodwin. There was no moon when we crossed the river, and following our guide, we soon found ourselves in the midst of about two hundred natives, stretched around their camp-fires, which formed a semi-circle, the middle being occupied by "old Jacob," the famous chief, who appeared to keep them merry by telling a number of tales; all were busy except Jacob. Some tried to straighten young shoots of the Myall, by heating them in the ashes, and then bending the wood into shape—keeping their feet and the whole weight of their body upon it; others were occupied knitting nets, using the same instrument as our fishermen do, and working with their hands and feet; the women were cooking fish, of which a large supply had been obtained during the day,—carefully reserving the taboo'd fish called Manor, for the use of the aged, no youth or lass being permitted to partake of it;—carving their waddies, or preparing opossums' skins for their rugs, kept others busy, and all this time the sonorous voice of old Jacob could be distinctly heard, and shouts of laughter testified how well the old man's tales were appreciated.

When the moon rose, the men left their occupation, some ascending trees to cut down branches, others painting themselves with gypsum, for the forthcoming corobboree, and shortly after the dance commenced,—performed by some fifty or sixty men, with bushes tied to their ancles. Their ribs, arms, and thigh-bones, were traced with gypsum upon the dark skin, and made them appear as so many skeletons; the women and young girls formed a sort of orchestra, beating opossum rugs, and singing their monotonous airs; all the dancing men, and some of the more aged ones who sat near the women, were provided with two short thick pieces of hardwood, which they beat to the time of the song. All this time one of their "doctors," as he was termed, experimented upon another blackfellow, as it would appear, in trying to deliver him of an immense worm which he seemed to pull out of his patient's mouth; I found afterwards that this worm was part of the intestines of an opossum; they went on enjoying themselves when I left, keeping the dance up until the small hours, and, of course, sleeping far into the day.

The following morning we inspected their fishing gear, which was simple enough. For river or lagoon fishing, when the water is clear, they have a three-pronged spear, with which they strike the fish, either from their canoes or from logs in the water. Sometimes they fish at night, as mentioned before, and then a fire is lit in the bow of the canoe to attract the fish. They also have iron spears, and I was told that they would dive, and take up a position alongside a sunken log, keeping the spear horizontal with the right hand and the big toe, and running it through every fish which came within range; sometimes five or six fish have been speared during the sixty or eighty seconds they remain under the water.

I do not think that they use large nets for fishing in the river, but the women are very expert with hook and line, and with a sort of flat net fixed to a bent stick about 6 or 8 feet in length, similar to a dredge; this, of course, is only fit for shallow lagoons, the outlets of which, when the flood-waters begin to fall, are closed with sticks or basket-work to prevent the fish escaping, thus creating a considerable reserve for the following months.

The principal fishes used as food by the natives are the Murray Cod, (*Oligorus macquariensis*); Silver Perch, (*Lates colonorum*); Cat Fish, (*Copidoglanis tandanus*); and Manor, (*Chatoëssus come*); most of the other species are small; I believe however, that both kinds of Australian Mullet (*Mugil dobula*, and *Mugil compressus*), and another species of so-called Perch inhabit the Murray, and its tributaries.

As I am speaking about nets, I may as well mention their contrivance for catching water-fowl, in particular ducks. Wild ducks are as much prized by the natives as they are with us, and having studied the habits of these shy birds well, they have at last contrived a plan to catch them, which is a complete success. A large net, sometimes 20 feet deep by 100 feet long, is spanned across a creek or river, to the two ends to which a string is fastened, resting upon some branch of a tree, being kept in readiness by two natives, who are posted beneath this tree, and the net completely immersed in the water. Some two or three miles higher up the creek, a party of natives start the birds, which invariably follow the bend of the creek, though sometimes at a height of a hundred feet or more; as soon as they are nearing the net, another native who is posted in the scrub gives a peculiar whistle—similar to a species of hawk—throwing a flat piece of wood or a boomerang among the startled birds, which immediately stoop to the level of the water's edge; quick as lightning the net is raised, the ducks get entangled in its meshes, and become an easy prey to the women and children, who jump in to secure them.

I have seen from 50 to 100 ducks taken in this manner at a haul. Black Duck, (*Anas superciliosa*); Shovellers, (*Spatula rhynchotis*); Teal, (*Anas punctata*); Pink-eyed or Whistling Ducks, (*Malacorhynchus membranaceus*); Wood Ducks, (*Bernicla jubata*); and White-eyed Ducks, (*Nyroca australis*); being the species most common.

Of fresh water crustaceans, we find the large river Cray-fish, (*Potamobius serratus*,) distinguished by its spiny back and white pincers, and a species of Prawn, which is frequently eaten raw by the natives.

The large cray-fish is secured in a very simple manner: a canoe is fastened in the stream, and two or three natives paddle with their hands in the water, the great crustacean makes a dart at their fingers with its pincers, and before he finds out his mistake, he is safely landed into the canoe—the pincers being immediately broken off.

Other kinds of food which the lagoons or river supply are tortoises, (*Chelodina*), generally taken during the hot summer days when the water is low, also muscle shells (*Unio*) large mounds of which may be traced upon the river banks at intervals for hundreds of miles.

Most of the natives being supplied with guns, they are able to surprise almost every kind of bird, though they generally shoot water-fowl only. The Emu is still hunted in the primitive style by hunters carrying bushes in their hands, and so trying to steal a march upon the rather stupid bird; as soon as they are within range their spears are thrown and the bird secured.

Fishes, cray-fish, insects, frogs, lizards, snakes, all birds, and the smaller mammals, are generally roasted upon the coals; whilst emus are treated in the following manner :—The feathers are singed off, and a large hole is made in the ground, filled with leaves, dry branches, &c., the fire being well supplied with fuel for an hour or so; the ashes and embers are then cleaned out, the bottom covered with fresh gum-leaves; the carcase is put upon these, covered over with leaves again, and the whole with earth and lumps of clay (the size of a man's fist) which have previously been heated; a fire is again lit upon the top, and after another hour the bird is done, tasting as sweet as if prepared by the best professed cook.

Of Mammalia which are hunted by the native for the sake of their skins or their flesh, the common opossum (*Phalangista vulpina*), stands first. In the Mallee scrub, where the trees are of stunted growth, these animals are plentiful, and easily secured: whilst upon the river banks, where gum-trees one hundred or two hundred feet in height give them shelter, this is a more laborious task; still even upon the highest tree poor 'Possum is never secure. I have seen one of these nimble blacks after a rainy day, when his stomach called loud for meat, carefully scan every tree along the river bank, until the trace of 'Possums' nails were found in one of the old "gums;" tomahawk in hand, he mounted it, the first branch being about sixty feet above ground; even then, he had to cut through a thick branch, and it was almost dark when he extracted an old opossum, which however, before it could be killed, dropped into the river below; his wife had been watching him, however, and plunging into the stream, she secured their supper for that night.

If nothing is to be had in the shape of meat, the last resource is, in summer time at least, to light a few branches and hunt for frogs, which may also be secured, summer or winter, beneath the bark of the flooded gum trees. Native cats, (*Dasyurus geoffroyii*) all species of rats and mice, and the smaller wallabies, (*Halmaturus*,) are also eaten, and some of them obtained almost every day. The large kangaroos (*Macropus major* and *Osphranter rufus*) are generally hunted by a number of men with their dogs, the time chosen being after a heavy shower of rain, when the large animals sink deep into the chalky soil of the Mallee scrub.

After a kangaroo has been killed, the successful hunter secures the kidney fat, which however is very small in quantity, it is generally attached to a string around the neck, and of course women and children who see this sign rejoice, and bring home the carcass, if it is not too far; or should more than one animal have been slaughtered, the tribe removes for a day or two, to eat the meat on the spot.

A species of burrowing kangaroo-rat, (*Bettongia campestris*) and a sort of bandicoot, (*Peragalea lagotis*), are dug out occasionally.

The kangaroo-rat, called Booming, is common in the scrub, and its burrows often cover a couple of acres of ground: the natives trace the direction of the holes, by inserting long slender twigs, and then sink a shaft, which sometimes requires to be from ten to twelve feet deep; when they labour, they work with a will, and more than once I have noticed a couple of natives to sink three such shafts in a day. A pointed stick to loosen the earth, a sort of scoop to throw it up, or if too deep, to fill a kangaroo skin with it, are all the digging utensils they require.

The burrowing bandicoot, known as Wuirrappur to the natives, is dug up in a similar manner. In fact there is scarcely a living animal from the grub of a large beetle to a whale, which an Australian rejects. The vegetable kingdom does not offer, however, a great variety of food.

One or two herbs,—the Quandong, and a root the size of a radish, are all the vegetables I have ever noticed these people to eat, though the so called "Pigface" (*Mesembryanthemum æquilaterale*), must not be forgotten; it appears to be the only substitute for salt they have, and whenever their women have been out, they invariably return with some bunches of this plant.

Being dependent upon a variety of food which is not always in season, or more plentiful at one time than at another, they lead of course, a wandering life, and on this account do not erect any permanent dwelling. A simple break-wind of gum-branches is all they require, and sometimes a few sheets of bark are stripped to make their huts more comfortable, but beyond this they do not go; these light structures are shifted, or rather turned, should there be a change of wind, or they are left altogether in case the vermin become too troublesome.

Their weapons are just as simple; a few reed-spears with hardwood ends, a throwing stick, a sort of shield, besides clubs or waddies and boomerangs, comprise the whole of their armoury. The boomerang appears to have been a late introduction, and I have never seen a native on the Murray who made use of it as a defensive weapon.

Their social position is naturally a very low one; they do not appear to have any idea of a Supreme Being, they possess no religious rites, and every man who is strong and cunning enough to enforce his authority and to subject the weak, will always be a chief among them. Marriage ceremonies they have none, and when a native takes a lubra to himself for good, it is pretty certain that, however young she may be, she has had connection with most of the men of the tribe. These women are often obtained by stealing them from another tribe, in which case the unhappy creature is generally beaten into a state of insensibility, or they are exchanged, any man giving his own sister for that of another; thus many young men who have no sister to offer, are deprived of the blessings of the conjugal state, or rather they possess no lubra which they may order about, or make a slave of.

They exchange wives out of compliment to visitors of other tribes, during the time of their stay; and they freely offer both their wives and daughters to any European who may have a piece of damper, a fish-hook, or any other present to bestow. They treat their children kindly, though they do not hesitate to destroy them sometimes at their birth, and particularly if the babe is a cripple; still I remember a man, named Piper, with malformed feet, who was then about twenty-five years of age, and able to make a living as well as any other blackfellow.

The children do almost what they like; it sounds ridiculous, though it is a fact, when I say that they often leave the mother's breast, to take the pipe out of her mouth, and have a smoke; they suckle their children often for four years and more. Of their dogs the natives are almost as fond as of their children. Women do not hesitate to suckle pups; and it is not to be wondered at, that under such circumstances, the dogs become much attached to the aboriginals: and if only with them for a few nights, they seldom follow their white master again. They sleep with their dogs, gnaw at the same bone with them, and though they do not feed them well, the kind treatment makes up for the rest; and as I mentioned before, a well-bred dog left with blackfellows for a few days, is a lost dog for ever.

It has been stated that they were in the habit of killing their aged men and women; this, however, must be a mistake, as I have noticed them to carry an old man about from place to place, who had been a cripple for 8 or 10 years. Cases of insanity are, I believe, of very rare occurrence; though I remember a single instance,—a boy about 14 years of age was pointed out to me as a "silly boy:" but I had not sufficient time to observe him, he played football with the other boys of the tribe and appeared to be the most expert of them.

Though they have not the faintest idea of religion, they are yet very superstitious: the universal belief that every death in their own little circle is caused by a member of a neighbouring tribe, and that vengeance will be taken accordingly is one of the principal causes perhaps of their rapid disappearance from among us. As soon as a native has breathed his last, messengers are sent to friendly families in the neighbourhood, and if bad news travels fast in civilised countries, it appears to travel much faster in the Australian bush. It is only with great reluctance that they pronounce the name of a departed friend, and if their wailings and the personal chastisement they inflict upon themselves, upon such occasions are proofs of their sorrow, their feelings must be intense.

The men seldom if ever wail, though they often inflict fearful gashes, principally upon their heads, mixing the blood with gypsum and thus cause the formation of a thick crust or skull cap which is frequently renewed. I have noticed a fine young fellow mourning the death of a young girl, (neither sister nor bride), stretch like Mucius Scævola his right arm into the fire until that limb was almost roasted, the skin cracked and hanging around it in large patches.

The women perform the noisy part of the business, howling incessantly for days and weeks, and only leaving off during meal time, and when tired out they fall asleep for a few hours. The deeper they mourn the more gypsum is laid on, so that sometimes nothing but the eyes, ears, and mouth, remain uncovered. Their burial rites I have had no opportunity to observe, but always found the graves well kept, and have generally seen the most romantic spots selected for the last resting place of their departed.

On the Lower Darling these sepulchres were generally made in some shield-like enclosure of brush wood, shaded by drooping acacias or cypress-pines, and covered with a rude hut of bark or brush wood, into which for a long period afterwards casual passers-by—friends of the lost one—implant a green bough, so that by the number of these boughs one may judge in what estimation the poor creature was held who rested beneath. Their strong belief that they will re-appear as white men, is well known, as also the desire to see a certain likeness in white men with one or another of their lost friends. The way in which they try to find out in which direction to take vengeance for a deceased member is singular. After the sand has been smoothed around the grave and the brush enclosure is formed, they leave the ground, returning from time to time until by some insect or other accidental cause the smooth surface has been disturbed, and in that direction retaliation is sought; of late they are satisfied to throw a waddy or a few harmless spears at the first unlucky strange black they may thus encounter; while formerly they tried to shed blood at least, if not able to kill their victim.

Before concluding I shall say a few words about their artistic skill, which is confined to the embellishment of their rude weapons and skin coverings; they seldom go beyond a series of straight lines at various angles, red and white being the usual color to set off the pattern. They are however tolerably good observers, as there is no difficulty whenever they carve the figure of a fish, a bird, or a mammal, upon a sandstone rock, or trace the same on a piece of blackened bark, to recognise the genus of the animal thus represented. The numerous bays and inlets of Port Jackson abound with such carvings, but on the Murray I have never seen any thing beyond a few tracings on sheets of blackened bark, probably done during a rainy day.

www.ingramcontent.com/pod-product-compliance
Lightning Source LLC
Chambersburg PA
CBHW021941240426
43668CB00037B/356